Hunter Museum of Art

A Catalogue of the

AMERICAN COLLECTION
Hunter Museum of Art
Chattanooga, Tennessee

William T. Henning, Jr.

Curator of Collections

*This project was supported by grants from the Lyndhurst Foundation of Chattanooga
and the National Endowment for the Arts, Washington, D.C., a Federal agency.*

Introduction to the 1999 Edition

One of the most exciting challenges and certainly pure joys of working in a museum is building the collection. Let us not forget that among the myriad of activities undertaken by art museums, above all in importance is the collecting of the art objects which essentially makes the institution a museum. In today's society, the Hunter Museum of American Art assumes many roles in the community, only one of which is the collecting and preservation of works of art. The interpretative and educational roles of the museum are extremely important but are blurred by the necessity to compete for audiences with the numerous other institutions which have become entertainment attractions as well as educational facilities, creating the need for ever growing numbers of participants. This atmosphere has necessitated the forging of a new multifaceted mission for the contemporary museum. Other circumstances created by the emphasis on political correctness, the pressure to attract a more diverse audience and the need to focus on underserved audiences have caused a completely new posture for the modern museum. Faced with these challenges and a drastically changing philanthropic landscape and changing funding sources, the primary functions of collecting and interpreting works of art have become only two of the many strategies now included in the mission statement of most museums. Most of us in the field know that change is inevitable and nothing remains the same, and if it does it usually becomes extinct. Most of the staff at the Hunter have looked upon these changes in the museum field as a challenge and even an inspiration as we have sought to meet these problems with creative solutions. Nonetheless it is gratifying, even exciting, to work on a traditional project such as a collection catalogue and look ahead with anticipation to the publication of a new document which will complete to date the scholarly work that began with the establishment of the curatorial department at the Hunter in 1980.

The republication of this 1985 catalogue of the permanent collection is a preamble to the upcoming publication of a new collection catalogue of artworks acquired since 1985. This new catalogue will complete a major goal set by the museum in the early 1980's. In 1997 the Hunter Museum received a grant from the Henry Luce Foundation of New York which, among other projects relating to the collection, included funding of a new catalogue documenting almost as many artworks as this earlier publication. Ellen Simak, Curator, and her assistants have been working diligently for the past year and a half and plan to complete their research and preparation for the new catalogue some time in the year 2000 with publication scheduled for 2001. Ms. Simak, who succeeded William Henning, Curator 1980 - 1987 author of this volume, has indelibly placed her own individual stamp on the scholarship of the new catalogue. The museum trustees, the curatorial staff, the administration and specifically the acquisition committee of the museum has essentially reached the goal of building the finest collection of American painting and sculpture in the Southeastern United States and one that is respected throughout the nation. Included in the collection are major works by the most important American artists, works that would be stars in any collection, public or private, anywhere. The task of building on this fine body of works will be ongoing and this milestone is only a beginning to what future years will reveal.

The quest of collecting for the Hunter Museum has been facilitated by many individuals, institutions and foundations and it would be inappropriate if not impossible in this short forward to try to give credit to all of those involved. On the other hand I would like to call attention to the enduring efforts on the part of the chairman of the acquisition committee who has served in that capacity since 1975, Mr. Scott L. Probasco, Jr. for his dedicated service in acquiring the museum's collections. In his own right, he is one of the most noted collectors of American painting in the region, and the zeal that he has exerted toward so many of his accomplishments, including building his own collection, has carried over into his dedication to the Hunter. Without the early support and later the establishment of a substantial acquisition endowment by the Benwood Foundation in 1988, the Hunter would not have made such remarkable progress in acquiring high quantity works. Behind every great collection, public or private, there is usually a significant dealer who plays a major role in finding and securing the majority of quality works of art. That dealer for the Hunter Museum is Douglas James, who has had an exemplary and appreciated relationship since 1975 when he negotiated the milestone purchase for the Hunter by the Benwood Foundation of 33 major American paintings from the Cohen Collection. This collection, along with a nucleus of quality paintings earlier acquired, created the basis and inspiration for the fervent collecting by the Acquisition Committees of the eighties and nineties. Other individual efforts and contributions have certainly been forthcoming, too numerous to describe here, but nonetheless significant in their numbers and their magnitude. Collectively, every gift of funds or works of art has been important and illustrates the broad base of support the museum's collecting program has attracted. On behalf of the Hunter's Board, staff and volunteers, I am pleased to take this opportunity to express our heartfelt gratitude to every one of the Museum's friends for their sincere dedication and out-pouring of generosity which enabled the soaring success of the Hunter Museum of American Art.

Cleve K. Scarbrough
Director

Foreword

Since 1897, when Chattanooga was a rail and industrial center of some 30,000 people, art has had a special place in the city's life. The Art Study Club organized in that year, followed by the Chattanooga Art Association in 1924, sponsored frequent exhibitions, lectures and workshops. Both groups worked closely with the art department of the University of Chattanooga (now The University of Tennessee at Chattanooga), where most of the activities took place.

It was in 1951, however, that the visual arts in Chattanooga found a home of their own. George Thomas Hunter, a Coca-Cola bottling magnate and cultural patron, bequeathed his residence at 10 Bluff View to the Chattanooga Art Association. The Benwood Foundation, the principal beneficiary of Mr. Hunter's estate, provided funds to renovate the building, and a year later it opened as the George Thomas Hunter Gallery of Art.

The focus was still on changing exhibitions, lectures and classes, although 1952 also brought the first acquisition of a major American painting for the Museum's collection, *The Huntsman's Door* by Richard LaBarre Goodwin. Acquisitions were only occasional, however; recognizing those limits, a consultant's study commissioned by the Art Association board of trustees in 1967 recommended that the Hunter Gallery collection focus exclusively on American art. That proposal set the course for today's collection. By the time the original gallery outgrew its facilities in the early 1970s, it could claim a fledgling collection of American paintings, with a small nucleus of museum-quality major works.

Work on a new building began in 1972. The award-winning structure adjoined the Hunter mansion, leaving the original building intact and complementing it in a way that brought universal praise. Through the generosity of the Benwood Foundation, a major group of American masterpieces was acquired and on display for the new museum's opening in 1975. The final name change was adopted then: the Hunter Museum of Art.

The enlarged museum and the enhanced collection spurred new interest in acquisitions for the Hunter, with the focus on works by living American artists and works produced during the post-war era. The Collectors' Group, museum patrons who have organized an annual buying trip to New York since 1982, has become a special feature of the acquisition program. In a relatively short time this has helped build one of the finest collections of American contemporary art in the Southeast.

Building a significant collection is possible only through the generosity of individuals, foundations and businesses and with the support of dedicated volunteers and staff. The Volunteer Associates has played a major role for acquisitions through fund raising efforts. The board of trustees has consistently underwritten an aggressive acquisition program for the continued excellence of the museum. The Hunter Museum's many benefactors, important as each has been, are too numerous to mention individually.

The strength of the permanent collection, coupled with an imaginative program of changing exhibitions and other art activities, makes the Hunter Museum a resource for the community unsurpassed in the Southeast.

We are pleased now to be able to offer this catalogue of the permanent collection. It has been made possible through a generous grant from the Lyndhurst Foundation, which underwrote the establishment of a curatorial department for three years. The scholarly work of curator William T. Henning and his assistants and the intelligent oversight of director Cleve Scarbrough and his dedicated staff have produced a publication of excellence. It is a superb reflection of the commitment to quality of the Hunter Museum of Art.

Llewellyn Boyd
Chairman, Board of Trustees

Staff (1985)

Administration

Cleve K. Scarbrough
Director
Charlotte B. Jurczak
Financial Assistant
Phyllis P. Bruce
Program Coordinator
Margaret L. Clark
Membership Coordinator
Janice Hayes
Secretary
Shirley Graham
Secretary
Ana P. Corbin
Receptionist
Karen Weed
Receptionist
Louise Crawford
Receptionist

Collections and Exhibitions

William T. Henning, Jr.
Curator of Collections
Kay T. Morris
Registrar
Elizabeth L. O'Leary
Collections Assistant
Timothy L. Flick
Chief Preparator
Robert B. Wright
Preparator

Education

Andrée Markoe Caldwell
Curator of Education
Elizabeth Evans Donahue
Assistant Curator of Education
Elizabeth M. Aplin
High School Program Coordinator
Jacquelyn Casey
Education Assistant

Physical Plant

William F. Baggett
Building Manager
Floyd L. Baggett
Head Custodian
Rick Turner
Custodian

Security

John T. Brett
Security Chief
David R. Turner
Custodian and Guard's Assistant

Staff (1999)

Administrative

Cleve K. Scarbrough
Director
Linda Tate
Accounting Manager
Dianne Linam
Accounting Assistant
Alicia Hyde
Accounting Assistant
Eileen Henry
Administrator
Terry Rigsby
Administrative Assistant
Christe Land
Membership Coordinator
Dotty Dunstan
Marie Rogers
Louise Crawford
Receptionists
Evelyn Richards
Angela Dittmar
Alice Campbell-Orde
Cashiers

Collections and Exhibitions

Ellen Simak
Curator of Collections
Elizabeth Le
Registrar
Theresa Slowikowski
Collections Assistant
John Hare
Exhibits Designer
Eric Keller
Assistant Preparator

Education

Sherry Babic
Education Curator
Helen Johnson
Coordinator of Studio Programs
Laura Woolsey
Education Assistant
Gretchen Davenport
Docent Coordinator

Physical Plant

Rick Turner
Maintenance Supervisor
Freddie Baggett
Maintenance

Security

John Ross
Chief of Security
Bill Shirley
Leonard Penley Jr.
Security Guards

Introduction

Producing a comprehensive catalogue of the American collection at the Hunter Museum of Art is the culmination of an intensive effort that has required the attention of almost every museum staff member. Over the last four years the collections department has exerted considerable effort and committed many diligent hours to the creation of this important publication. Curator of collections Bill Henning, author of the catalogue, has dedicated his time and skills as a scholar to ensure that the catalogue is a significant contribution to the museum and to the academic community.

Impetus for the project came from the Hunter's dedicated board of trustees. From the beginning, the board charged the administration to build a full-service art museum for the Chattanooga community and the surrounding region. Incorporated in this plan was the creation of a fully staffed curatorial department headed by a scholar in American art. The board of trustees has been committed to this project since its inception, with funding and support through approval of grant applications and, even more importantly, with a keen understanding of the significance and magnitude of the undertaking. The Lyndhurst Foundation of Chattanooga was a major funding source, as was the National Endowment for the Arts, a Federal agency. The Allied Arts of Greater Chattanooga has also played an important role in funding the curatorial department through its expanded support for operations after the three-year Lyndhurst grant concluded.

An additional consequence of the catalogue project has been improved professional practice throughout the museum. The collections department has assumed responsibilities that have permeated the museum program, from the handling of art works in the changing exhibitions to the quality of communication in education. All of these factors have brought the museum to the level of excellence aspired to by the board, the staff, and the volunteers.

With the publication of this catalogue, the Hunter Museum enters a new era and level of visibility as a major collection institution in the Southeast. Although collecting has been an important part of the museum's program since its beginning in 1951, extraordinary advances have been made recently in both the early twentieth century and contemporary periods. In fact, some thirty major works of art have been added to the collection during the period of time this catalogue has been written and published. The importance of a museum's collection has long been recognized, and is unquestionably the major reason for a museum's existence. The people of Chattanooga and the regions beyond served by the Hunter have experienced the advantages of the permanent collection as well as the changing exhibition schedule. Through interpretative programs, citizens of the area have become aware of the rich and varied contributions of America's artistic heritage. The museum has grown to be the "people place" that it should be — an institution serving as wide a public as possible through continual involvement with the schools and people of all ages in the community.

Interpretation of the collection will be greatly enhanced by this scholarly document, enabling the Hunter to fulfill its mission to the public in a very tangible way. The catalogue will give assistance to the other museums both as an informative manual as well as an aid in planning exhibitions of American art. The extensive documentation of works in the catalogue will also be very helpful to other scholars in their research and writings, ultimately contributing to the body of American art history knowledge.

If this volume expands the artistic knowledge of even a few students, or inspires one young artist to excellence, the efforts of the staff will be well rewarded. People in many institutions will benefit from the work that has gone into the creation of this book as, to an even greater extent, will the Hunter Museum of Art.

Cleve K. Scarbrough
Director

Preface

At the time the Hunter Museum of Art was organized, nearly three and a half decades ago, American art was neither the popular academic study nor the highly collectible commodity (with soaring prices for important pieces) that it has become today. It used to be, as Paul C. Mills, former director of the Santa Barbara Museum of Art, observes, that our native art "suffered a surprising amount of resistance, opposition, and neglect . . . when it was necessary to make a valiant, pioneering effort to be involved with American art at all." The predicament began to change in the 1950s with the publication of several works of distinguished scholarship: Oliver W. Larkin's *Art and Life in America* in 1949, for example, or Alfred Frankenstein's *After the Hunt*, in 1953, or E. P. Richardson's *Painting in America*, in 1956. Richardson, moreover, was a co-founder of the Archives of American Art in 1954 (now administered by the Smithsonian), a repository of artists' letters, personal papers, records, and other documents that researchers have found enormously useful.

Interest in our nation's art was also stimulated when, in the late 1940s and '50s, a new American avant-garde, the abstract expressionists, achieved international notoriety, and New York displaced Paris as the leading progressive art center of the Western world. Scholars and critics, in turn, were moved to consider how it came about, to explore what roots in American art history may have led to the post-World-War-II success of modernism.

When early Hunter Museum trustees elected to define the institution's specialty as American art, they demonstrated a timely belief in the worthiness of the nation's cultural heritage—not to mention extraordinary foresight! Now, with thirty-four years of astute collecting, the museum has developed what is perhaps *the* finest institutional holding of American art in the Southeast, and certainly *one* of the finest such collections anywhere. All major periods are adequately represented (even if not every "ism" or variation), and recent trustees have affirmed a commitment to support and collect works by accomplished contemporary artists.

Still, to this writing, the breadth and quality of the Hunter collection are not as widely known among museum professionals, patrons, and visitors as they deserve to be. For that reason alone, it is fitting that this catalogue be published. Its circulation, advancing the collection to broader public awareness, should in turn bring the Hunter increasing, rightfully deserved recognition. The chief purpose of the catalogue, however, is to offer interested readers an accessible and informative survey of the major pieces in the collection and the respective artists represented, and to provide scholars in American art history a creditable resource. Throughout the research and writing, I have kept in mind one special constituency: I particularly hope the museum's fine docents will see the catalogue as a helpful reference for the responsible service they perform in interpreting collection objects to gallery visitors, many of whom are young people.

Of nearly a thousand items in the museum's American collection, 141 are featured in the catalogue by illustrations and accompanying explanatory texts. Determining *which* works to highlight was no easy task. In the light of art-historical criticism by respected authorities, I endeavored to weigh the reputations of artists and the relative merits of individual pieces. Many of the artworks selected were obvious choices. But for many others the decision was admittedly subjective. To the reader familiar with the collection, I regret sincerely if certain works you especially like or believe significant are not featured. Perhaps such works will be added in future catalogue editions.

The main body of the catalogue is divided into five historically chronological sections, though there is some overlap of times to accommodate the conclusion of various movements or stylisms. Each section begins with an introductory overview of events and creative activities that bear upon the period. Feature articles follow, arranged by artist, and in chronological order of the artwork described. A "provenance" (that is, as thorough a history as has been possible to gather on the individual piece: ownership, exhibition, and publication) appends each of the artworks pictured and discussed in the text. Rather like an abstract of title for real property, this accessory information is often valuable to scholars, biographers, and exhibit planners. A complete index of the entire American collection—listed alphabetically by artist and naming every object acquired from 1951 through July 1985—follows the main text.

6

I am supposing that most readers of this catalogue will review those individual articles that are of interest at any given time, and will not likely follow any prescribed order. Consequently, I have endeavored to make each a fairly independent entity. This means, on the other hand, that some pieces of information are occasionally repeated as they apply to separate artworks. Though I have tried to restate such information with a slightly different slant, point-of-view, or choice of words, I hope those few readers who proceed through the book page by page will pardon the periodic redundancies.

William T. Henning, Jr.
Curator of Collections

Acknowledgments

Soon after Hunter director Cleve Scarbrough came to the museum in 1976, he saw a need to develop an academic and registrarial department that would be responsible for care, records, study, and interpretation of the institution's outstanding art holdings. The board of trustees readily concurred. With three-year underwriting assistance from Chattanooga's Lyndhurst Foundation, a collections department—with curator, registrar, and assistant—was established in 1980, and when the grant expired in 1983, the Allied Arts organization moved to assure ongoing financial support. Production of a comprehensive catalogue of the American collection, a long and earnestly desired goal of many of the museum's patrons, became a major charge to the new department.

A portion of the original Lyndhurst grant specifically supports publication of the catalogue, as does a separate grant from the National Endowment for the Arts, a Federal agency. The museum is most grateful. And I, personally, am grateful to have been entrusted by the board and director with so worthy a research and writing opportunity.

This four-year undertaking came to fruition with the help of many persons, both within and without the museum, whom I would formally recognize and thank. I am most grateful to the private collectors, gallery and museum staff personnel, curators, archivists, and librarians—all over the United States—who graciously responded to research inquiries. Naturally, certain of my Hunter Museum colleagues have been closely involved with many facets of the project, and have made real and significant contributions to the catalogue end result. I am particularly grateful to registrar Kay T. Morris, who maintains the museum's extensive art-object records—much vital primary-source information. Further, she has carefully monitored the color photo reproduction processes, from original camera work through balancing the printing plates, to assure image sharpness and tone and hue fidelity to the actual artwork. Collections department assistants Linda DeVane Williams, from 1980 to '82, and Beth L. O'Leary, from 1982 to the present, provided substantial research assistance, especially of provenance matters, and dutifully, even good-naturedly, typed the seemingly interminable text manuscript.

J. Bradley Burns, Robert B. Wright of the Hunter Museum, and William L. Parsons of Photography, Inc. provided professional photographic services. Former Hunter program coordinator Kay S. Parish, now executive director of the Chattanooga Museum of Regional History, has written a short, yet remarkably comprehensive and thoroughly readable history of the museum. What is more, before leaving the Hunter, Ms. Parish devised the catalogue's striking graphic-design format, and assisted with considerable proofreading and editing. Linda and Paul Neely have given generously of their journalistic skills to proofreading and editing the entire type-written and later, type-set text. I much appreciate their many constructive comments and suggestions. The technical staff at Chattanooga's Jones Printing Company, particularly Anita Godfrey, Marvin McClain, and Gary R. Russell, have accorded this project an extra measure of interest and care. Finally, for abiding patience and encouragement, I thank my wife, Eleanor, and our family.

W.T.H.

A Short History of the Hunter Museum of Art

by Kay S. Parish

The Hunter Museum of Art has a physical presence as arresting as the fine collection of American art housed within its galleries. Situated on a ninety-foot limestone bluff overlooking the Tennessee River on one side and downtown Chattanooga on the other, the museum is a prominent feature of the cityscape to residents of the area. It operates in two very different buildings which function as a unit while retaining their unique visual integrity. A 1904 classical revival mansion and a contemporary structure completed in 1975, the buildings are linked by an ingeniously designed elliptical stairwell and an outdoor sculpture garden.

The museum's setting has been significant throughout the region's history. To the early Cherokee people who inhabited the area, the bluff was said to be sacred as the home of a mythical hawk-like giant known as "tla' nuwa". In 1854, one of the earliest industrial enterprises in the Southeast occupied the site. An iron smelting plant known as Bluff Furnace stood below the present northwestern corner of the museum until being demolished during the War Between the States. The furnace is the location of a present-day archeological dig for anthropologists from The University of Tennessee at Chattanooga. Because the site commands a sweeping view of the river and surrounding territory, it was used at various times by both Confederate and Union forces during the Civil War as a lookout and garrison.

The bluff's significance to what would later become the Hunter Museum began in 1904, when a wealthy insurance broker named Ross Faxon engaged the Cincinnati architectural firm of Mead and Garfield to design a new home for his family. Completed in 1905, it occupied a choice lot on what was by then known as Bluff View. The house was lavishly embellished with classical and renaissance motifs inside and out: egg and dart, acanthus leaf, reliefs of fruit, fanciful heads, and dentil moldings of plaster and wood. The Faxon family lived in the home until 1914, when it was purchased by Walter Henson, an exporter of oil and grease. Again in 1920 the home was sold, this time to the widow of Benjamin F. Thomas. Thomas had been the founder of the world's first Coca-Cola bottling franchise, the phenomenal success of which earned a substantial fortune.

The same year the Hunter mansion was designed, Thomas' young nephew, George Thomas Hunter, arrived in Chattanooga to work as a clerk in the Coca-Cola Thomas Company. Destined to inherit the franchise and the entire Thomas estate, Hunter rose rapidly through the managerial ranks from clerk to secretary, president, and, finally, chairman of the board of his childless uncle's business. He also became one of Chattanooga's most respected community advocates, known widely for his philanthropic interests.

When Hunter died, unmarried, in 1950, he had already organized the Benwood Foundation, a private charitable and educational trust. Funds from Benwood, along with the gift of the Hunter mansion, were donated to the Chattanooga Art Association in 1951. The Association used the money to transform the home into space suitable for showing artwork, then, on July 12, 1952, opened Chattanooga's first permanent exhibiting institution as the George Thomas Hunter Gallery of Art.

The members of the Chattanooga Art Association were integral in setting high standards for the visual arts in Chattanooga and in guiding the institution's early years. The roots of the Art Association reached back to the establishment of the Art Study Club in 1897 by some of the city's culturally concerned citizens. By 1924, the club was interested in introducing newer, younger blood to the visual arts and met to incorporate an organization devoted to "encouraging and advancing culture in Art, Painting, Drawing, Sculpture and Carving, Engraving, Etching, Statuary, and Designs." The group, named the Chattanooga Art Association, grew rapidly, sponsoring exhibits, speakers, fund raisers, and local art fairs. One of only three exhibiting organizations in the entire state of Tennessee during the 1930s, the CAA at first utilized rooms at the public library, then showed at a small gallery in the fine arts building at the University of Chattanooga (now The University of Tennessee at Chattanooga). During that period the CAA was able to attract such outstanding visiting artists and lecturers as, for example, the prominent American regionalist painter, Grant Wood. This energetic group was only too delighted to address its efforts to the Hunter Gallery's management. The CAA appointed Russell B. Thornton first director. Former curator at the Corcoran Gallery in Washington, DC, Thornton organized an impressive inaugural exhibition, bringing art treasures to Chattanooga from many of the nation's major museums. Exhibitions, films, lectures, and occasional gifts to a fledgling collection kept the Gallery busy. In 1959, the Hunter Annual visual arts competition was established; thereafter, it brought fine regional art to the Chattanooga area for twenty consecutive years.

During the 1960s, art classes and musical recitals were added to the public program of the Hunter Gallery, encouraging the growth of young artistic talent. In '66, Thornton retired, and Frank Baisden, former art department head at the University of Chattanooga, served as interim director until Budd H. Bishop was named director in the fall. Under Bishop, the Hunter mansion was extensively remodeled and education programs were expanded to include an art slide presentation that took art out of the gallery and into the public school classroom. Not only did programming increase, but so also did the size of the collection. In 1968 the Hunter made its first major acquisition by gift and purchase, when nine American paintings known as the Hayes Collection were added to its holdings. The CAA reorganized in the same year, establishing a board of trustees and an associate board of volunteers and advisors. The institution's standing as one of the leading cultural resources in Chattanooga solidified in 1969 with the chartering of Allied Arts of Greater Chattanooga. Hunter Gallery was one of six groups supported by this united-drive funding agency for the arts in the city.

With a growing membership and collection, an active docent program and a variety of community groups clamoring to use Gallery facilities, the 10,000-square-foot mansion began to seem cramped. In 1971 the trustees visited and studied museum facilities in other cities, then engaged the local firm of Derthick and Henley to design a new complex around the Hunter Mansion. In the ensuing two years, the Chattanooga community raised over two and a half million dollars for the new structure in what was then the most extensive capital campaign ever for the arts in the state of Tennessee.

1973 saw the CAA in temporary galleries downtown in a storefront, where exhibitions and educational programs continued uninterrupted while construction took place on Bluff View. The trustees voted new bylaws and a name change that would become effective when the building was finished: the George Thomas Hunter Gallery of Art of the Chattanooga Art Association was to be consolidated as the Hunter Museum of Art. Derthick and Henley's plan was for maximum utilization of the bluff site. Old fill dirt was removed, and the mansion braced and girded. Then blasting began next door for the building that would occupy land beside the older one. Much of the new facility would be underground, so as to avoid visually overpowering the mansion. It was built of cast-in-place architectural concrete with a sandblasted exterior, and designed to be compatible with the mansion and at the same time to blend with its location on—and, literally, in—the rocky bluff.

In fall 1975, the new complex opened, featuring as its first exhibition a collection of 100 of the finest paintings owned by forty-six Southern museums. The Hunter mansion underwent a facelift, too, and became a showplace for the permanent collection. In addition to artwork gifts that had trickled in during the gallery's early years and to the Hayes Collection purchase, in 1975 the Benwood Foundation made an extraordinary gift to the new museum of forty fine American works of art worth more than one million dollars; a collection with the stature of the Hunter's was indeed worthy of a showplace at that point! The new building hosted changing exhibitions, public programs, education activities, storage and preparation, and staff offices. Soon after the transition from gallery to museum was completed, Bishop resigned to accept the directorship of the Columbus (Ohio) Museum of Art. Cleve K. Scarbrough, formerly director of the Mint Museum of Art in Charlotte, North Carolina, was named the Hunter's third director in 1976.

With National Endowment for the Arts funding, the Hunter Museum set about bringing its now fine collection "up to date" with intensive acquisition of works on paper by living American artists and with commissioned works to be installed in areas of the new building and grounds. By that time, collecting efforts were being accomplished by an acquisitions panel of trustees, the director, and outside scholars and experts.

The late 1970s were years of growth for the Hunter. Funding from the Allied Arts was consistent, volunteer commitment was strong, and the collection was rapidly gaining exposure and respect in the museum community. Programming efforts expanded with the opening of the new facility to include a high school art enrichment group called ArtScene, a revamped education system based on sensory enjoyment of visual art, and studio classes in cosponsorship with The University of Tennessee at Chattanooga, in addition to the ongoing programs of the museum.

In 1979 the Lyndhurst Foundation of Chattanooga opened another door for the Hunter with a three-year grant providing for the establishment of a collections department staffed by a curator, assistant, and registrar. With a resident scholar for the first time, the museum could commence research and documentation of the collection. The goal was this 300-page catalogue, designed for the casual reader as well as the art history scholar.

The National Register of Historic Landmarks added the "Faxon-Thomas Mansion" to its rolls in 1980, the same year that the Hunter became one of 405 museums out of 1500 applicants awarded federal education funds from the Institute of Museum Services. Again in 1981 the IMS granted support to Chattanooga's art museum for general operating purposes, and the American Association of Museums bestowed its seal of approval with professional accreditation.

GEORGE THOMAS HUNTER
Paul A. Trebilcock
1954
oil on canvas
36 x 28¼ inches
signed lower right
Museum commission

Provenance
Hunter Museum commission.

Confidence in the museum's mission as a top quality regional institution ran high among trustees, staff and the extensive corps of volunteers. The Collectors' Group, composed of community patrons, amassed donations and banded together in 1982 for the first in an annual series of group buying trips to New York galleries for the purpose of adding to the Hunter's contemporary collection. Their first effort drew such acclaim that roughly three dozen other works have been either purchased in the same manner or donated in addition to the objects with which they returned from New York that first year, as a wave of enthusiasm carried over into the wider community. The growth of the Hunter collection at that point necessitated its expansion into the new building, which until then had been devoted to the display of changing shows. To maintain the quality of the changing portion of exhibits programming—and add space for the public to use—a large classroom was renovated to a multi-function gallery in late 1982.

The Chattanooga community had long supported the Hunter through its enthusiastic response to Allied Arts' fund drives, but in 1984 tangible signs of the local government's confidence in the museum became evident. The Hamilton County Tourist Development Agency granted the Hunter a sizable amount for use in visitor introductions to its galleries in a small video theater, and for publication of a brochure designed to inform tourists of its facilities. Since over one million people visit the Chattanooga area each year, the Tourist Development projects have the potential of attracting a large, new audience to the museum.

From beginnings in 1897 with the Art Study Club, through years as the all-volunteer CAA and Hunter Gallery, the Hunter Museum of Art has grown into a professionally acclaimed regional arts center with an important collection and extensive public services. It has the generous spirit of Chattanooga leaders and residents to thank for its existence and prosperity.

Featured Artists and Artworks

The Colonial Period and the Young Republic

"Man lives by habit except when circumstances force him to do otherwise," art historian Daniel Mendelowitz reminds, "and habit directed the colonist to attempt to recreate familiar patterns of living. Each of the national groups that settled America, as soon as the barest foothold had been established in the new land, tried to duplicate its former way of life." But there were indeed circumstances that mitigated against the colonials living life as they had in the several "old countries." The colonists' foremost concern in the seventeenth and early to mid-eighteenth centuries was conquering wilderness and enduring the hardships of frontier existence. Little time or energy was left to pursue the fine arts, either as producers or collectors. What is more, the predominantly Protestant settlers from northern and western Europe, as Lloyd Goodrich succinctly points out, tended to be "more word conscious than image conscious, more verbal minded than visual minded." Especially in Puritan New England, Mendelowitz continues, "antagonism towards the arts as expressions of courtly extravagance and vanity did not provide an atmosphere conducive to artistic production. It comes therefore as something of a surprise to find artists working in America almost from the moment the continent was discovered."

It is all the more remarkable to find artists actively producing, because colonial America offered virtually none of the traditional bases of support—no centralized government, no cultivated nobility, no royal court, no official academies, no state religion*—in short, none of the forms of reliable patronage that sustained European artists.

Colonial artists were further handicapped by their distance from metropolitan cultural centers (even though Philadephia grew steadily to become the second largest city in the British Empire at the time of the Revolution) and professional schools. The majority of native-born talents, not surprisingly, were self-taught, and most doubled as enamelers, house painters, sign painters, carriage decorators, carpenters, and shipwrights. Standards of proficiency, such as they were, came about either in the colonial artists' imitating what Samuel M. Green calls "second-hand or second-rate sources," that is, engraved reproductions of European work or original work by a few artists of European origin and training, typically persons of limited abilities who were unable to compete successfully in their native countries.

The prevailing colonial styles in painting, for example, reveal an awareness, but far from a mastery, of the fashionable late rococo trends set by Godfrey Kneller, Peter Lely, Thomas Hudson, Joshua Reynolds, Thomas Gainsborough, and other prominent Europeans. At the same time they manifest a clearer understanding of the earlier English Tudor style, with its characteristic decorative, flat patterning, simplified shapes, and even lighting—a mode better suited to emulation by untrained craftsmen-folk artists. This is the underpinning of the limner tradition that dominated the earliest colonial painting and bore strongly on American art well into the nineteenth century.

The principal topic of colonial painting, as it had been in predominantly Protestant and thoroughly secularized northern Europe, was portraiture. As an upper class began to emerge throughout the colonies—planters in the South, merchants in the middle region, landowners in New York, industrialists in New England, and shipmasters from all along the Atlantic seaboard—representatives of both established wealth and the newly prosperous demanded replicas of their faces. Particularly if the artist plied handicrafts as well as painting, a "likeness maker" could have an adequate living in colonial times. The painters' status in society, however, unlike Europe, was never greatly esteemed. Boston's John Singleton Copley, probably the most accomplished and successful painter in America before the Revolution, would still write disgruntledly in the 1760s that it was "not a little mortifying that the people regarded painting no more than any useful trade, as they sometimes term it, like that of a carpenter or shoemaker."

During the War for Independence and the first years of organizing a new government—though progress in the visual arts was interrupted—America's character was transformed and its culture given a new direction. The greatest single factor distinguishing the early republic from the previous era was the consciousness of self-determination. Americans defined their new role with a near-fatalistic belief in the righteousness and historical necessity of the nation—Manifest Destiny, historians would name it, as vast territories to the west were added to the original thirteen states. Art and architecture should therefore express the stability of establishment on the one hand, and the future promise of America on the other. Influential tastemakers like Thomas Jefferson saw representative government and social egalitarianism embodied not in the art forms of the Church that had been a guiding force in European society for centuries, certainly not in the ostentation of kings, but rather in the stately forms of democratic ancient Greece and republican Rome. American art entered upon an ideological preference for classic revival architecture and decorative arts and what E. P. Richardson identifies as "neoclassic realism" in painting. "The American republic was born in an age saturated in the dream of classical antiquity," Richardson notes.

Portraiture continued in the early republic as the main purpose for painting. But significantly, subject types—even national heroes—are typically depicted as self-reliant, unassuming individuals rather than members of an eminent ruling class. Incidentally, in the wake of both the American and French Revolutions, a similar classic revival spread over much of Europe. The aristocratic frivolity of the rococo style no longer expressed the reality of the age.

It may at first seem ironic that artists in the new nation would rediscover Europe's magnetic cultural attraction. With the conflict behind and the immediate euphoria of independence subsiding, Americans reckoned the shallowness of their native cultural traditions. In Europe were the great old cities (including those admired ancient places), the great art masterpieces, the great conventions of patronage, the great art academies and teachers. (No regular art school operated in America until the founding of the Pennsylvania Academy of the Fine Arts in Philadelphia in 1805.) Would-be serious artists realized the best available instruction lay abroad. Philadephian Benjamin West, in 1759 the first native-born American artist to go to Europe for study, remained and eventually became a leading member of the Royal Academy in London, even the organization's director from 1792 until his death in 1820. Yet, always cognizant of his American nationality, he generously took many young American painting students into his studio, including Matthew Pratt, Charles Willson Peale, William Dunlap, Gilbert Stuart, John Trumbull, Samuel F. B. Morse, Washington Allston, and Thomas Sully. In time, each returned to the United States with refined technique, expanded vision, and perhaps most importantly, awareness of other worthy purposes for art beyond portraiture, especially allegorical and historical work.

---

*Though the Church of England was sanctioned in nine of the original thirteen colonies, it was far from preponderant. And while it might be argued that in those areas where Puritans dominated, a theocracy was thereby established, it was of no particular benefit to the arts.

Unknown artist

GIRL WITH A BIRD AND CAGE
Unknown artist
c. 1735-1740
oil on canvas
36½ x 24½ inches
Gift of Mr. and Mrs. Harold
Cash

Provenance

Rowena Cuell, Marietta, Ohio
Francis Mason, Marietta, Ohio
Mr. and Mrs. Harold Cash, Chattanooga,
Tennessee.

Little is known about those remote, largely self-taught, and typically anonymous artists who provided the earliest paintings in colonial America. In letters and documents from the seventeenth and first half of the eighteenth centuries they are often described as itinerants who just as surely could decorate wagons, enamel furniture, or paint shop signs. Frequently they are called "limners." In the parlance of the time to "limn" meant to make a likeness, that is to say a portrait, and such was far and away the predominant subject for painting in this country throughout the colonial period. As E. P. Richardson observes:

> The Dutch and English settlers, sturdy Calvinists all, felt no need for the religious paintings which were the first desire of the French and Spanish missionaries. But family feeling and personal pride were prominent among these strong-willed people, and among the skills which were normal features of seventeenth century middle-class life in both Holland and England was that of portrait painting. It accompanied the earliest settlers to America.

17

It is further interesting to note that the word "limn" is derived from "illumine." During the Middle Ages illustrated manuscripts (as opposed to those with written text only) were said to be "illumined." An inference one can rightly take here is that American limner painting is not a provincial version of the fashionable Baroque modes that were then current in Europe. Instead it is a continuation of the English Tudor school of 150 years earlier which is indeed late Medieval in style, characterized by a quality of decorative two-dimensionality in both the modeling and lighting of form. It is of course a manner more readily adapted to the naive capabilities of the untrained colonials.

The Hunter Museum's *Girl with Bird and Cage* is a splendid example of the late limner tradition. The work is essentially linear with limited color filled in flatly. The pleasant girl looks directly out of the picture, greeting the viewer with crisply rendered eyes — perhaps the strongest single aspect of the painting. Her facial features generally are in a developed state, in contrast to the casual slapdash brushwork of the skirt. And the artist was more alert to the correct proportion of the facial parts than the scale of face to hands. This selective and uneven degree of finish is a common characteristic of primitive artists. The painter's fascination with surface detail is further apparent in the meticulous rendering of the neckchain and the flower on the low-cut neckline of the bodice.

Showing the cage and the bird may represent family possessions, but more likely the artist employed these effects to "motivate" the pose, to give the subject something to do with her hands, and to give the picture additional variety and curiosity. Despite its small size the bird is an important element for the composition. In that it is turned to the right, it helps bring the viewer's eye into the scene. The angle of the pet's stance optically is continued in the girl's right shoulder line, which in turn leads one's glance to the face. Subjectively, the bird may also allude to the girl's position as one of quality gentry, whose gracious lifestyle makes possible the indulgence of such a dalliance.

John Wollaston (c. 1710-c. 1770)

The Hunter's portrait of an unidentified gentleman by John Wollaston is one of approximately three hundred paintings the English-born artist is estimated to have done during his ten-year sojourn in the American colonies. Little is known of his background. He was probably born in London about 1710. His father, John Sr., was a portrait painter who doubtless taught his son the fundamentals of technique and "likeness taking." According to a reminiscence written by American artist Charles Willson Peale, Wollaston also studied with an unnamed drapery painter in London, that is to say with one whose responsibility was to fill in the clothing and background hangings after the principal artist rendered the all-important face and hands of portrait subjects.

By contemporary English standards Wollaston was at best a moderate talent, and he almost certainly would have had difficulty competing in the circle of sophisticated and dexterous rococo portrait masters which included Joseph Highmore, William Hogarth, and Thomas Hudson. On the other hand, many colonial American merchants, ship owners, planters, and professional men had grown sufficiently prosperous to establish a ready clientele for portraiture and which in turn attracted lesser European painters who had probably only modest success in their native countries. This is likely the circumstance that brought Wollaston to America in 1749. He worked in New York City until 1752, in Annapolis until 1754, in numerous Virginia towns until 1757, and then on to Philadelphia in 1758. At this point he abruptly changed careers by accepting a position in Asia with the British East India Company in which capacity he continued service over eight years. He was back in the colonies in 1766, reestablished in Charleston, South Carolina, where he resumed portrait painting for about six months. Then in late May 1767 he sailed for England, never to return to America. Nothing is known of his subsequent years, except that he settled at Bath and died there about 1770.

PORTRAIT OF AN UNKNOWN
GENTLEMAN
John Wollaston
c. 1755
oil on canvas
22⅛ x 18⅛ inches
Gift of Hirschl & Adler
Galleries, Inc.,

Provenance
Hirschl & Adler Galleries, Inc., New York,
New York.

While in America Wollaston painted several large, three-quarter-figure portraits that demonstrate his awareness of the elegant poses, surface finery, and flamboyant handling characteristic of the English rococo style. But most of his paintings, like the Hunter's portrait, are bust views of gentlemen clad in mute-colored garments that effectively set off their white collars and glowing faces. They are recorded without flattery or character penetration — as Oliver Larkin has noted, "painted from the outside in." There is enough individual differentiation from one work to another to suppose that the subjects are fair likenesses. Still, Wollaston modeled facial features somewhat by formula, particularly a mannerism of slanting the eyes downward toward the inside with such obvious result that he came to be called the "almond-eyed artist." This trait grew increasingly more pronounced as time went on; and it is on this basis that the Hunter's portrait, showing only a slight eye slant, is dated to the comparatively early 1755 and thought to have been painted in Virginia.

Despite his deficiencies, Wollaston was one of the most skilled painters working in America at the middle of the eighteenth century. He had marked influence on Benjamin West, Matthew Pratt, John Hesselius, and other native colonial artists who rose to prominence after his departure.

John Trumbull (1756-1843)

John Trumbull's career spans the time of the nation's founding, Revolutionary War, early republic, War of 1812, and the Jacksonian era, and perhaps no other American artist of the period so determinedly linked his own destiny with that of his country (though Benjamin West, Charles Willson Peale, and Gilbert Stuart were similarly motivated). Having been a witness to decisive junctures in the young land's development, he considered himself first and foremost a historical painter. Today his heroic depictions of such events as *The Battle of Bunker's Hill* (1786), now at the Yale University Art Gallery, *The Declaration of Independence* (1818), *The Surrender of Lord Cornwallis at Yorktown* (1820), *The Surrender of General Burgoyne at Saratoga* (1821), and *The Resignation of General Washington* (1824), all in the Rotunda of the United States Capitol, are accorded virtually the status of cultural icons.

Besides historical subjects, Trumbull also painted religious themes, genre, landscapes, and portraits — including those of Presidents Washington and Jefferson, and what is probably the best known likeness of Alexander Hamilton, now in the collection of the National Gallery of Art in Washington. *Bartholomew Dandridge* (1773-1802), the subject of the Hunter's portrait, was born into a prominent colonial family. His father, a judge, was elected to the Virginia House of Burgesses, and his widowed aunt, Martha Dandridge Custis, had become Mrs. George Washington in 1759. At the time the portrait was commissioned, the twenty-seven-year-old Dandridge was a diplomatic envoy in London where coincidentally his friend Trumbull was also then working in the diplomatic service. That Dandridge was as severe a person as Trumbull represented is unlikely; most of the artist's larger portraits, while precise and dignified, lack warmth or characterization.

Trumbull was born in Lebanon, Connecticut, in 1756. His lawyer father, Jonathan Trumbull, was governor of the state from 1769 to 1784, (the elder Trumbull was, in fact, the only pre-Revolution colonial governor to back the American patriots, and during the war he helped supply the Continental Army with food, clothing, and munitions.) When he was five years old he was injured in a fall which resulted in the permanent loss of sight in the left eye. Intellectually precocious, he was admitted to Harvard University when he was fifteen, and when he graduated with honors in 1773, he was at seventeen the youngest member of the class. While at Harvard Trumbull had opportunity to visit John Singleton Copley's studio in Boston, an experience that contributed substantially to his decision to pursue a career in painting. His father objected strongly, believing art an unseemly occupation for a gentleman. Nonetheless it was the onset of war with Britain that provided a timely and compelling chance for the young artist to use his talents in the service of the Army. Trumbull's skill in drawing and mapmaking proved invaluable. He became aide-de-camp to Generals Washington and Gates and swiftly rose to the rank of colonel. Then abruptly in 1777 the oft-temperamental Trumbull resigned his military commission to resume art studies in Boston.

In 1780 Trumbull went to London to continue his training with the venerable West, who had established a teaching studio there in 1763. But because of Trumbull's known military background and because hostilities with the Americans were still going on, British authorities suspected he was a spy. He was arrested, imprisoned, and after several months deported back to the United States. In 1784 he was at long last able to return to London and undertake West's instruction. West doubtless impressed upon the then twenty-eight-year-old artist the importance of grand-scale history painting; it was at about this time that Trumbull began to conceive of a great "national work." However in 1794 he largely put aside his art when he was asked to take the position of diplomatic secretary to Chief Justice John Jay, who had been sent to England to negotiate what a year later was called the Jay Treaty. Trumbull stayed on to become an official on the Ambassador's staff and remained to serve in London until 1804. The portrait of Dandridge was done during this term of duty.

After a third extended residence in England between 1808 and 1816, Trumbull returned to New York, established a studio, and painted actively for the next twenty-one years. The year 1817 was an important time in his life. Congress commissioned his "national work," the historical series for the Capitol Rotunda, a project that was completed in 1824. It was also in 1817 that he was elected president of the American Academy of Fine Arts. His nineteen-year administration was stormy, fraught with charges of poor judgment, mismanagement, and

BARTHOLOMEW
DANDRIDGE
John Trumbull
c. 1800
oil on canvas
29⅜ x 23⅜ inches
Anonymous gift

Provenance

Mrs. J. Burbidge Halyburton, Richmond, Virginia
Mrs. Holis E. Suits, Kirkwood, Missouri
American National Bank and Trust Company, Chattanooga, Tennessee
Private Collection, New York, New York

Publications

Theodore Sizer, *The Works of Colonel John Trumbull: Artist of the American Revolution,* New Haven: Yale University Press, 1950, p. 23.

self-aggrandizement. Holding that he showed favoritism to the association's older and more conservative artists, many younger members bolted in 1826 to organize the rival National Academy of Design.

In 1837, the year after his resignation from the American Academy and with personal and professional fortunes in decline, a bitter and resentful Trumbull retired to New Haven, where seven years before he had made an agreement with Yale University to receive a large collection of his paintings in return for a pension. The transaction, in effect, resulted in the founding of America's first college-affiliated art gallery. Trumbull missed New York and after four years in New Haven decided to move back to the city. There he lived the last two years of his life; he died in 1843.

James Peale (1749-1831)

The urbane subject of this painting by James Peale has long been identified as the prominent Philadelphia printer and publisher Zachariah Poulson (1761-1844). As a young man Poulson had learned the rudiments of the printer's trade from his Danish immigrant father. Subsequently he became a journeyman with the Christopher Sower firm of Germantown, Pennsylvania, (which at the time enjoyed considerable prestige for having printed the first Bible published in the United States). By 1789 he was in business for himself, publishing a popular journal called the *Town and Country Almanac.* In 1800 he purchased the already successful *American Daily Advertiser*, which was, significantly, the nation's oldest daily circulated newspaper. By the time the portrait was commissioned, about eight years later, he had gained substantial wealth. He continued as owner and editor until the paper was

ZACHARIAH POULSON (?)
James Peale
c. 1808
oil on canvas
36 x 28½ inches
Museum purchase with funds
donated anonymously

Provenance

Poulson family, Philadelphia, Pennsylvania
Hirschl & Adler Galleries,Inc., New York, New
York

Exhibitions

*The Painter in the New World: A Survey of Paint-
ing from 1564 to 1867,* The Montreal Museum of
Fine Arts, Montreal, Quebec, June 9-July 30,
1967.

Early American Painting, Sheldon Memorial Art
Gallery, University of Nebraska, Lincoln, NE,
Oct. 17-Nov. 12, 1967.

*American Paintings for Public and Private Collec-
tions,* Hirschl & Adler Galleries, Inc., New York,
NY, 1967.

Publications

*The Painter in the New World: A Survey of Paint-
ing from 1564 to 1867,* exhibition catalogue,
Montreal: The Montreal Museum of Fine Arts,
1967, no. 134.

*American Paintings for Public and Private Collec-
tions,* exhibition catalogue, New York: Hirschl
& Adler Galleries, Inc., 1967, no. 23.

disbanded at the end of 1839. For twenty-one years he served simultaneously as librarian for the Library Company of Philadelphia; for six years he was also its treasurer. A portrait of Poulson by Thomas Sully, painted almost forty years after Peale's, still hangs in the Library's building on Locust Street.

Poulson would have been in his mid-forties, however, to have sat for Peale at the time the painting is believed to have been done. The subject appears obviously younger, suggesting that Peale either flatteringly idealized the visage (which is inconsistent with the artist's other portraiture), or the subject is another member of the family (whose identity is yet to be determined). In any case, the softly modeled hands and face, devoid of age lines, provide an effective foil for the dark, penetrating eyes, probably the subject's most engaging feature. The narrow, refined lips, slightly turned up at the corners of the mouth, mollify what might otherwise be a severe expression. In contrast to the prevailing style before the turn of the century, the subject wears his hair combed to the front, descending over the forehead in wispy ringlets—a fashion recently arrived in America from the French court of Napoleon (and which in turn was an emulation of ancient Roman hairstyles). He is posed in a manner balanced between formal stiffness and casual receptiveness. The book in the left hand, with the index finger marking a place, suggests that he has momentarily paused from his reading to acknowledge the viewer's entrance. The book further intimates that he is a man of letters or academic achievement.

The heavy crimson drapery in the left background, a stock property in much European and American portraiture since the 1600s, counters the subject's off-center positioning to the right. It repeats some of the design configuration of the shirt and tie, helps move the viewer's eye around the corner and back toward the rendering of the head, and generally reinforces a sense of clockwise compositional rhythm.

James Peale was born in Chestertown, Maryland, in 1749, the fifth and youngest son of an English-born schoolmaster who died the year after his birth. His widowed mother moved the family to Annapolis, where as a youth he learned saddlery and carpentry from one in whose shadow he would pursue his entire professional life, his eldest brother Charles Willson Peale. It was from Charles too that James received his basic art instruction. Before the Revolutionary War Charles had studied painting, first with the colonial portraitist John Hesselius and later, for eighteen months, with Benjamin West at the Royal Academy in London. He developed a sophisticated portrait style which at first James sought to imitate. After the War (in which both brothers served with distinction in the Continental Army and both rose to the rank of Captain), Charles, then established in Philadelphia, became one of the most sought after portrait artists in the new nation.

James had likewise settled in Philadelphia, but realizing his brother's greater facility in portraiture and not wanting to compete with him in any case, about 1782 began working mainly in miniatures. After fifteen years of such specialization he abandoned the meticulous craft because of acute eye strain. In the early nineteenth century he undertook numerous original portraits, one of the most successful of which is the *Zachariah Poulson*. In his later years he also painted landscapes and a number of very sensitive fruit still lifes for which, after the miniatures, he is perhaps best recognized. Peale died in Philadelphia in 1831, at age eighty-two.

Thomas Sully (1783-1872)

English-born Thomas Sully came to America with his parents in 1792, at age nine. He was brought up in Charleston, South Carolina, where his first art teachers were his older brother Lawrence, a miniature painter, and his brother-in-law, Jean Belzons, who was also a miniaturist as well as a drawing teacher and a theatrical scene designer. When Sully was eighteen he decided to pursue a career as a professional portrait artist and moreover to do so in a larger community where he believed there could be greater potential clientele. After working in Norfolk, Richmond, Boston — where he also studied with Gilbert Stuart — and New York, in 1808 he established a home and studio in Philadelphia, which at that time was still the young nation's leading art and publishing center. In 1809 he went to London to study with Benjamin West. While there, however, he was far more influenced by England's leading portraitist of the period, Sir Thomas Lawrence, whom he had met. Much of the aristocratic verve, casual elegance, and flowing lines of Lawrence's portraits would thereafter be evident in Sully's work, though suitably adapted for more restrained American tastes. Back in Philadelphia in 1810, he was increasingly successful. After the death of Charles Willson Peale in 1827, Sully was the undisputed foremost portraitist of the city for four and a half decades (he lived to age eighty-nine). Five Presidents—Washington (posthumously), Jefferson, Madison, Monroe, and Jackson are among the more than 2,000 portraits he painted.

Sully's half-length portrait of *Martha Wade Young* from 1835 demonstrates his mastery of what may be called the decorative romantic style of Lawrence. The slightly askance turn of the head, the eyes that not quite meet those of the viewer, the bemused expression, soft lighting and shadows all add to the subject's gracious bearing. The left arm and hand gently bent so as to hold the wrap and ever so lightly touch the smooth feminine torso is not only a piquant gesture but also an element of verticality which, in continuing on into the line of shoulder, neck, and head, adds an air of eminence and gentility. Mrs. Young was the wife of a prominent Mississippian who, according to family records, made the long journey by overland coach from her home to Philadelphia for the expressed purpose of sitting for Sully. It would have been a particularly arduous journey at the time.

Sully also did other subjects, however, including what were called "fancy" (meaning fanciful) pictures in which typically children are depicted in quaint, sentimental, sometimes mildly amusing situations. The fashion originated in Europe and was popular on both sides of the Atlantic in the first half of the nineteenth century. Such a work is the Hunter's *Juvenile Ambition* (color plate 1). A precocious lad is shown playing the role of an adult; he has climbed into his father's chair, seated himself on a book to increase his stature, put on the elder's tricorn hat and spectacles, and pretends to read a newspaper.

(color plate 1)
JUVENILE AMBITION
(Also known as *Grandfather's Hobby*)
Thomas Sully
1825
oil on canvas
36¼ x 28¾ inches
initialed and dated on reverse
Gift of Mrs. Roana B. Hayes in memory of her husband, Henry H. Hayes

Provenance

Joseph Howe, Boston, Massachusetts
Henry H. Hayes, Chattanooga, Tennessee (great-grandson of Joseph Howe)

Exhibitions

The Paintings of Charles Bird King, (1785-1862), National Collection of Fine Arts, Smithsonian Institution, Washington, D.C., Nov. 4, 1977-Jan. 22, 1978.

With a Little Help from Our Friends, The Mississippi Museum of Art, Jackson, MS, April 21-July 16, 1978.

(Continued on page 24)

The artist kept an elaborate register of his paintings and he recorded that *Juvenile Ambition* was derived from a work by his good friend, Charles Bird King. In fact, he noted that it was begun in December 1824, while he was on an extended visit in King's Washington, D.C. home. It is a remarkably faithful copy, although Sully's technique is rather more crisp and his lighting more dramatic.

King's picture (Winterthur Museum, Delaware) has traditionally been called *Grandfather's Hobby*, though there is no evidence that this was King's original designation. Sully's painting likewise in the past has been known by that same title. Subsequent owners may have taken the liberty of renaming either or both works to suit their own preferences. But more probably the newer identification followed upon the publication of an engraving after the Sully version and an attendant narrative poem titled *Grandfather's Hobby* in the 1830 issue of *The Token*, an attractive Christmas gift magazine that was printed annually in Boston during the 1820s and '30s. The unidentified rhymer first speaks of a venerable "sage" from whose lips "we love to learn" telling his grandson about an "olden time when all was heroic, bold and new." Then follows a description of the boy's wonder and fascination at the old man's magical tales and finally the vision that more specifically relates to the painting:

> How on the morrow will that boy/With swelling thought resign his toy,
> Steal the cocked hat, and on his nose,/The reverend spectacles impose,
> Mount to the vacant chair, and place/The wise gazette before his face,
> And there half sly, half serious pore/The last night's legend o'er and o'er,
> And deem himself in boyish glory,/Like the old man that told the story!

(Continued from page 23)

Publications

Edward Biddle and Mantle Fielding, *The Life and Works of Thomas Sully*, Philadelphia: Wickersham Press, 1921, p. 363, no. 2353 (re-print of Sully's own account book).

Ruth Davison, "Museum Accessions." *Antiques*, June, 1969, pp. 774-864, illus. p. 790.

Andrew F. Cosentino, *The Paintings of Charles Bird King, 1785-1862*, exhibition catalogue, Washington, D.C.: The Smithsonian Press, 1977, p. 94, no. 94.

With a Little Help from Our Friends, exhibition catalogue, Jackson, MS: The Mississippi Museum of Art, 1978, p. 9, illus. p. 24, no. 9.

Diana W. Suarez, *Bluff and the Magic Mansion, A Children's Guide to the Hunter Museum of Art*, Chattanooga: Hunter Museum of Art, 1980.

MARTHA WADE YOUNG
(Also known as *Mrs. Benjamin Young*)
Thomas Sully
1835
oil on canvas
30 x 25 inches
initialed and dated on reverse
Gift of Mr. Jo Conn Guild, Jr., in memory of May Young Guild

Provenance

Mrs. Martha Wade Young, Mississippi
May Young Guild, Lookout Mountain, Tennessee (great-granddaughter of Martha Wade Young)
Jo Conn Guild, Jr., Chattanooga Tennessee

Publications

Edward Biddle and Mantle Fielding, *The Life and Works of Thomas Sully*, Philadelphia: Wickersham Press, 1921, p. 325, no. 2016 (reprint of Sully's own account book).

The *Hobby* thus conveys several levels of meaning. It obviously alludes to the small and curious toy rocking horse that hangs from the arm of the chair and occupies a position of particular importance near the front and lower center of the composition. On a more subjective plane, *Hobby* — especially in the parlance of the period — refers to an aspiration or imaginary pursuit. Finally, toward one given to such fanciful flights, it becomes an assigned nickname, in this instance, the boy himself.

William Matthew Prior (1806-1873)

GEORGE WASHINGTON
William Matthew Prior
c. 1850
reverse glass painting
24 x 18 inches
Gift of Mrs. A. M. Patterson
and Elizabeth Patterson

Provenance
Mrs. A. M. Patterson and Elizabeth Patterson, Chattanooga, Tennessee.

If William Matthew Prior's reverse-glass painting of *George Washington* seems suspiciously akin to the well-known "Athenaeum" portrait by Gilbert Stuart, the similarity is no accident. But neither is it a blatant unauthorized plagerism. In 1850 the artist had secured permission to do reproductions on glass and — taking advantage of the extraordinary veneration still accorded the first president sixty years after his death and the widespread demand for his likeness in home and business decoration — Prior produced many, many such paintings. Though somewhat larger than most of his other Washingtons and though the face is turned to the right rather than left as in the Stuart original, the Hunter's version is important not so much as a singular artwork, but as a collectible, a curious object of Americana.

Reverse-glass paintings were particularly popular with Americans in the nineteenth century. The technique in part grew out of the European stained-glass window tradition in the 1500s; strong centers for the craft developed in Austria, Bavaria, and Bohemia. But Prior's work was doubtless inspired by a more direct antecedent. About 1800 a trader named Blight took a Stuart Washington (not the Athenaeum piece, but one of the many other Washington portraits Stuart painted) with him on a voyage to China. There Blight commissioned a reverse-glass painting workshop to produce numerous facsimiles, which in turn were brought back and offered for sale in Philadelphia. At that event, however, Stuart was able to get an injunction to prohibit the continued marketing of the works in the United States. This action did not eliminate those original imports and it did not enjoin other glass paintings that the Chinese produced, also as early as 1800, depicting Washington as hero or protagonist in narrative scenes. The fashion for reverse-glass painting then was well established by the time Prior began his series and he would certainly have been aware of the earlier Chinese Washington prototypes. In its best execution the medium is quite difficult because the rendering must be handled just the opposite of the way it would be conceived for paper or canvas, that is to say highlights and details must be painted first, general shapes and backgrounds last. Prior's method is less remarkable in that the entire surface is thinly painted rather than built up in successive layers.

Prior was born in Bath, Maine, in 1806, the son of a shipmaster who was lost at sea in 1816. Essentially self-taught, he lived and worked in Portland from 1831 to 1840. His advertising at the time offered everything from "likenesses" to varnishing, mirror decorating, embellishing military standards, delineating machinery, and painting fool-the-eye carved woodwork. In 1841 he married into a family of sign-painters named Hamblen. With his new wife and two brothers-in-law he moved to Boston and set up what not facetiously might be called a "factory" for portrait painting. Perhaps droll to present-day viewers, many works from the studio were signed "William M. Prior, Artist, and His In-Laws, the Painting Hamblens." Prior had the ability to paint conventional academic portraits, but to attract customers and to accommodate their varying pocketbooks, he also offered the "flat picture . . . without shade or shadow at one quarter price." For approximately three dollars each, he turned out so many pictures in the latter category that some historians have unfairly classified him as a "primitive" in the tradition of the eighteenth century limner. Prior traveled extensively, offering his portrait service as far away as Annapolis and Baltimore. He died in Boston in 1873, at age sixty-seven.

The Democratic Ideal:
the Mid-Nineteenth Century

In 1836, during President Andrew Jackson's second term, novelist James Fenimore Cooper wrote his friend, sculptor Horatio Greenough: "You are in a country in which every man swaggers and talks, knowledge or no knowledge; brains or no brains; taste or no taste. They are all *ex nato* connoisseurs, politicians, religionists, and every man's equal and all men's betters." Jackson was elected in 1828 as the champion of the common man—the frontier farmer, backwoodsman, laborer, and mechanic. (Cherokee Indians of the time, however, would doubtless have disagreed.) Political opponents called his administration "mobocracy," but Jackson's policies fostered national expansion, development of public education, growth of printing and publishing, equal social and business opportunity, and more widely distributed wealth. Wendell D. Garrett, art historian and editor of *Antiques* magazine, effectively summarizes the broader implications of the seventh president's democratization program:

> The whole period of the "great experiment" in Jackson's America was one of change. The steamboats and canals, the new railroads, the revolutionary factories, the growing cities were at once causes and symptoms of the upheaval through which the old order was passing. New influences, partly emanating from Europe and partly indigenous, were at work. The very intellectual underpinnings of the eighteenth-century Enlightenment were being knocked out. The ideals of the previous age — urbanity, precision, reason — were under attack from the Romantic cult of the natural, the simple, and the ordinary.

The new influences of which Garrett speaks, those causes for upheaval that gave impetus to the movement cultural historians catalogue loosely beneath the umbrella term "romanticism," spring from events of extensive consequence. In Europe, the failure of reason demonstrated by the Reign of Terror following the French Revolution and the breakdown in the original utopian ideals of the cause, the long turmoil of the Napoleonic Wars, the negative ramifications of the Industrial Revolution—urban ugliness, slums, and poverty—all contributed to widespread disillusionment. In America, too, growing revulsion against burgeoning industrialization (hastened by improvements in steam-engine technology and the inventions of the reaper and cotton gin), the rude shock of the War of 1812, the economic Panic of 1837, the Mexican War of 1846-48, and the social and political problems leading to the secession of Southern states and tragic Civil War—all combined to generate, in Charles Coleman Sellers' view, "a sense of sinister powers beyond human control."

Unconvinced of mankind's supereminence and skeptical of materialism, proponents of what Kenneth Clark calls the "romantic rebellion" tended to trust emotion and subjectivism over intellect and objectivism. Developing more contemplative frames of mind, they queried the mysteries of life, the universe, and God. In America the movement found a philosophical base through the eloquent writings of Ralph Waldo Emerson, Henry David Thoreau, and other transcendentalist thinkers. William Cullen Bryant, Washington Irving, James Fenimore Cooper, Herman Melville, Nathaniel Hawthorne, and Edgar Allan Poe expressed a comparable spirit in literature and poetry. So-called "Gothic" novels were written to impart adventure, intrigue, and trepidation. Gothic and Romanesque Revival architecture, picturesque in its evocation of the Middle Ages, displaced Classical Revival styles (except for many government buildings, where strong precedent dictated, affecting public statuary as well).

Though portraiture continued to serve as a major function of painting and sculpture for expanding middle and upper classes throughout the nineteenth century, the American public opened its tastes in the 1820 and '30s to subjects that in the previous era would have been seen as vulgar and inappropriate for the serious artist. Genre, scenes of everyday experience, emerged as an altogether fitting, vernacular, romantic expression of democratic society. "Paint not for the few but the many," genre artist William Sidney Mount admonished his peers. John Quidor, David Gilmore Blyth, George Caleb Bingham, Eastman Johnson, John George Brown, and the Currier and Ives company are among the best known who addressed American popular taste.

At the same time, landscape evolved from subordinate backgrounds in history painting and some portraiture to an autonomous statement. "Widespread acceptance of a
romantic view of nature was significant," Garrett explains, "for it was believed that nature revealed its truth and beauty not to a limited few but to the mass of men." Nature in
its own terms would come to symbolize, on the one hand, the vast geophysical asset,
the challenge and adventure of exploration, the present and the *future* of the nation
(particularly appropriate for a country deficient in long historical traditions). On the other
hand, to the anti-urban, anti-industrial naturalist, landscape was the glorious demonstration of God's handiwork and benevolence. "Nature is God's art," extolled painter, critic,
and collector James Jackson Jarves—in so doing, characterizing landscape as of the
highest worthiness for the artist's consideration. Not surprisingly, in much writing of the
period, the word nature is reverentially capitalized, as though proceeding from Deity just
as certainly as the Son and Holy Spirit of the Trinity. Thus landscape was potentially more
than mere topographical recording; it could be overlaid with moral and theological
significance.

"America's first homegrown, coherent, and sizable group of landscape artists," the
Metropolitan Museum of Art's John K. Howat explains, "began in the 1820s . . . It grew
rapidly, developed its own theorists, and occupied the center of the national art stage until it
faded in the 1870s and 1880s." Though many of its members traveled widely and painted
deep into frontier and uncharted territory, the movement has been called the Hudson River
School* because a majority of the artists, as well as their patrons and promoters, lived in or
near New York City, and found much of their inspiration up the waterway to the relatively
nearby Catskill and Adirondak Mountains of New York State, Green Mountains of Vermont,
and White Mountains of New Hampshire. Interpretation of the natural wonders took
remarkably diverse forms: the subdued pastoral views of Alvan Fisher, Thomas Doughty,
and Jasper Cropsey; Thomas Cole's epic scenes, laden with philosophical meaning; the
light-bathed (indeed "luminist") treatments of Sanford Robinson Gifford, Fitz Hugh Lane,
and Martin Johnson Heade; the grandiose and often outsized vistas of Frederic E. Church,
Albert Bierstadt, and Thomas Moran. Though varying in pictorial and emotional intensity,
each version was, and is still, a pantheistic celebration.

*According to Thomas Worthington Whittredge, a leading member of the Hudson River School, the designation was first
coined by an unnamed critic for the New York Herald, who intended it as a barb on what was seen as the group's
provincialism. Other accounts hold that the term originated with Clarence Cook, a nineteenth-century critic for the
New York Tribune.

Thomas Doughty (1793-1856)

Born in Philadelphia in the last decade of the eighteenth century, Thomas Doughty was as a young man apprenticed to a leather merchant and eventually succeeded to his own profitable leather business. Therefore it must have astonished his friends when in 1820, at age twenty-seven, he abandoned his established trade in favor of painting — an area in which he had no formal training. What at the time would have seemed even more audacious, he aspired to the virtually unheard of profession of "landscape artist." But Doughty obviously had both insight and foresight. With the acquisition of the Northwest Territory in 1787 and the Louisiana Purchase in 1803, the geographic limits of the United States had been expanded enormously. People were awed and intrigued by the vast territorial holdings of the still young nation. Meanwhile poets and essayists like William Cullen Bryant and Ralph Waldo Emerson were extolling the God-given blessing of the American land.

Doughty was one of the first Americans, along with Alvan Fisher, Thomas Birch, and Washington Allston, to specialize in scenery painting. He began his career by recording topographical views of gentlemen's estates — not landscapes in the strictest sense, but in effect, "portraits" of specific lands ordered in much the same spirit as the respective owners had commissioned portraits of themselves. Doughty's early works therefore occupy a curious transitional position between conventional portrait and pure landscape. He received his first public recognition in 1822 when eight of his landscapes were shown at the Pennsylvania Academy of the Fine Arts. Two years later he was elected to membership in that institution, an occasion marked by the exhibition of eight additional paintings. (Upon seeing these works the young Thomas Cole was reported to have felt profoundly moved and humbled.) In 1826 Doughty submitted to the first exhibition of the National Academy of Design. The *New York Mirror*, reviewing the show in its June 10th issue, acclaimed two Doughty canvases "the most beautiful in the room."

Except for a brief period of 1826 when he was teaching in Boston, Doughty lived in Philadelphia until 1837. He toured Europe in 1837 and '38. Upon his return to the United States he settled in New York City where, but for his periodic travel, he spent the remainder of his life. Increasingly his work grew in popularity, evidenced by the fact that the American Art Union alone purchased more than fifty of his paintings for distribution through its periodic members' lottery.

Many of Doughty's paintings seem repetitive and uninspired. Yet at his best he produced charming and poetic pastoral images. Rather than the grand panoramas that typify the work of several of his successors in The Hudson River School, Doughty's paintings are intimate and approachable. As in the case of *Near Little Point* (color plate 2), his composition often centers on a tranquil body of water surrounded by trees in the foreground and gently rolling hills in the distance. His light and color is nearly always subdued. One or two human figures may be included, rarely more; and in terms of the total picture area they are typically small in scale. Like the youthful fishermen in the Hunter Museum's painting, the characters in some way "commune" with their rustic surroundings. The ideal of harmony between humankind and nature is a major theme in Doughty's art.

(color plate 2)

NEAR LITTLE POINT,
CATSKILL MOUNTAINS
Thomas Doughty
c. 1840
oil on canvas
36 x 50 inches
signed bottom, left of center
Gift of the Benwood
Foundation

Provenance

Van Loan Family, Athens, New York
Hirschl & Adler Galleries, Inc., New York, New York
Benwood Foundation, Chattanooga, Tennessee

Exhibitions

The American Scene: A Survey of the Life and Landscape of the 19th Century, Hirschl & Adler Galleries, Inc., New York, NY, Oct. 29-Nov. 22, 1969.

Publications

The American Scene: A Survey of the Life and Landscape of the 19th Century, exhibition catalogue, New York: Hirschl & Adler Galleries, Inc., 1969, no. 24.

Diana W. Suarez, *Bluff and the Magic Mansion, A Children's Guide to the Hunter Museum of Art*, Chattanooga: Hunter Museum of Art, 1980.

Charles Loring Elliott (1812-1868)

Charles Loring Elliott was born in 1812 at Scipio, in central New York State. His father, a sometime architect and merchant, moved the family to Syracuse, the nearest large community, the better to pursue his trades. Young Charles served his father in both occupations, but it soon became evident that he had a greater interest in drawing and painting. At seventeen he went to New York City, where he apprenticed briefly in John Trumbull's studio, followed by a six-month period of study with portrait and humorous genre painter John Quidor. After mastering the basics of oil technique and improving his skill at likeness taking, he left the city for his native region, where for the next ten years he worked as an itinerant portraitist. His paintings of the decade show the influence of his teachers and also the idealizing romantic style of Gilbert Stuart, who was doubtless the most popular American portraitist of the early nineteenth-century. During his wanderings, Elliott acquired a Stuart painting that became for him a constant reference for paint application, lighting, and modeling of form.

About 1839, Elliott returned to New York City, where he quickly gained a reputation not just for achieving in his portraits convincing image, but also for capturing aspects of the subjects' personal character and a certain immediacy of effect. He was eminently successful. His work was regularly shown at the National Academy of Design, where he was elected an associate in 1845 and made full academician the year following. In the 1840s, Elliott's style had evolved to the rather more slick-mannered romanticism of the period characterized by Sully, Healy, and — particularly in Elliott's case — the facile but somewhat saccharine style of Henry Inman, who at the time was New York's most fashionable and highest-paid portrait painter. When Inman died in 1846, the contemporary art historian and critic Henry Tuckerman dubbed Elliott Inman's successor as portraitist-par-excellence of the city.

JOSEPH HOWE
Charles Loring Elliott
1847
oil on canvas
29¾ x 24¾ inches
Museum purchase

Provenance

Joseph Howe, Boston, Massachusetts
Henry H. Hayes, Chattanooga, Tennessee
(great-grandson of Joseph Howe).

(Continued on page 31)

The next year, 1847, Mr. and Mrs. Joseph Howe of Boston sat for the companion portraits now in the Hunter Museum collection. Both subjects quietly project an air of self-confidence and refinement consistent with having achieved ranking social position in that auspicious time of general well-being before the Civil War — what art historian Virgil Barker calls "the reign of the genteel." Howe, a prominent businessman, was manager of the New England Glass Works. He and his wife Maria were discriminating collectors of American art — to the Hunter's eventual good fortune. Besides the two portraits, Kensett's *View at Conway*, Blauvelt's *The Immigrants*, and Lane's *The "Constitution" in Boston Harbor* were first acquired by the Howes and displayed in their fashionable Beacon Hill residence. The artworks descended to their great-grandson, the late Henry H. Hayes of Signal Mountain, Tennessee, and then through the generosity of his widow, Roana Bass Hayes, were offered to the Museum.

Elliott's most competent portraits are, like the Howe pair, the conventional bust or head-and-shoulder view. Though he occasionally painted full-length figures, the composition and draftsmanship of those are comparatively awkward. With the advent of the daguerreotype and increasing use in the 1850s of photography for portraiture, Elliott (not alone in the practice) often copied in part and in many cases wholly from photo prints. In the process he lost much of the presence and vitality that characterize his work done directly from life. Still, he was held in esteem by many of his fellow artists, as evidenced by the large number of portraits painted *of* him and by the numerous portraits *he* painted of them — including Frederic E. Church, Asher B. Durand, and photographer Matthew Brady.

According to Tuckerman, Elliott did nearly seven hundred paintings, though today less than a quarter of these have been located. They show him as an uneven artist, but one who at his best produced portraits that by virtue of their strength and characterization stand well above the often tame, sweet, sentimental depictions by many of his peers. Elliott moved to Albany in 1867; he died there the following year at age fifty-six.

Charles F. Blauvelt (1824-1900)

Charles F. Blauvelt was an important genre and portrait painter in the mid-to-late nineteenth century. Judging from both the frequency and the empathy with which he painted immigrant subjects, especially in the 1850s, one might suppose that he was an immigrant himself. But he was born and reared in New York City. On the other hand, New York was the main portal through which approximately 4,000,000 immigrants entered the United States in the two decades between 1840 and 1860. Immigrants and their immediate descendants accounted for a large portion of America's phenomenal population increase during that same period, from 17,000,000 to 31,000,000. The greatest growth and the greatest immigrant settlement took place in the larger cities. New York's population, for example, quadrupled, jumping from just over 300,000 persons to 1,250,000 at the onset of the Civil War.

For Blauvelt, the stream of newcomers was a picturesque cavalcade of representative human types and cultures. It was also a story of patience, tribulation, and courage as many of the arrivals from foreign lands, impoverished and incapable of speaking English, endeavored to get about in their adopted country. Blauvelt's immigrant narratives fall chiefly into two thematic categories: (1) asking for directions and (2) a family's interminable waiting for transportation at a dock or depot, usually surrounded by their meager possessions. The Hunter Museum's small oil, *The Immigrants* (color plate 3), of c. 1850, is obviously in the latter group.

Blauvelt's rendering style is finely drafted and smoothly painted, while his genre subjectively tends to the sentimental—characteristics he probably learned from his principal instructor, Charles Loring Elliot. In *The Immigrants* (which by their physical appearance have been sometimes identified as Dutch) the sober-faced young mother looks directly out of the picture to make eye contact with the viewer. She seems to wonder if the viewer might be the person for whom the family has waited. (Or, in any case, he arouses sympathy.) The dramatically lighted woman sits resolutely, holding an infant to her bosom. Like a domestic icon, the motif is reminiscent of the Madonna and Child theme in religious art. Another

(Continued from page 30)

MARIA HOWE (MRS. JOSEPH HOWE)
Charles Loring Elliott
1847
oil on canvas
29⅞ x 24¾ inches
Museum purchase

Provenance
Joseph Howe, Boston, Massachusetts
Henry H. Hayes, Chattanooga, Tennessee
(great-grandson of Joseph Howe)

Publications
Ruth Davidson, "Museum Accessions." *Antiques*, June, 1969, pp. 774-864, illus. p. 790.

(color plate 3)
THE IMMIGRANTS
Charles F. Blauvelt
c. 1850
oil on canvas
21¼ x 17 inches
signed bottom, left of center
Museum purchase

Provenance
American Art Union, New York, New York
Joseph Howe, Boston, Massachusetts (awarded to him through the monthly drawing of the American Art Union, year uncertain)
Henry H. Hayes, Chattanooga, Tennessee (great-grandson of Joseph Howe)

Exhibitions
Family Time, The Tampa Museum, Tampa, FL, Aug. 4-Oct. 17, 1984.

small child, seated nearby, looks up inquiringly at the mother and points outward, again toward the viewer. The composition is simple, but poses and properties are carefully arranged so as to lead the eye to the mother's embrace. The angle of the bale resting diagonally at the right is continued in the reclining position of the infant. The angle of a second bale, partially hidden and between the older child and the mother, similarly is continued by the woman's left arm. The four central figures together also form a pyramidal grouping, an often used pictorial device to create a sense of monumentality and stability.

The artist was active in his native New York City from 1847 to 1862. In 1859 he was elected to full membership in the National Academy of Design, and he was a frequent participant in Academy exhibitions. He worked in Philadelphia from 1862 to '67, and there in 1864 was elected to membership in the Pennsylvania Academy of the Fine Arts. He returned to New York in '67 and two years after moved to the adjacent city of Yonkers. In 1878 Blauvelt joined the faculty as assistant professor in the art department at the United States Naval Academy in Annapolis. He died in Greenwich, Connecticut, in 1900.

John Frederick Kensett (1816-1872)

John Frederick Kensett holds an important position in mid-nineteenth-century American landscape painting. Highly talented and enormously well-liked by colleagues, he was both a creative and spiritual leader for artists of the second generation Hudson River School. Further, because many of his best works are scenes bathed in a soft poetic light and imparting a sense of contemplative quietude, he is also regarded as one of the most adept of the numerous figures identified with luminism.

Kensett was born in Cheshire, Connecticut, the son of an English immigrant engraver in whose New Haven shop a few years later he received his first instruction in drawing and engraving. In 1829, at age thirteen, he was supporting himself as an apprentice engraver at the shop of Peter Maverick in New York City, but he returned home later that same year upon his father's unexpected death. Back in New York in 1837, he was employed as an engraver of bank notes for Hall, Packard, Cushman and Company. These early experiences in intaglio graphics had substantial effect on young Kensett's developing style; later his paintings would be noted for their exceptional draftsmanship, precise detail, and pictorial accuracy.

In the late 1830s Kensett attempted, with good result, his first oils. He was greatly encouraged in 1838 when one of his works was accepted for exhibition at the National Academy of Design. At the Academy he befriended several prominent first generation Hudson River painters. With three of their number — Asher B. Durand, John W. Casilear, and Thomas P. Rossiter — he set out on a study and painting tour of Europe in 1840. Kensett remained in Europe until 1847, traveling in Britain, France, Germany, Switzerland, and Italy. He was particularly impressed on seeing English School landscape painting and in France by the arcadian country views of Claude Lorrain.

Upon his return to the United States he took a studio in a New York University building on Washington Square and he began making trips to paint the New England mountains and the Atlantic coast. His work met with swift and remarkable success. In 1848, only a year back from Europe, he was elected an associate of the National Academy and just a year after that elevated to full membership. In 1859 President Buchanan named Kensett one of three advisors for the decoration of the U.S. Capitol, an appointment that was suspended at the onset of the Civil War. In 1870 he was a founding trustee of the Metropolitan Museum of Art.

Many Hudson River School painters from both first and second generations — Thomas Cole, Albert Bierstadt, and Frederic E. Church for example — were caught up in the vastness, grandeur, and terrible power of nature; accordingly their better known works are grandiose scenic panoramas. Kensett on the other hand shared much with his older mentor Durand in the appreciation of nature close up, perceived in terms of human scale, readily approachable: nature to marvel and enjoy for its manifold intricacy rather than its breathtaking vista. (Kensett traveled extensively to the West in the 1860s. He visited the Rocky

VIEW AT CONWAY
John Frederick Kensett
c. 1850
oil on panel
12 x 10 inches
Museum purchase

Provenance

American Art Union, New York, New York
Joseph Howe, Boston Massachusetts,
(awarded to him through the monthly drawing of the American Art Union, 1851)
Henry H. Hayes, Chattanooga, Tennessee
(great-grandson of Joseph Howe).

Mountains, but found them too immense and imposing and therefore unsuited to his more personal and intimate landscape sensitivities.) Consequently, Kensett produced not only conventional landscape overviews but also many small oils where the viewer feels enclosed by a private nature hideaway, where one becomes aware of the nuances of sunlight filtering through tree branches, striking colors, textures, and shapes of subtle yet infinite variety. Such a painting is *View at Conway*, a tranquil wooded spot in east central New Hampshire near the White Mountains and the Maine border. The piece is believed to have been painted about 1850. In 1851 it was purchased by the American Art Union to be awarded as a prize in the Union's periodic lottery for its membership.

Unfortunately, Kensett did not have a strong physical constitution. After a vain attempt to save the drowning wife of artist-friend Vincent Colyer in Darien, Connecticut, he contracted pneumonia and died of heart failure in 1872. He was only fifty-six years old and his death was widely mourned. For the estate settlement a short while later, the contents of his studio, about five hundred paintings and drawings, were auctioned for $136,312 — an extraordinary sum for the time, which additionally attests to the high regard that his contemporaries held for him and his work.

George Peter Alexander Healy (1813-1894)

PORTRAIT OF A MAN
George P. A. Healy
c. 1850-1860
oil on canvas
30 x 25⅛ inches
Gift of Dr. and Mrs. Cecil E. Newell

Provenance

Dr. Isaac M. Cline, New Orleans, Louisiana
Frank Schneider, New Orleans, Louisiana
Dr. and Mrs. Cecil E. Newell, Chattanooga, Tennessee.

   Though George Peter Alexander Healy's *oeuvre* includes genre and historical subjects, he established his reputation chiefly as a painter of fashionable portraits for the socially and politically prominent. The Boston-born artist had no formal training when at age eighteen he opened a studio in his native city. A year later, 1832, in what must have seemed an incredibly presumptuous move, the young artist called at the home of the eminent Mrs. Harrison Gray Otis and announced that he intended to do her portrait because it was his ambition "to paint a beautiful woman." She is reported to have laughed at first, but ultimately consented to the sitting. The remarkably successful outcome earned her abiding rapport, subsequent patronage, and perhaps even more importantly, referrals that led to numerous other commissions. Then, encouraged by artist Thomas Sully and with money saved from his painting activity, he went to France in 1834 — still just twenty-one years old — to study under Baron Antoine Gros. When the melancholic Gros committed suicide the following year, Healy came to be most influenced by the romantic-classicist French painter Thomas Couture, whom he had met in Gros' atelier and with whom he formed a life-long friendship. (Couture, incidentally, would later be Manet's teacher.) From Couture, Healy learned the effective ploy of rendering light-colored areas in relatively heavy impasto and dark tones in thin transparent glazes. In that the heavier paint optically advances while the flattened areas recede, an augmented sense of roundness results in the modeling of the head and other spherical or cylindrical forms. An enhanced chiaroscuro also ensues, which provides inherently dramatizing contrasts of light and shadow. One can see these devices aptly applied in the Hunter's portrait of a mid-nineteenth century man whose identity has unfortunately been lost.

During an eight-year residency on the Continent and in England, Healy attained international recognition not only for his ability to paint convincing likenesses but also for characteristically imparting in these portraits the pride, vigor and dynamic personality of individuals who were among the most distinguished and successful of their time. His introduction to the U.S. Ambassador to France, Lewis Cass, in 1838 brought him many patrons including King Louis Philippe. In 1844 the king commissioned Healy to produce a portrait series of the American presidents which was planned for installation at the art gallery of Versailles. Healy returned to the United States and enthusiastically undertook the project; but Louis Philippe was deposed in 1848 and the paintings were never delivered. In 1860 Thomas B. Bryan of Chicago (where Healy had moved in 1845 at the invitation of Mayor William B. Ogden) purchased the paintings completed to that time, and commissioned Healy to add the intervening Presidents to the series. The Corcoran Gallery acquired the portraits, fourteen in all, and added a final commission to paint President Arthur. It was in sum an extraordinary venture. Healy painted five posthumous portraits based on earlier works by other artists, but *ten* presidents were actually painted from life (J. Q. Adams, Jackson, Van Buren, Tyler, Polk, Fillmore, Pierce, Buchanan, Lincoln, and Arthur). Other notables Healy painted in his long career include Henry Clay, Daniel Webster, Henry Wadsworth Longfellow, Franz Liszt, and Jenny Lind. He had a penchant for working rapidly; at the height of his productivity, between 1850 and 1860, he completed as many as a hundred portraits per year.

Healy returned to Europe after the Civil War. He lived and worked in Rome from 1867 to 1872, and in Paris from 1872 to 1892. Toward the end of his life his popularity declined and his vision deteriorated. He returned to Chicago where in 1894 he died at age eighty-one.

James Cameron (1817-1882)

VIEW OF MOCCASIN BEND, CHATTANOOGA
James Cameron
1857
oil on canvas
40 x 60 inches
signed and dated lower left
Gift of the Chattanooga Public Library

Provenance

W. C. Boswell, Pensacola, Florida
Edward Y. Chapin, Sr., Lookout Mountain, Tennessee
Chattanooga Public Library, Chattanooga, Tennessee.

James Cameron, an artist who figured significantly in the history of Chattanooga the decade before the Civil War, was born in Greenock, Scotland, in 1817. He came to America with his family about 1833, settling in Philadelphia where he also received his earliest art instruction. When he was twenty-two he moved to the then small town (less than 3,000 population) of Indianapolis, Indiana. He hoped to achieve portrait commissions sufficient to sustain a studio; sadly, however, no surviving works have ever come to light in Indiana, or depicting Indianians, that would verify his success. He is known to have been back in

Philadelphia at least by 1847 when he married Emma Alcock, an artist in her own right from a family of some means. The Camerons combined an extended wedding trip to Italy with painting. The following year, listing himself as a resident of Rome, James sent a painting back to New York for exhibit at the American Art Union. In 1849 and again in 1851 Cameron showed what were designated "Italian subjects" at the Pennsylvania Academy of the Fine Arts. By the latter exhibition he had returned to the United States. Sometime in the early 1850s he moved to Nashville with much the same objective as that which previously took him to Indianapolis. He had not been long in the Tennessee capital when he met Colonel James A. Whiteside, a prominent Chattanooga businessman, industrialist, land developer, former lawyer and state legislator, and a past (1848) mayor of the city. Whiteside persuaded Cameron to come to Chattanooga; as an added inducement he even offered the artist and wife the guesthouse on his large Poplar Street estate for use as a residence and studio. Whiteside also extended his influence to generate portrait commissions. Eventually the artist purchased, probably with financial assistance from his wife's family, thirty acres on a knoll just west of the downtown. Near the crest, just above West 6th Street, he built an Italianate stucco mansion that commanded an impressive view in all directions. That area of the city, incidentally, is still known as Cameron Hill.

Colonel Whiteside, his second wife, Harriett, their son Charles, and two black servants are the subjects of a large and elaborate "conversation-type" group portrait that Cameron painted in 1859. By some accounts the painting, now in the collection of the Hunter Museum (color plate 4), was originally a gift from the artist to the colonel in appreciation for his long patronage and support. The figures occupy an imagined veranda of the type Cameron would have seen in Italy. The principal couple is seated by a marble-topped table near the center of the composition. Both are dressed in the finery of the period: he in a distinguished dark suit, she in an elegant full-length brown satin dress, the material of which reflects the sheen highlights off the dexterously painted skirt. With his right hand the colonel points to a letter that has been carefully opened and unfolded upon the table. The writing is a matter of brushwork suggestion, too small to be legible, except the envelope, which is clearly addressed to Colonel Whiteside, with the sender's name "J. Cameron" in the upper left corner. This is not only the sole signature for the painting, but also an allusion to the artist's acceptance of Whiteside's invitation nearly a decade earlier. The neatly attired slave woman in the right foreground holds the infant Charles, whose cherubic face is mysteriously enhanced by added spot illumination. (Charles was actually the eighth of nine children Harriett bore her husband. The Colonel also had five children by his previous marriage.) On the left a youthful male slave steps into the scene, bearing refreshments in silver goblets upon a silver tray.

The painting is at once sophisticated and naive. Cameron obviously had difficulty with the perspective of the checkered floor. Yet he was capable of extraordinary flourish in rendering garments and facial features, and was particularly adept in handling the landscape background. As from the point on Lookout Mountain — property Whiteside also then owned — one sees the Tennessee River, Moccasin Bend, and to the right, ante-bellum Chattanooga which, like Indianapolis, was at the time a town of just a few thousand people. Cameron took artistic license in moving the landmark formation called Umbrella Rock from its true site well to the left of the picture to hold a central, if not psychologically menacing, position between and above the couple.

Nearly the same vista, but without the Umbrella Rock, portico, and portrait group, is seen in a Cameron work of two years earlier, now also in the Hunter collection. It is in many ways a more successful painting than the Whiteside ensemble, confirming perhaps what Cameron himself declared, that landscape was his first preference, and reflecting moreover his formative training in the East by teachers representative of the Hudson River School. This view of the Chattanooga Valley is especially impressive for the phenomenal sky in which sensitively rendered clouds, built up in overlapping planes to the left and right while diminishing to the center, create a one-point perspective effect that substantially augments the feeling of vastness and depth.

In 1860, at the onset of the Civil War, Cameron realized he would not likely be able to maintain his career while the small Southern community was preoccupied with the conflict. He and his wife therefore returned to Philadelphia for the duration of hostilities. In 1865 they were back in Chattanooga, but were dismayed at the destruction the war had inflicted upon the town and the surrounding countryside. Thoroughly depressed, Cameron never

(color plate 4)

COLONEL AND MRS.
JAMES A. WHITESIDE,
SON CHARLES AND
SERVANTS

James Cameron

c. 1858-1859

oil on canvas

53 x 75 inches

signed center on letter

Gift of Mr. and Mrs. Thomas
B. Whiteside

Provenance

Col. and Mrs. James A. Whiteside, Lookout Mountain, Tennessee
Charles Whiteside, Lookout Mountain, Tennessee
Mrs. Helen Whiteside Heiser, New York, New York
Mr. and Mrs. Thomas B. Whiteside, Chattanooga, Tennessee

Exhibitions

Painting in the South, 1564-1980, Virginia Museum of Fine Arts, Richmond, VA, circulating exhibition: Virginia Museum of Fine Arts, Richmond, VA; Birmingham Museum of Art, Birmingham, AL; National Academy of Design, New York, NY; Mississippi Museum of Art, Jackson, MS; J. B. Speed Museum, Louisville, KY; New Orleans Museum of Art, New Orleans, LA; Sept. 11, 1983-Feb. 3, 1985.

Publications

"The Whiteside Portrait." *The Lookout*, Jan. 16, 1953, cover illus.

The Lookout, June 26, 1915, page 1.

Penelope Allen, *Genealogy of a Branch of the Johnson Family,* Chattanooga: H. B. Miller, 1967, pp. 413-419, illus. p. 414.

Budd H. Bishop, "Art in Tennessee: The Early 19th Century." *Tennessee Historical Quarterly,* Winter, 1970-1971, pp. 379-389.

Budd H. Bishop, "Three Tennessee Painters: Samuel M. Shaver, Washington B. Cooper, and James Cameron." *Antiques,* Sept. 1971, pp. 432-437, illus. p. 437.

Kay Baker Gaston, "The Remarkable Harriet Whiteside." *Tennessee Historical Quarterly,* Winter, 1981, pp. 333-346, illus. on cover.

Painting in the South: 1564-1980, exhibition catalogue, Richmond: Virginia Museum of Fine Arts, 1983, p. 80, illus. p. 81, illus. p. 239, no. 75.

"Painting in the Southland." *American Heritage,* June-July, 1983, pp. 28-41, illus. pp. 32-33.

Cindy Graft Hobson, "South's Charm Captured on Canvas, 1564-1980." *Antique Monthly,* Sept. 1983, illus. p. 16A.

(Continued on page 37)

again painted. After a short business venture ended in bankruptcy, Cameron elected to follow a quite different, but for him quite serious calling. Always devoutly religious, the then almost-fifty-year-old former artist decided to study for the Presbyterian ministry. About 1870 he moved to California where he served pastorates both in San Francisco and Oakland. His health gradually deteriorated, however, in the cool, damp climate of the Bay Area so that, on the advice of physicians, he was making arrangements to move to Hawaii when he died tragically in 1882, at age sixty-four. While recovering from minor foot surgery at his Oakland home, his wife unwittingly gave him the wrong medicine: instead of a tonic he took regularly for gastric distress, she poured from an apparently similar bottle a similarly colored liquid dose of the carbolic acid that had been prescribed as a wash for the foot. Cameron reportedly commented on the strange taste, but dutifully drank it down. Despite immediate efforts to administer an antidote, within fifteen minutes he was dead. A coroner's inquest afterwards ruled the poisoning accidental and absolved Emma Cameron of any wrongdoing.

(Continued from page 36)

James Cassell, "The South Rises Again Through its Paintings." *USA Today,* Sept. 14, 1983, illus. p. 4D.

Paula S. Rackous, "Museums this Month — The South's Vibrant Art Scene." *MD Magazine,* Oct. 1983, p. 254.

George Caleb Bingham (1811-1879)

George Caleb Bingham was one of the leading American genre painters of the mid-nineteenth century. Yet his fame rests on fewer than twenty pictures that describe aspects of life on what was then the nation's frontier, the Mississippi River valley and his home state of Missouri. His best known paintings fall into two topic categories: activity on the river, including such works as *Fur Traders Descending the Missouri* (1845), *The Jolly Flatboatmen* (1846), *Raftmen Playing Cards* (1847), and frontier politics, including *Canvassing for a Vote* (1852), *County Election* (1852), *Stump Speaking* (1854) and *Verdict of the People* (1855).

Surprisingly, what is not as well recollected is that Bingham was a prolific portraitist; it was in fact his chief livelihood. Biographers estimate he painted at least a thousand portraits over a forty-five year span. The Hunter's companion portraits of *John R.* and *Elizabeth Carpenter Griffin* are believed to have been done about 1860, when the artist is known to have temporarily resided in Independence, Missouri, where Mr. Griffin was the manager of the Barlow-Sanderson Stagecoach Line. Bingham's portrait style changed little over his lifetime and it lacked the expressive vigor and social consciousness of his genre pieces. As the Griffin pair fairly demonstrate, his portraits typically were painted by formula, using standard, rather wooden three-quarter-length poses as well as other such stock devices as heavy corner draperies, classical columns, and distant landscape vistas seen through a window or portal. More typical of a primitive or self-taught artist, the rendering is uneven. Though stiff and linear, the faces are carefully detailed, in marked contrast to the hands, which are only summarily recorded.

Bingham was born on a farm near Charlottesville, Virginia. When he was eight the family moved to the frontier town of Franklin, Missouri, where he grew up. He was apprenticed to a cabinetmaker and is also thought to have studied briefly with an unidentified itinerant portrait painter about 1832 (not the artist Chester Harding as some early biographies have held). In 1838 he studied three months at the Pennsylvania Academy of the Fine Arts. He returned to Missouri, but in the fall of 1840 he moved to Washington, D.C., established a studio in a basement room at the U.S. Capitol, and set up to paint portraits of public figures. All the while he was in the East, Bingham had ample opportunity to see works by the better American painters as well as engravings and copies of Renaissance and Baroque masters. He had an astonishing ability to absorb lessons on drawing and composition through such perusal.

By late 1844 Bingham was again in Missouri. In the decade that followed he produced the best and most famous of his genre paintings as well as many portraits. It was during this period too that he became personally involved in politics. He ran for office several times, and was elected to the state legislature in 1848.

From 1856 to 1859 Bingham was in Germany to attend the renowned Düsseldorf Academy. Many critics feel that this experience was ultimately detrimental in that he seemed to lose his native American vision and strong genre style in favor of an affected or overly refined manner. In any case, during and after the Civil War his renewed interest in politics and public service diminished his productivity as a painter. In 1862 he was appointed state treasurer for a two-year term. In 1875, he was named state adjutant general. Perhaps one of the most important elections in which Bingham was called upon came near the end of his life and was not political. In October 1877 he was invited to the faculty at the University of Missouri in Columbia as professor of art. It was largely an honorary position and though he was provided a studio at the campus, he was allowed to divide his time among Columbia, Jefferson City, and Kansas City. He died in Kansas City in 1879 at age sixty-eight.

JOHN R. GRIFFIN
George Caleb Bingham
c. 1860
oil on canvas
40 x 32¼ inches
Gift of Mr. and Mrs. Walter T. Wood

Provenance

Mr. and Mrs. John R. Griffin, Independence, Missouri
Henry Carpenter, Roanoke, Virginia
Mr. and Mrs. Walter T. Wood, Chattanooga, Tennessee

Exhibitions

America and the New South, Birmingham Museum of Art, Birmingham, AL, April 15-June 15, 1959, no. 15.

ELIZABETH CARPENTER GRIFFIN
George Caleb Bingham
c. 1860
oil on canvas
40 x 32¼ inches
Gift of Mr. and Mrs. Walter T. Wood

Provenance

Mr. and Mrs. John R. Griffin, Independence, Missouri
Henry Carpenter, Roanoke, Virginia
Mr. and Mrs. Walter T. Wood, Chattanooga, Tennessee.

38

Thomas Worthington Whittredge (1820-1910)

TROUT FISHING IN THE
ADRIONDACKS

Thomas Worthington
Whittredge

c. 1862

oil on canvas

22¼ x 18¼ inches

signed lower right

Museum purchase and partial
gift of Leon and Marjorie H.
Marlowe, Miss Margaret
Thomasson and the estate of
Billie Fitts Durham (by
exchange)

Provenance

Mr. and Mrs. Dan Lard, Erie County, New York
Lake View Gallery, Lake View, New York
Douglas James & Co., Signal Mountain,
Tennessee
Scott L. Probasco, Jr., Lookout Mountain,
Tennessee
Private Collection, Chattanooga, Tennessee
Dr. W. K. Striker, Chattanooga, Tennessee
Douglas James & Co., Signal Mountain,
Tennessee

Exhibitions

*The Four Seasons, American Landscape Paint-
ings,* Columbus Museum of Arts and Sciences,
Columbus, GA, March 17-May 20, 1984.

Publications

Anne Russell King, *The Four Seasons, American
Landscape Paintings,* exhibition catalogue,
Columbus, GA: Columbus Museum of Arts
and Sciences, 1984, p. 27.

One cannot help but notice the similarity between Thomas Worthington Whittredge's *Trout Fishing in the Adirondacks* of ca. 1863 and John Frederick Kensett's *View at Conway* (see pp. 32-33) of about twelve or thirteen years earlier. Both paintings are what may be called "interior" wooded scenes. The viewer stands within an enclosure of rocks, trees, and brush relatively near at hand. More specifically, both environments feature a stream, that rushes forward toward the viewer from the center recesses; both depict sunlight softly filtering through dense foliage; and both works are highly tactile. The presence of a fisherman at mid-ground in the Whittredge picture imparts a suggestion of the intimate scale.

That the two paintings are so alike may not seem too remarkable when one considers the artists were very good friends. (In 1866 and 1870 they traveled together, along with Stanford Gifford, on trips to the American West.) In that both men were enthralled with the nuance and intricacy of nature, they shared a common pictorial purpose. Whittredge, four years younger and largely self-taught, was doubtless influenced by the amiable and persuasive Kensett. More significant perhaps, both artists were aesthetic disciples of Asher B. Durand, a leading figure of the first-generation Hudson River School who innovated the close-up landscape.

Whittredge was born in a log cabin on a farm near Springfield, Ohio, in 1820. In 1837 he left home for Cincinnati, where first he worked as a house painter, advanced to sign painting, then to making daguerreotype photographs, and, still less than three years in the southern Ohio city, began portrait painting. About 1843 he turned to landscape. His earliest surviving paintings, from about 1845, already reflect the influence of Thomas Cole, Thomas Doughty, and most especially Durand, whom he had met and who had greatly encouraged his ongoing professional pursuit. Following the pattern of serious artists of the time, in 1849 he went to Europe, eventually settling in Düsseldorf, Germany. Though he never actually enrolled at the renowned Academy there, he studied independently with two of its masters, Emmanuel Leutze and Karl Friederich Lessing. After a sketching trip through Switzerland in 1854, he went on to Rome where he lived and worked for an additional five years. When he returned to the United States in 1859, he established himself in New York City and took a space in the Tenth Street Studio Building. He was elected to membership in the National Academy of Design in 1861, and he served as that organization's president first in 1865 and again from 1874 to '77.

Whittredge was an inveterate traveler and though his trips took him to the stupendous Alps of Europe and Rockies of America, like Kensett he found them *too* grand, *too* immense. His favorite area always remained the Catskills. Never really fond of New York or other large cities, in 1880 Whittredge moved to the rural community of Summit, New Jersey. His landscapes from that time forth became somewhat richer and more tonal. From Summit he also began work on his *Autobiography*, which was published in 1905. It is not only a fascinating account of his own art, travels and experiences, but because it comments extensively on many artist associates, it also has become a valuable resource for students of the Hudson River School. Whittredge died in 1910, closing a life that spanned nine decades and a painting career that spanned seven.

Albert Bierstadt (1830-1902)

Albert Bierstadt was born in Solingen, Germany, in 1830. When he was two years old his family emigrated to the United States and settled in New Bedford, Massachusetts. He received his early education in that New England community, all the while showing increasing talent for drawing and painting. In 1853 he returned to Europe to undertake serious art instruction at the renowned Düsseldorf Academy. Three years later he went on to Rome, where he spent the winter and spring of 1856-57 sketching and painting with his friend, the American landscapist, Worthington Whittredge. He returned to New Bedford the following summer.

In April 1859 Bierstadt was one of several artists and photographers who joined Colonel Frederick Lander's expedition to find a suitable rail route from the Mississippi to the Pacific Coast. An unforgettable experience for him, it would be the first of many such treks the artist would take to the then vast, largely uncharted, and sparsely settled American West. That first-hand witness to the frontier provided a principal source of subject matter for the remainder of Bierstadt's life. In fact it was 1864, the year following his second western journey, that he painted the Hunter Museum's fine oil, *Across the Prairie* (color plate 5), which depicts an autumn scene on the Great Plains. To the left of the picture, cottonwood trees rise above the bank of a tranquil stream that winds forward from the center rear depth. A warm light pervades the entire vista as a setting sun near the middle of the composition glows golden through the diffusion of clouds. The sky seems particularly large and the distances great owing in part to the low horizon line. Delicate touches of paint dot the foreground and represent grasses and flowers.

Bierstadt's work is closely allied to the style of the Hudson River School (a designation coined by the nineteenth-century art critic for the *New York Tribune*, Clarence Cook), a group of artists who sought to express in their painting the beauty and magnificence of landscape. The School's views reflect those of the American transcendentalist philosophers who glorified nature as a manifestation of God and a providential gift to humankind. Bierstadt was an important figure in the School's third and final generation; it was rather a sensationalist phase whereby colossal scale and grandiloquent depictions overwhelm the viewer. Bierstadt's large theatrical canvasses of the period do indeed impart a certain awesome grandeur. But it is in his smaller work and oil sketches that the artist's accomplishment can be best seen. Writing in his Pulitzer Prize winning *Art and Life in America* in 1960, Oliver Larkin declares: "From time to time the freshness and immediacy of his early work reappeared in small-scaled landscapes which now seem the true measure of his talent."

(color plate 5)
ACROSS THE PRAIRIE
Albert Bierstadt
1864
oil on canvas
12⅞ x 19¼ inches
signed and dated lower right
Museum purchase with funds donated anonymously

Provenance
Hirschl & Adler Galleries, Inc., New York, New York.

The more intimate pieces, such as *Across the Prairie*, possess a directness of vision and sense of spontaneity lacking in the labored large paintings. Nonetheless those outsized works were in popular demand by the wealthy of their day. At the height of his career Bierstadt was able to command $25,000 a canvas, then the highest sum ever paid for American painting. He lived in baronial splendor above the banks of the Hudson at Irvington. When his home was destroyed by fire in 1881, he and his wife moved to New York City. By the 1880s the artist's fame was eclipsed by his patrons' new fascination with European art, and particularly the style of impressionism. Only in the past twenty or so years has Bierstadt been critically re-accorded the credit he deserves as a major figure in nineteenth-century American art.

William Louis Sonntag (1822-1900)

William Louis Sonntag was born in 1822 at East Liberty, Pennsylvania, which is today a part of greater Pittsburgh. He was the second of nine children. In 1823, his father, a "druggist and apothecary" according to later city directories, moved the family to Cincinnati, Ohio. Like fathers of many other aspiring young artists, the elder Sonntag saw art as an unseemly and gainless occupation, and he tried to deter his son from such a career. Conceding finally that if young William was determined to be an artist, he should at least be a "practical" one, the father arranged in 1840 for his eighteen-year-old to undertake an apprenticeship with an architect named Jolasse. It lasted just three months. Reportedly Sonntag would not apply himself to the discipline and was always freehand sketching on the job. Thereafter he began seriously to pursue his art. He probably either took lessons from a minor or itinerant artist as yet unknown, or was self-taught. It was common at the time for beginning artists to study by copying available prints, often etchings and engravings after master paintings. No matter how it was accomplished, Sonntag developed such sufficient skill that by 1846 a work was accepted for exhibit at the American Art Union in New York. A year later the newly formed Western Art Union (patterned after the New York organization) in Cincinnati purchased and distributed eight of his paintings; over the next three years it purchased an additional twenty-two works.

Sonntag continued to live in the bustling riverside city until he was thirty-four, and the early 1850s can be called the height of the Cincinnati phase of his career. In October 1851 he placed some paintings on view in a storefront gallery with two particularly propitious results. They attracted the attention of a director for the Baltimore and Ohio Railroad, who in turn commissioned the artist to paint a series of landscape views along the line's routes. At about the same time, the exhibit was seen by sixteen-year-old Mary Ann Cowdell of Delaware, Ohio. She was captivated by the paintings, and after being properly introduced by the store proprietor, she was even more captivated by the artist. Three weeks later they were married. He, by the way, was twenty-nine at the time. The railroad's assignment provided the couple a kind of extended honeymoon vacation. Into the following summer they rode the trains to destinations in the wild throughout the B & O system, camping out overnight, or nights, until another train would stop to pick them up. Sketchbook, canvases, paints and brushes in hand, Sonntag idylically pursued his commission—although, strangely, the railroad's historical archives have no record of what the artist painted, nor does it own any of his works. What is more, inasmuch as Sonntag infrequently dated his paintings and often as not gave them indefinite generic titles, no works can be attributed with certainty to the "honeymoon" series.

In 1856 Sonntag went abroad to study in Florence, a pivotal stage in his development. From that time forth his work shows a characteristically Florentine school interest, both in the tactile quality of the oil paint medium and in the luminosity of atmospheric light — factors quite evident in the Hunter's *Chenago Valley, New York* (color plate 6), a place in the south central part of the state, near Binghamton. Though the work is undated, based on the overall tonality of the scene (Sonntag's palette became progressively more muted as time went on), it can be fairly ascribed to about 1865-70. The imagery follows a formula seen over and over in his paintings: a panoramic view with a lake in the center, out of which a rivulet flows toward the viewer. A fisherman, or two, in the distance is shown as a small component in the vast scheme of nature. The color is highly keyed, and a slight bluish haze, as from

(color plate 6)

CHENAGO VALLEY, NEW YORK

William Louis Sonntag

c. 1865-1870

oil on canvas

30 x 50 inches

signed lower left

Museum purchase with funds donated anonymously

Provenance

Private collection, Washington, D.C.
Hirschl & Adler Galleries, Inc., New York, New York

Publications

Nancy Dustin Wall Moure, *William Louis Sonntag, Artist of the Ideal, 1822-1900*, Los Angeles: Goldfield Galleries, 1980, p. 125, no. 350.

a far away chimney or campfire, tints the air above the valley in later afternoon. Though not considered a major figure of the group, Sonntag created work fitting the precepts of the Hudson River School.

After returning from Florence in 1856, the Sonntags settled permanently in New York City, except for shorter tours of Italy again in 1860, '61, and '62. He was elected an associate of the National Academy of Design in 1860 and full academician the year following. He actively continued his career in New York until his death in 1900.

Fitz Hugh Lane (1804-1865)

Numerous American artists before Fitz Hugh Lane depicted the sea occasionally, but they were mainly painters of portrait, history, allegory, and landscape. Lane, on the other hand, made marine painting his essential stock-in-trade. Of about 190 oils he painted, fewer than a tenth are other than sea and coastal subjects. He rightly deserves art historian John Wilmerding's high regard as "our first native marine painter of real stature." Lane sailed often. He was keenly aware of the ocean's manifold appearances and he developed a thorough knowledge of ship architecture. His painting is distinguished for accuracy and detail. He was also fascinated by the cool, hazy, radiant atmosphere of the New England offshore region; for his adeptness in portraying it, he is considered one of the foremost American luminists. Richard McLanathan observes:

> . . . his work reflects a new sensitivity to the special quality of American light. Though a hushed quiet pervades almost all his paintings, and his compositions in general have a marked sense of repose, there is nevertheless an intensity in the concentration with which he records what he sees that equally expresses his poetic feelings about the scene.

Lane's origins, not surprisingly, were near the sea. The second of four children, he was born in 1804 at Gloucester, Massachusetts. His father, Jonathan Dennison Lane, was a sailmaker. Earlier ancestors had been among Gloucester's first settlers in 1623. A childhood disease, probably polio, left his legs partially crippled. While debilitated he began making sketches, and as his condition improved, he took to drawing the dramatic coast around Cape Ann. It was not until he was twenty-eight years old, however, that he had any kind of professional instruction. On the strength of his natural drawing ability, he was admitted in 1832 as an apprentice draftsman for the William S. Pendleton lithography firm in Boston. Becoming a master lithographer, he remained with Pendleton until 1837, when he joined the new company of Keith and Moore. In 1845 he formed his own lithographic shop in partnership with marine painter John W. A. Scott. The association continued through summer of 1848, when Lane moved back to Gloucester.

Lane produced his first oils about 1840, and his training as a printmaker is especially evident in the meticulous, comparatively hard manner of his earliest paintings. But the greater influence upon his style was the English-born land and seascape painter, Robert Salmon (1775-1844), who came to the United States in 1828 and resided in Boston until returning to Europe in 1842. Unquestionably the best marine artist in America during the years of Lane's early progress, Salmon brought forth the atmospheric effects of J. M. W. Turner, Horace Vernet, and other European romantics. Salmon's *Boston Harbor from Constitution Wharf* of c. 1829 (Naval Academy Museum, Annapolis) seems a definite inspiration for Lane's piece in the Hunter collection *The Constitution in Boston Harbor* (color plate 7), painted in the late 1840s. The format of the two works is remarkably similar, particularly the positioning of the great American frigate in the water. Lane's horizon line is characteristically at the lower fourth of the composition (Salmon's typically would be at the lower third), so that the sky is vast. The swelling cloud bank behind the *Constitution* seems halo-like, setting the ship apart both visually and psychologically as the hallowed national monument it had become. The ship gained fame during the War of 1812, winning sea engagements against the British. Watching enemy shells bounce off its sturdy oak hull, American sailors dubbed the ship "Old Ironsides." It had long since been retired from combat readiness when Lane did the painting, though at mid-century it was still a commissioned Navy vessel, used primarily for training.

(color plate 7)

THE *CONSTITUTION* IN BOSTON HARBOR

Fitz Hugh Lane

c. 1848-1849

oil on canvas mounted on panel

15¾ x 23¼ inches

Museum purchase

Provenance

Joseph Howe, Boston Massachusetts
Henry H. Hayes, Chattanooga, Tennessee (great-grandson of Joseph Howe)

Publications

John Wilmerding, *Fitz Hugh Lane*, New York: Praeger Publishers, 1971, p. 180.

The Boston harbor is identified by the several structures faintly visible in the distance. In the matters of historic documentation and civic pride, harbor scenes would come to constitute an important division within the broader category of marine painting. They were as much in demand as the familiar scenes of gentlemen's estates or the bird's eye city views. Robert B. Stein explains:

> The harbor view tradition reinforced the romantic sense of voyaging out into seascape space at the same time that it harnessed that impulse for national purpose, defined it as specifically American by situating it within a particular American harbor.

Probably three-fourths of Lane's marines depict seaports — at Boston, Gloucester, New York City, the Maine coast, in Puerto Rico, and other places. As Wilmerding again points out, he was truly one of the best of the harbor painters.

Lane was popular in his lifetime. But after his death in 1865, his reputation, his work, even his person (that is, his mortal remains) fell into oblivion. Never married, without family, alone at his passing, his grave at the Oak Grove Cemetery in Gloucester remained unmarked for almost a century. In 1960 members of the Cape Ann Historical Association arranged for a stone to be cut and put in place. That belated gesture followed upon the rediscovery of Lane's extraordinary achievement by such art historians as John I. H. Baur, who wrote the first definitive essay on American luminism in 1949.

Sanford Robinson Gifford (1823-1880)

Like his close personal friends, John Frederick Kensett and Worthington Whittredge, Sanford R. Gifford was devoted to painting the Hudson Valley landscape and was fascinated by the region's subtle and variable qualities of light. He is therefore identified both with the second-generation Hudson River School and luminism. Speaking with favorable intent of the artist's mature style, nineteenth-century critic James Jackson Jarves said that Gifford "painted as if he were looking through a pane of colored glass." And art historian James Thomas Flexner, analyzing Gifford's method, observes: "He resolved to bring down from the sky in each picture a single hue that would mollify all local colors." Depending upon the season, weather condition, or time of day recorded, that might be a cream, or golden, or bluish tone. Though the landscape elements are precise and solidly rendered, the scenes convincingly impart the material presence of atmosphere. George W. Sheldon explains how this effect was achieved in his 1879 book, *American Painters*:

> Mr. Gifford varnishes the finished picture so many times with boiled oil, or some other semi-transparent and translucent substance, that a veil is made between the canvas and the spectator's eye — a veil which corresponds to the natural view of the atmosphere.

The Hunter Museum's *South Bay on the Hudson, near Hudson, New York*, (also known as *Autumn Sailing*), of 1864, presents an idyllic scene of casual recreation not far from the artist's childhood home, a place about a hundred miles north of New York City. It is late afternoon, judging from the length of cast shadows, and the suffusive atmospheric hue is a warm blue-grey. The viewer stands as if on a dirt road that leads one into the picture to the left. Strolling figures ahead lend a sense of scale and distance. The river is tranquil and smooth, and the far-away boats — their white sails reflecting the low sun — seem motionless in the water. The few clouds in the sky are long horizontal wisps that visually repeat and reinforce the restful plane of the river below.

Gifford was born at Greenfield, near Saratoga Springs in upstate New York. When he was small, the family moved south to Hudson. He attended Brown University from 1822 to '24, but withdrew to pursue art. He enrolled at the National Academy of Design, where he studied with watercolorist John Rubens Smith. Following a sketching trek through the Berkshire and Catskill mountains in 1846, he turned exclusively to landscape painting. He admitted, at the same time, a great admiration for the work of Thomas Cole. Gifford was much encouraged when the American Art Union purchased one of his paintings in 1846, and an additional eight the next year. In 1846 he also began showing regularly at the National Academy. He was elected an associate member in 1851, and made full academician in 1854.

Gifford traveled to Europe in 1851 and again from 1855 to '56. On the particularly eventful second journey, he accompanied Albert Bierstadt on trips about Italy, became aware of the Barbizon painters in France, met critic John Ruskin in London, and there too was profoundly impressed upon seeing late paintings by J. M. W. Turner. His own work thereafter took on a lighter, Turner-esque palette.

Upon his return to the United States, Gifford established himself in New York at the Tenth Street Studio building, which housed many other well-known artists of the period. He continued to travel extensively and even served briefly with the Union Army during the Civil War. He went abroad again in 1868, touring for more than a year in Europe and the Near East, and in 1870 he joined Kensett and Whittredge on a westward trip to the mountains of Colorado and Wyoming. He concurred with his companions that the Rockies seemed too large and vast; his preference was for the more intimate scale of the Adirondacks and Catskills.

In 1876 Gifford received special commendation at the Philadelphia Centennial Exposition for his outstanding achievement in landscape art. It was the high point of his career. He had many friends and was well regarded by his peers. His work was enthusiastically sought by wealthy and influential patrons. Just four years later, in July 1880, Gifford contracted a cold while on a sketching trip to Lake Superior. His condition worsened and he was forced to return to New York, where in August he succumbed to pneumonia and complications. He was fifty-seven. Shortly after his death, the Metropolitan Museum of Art honored him with a memorial exhibition.

SOUTH BAY, ON THE HUDSON, NEAR HUDSON, NEW YORK
(Also known as *Autumn Sailing*)

Sanford Robinson Gifford

1864

oil on canvas

12¼ x 25¼ inches

Museum purchase

Provenance

Robert Gordon, New York, New York
Mrs. Lucy Tinker, New Milton Village, Hampshire, England
Kennedy Galleries, Inc., New York, New York

Exhibitions

Loan Collection of Paintings in the West and East Galleries, Metropolitan Museum of Art, New York, NY, 1880-1881.

Mt. Merino, Columbia County Historical Society, Kinderhook, NY, 1978.

The Four Seasons, American Landscape Paintings, Columbus Museum of Arts and Sciences, Columbus, GA, March 17-May 20, 1984.

Publications

Loan Collection of Paintings in the West and East Galleries, exhibition catalogue, New York: Metropolitan Museum of Art, 1880, no. 75.

Gifford Memorial Catalogue, New York: Metropolitan Museum of Art, 1881, no. 378.

Ruth Piwonka, *Mt. Merino*, Kinderhook, NY: Columbia County Historical Society, 1978, no. 31.

Anne Russell King, *The Four Seasons, American Landscape Paintings*, exhibition catalogue, Columbus, GA: Columbus Museum of Arts and Sciences, 1984, p. 27.

Jasper Francis Cropsey (1823-1900)

UNTITLED (Rural Landscape)
Jasper Francis Cropsey
1867
watercolor on paper
20½ x 28 inches (sight)
signed lower left
Gift of Carl D. Hagaman and
museum purchase funds

Provenance

Maurice Sternberg Gallery, Chicago, Illinois
Mr. and Mrs. Noel Wadsworth, Marietta,
Georgia
Carl D. Hagaman, Chickamauga, Georgia.

Jasper Cropsey was born to Dutch and Huguenot immigrant parents at Rossville on Staten Island, New York, in 1823. His earliest creative interest was in architecture. At age fourteen he won an award from the New York Mechanics Institute for a model he had made of a house based on his own design. The following year he began an apprenticeship under Manhattan architect Joseph Trench. He continued study for five years and then received several commissions, perhaps the most notable of which was for Queen-Anne-style stations of New York's Sixth Avenue elevated railway. During that same period he also took art lessons with painter Edward Maury, chiefly to improve his skills at rendering attendant backgrounds for his architectural illustration. This would be the genesis of his landscape style. When he was unable to obtain sufficient architectural commissions to support himself, he turned more and more to painting. In 1843 he exhibited for the first time at the National Academy of Design. Thus encouraged, he thereafter concentrated on painting. As an indication of how rapidly he developed, in less than a year the Academy elected Cropsey to associate membership.

Cropsey greatly respected Thomas Cole, who was probably the leading figure of the first-generation Hudson River School. Cropsey's painting to about the 1850s, generally considered his formative period, shows the influence of Cole in its vigorous brushwork, rich tonalities, and panoramic, idealized view of nature. When he went to study in Rome between 1847 and '49, he even took the same studio Cole had used six years earlier.

On his return to America, Cropsey discovered other picturesque areas to paint in the northeast: the White Mountains of New Hampshire, Atlantic shore in Rhode Island, and western New York State, including especially Niagara Falls. Significantly, in 1856 Frederic E. Church, Cole's only student and one whom many accepted as the leader of second-generation Hudson River School painters, was at the Falls making studies for the grandiose painting that was completed the following year (now at the Corcoran Gallery, Washington, D.C.). Just previously, Church had finished the large-scale, cloyingly romanticized *The Andes of Ecuador* (Reynolda House, Winston-Salem, North Carolina). Determined to show the Hudson River valley equal in grandeur to that of South America or even Niagara, Cropsey painted a series of effusive vistas, including what may be his best-known work, the five-by-nine-foot *Autumn in the Hudson* of 1860 (National Gallery, Washington, D.C.). As the title of this and numerous other Cropsey paintings suggest, the artist favored warm, often vivid fall colors to picture the beauty of his preferred American landscape all the more eloquently. Perhaps at the same time he reminded viewers of Thoreau's contemporary statement on the season when "every tree is a living liberty pole on which a thousand bright flags are flying." Cropsey is chiefly recalled today as the Hudson River School's "autumn" master.

A year before doing the Hunter's painting, 1866, Cropsey had been a founder of the American Watercolor Society. He had achieved full membership in the National Academy of Design in 1851 and in 1854 was made an honorary member of the Pennsylvania Academy of the Fine Arts. From 1856 to '63 he was again working in Europe. (In fact, *Autumn in the Hudson* was painted and first shown publicly in London.) Queen Victoria appointed Cropsey to the American Commission for the London International Exposition in 1862, a high honor. When he returned to the United States in 1864 he settled at Hastings-on-Hudson, in the lower river valley just north of Yonkers, New York. He resided there the remaining thirty-six years of his life.

In recent years, Cropsey's pencil and watercolor works have been increasingly admired. They demonstrate the proficient draftmanship he learned as an architectural student. Further, by comparison to his oils, they tend visually to be more immediate and accessible. One of these, the Hunter's untitled rural landscape of 1867, features stock motifs seen in much other painting of the period: an easy moving stream, a bucolic field in the distance, a pair of young fishermen who represent mankind's finite presence in the grander scheme of nature. Restrained color and diaphanous light impart a casual charm and idyllic longing.

Currier and Ives (active 1835 to 1907)

Lookout Mountain, Tennessee, and the Chattanooga Rail Road is one of fifty-one Currier and Ives prints in the Hunter Museum's permanent collection. Unfortunately, most of the other works are in poor or marginal condition, so that they are rarely shown publicly. They nonetheless remain interesting study pieces and diverse examples from the vast production of this best-known of nineteenth-century American commercial lithographic shops.

The firm's founder, Nathaniel Currier (1813-1888), was born and raised in Roxbury, Massachusetts. At age fifteen he began a five-year apprenticeship with William and John Pendleton of Boston, who operated one of the earliest successful lithographic firms in America. In 1834 he accompanied John Pendleton to New York City, where the two men had intended to establish a new partnership. Shortly after their arrival, however, Pendleton was lured into a different venture. He sold his interest to Currier, who in turn took on as partner a man named Stodart, about whom little is known. The second arrangement likewise did not work out, so that Currier, then only twenty-two, began business entirely on his own.

His first print, published in 1835, depicts a disastrous fire at New York's old Merchants Exchange Building. Remarkably, the picture was designed, printed, and circulated within a few days of the conflagration. In that period before the advent of photojournalism, public response to Currier's relatively prompt "illustrated" reporting was substantial. He realized at once that a ready market existed. To meet the demand, he continued to produce such pictorial news accounts throughout his long career. Scarcely a contemporary event of any importance failed to be recorded as a Currier print. Disasters at sea, death-bed scenes of famous persons, Indian uprisings, political squabbles, Civil War battles, the advance of steam power, spread of the railroads, westward migration, women's suffrage, and many other noteworthy news matters were covered. Particularly with its historic-site implications following the Civil War, the 1866 print of *Lookout Mountain, Tennessee, and the Chattanooga Rail Road* fits well within this category of production.

LOOKOUT MOUNTAIN,
TENNESSEE, AND THE
CHATTANOOGA RAILROAD
Currier and Ives, publishers
F. F. Palmer, illustrator
1866
handcolored lithograph
image: 16¼ x 20½ inches
Gift of Mrs. Arthur Hays
Sulzberger in memory of
William McKenzie

Provenance
Kennedy Galleries, Inc., New York, New York.

Currier was shrewd enough to know that his clientele would have interests other than news. Catering to the strong sentimental inclinations characteristic of the era, he turned out many views of domesticity: homelife, courtship, marriage, children playing, flower arrangements, simple farm or village scenes, religious subjects, mottos and slogans. Vicariously experienced adventure was provided in pictures of sporting activities, horses, and sailing ships.

Manhattan-born James Merritt Ives (1824-1895) joined the company as a bookkeeper in 1852. Currier found his service so valuable that soon he was promoted to office manager, and in 1856 he became a full partner. It is only after this time that pictures carried the imprint "Currier and Ives," although today all prints produced by the firm, whether before or after the partnership was formed, are commonly called by both names. Essentially, Ives was an astute businessman with a keen knack for discerning the public's preferences, but he also learned lithography on the job and actually helped produce numerous works.

The prints were distributed by direct mail, by franchised dealers all over the nation, and by authorized itinerants. They were available generally in three approximate sizes: small (image 8 x 13 inches), medium (image 13 x 20 inches) and large (image 18 x 27 inches). In catalogues, Currier and Ives unabashedly referred to their company as "makers of cheap and popular prints for the American people" or to their product as "the cheapest ornaments in the world." They were indeed inexpensive, even for the time. Prices began at about 25¢ for the smaller size; the larger were proportionately more, up to about $3 each. A select number of the larger folio works sold for $4 each. Individual subjects typically were issued in editions of several thousand. Some of the more popular themes, astonishingly, were issued in as many as a hundred thousand copies. From 1835 until surviving sons Edward Currier and Chauncey Ives disbanded in 1907, the firm published nearly *seven thousand* different titles.

Currier and Ives deserve further recognition for having reproduced works of many important artists of the period: Eastman Johnson, George Catlin, Arthur Fitzwilliam Tait, George Durrie, and Thomas Nast, to name a few of the better known. They also employed several staff artists, including the prolific Fanny Palmer (1812-1876) who drew the *Lookout Mountain, Chattanooga Rail Road* scene. Mrs. Palmer had come with her husband to the United States from Leicester, England. Sadly for her, the husband fancied himself too much a gentleman to work for a living. She therefore labored dutifully and diligently to support the family. She is known to have been in Currier and Ives' employ from 1852 until near her death twenty-four years later at age sixty-four.

(Continued on page 50)

Color plate 1. Thomas Sully, *Juvenile Ambition*, 1825, oil on canvas, 36¼ x 28¾ inches. Gift of Mrs. Roana B. Hayes in memory of her husband, Henry H. Hayes. (See article, page 23.)

Color plate 2. Thomas Doughty, *Near Little Point, Catskill Mountains*, c. 1840, oil on canvas, 36 x 50 inches. Gift of the Benwood Foundation. (See article, page 29.)

(Continued from page 47)

Lithography, the method which Currier and Ives pictures were printed, is a process of transferring the image to paper from a specifically prepared flat-surfaced stone. A German craftsman named Alois Senefelder is credited with developing the technique in the late 1700s. Briefly, the artist first draws a design with a grease crayon on the stone. In printing, the stone face is moistened with water, then inked with a grease or oil-based ink. The ink adheres to the areas previously touched by the crayon, but having no affinity for water, does not stick to the part where nothing is drawn. Paper pressed against the stone will pick up the ink, an impression of the artist's design. The procedure can be repeated, not indefinitely, but in numbers far greater than other conventional print processes: relief (block printing) or intaglio (etching, engraving).

At the Currier and Ives studio, most prints were lithographed in black only: Colors were added by hand in an ingenious assembly-line manner. Watercolorists sitting at a long table passed the print from one person to the next. Each had a single hue to apply. When it reached the end, it was complete.

In the latter part of the nineteenth century the development of chromolithography, photography, photoengraving, halftone printing—and the concurrent wide circulation of newly popular "illustrated" magazines—signaled the decline and eventual demise of the Currier and Ives company. Moreover, because their prints had cost patrons so little, they were not greatly prized when newer and more fashionable pictures supplanted them. Thousands upon thousands of copies were neglected, lost, destroyed, or discarded. Today many of the images are quite rare and, as a consequence, surprisingly valuable. Though critics have never held Currier and Ives prints as high art, the works nonetheless are important as pictorial American history, as a record of the nation's growth, and as a guide to its culture and taste during the nineteenth century.

William M. Hart (1823-1894)

"Mr. Hart's landscapes present the sunny and peaceful aspects of nature — the sylvan stream, the refulgent sunset, pleasant trees, honest cows, and lush green grass," wrote George W. Sheldon in his *American Painters*, published in 1879. Indeed "honest cows" are featured in so many of William M. Hart's Hudson River School paintings that Henry T. Tuckerman and other critics of the day called him a "bucolic" scene painter. He chose to paint the long-settled, genial, cultivated areas of the rural East, areas that show man's occupation of and partnership with the land. Oddly enough, the views were especially popular among urban patrons — among those perhaps who had come out of agrarian backgrounds or those who, suspicious of increasing industrialization, looked fondly to the relative simplicity of a pastoral life.

In the Hunter's *Autumn Landscape* of 1870, cows are suggested only as specks in the distant meadow. But the farm couple in the nearer ground, though indistinct likenesses, have a role akin to the humble but proud peasants in French genre painter Jean-Francois Millet's nineteenth-century Barbizon settings. Colors in the painting tend to the warm spectrum. The sky modulates from a greenish-blue overhead to a soft, pale gold at the horizon. The foliage provides accents of brown, red, and orange. The artist made a specialty of recording the mellow atmosphere and rich tonalities of Indian summer landscape. Like his good friend, Jasper Cropsey, Hart came to be known for his autumnal views. "At his best," wrote John Paul Discoll, "he was a charming painter, able to endow his compositions with a quietly lyrical and romantically poetic sense of hour and locale."

Hart was born in Paisley, Scotland, in 1823. (His younger brother, James MacDougal Hart, was also a recognized landscape painter.) In 1831 the family came to the United States and settled in Albany, New York, which at mid-century supported a small but active community of artists. When he was fifteen, he worked as a decorator of coaches for the Eaton and Gilbert Carriage Company at nearby Troy, New York. A surprisingly large number of artists during the period started in the carriage trade, where they learned the technical skills of using enamels and varnishes and the design skills for arabesque and floral embellishment. About 1840, at age seventeen, he became seriously ill and was forced to discontinue his work at Eaton and Gilbert. While recuperating he was said to have read William

AUTUMN LANDSCAPE
William M. Hart
1870
oil on canvas mounted on panel
14½ x 24¼ inches
signed and dated lower right
Gift of Dr. Arch Y. Smith

Provenance
Schweitzer Gallery, New York, New York
Dr. Arch Y. Smith, Signal Mountain, Tennessee.

Dunlap's extensive *History of the Rise and Progress of the Arts of Design in the United States* (published in 1834) and was inspired to become a portrait painter. Following his recovery, he set himself up in a studio near Troy. He also endeavored to further his career as an itinerant portraitist. He traveled widely and spent about three years in Michigan before returning to open a studio in Albany in 1848. With the support of a local patron, one Dr. Ormsby, in 1849 Hart made his first and only trip abroad, visiting his native Scotland, where he studied art briefly. He returned to Albany, but in 1853 moved to New York City. By this time he was mainly producing landscape, and was exhibiting regularly at the National Academy of Design. In 1855 he was accorded full membership in that organization. He moved to neighboring Brooklyn in 1865, when he became president of the Brooklyn Academy of Design. He was a charter member of the American Watercolor Society at its founding in 1866, and he served as its president from 1870 to '73. Hart spend his later years in Mt. Vernon, New York, and he died there in 1894.

Color plate 3. Charles F. Blauvelt, *The Immigrants*, c. 1850, oil on canvas, 21¼ x 17 inches. Museum purchase. (See article, page 31.)

Color plate 4. James Cameron, *Colonel and Mrs. James A. Whiteside, Son Charles and Servants*, c. 1858-59, oil on canvas, 53 x 75 inches. Gift of Mr. and Mrs. Thomas B. Whiteside. (See article, page 35.)

James Hope (1818-1892)

CHATTANOOGA FROM
LOOKOUT MOUNTAIN
James Hope
1878
oil on canvas
25¼ x 20⅛ inches
signed and dated lower right
Museum purchase

Provenance

Family of the artist, Watkins Glen, New York
Kennedy Galleries, Inc., New York, New York

Exhibitions

Civil War Centennial Exhibition, Washington
County Museum of Fine Arts, Hagerstown,
MD, Sept.-Oct. 1962.

Publications

James Hope, *Catalogue of Eighty-three Famous
Canvases by James Hope, A.N.A.*, Watkins
Glen, NY: Hope's Art Gallery, undated, re-
printed 1961.

Larry Freeman, *The Hope Paintings*, Watkins
Glen: Century House, 1961, p. 33, p. 69.

Rudolf Wunderlich, "Artists of the Civil War,
Part I." *The Kennedy Quarterly*, New York: Kennedy Galleries, Inc. May, 1961, p. 55, no. 68.

Civil War Centennial Exhibition, exhibition
catalogue, Hagerstown, MD: Washington
County Museum of Fine Arts, 1962, no. 26.

The Kennedy Quarterly, New York: Kennedy
Galleries, Inc., April, 1971, p. 216, illus. p. 223,
no. 312.

During the Civil War, artist James Hope served as a Union officer with the Second Vermont Infantry until the summer of 1863, when he was discharged in ill health. He had been present at twelve armed engagements, including the first battle at Bull Run, Antietam, and Gettysburg. Because of his natural drawing ability, he was assigned as a "topographical engineer," responsible for making careful illustrated studies of encampments, tactical or strategic positions, battlegrounds, or other places of military significance. Immediately after the war, he was taken with the idea of using his sketches to paint documentary canvases, not just of the actions in which he had been part, but also of other important events as they could be reconstructed from post-war trips to the sites, written records, and eyewitness accounts. His plan was to show these "historic" accounts as an adjunct operation of his painting studio, charging a reasonable admission (which, in that era before widespread photojournalism, people were not adverse to paying), and thereby making a modest additional income. He undertook the project and eventually exhibited the pictures, several of which were approximately six by twelve feet in size, first at his studio in New York City, then after 1872, in a gallery he built specially at Watkins Glen, in the Finger Lakes region of New York State.

When Hope visited the Chattanooga area cannot be determined with certainty. He had been discharged from the army for several months and presumably was convalescing when the major Civil War engagements took place at Missionary Ridge, Lookout Mountain, and Chickamauga. Most likely it was 1870, a year in which he is known to have traveled extensively to sketch the terrain at important battle locales he had not previously or recently seen. The Hunter Museum's detailed oil, *Chattanooga from Lookout Mountain,* was painted in 1878, probably at the Watkins Glen studio, and derived from earlier drawings. What is more, it was obviously painted for scenic appeal rather than military history. Whatever the time the artist was actually on site, if one compares Hope's view with either of the two pre-war paintings from nearly the same vantage point by James Cameron (pp. 35 and 53, color plate 4), it is apparent that the town in the distance grew considerably through the interim.

Hope was born in Drygrange, Scotland, in 1818. His mother died when he was two, and he emigrated with his father to Canada when he was nine. Six years later, when the father died of cholera, a displaced and companionless young Hope walked 150 miles in search of a new home and security. He finally stopped at Fairhaven, Vermont, where he began a five-year apprenticeship with a wagonmaker. In 1839 he took art courses at the nearby Castleton Seminary, and shortly after began producing portraits professionally. His portrait style is distinct, but primitive compared to his later landscape work. He married in 1842 and established a home and studio at Rutland, Vermont. In 1845 he returned to Castleton to teach at that same school he had earlier attended as a student. For two years, 1848-50, he worked in Montreal, Canada. Back in Castleton between 1850 and '52, Hope met and received encouragement from the Hudson River School masters, Asher B. Durand and Albert Bierstadt. Thereafter he devoted increasing effort to landscape painting. In 1852 he moved to New York City, but he continued to summer in Vermont. When the Civil War broke out, Hope was Castleton's first army volunteer. He actively recruited others, which resulted in the formation of an infantry company, and was rewarded by being designated its captain.

After Hope died in 1892, his son, who had become a professional photographer in Watkins Glen, replaced the old picture display building with a larger gallery that also provided space for a photographic studio. But when the son died in the early twentieth century, the property went to the artist's two grandchildren who kept the gallery open, but tended to neglect the collection of more than eighty paintings. Then in 1935, a dam just above the town burst, and a disastrous flood went through the complex. Debris, silt, and water stood about four feet deep in the gallery, and several of the paintings fell into the mire. Many smaller paintings, fortunately including *Chattanooga from Lookout Mountain,* were removed at that time and subsequently sold. No attempt was made to clean and restore the space. Sadly, the remaining artworks, more than forty pieces, were left in the gallery. The facility was closed tight and was, for the most part, unattended and forgotten. Twenty-five years later, a local amateur historian Dr. Larry Freeman, after a long period of negotiation with the Hope heirs, was instrumental in removing seventeen paintings to the nearby Yonker Yankee Village Museum. All the other remaining works had deteriorated beyond reclamation.

Color plate 5. Albert Bierstadt, *Across the Prairie*, 1864, oil on canvas, 12⅞ x 19¼ inches. Museum purchase with funds donated anonymously. (See article, page 40.)

Color plate 6. William Louis Sonntag, *Chenago Valley, New York*, c. 1865-70, oil on canvas, 30 x 50 inches. Museum purchase with funds donated anonymously. (See article, page 41.)

Winslow Homer (1836-1910)

SHEPHERDESS AND SHEEP
Winslow Homer
1879
pencil and gouache on paper
9½ x 14⅞ inches
signed and dated lower right
Bequest of Margaret Caldwell
Morrison (1895-1984)

Provenance

Macbeth Galleries, New York, New York
Mr. and Mrs. Dunbar Bostwick
Margaret Caldwell Morrison, Chattanooga,
Tennessee.

Critics and art historians unanimously hold Winslow Homer as one of the independent giants of American painting in the last third of the nineteenth century and early years of the twentieth. He is "independent," or as Robert Hughes calls him, an "isolate," in that he worked in a *narrative* realist style when most other serious American artists were involved either with the later phases of the Hudson River School or the *trompe l'oeil* still life, or were responding to recent trends from Europe, particularly impressionism. He was undoubtedly aware of these various directions, but was influenced by them only slightly. As Lloyd Goodrich has noted: "Homer looked more at nature than at other art, painted by eye rather than tradition." His work was based on direct observation. It is frank and honest, presented without contrivance, triviality, or exaggeration. Homer once remarked that after he had carefully selected what he wanted to paint, he simply recorded it as exactly as he was able. Considering his extraordinary achievement, the statement may seem modest and over-simplified, but, significantly, it reveals his early grounding as a news illustrator.

Homer was born in Boston and spent most of his childhood in neighboring Cambridge, Massachusetts. Initial encouragement as an artist came from his mother, who was an amateur painter, mainly of flowers and birds. At age nineteen he began a two-year apprenticeship with the Boston lithography shop of J. H. Bufford. He resigned Bufford's in 1856 to pursue free-lance illustration. On his strong drawing skill and instinctive ability to picture the essential action, character, and setting of a story or event, he won commissions from two of the period's widely circulated journals, *Bellow's Pictorial* and *Harper's Weekly Magazine*. He moved to New York City in 1859 and studied briefly at the National Academy of Design. In 1861 *Harper's* assigned Homer to cover Lincoln's inauguration and, at the onset of the Civil War, sent him into Virginia with McClellan's Army of the Potomac. Chiefly for the merit of his war illustrations, he was elected to full membership in the National Academy in 1865. His 1866 oil, *Prisoners from the Front* (Metropolitan Museum of Art), which is actually a composite based on earlier wartime sketches, brought Homer his first critical recognition as a painter. The work was highly acclaimed in the press and was selected for showing at the 1867 Paris International Exposition. As part of his first trip abroad, Homer attended the Exposition. He stayed in France nearly a year, during which time he was inspired to a lighter palette by the work of Monet.

A certain closeness and familiarity characterizes all of Homer's painting, including the few military subjects. But following his return to the United States in late 1867, he began depicting situations that are among his most intimate and personal: rural life, boating, children playing or idly passing time, and — especially between 1874 and 1880 — prepossessing young women in country settings, standing or walking alone, reading, gathering flowers, or lost in reverie. The Hunter Museum's *Shepherdess and Sheep*, a pencil and gouache drawing from near the end of this series, 1879, is a variation on a watercolor of the year before, titled *Fresh Air* (Brooklyn Museum). Standing into a stiff breeze, the wholesome miss maintains a certain demure and girlish mystique. The scene was first sketched at the rural property of the artist's friend, Lawrence Valentine, called Houghton Farm, near Mountainville in Orange County, New York. *Young Lady in Woods*, an 1880 watercolor, has in the past mistakenly been identified as a scene in Gloucester, Massachusetts, where the artist is known to have resided much of the summer. However, he also spent a portion of that season at Field Point in Greenwich, Connecticut. There he produced a number of small watercolors, including the Hunter's piece and at least eight other extant, showing the same young woman placed amidst trees or at water's edge.

In 1873, only a year before Homer commenced the young-woman studies, he produced his first paintings in the watercolor medium. And even though he continued also to work successfully in oils for the rest of his career, many critics feel that his watercolors demonstrate the greater mastery. James Thomas Flexner submits:

> *Homer was never more relaxed, more completely himself, than in his watercolors . . . What makes Homer's watercolors so outstanding is not their subject matter, but their simplicity and freedom, their transparency and luminosity, their extraordinary color sense, their celebration of the physical sensations.*

(Continued on page 62)

YOUNG LADY IN WOODS
Winslow Homer
1880
watercolor on paper
8½ x 11⅛ inches (sight)
signed and dated lower left
Museum purchase

Provenance

Mrs. Sally Turner, Plainfield, New Jersey

Publications

Gordon Hendricks, *The Life and Works of Winslow Homer*, New York: Harry N. Abrams, Inc., 1979, p. 144, p. 322, no CL-615.

Diana W. Suarez, *Bluff and the Magic Mansion, A Children's Guide to the Hunter Museum of Art*, Chattanooga: Hunter Museum of Art, 1980.

Color plate 7. Fitz Hugh Lane, *The "Constitution" in Boston Harbor*, c. 1848-49, oil on canvas, mounted on panel, 15¾ x 23¼ inches. Museum purchase. (See article, page 42.)

Color plate 8. William Trost Richards, *The Lion Rock*, 1885, oil on canvas, 34 x 60 inches. Gift of Mr. and Mrs. Scott L. Probasco, Jr. (See article, page 64.)

EIGHT BELLS
Winslow Homer
1887
etching
image: 18⅞ x 24⅜ inches
signed lower right
Gift of Mr. and Mrs. Scott L. Probasco, Jr.

Provenance

Anthony Olivo, Providence, Rhode Island
Douglas James & Co., Signal Mountain, Tennessee
Mr. and Mrs. Scott L. Probasco, Jr., Lookout Mountain, Tennessee

Exhibitions

An American Collection, Hunter Museum of Art, Chattanooga, TN, Sept. 9-Oct. 15, 1978.

Publications

Zane Probasco Brown, *An American Collection*, exhibition catalogue, Chattanooga: Hunter Museum of Art, 1978, no. 13.

(Continued from page 59)

Homer spent most of 1881 and '82 at Tynemouth, England, a rugged fishing port on the North Sea. The time marked a transition in his painting from tranquil genre topics to an interest in the ocean, the forces of nature, and their combined potential for human drama. Back in America in 1883, he settled at Prouts Neck, Maine, on the coast near Portland. There he continued to work in the "Tynemouth" vein, though for additional sea subjects he took periodic excursions to Florida, Cuba, Nassau, and other Carribean Islands. The etching *Eight Bells* of 1887, while not an exact copy, is based on a Homer oil painting with the same title from the preceding year (Addison Gallery, Phillips Academy, Andover, Massachusetts). Compared to the painting, the composition of the etching is cropped at top and right, so that the two figures fill a greater portion of the view. Because of the black-and-white format and the several areas of heavy inking, the etching is darker in tonality and more somber in feeling; the sense of swelling sky and choppy sea is more pronounced. In either painting or etching, Homer's seamen calmly, confidently, steadfastly, perilously perform the vital task of navigating against nature's recurring violence.

An extremely reticent person, Homer never married and lived alone. He died at the Prouts Neck studio in 1910. His work was popular in his own lifetime, especially with middle-class patrons, because it offered experiences with which the average person could readily identify and re-live. "What stirred his age, and pleases us," Oliver Larkin suggests, "is his re-creation of the self-sufficient moment when the American responds with his senses to weather, place, and season, with no time and no need for thinking."

John George Brown (1831-1913)

SOLID COMFORT
John George Brown
c. 1881
oil on canvas
30 x 25 inches
signed lower left
Gift of Mr. and Mrs. John T.
Lupton

Provenance

Duncan Graves Estate, Washington Depot,
Connecticut
Private collection, Great Neck, New York
D. Wigmore Fine Art, Inc., New York, New York.

John George Brown was born near Durham in northern England in 1831. He was apprenticed to a glass cutter and worked at this trade first in Durham and later in Edinburgh, Scotland, where he also took art classes at the Royal Scottish Academy. In 1853 he emigrated to the United States and initially supported himself as a glass worker in Brooklyn, New York. His employer (and future father-in-law) urged him to resume his art studies, which he did by evening courses at the National Academy of Design under the noted miniaturist Thomas Seir Cummings. Brown's characteristic rendering style — minute detail, precise draftsmanship, and meticulously smooth, almost lacquered finish — is in great measure an outcome of Cummings' instruction and example.

About 1855 Brown left the glass factory to set himself up as a portrait artist, and in 1860 he rented a space in the Tenth Street Studio Building in Manhattan where several other New York-based landscape and genre painters also worked. Brown early demonstrated particular adeptness in capturing the vigor and ebullient personality of children, a factor that probably led him to the specialty on which his reputation was eventually established. Brown became one of the most popular and successful genre painters of the late nineteenth century, based almost entirely upon his sentimental portrayals of street urchins, ragamuffins, newsboys, bootblacks, and the like. (In his own time the artist was called the "shoeblack Raphael.") The subjects appealed to a large middle-class American populace who, as Bruce W. Chambers points out, "fancied in them mischievous but ultimately harmless ragtag bands of potential Horatio Algers."

Though they were not nearly so well known as the juvenile subjects, Brown also painted numerous studies of elderly people that, while not lacking in poignancy, are inherently more trenchant. In *Solid Comfort*, for example, the viewer meets the stern gaze of a whiskered older gentleman. Yet in the casual ease of the cross-legged pose, the relaxed indulgence of the pipe, the nearby jug of spirits, the modest but sufficiently appointed surroundings, one senses reserved sociability. His comfort is realized partly in the setting itself — on a cushioned chair as securely and confidently as any monarch might sit a throne — and partly in the enjoyment of that leisure to which his age and experience have entitled him.

"Art should express contemporaneous truth," said Brown, attesting to the didactic intent of his painting. Finding nobility and virtue in the simple, honest, practical, hard-won attainments of life was an essential precept both of High Victorian morality and the American nineteenth-century pioneer ethic. In this respect Brown shared a fundamental purpose with certain of the English pre-Raphaelite painters, most notably Ford Maddox Brown and John Everett Millais, and with such earlier American genre artists as William Sidney Mount and Richard Caton Woodville. He was no doubt influenced by each of these traditions.

Brown was elected an associate of the National Academy of Design in 1861, raised to full membership two years later, and served as the organization's vice-president in 1889. He was also a member and vice-president of the American Watercolor Society. Respected and financially well-off, Brown died in New York in 1913.

William Trost Richards (1833-1905)

William Trost Richards, one of the leading American marine artists of the nineteenth century, was born in Philadelphia in 1833. As a youth he studied briefly with the portrait and landscape painter, Paul Weber; but by his late teens he had become a designer of ornamental ironwork, chandeliers, and gas fixtures. Still, he knew that he wanted to be a serious painter. At age twenty he elected to use his earnings for continuing study in Europe. From 1853 to '56 he enrolled in art academies successively at Florence, Rome, and Paris. Upon his return to the United States he married and established a home and studio in Germantown, Pennsylvania.

For the decade following, Richards was chiefly a landscapist. Landscape was, after all, the topic of painting in mid-nineteenth-century America critically accorded the highest degree of worthiness — reflecting the significant influence of such aesthetic theorists as British scholar John Ruskin, whose five-volume *Modern Painters* championed the cause of truth to nature in art as reverential and moralistic expression of God's sublime handiwork. Seascapes, of course, also demonstrated the power and drama of Creation, and numerous artists of the period produced extensively in that theme. Martin Johnson Heade, John Frederick Kensett, William S. Haseltine, James Hamilton, Robert Salmon, and Fitz Hugh Lane would later have some influence on Richards. And Richards himself declared a particular appreciation for the sea pictures of Thomas Cole and Frederic E. Church. But it was a profoundly moving single event that turned the artist to marine painting. The ship on which he was returning from Europe in 1867, after a year's study at the renowned Düsseldorf Academy, encountered a violent Atlantic storm off the coast of New Jersey. Tempered perhaps by his recent Düsseldorf training — which stressed emotional narrative, theatrics and drama, even to the state of melodrama — Richards was awakened to the picturesque might of the ocean, especially as it hammers against the shore. He was thoroughly captivated and shortly after a safe landing began an intense spell of close observation and sketching of water movement, wave patterns, coloring, and translucency.

Richards was fond of the British Isles, and he made numerous trips there in his lifetime. The Hunter Museum's impressive oil *The Lion Rock* (color plate 8) was painted in 1885 after a visit to the site, a place called Kynance Cove on the rugged Cornwall coast of southwestern England. The landmark derives its name from the middle of the three pictured major rock formations, which slightly resembles the head of a lion with heavy mane, in profile to the left, its jaws wide open.

(color plate 8)

THE LION ROCK
William Trost Richards
1885
oil on canvas
34 x 60 inches
signed lower right
Gift of Mr. and Mrs. Scott L. Probasco, Jr.

Provenance

Mrs. Herbert Richards, New York, New York
Dr. William B. Dunning, New York, New York
Mr. and Mrs. Scott L. Probasco, Jr., Lookout Mountain, Tennessee

Exhibitions

An American Collection, Hunter Museum of Art, Chattanooga, TN, Sept. 9-Oct. 15, 1978.

Publications

Zane Probasco Brown, *An American Collection*, exhibition catalogue, Chattanooga: Hunter Museum of Art, 1978, no. 15.

While the sea is far from heavy, one senses that it rolls to the land in endless percussion. The overall tonality is muted greens to blue-greens. The sky is mostly overcast, but low sunlight breaks through, bathing the upper surfaces of the water and the cliffs in a soft glow suggestive of the luminists' subtle gradations of light and atmosphere.* Despite the artist's meticulous attention to detail, his rendering technique is vigorous with individual brush-strokes coinciding with the movement of the water and the manifold facets of the rock forms.

Richards communicates a certain immediacy and the viewer seems definitely to be on and in the scene. Yet, typical of his painting, no human figures are visible by which to determine scale. The only implications of man's presence are the sailing ships in the distance to the left; but their diminutiveness also imparts the idea of man's finiteness and his relative helplessness before the awesome grandeur of the physical world, and by further association, man's humbling before the Almighty. Thirty years before *The Lion Rock* was painted, Richards wrote that he had "a higher purpose than to make a good picture." Art historian Roger B. Stein confirms: "What mattered to Richards, clearly, was not the mapping of a geographical location but the opportunity if offered for the interplay of the forces of nature." To be nearer the sea, Richards moved to Newport, Rhode Island, in 1890. He lived and painted there until his death in 1905, at age 72.

*Luminism, a term coined in 1954 by the late John I. H. Baur, was not a movement per se but rather a method of illuminating the scene, typically by a soft radiant light, variously employed by many important American painters of the nineteenth century, including Cole, Church, Gifford, Lane, Kensett, Salmon, Bingham, and Inness.

Restoration and Expansion: the Late Nineteenth Century

The thirty-five-year period between the restoration of the Union and the turn into the twentieth century was marked by changes that transformed the very fabric of American culture and society. Territorial annexation continued to the west, and twelve new states were added to the nation, bringing the number to forty-five. Some 3,000,000 American blacks, emancipated slaves, entered the body politic as free—though hardly economically and socially equal—citizens. The overall population increased one and a half times, growing from 31,000,000 to 76,000,000. 15,000,000 immigrants entered the country (and another 7,000,000 were children of the foreign-born). They came mainly from Germany, Ireland, Italy, central and eastern Europe. America moved from a predominantly British and Northern European heritage to an ethnically pluralistic heritage. The newcomers settled chiefly in cities, establishing a work force for industries, begun in wartime, that carried North and South alike into the modern mechanized world, and began the steady transition from an agricultural to a manufacturing economy.

America's remarkable growth and prosperity was not without serious economic, social, and political problems however. Depressions, widespread unemployment, and labor strife were recurrent. Large rural and urban poor classes became a reality. There would be blighted farms and city neighborhoods. Natural resources were despoiled in the cause of industrial progress. Democratic government frequently bent to accommodate the wealth and special interests of a small percentage of the populace. It was a time of "spectacular corruption in government and big business," notes art historian Richard McLanathan, "as tycoons fought ruthless battles for financial domination." James Thomas Flexner declares bluntly: "Greed appeared to have become the country's dominant emotion." And in Oliver Larkin's critical analysis:

> No man of ideals, whether critic, artist, or philosopher, could ignore the changed atmosphere around him. He saw that the word "competition" had acquired a more metallic ring. He discovered that inequalities of wealth and status which had once been looked upon as temporary—a moment in democratic time—were being perpetuated by every device the ruling clique could fashion. Money had once been regarded as that which gave the democrat his chance to take his place among his fellows. Now it was something to be wasted visibly by men who valued a house or landscape in terms of how much its owner had been overcharged.

Immense fortunes were made by the relatively few who controlled the stock market, banking, railroads, manufacturing, real estate, and such growth industries as petroleum, meat packing, and publishing. And these who were derisively called "robber barons" became the chief tastemakers and patrons for the arts. The well-to-do tended to acquire things, things in abundance, things that gratified their aristocratic notions: old masterworks, rare antiques, opulent jewelry, ornate decorative arts, first editions, and the like. Unfortunately for American artists, such "quality" was more often sought overseas. Flexner explains: "Their wealth made them seem in their own eyes to resemble less their own compatriots than the nobility, past and present, of Europe. What they wanted, they bought; they would buy European nobility." Little wonder that wry-humored Mark Twain would dub the period the "Gilded Age"—an epithet that stuck.

Portraits tended to be larger and more imposing than before, and patrons favored landscape that was similarly grandiose and theatric. Revivalisms continued in architecture with the emergence of modes aptly adapted to palatial living: neo-baroque, Renaissance, Venetian Gothic, Second Empire, and French chateau.*

As American millionaires vied with one another to collect European materials, most artists at home endured a long depression. To some, an obvious solution presented itself: If the cultural climate was more cosmopolitan, more fulfilling, and more lucrative in Europe—then why not reside in Europe? Many American artists went abroad for extended periods. Several—Mary Cassatt, James McNeill Whistler, and John Singer Sargent, among the best known—became expatriates. (How ironic that a substantially American clientele would flock to London to sit for a portrait in Sargent's fashionable studio.)

Even to those not inclined to live abroad, schooling with a European master or at one of the prominent European academies came to be held as near-essential for a young American artist's development and probable success. Both before and after the Civil War, such American painters as Albert Bierstadt, George Caleb Bingham, Richard Caton Woodville, and Eastman Johnson were learning the particular creative thrust of the Düsseldorf Academy: theatrics, sentimentality, poetic intensification of reality, and above all, insistence on precise detail. In the 1870s Munich eclipsed Düsseldorf as the leading art center in Germany. The persuasive young artist and teacher Wilhelm Leibl, who had devotedly studied masterworks at the Pinakothek, brilliantly revived the dramatic, painterly manner of Rembrandt, Franz Hals, Diego Valásquez, and Peter Paul Rubens. Such notable American painters as Frank Duveneck and William Merritt Chase learned from him the "Munich style," characterized by bravura brush technique, flashing highlights, diminishing into warm, dark backgrounds, and unidealized subject matter, typically scenes from everyday life. Of import for later American art, Duveneck and Chase passed on the Munich principles to Robert Henri and other members of the Ash Can group.

As Munich supplanted Düsseldorf, so in the last two decades of the century did Paris supersede Munich as the center of greatest impact on American visual arts. "By far, the largest contingent of American students went to Paris," E. P. Richardson writes. "From the seventies on, every French painter who gained prominence, every French movement which appeared collected a number of American pupils and followers." Most of those Americans, eager to adopt the European fashions that were selling back home, studied with the officially recognized Salon painters and sculptors such as Jean-Leon Gérôme, Jules Bastien-Lepage, and C-E-A Carolus-Duran, or at the conservative Colarossi and Julian academies. Flexner describes the regimen:

> In France, the Americans were caught up in a long drawn-out pedagogical system, much of which dated back to the 17th century. They had to draw from plaster casts and then from the nude model until they could reproduce every part of a human body in any conceivable position. The use of oil paint was a separate step, as was the composing of several figures, nude or clothed, into a logical picture.

Thus properly steeped in academic painting, or in eclectic combinations, or the refined Barbizon landscape style, or—in sculpture—a heroic or romantic realism, American students saw themselves returning to their native country as enlightened apostles of the grand European manner, ready to provide for the tastes of affluent patrons. But, as Flexner continues, it was a dubious homecoming for most:

> These students hoped, of course, that after their return to the United States they would sell their works to the plutocrats who had been importing pictures. However, shrewd businessmen preferred to acquire the real thing from Europe rather than imitations being created in their own cities by their own compatriots.

Not all Americans who studied abroad practiced what has sometimes been called "bastard" style academic art. Some had begun to do so, but in the course of their pedantic training at the "proper" academies, they became aware of revolutionary developments outside the officially approved Salon production—specifically impressionism and post-impressionism. One of the first, Mary Cassatt, befriended Edgar Degas and other French impressionists, and lived her mature creative life in France. A relatively small number of others—including Childe Hassam, John H. Twatchman, and Theodore Robinson—brought a distinctly American, less doctrinaire version of the style to America, albeit twenty years behind the zenith of the movement in Europe. American artists would not concertedly come to grips with modernism for yet another twenty years, in the second decade of the twentieth century.

---

*In fairness, it should be noted that by the latter fifteen years of the century, the nation's technological progress made possible the beginnings of more contemporary architectural invention, evidenced in the work of H. H. Richardson, Louis Sullivan, the firms of Burnham and Root, and Hollabird and Roche—all pioneers of the so-called "Chicago School."

J. Alden Weir (1852-1919)

HELEN WEIR STURGIS

J. Alden Weir

c. 1878

oil on canvas

49 x 36 inches

signed lower right: "J. Alden Weir per D. Weir"

Gift of M. R. Schweitzer in honor of his friends and clients in Chattanooga

Provenance

Helen Rutgers Weir Sturgis (sister of the artist)
Reginald Sturgis
Helen Sturgis Young
M. R. Schweitzer, New York, New York

Exhibitions

Fifty-third Annual Exhibition, National Academy of Design, New York, NY, 1878.

Publications

Fifty-third Annual Exhibition, National Academy of Design, exhibition catalogue, New York: National Academy of Design, 1878, p. 26, no. 453.

Maria Naylor, *The National Academy of Design Exhibition Record, 1861-1900,* New York: Kennedy Galleries, Inc., 1973, p. 1005, no. 453.

Art Journal, Spring, 1969.

Art Quarterly, Spring 1969.

Doreen Bolger Burke, *J. Alden Weir, An American Impressionist,* Newark: University of Delaware Press, 1983, p. 96, no. 3.9.

J. Alden Weir is best known as an impressionist-style artist and one of the founding members, in 1896, of The Ten American Painters, an association of like-minded Boston and New York impressionists. But impressionism marks only the phase of his career after about 1890. For twenty years prior to his conversion (and "conversion" is an apt term in his case), he worked seriously in an academic manner built variously on the styles of his father and first teacher, Robert W. Weir, a painter of portraits, landscapes, genre, and historical subjects, and, for forty-two years, a drawing master at the United States Military Academy; of his older half-brother, John Ferguson Weir, a painter, National Academician, and first director of the Yale University School of Fine Arts; of his instructors at the National Academy of Design between 1870 and '72; and particularly of Jean-Leon Gerome at the École des Beaux Arts in Paris, where young Weir studied assiduously between 1873 and '77. During that first European stay, he met Edouard Manet, whom he said could not draw, and James McNeill Whistler, whom he thought eccentric and called "a snob of the first water." Upon attending the third major French impressionist exhibition just before returning to America, he bemused: "I never in my life saw more horrible things." Slightly more than a decade later, he held Whistler in esteem, had purchased three Manet paintings, and was himself experimenting in the light-bathed, broken-color, brushed-daubed effects of impressionism.

When he painted the three-quarter-length oil portrait of his sister, Helen Weir Sturgis, in 1878, he was only twenty-six years old, and back from Paris just a year. The format reveals his admitted admiration for certain old masters, whose work he had seen in Europe: Raphael, Titian, and the early portraits of Franz Hals. As in numerous other Weir portraits of the period, Mrs. Sturgis is posed near-frontally, before a dark, non-descript background, even wearing dark clothing so that attention is directed to the illuminated face and hands. Drawing on gloves gives an implicit sense of movement and "motivates" the pose. (Though not greatly alike, the viewer may be reminded of Titian's *Man with the Glove*.) By the curious fern held in the right hand, the artist demonstrates his ability to capture delicate and fragile things. And he makes his sister a latter-day madonna; her head is accentuated by the thin encircling ribbon on the brim of the hat, a not-too-subtly disguised halo in the fine-spun Raphael fashion.

Weir was born at West Point, New York, in 1852, the youngest of sixteen children from his father's two marriages. While still a student at the National Academy in his early twenties, he began a life-long friendship with romantic-mystic painter, Albert Pinkham Ryder. He often took care of the reclusive, unmarried Ryder during the latter's illnesses, and when Ryder died in 1917, Weir paid the funeral expenses. He was also close to fellow impressionist and member of The Ten, John Twachtman, until Twachtman's untimely death in 1902. Weir taught many years at the Cooper Union in New York and at the Art Students League. He was a founder of the Society of American Artists in 1877; however, in 1897 he resigned, along with Twachtman and Childe Hassam, in dissatisfaction with the quality of recent Society exhibits. He was elected to full status in the National Academy in 1885; from 1915 to '17, he served as the organization's president. Though already moving toward a developed impressionist style, in 1893 he returned to an academic neo-classical mode for an important commission, the interior dome mural for the Manufacturers and Liberal Arts Building at the World Columbian Exposition in Chicago. Twenty years later, 1913, he submitted twenty-five impressionist works to the New York Armory Show. He was elected to the American Academy of Arts and Letters in 1915. He received an honorary degree from Princeton University in 1916, and another from Yale in 1917. As early as 1911 Weir suffered heart trouble, though it was not until 1919 that his health deteriorated rapidly. He died in New York City in December at age sixty-seven.

Richard LaBarre Goodwin (1840-1910)

Richard LaBarre Goodwin's finely detailed oil, *The Huntsman's Door*, (color plate 9), undated, though from stylistic comparison probably painted about 1890, was the first artwork to be formally acquired by the Hunter Museum of Art after its founding in 1951. In May 1952 Mrs. Otto K. LeBron donated the painting in memory of her late husband. Mr. LeBron, a Chattanooga jeweler for many years, recounted in a *Chattanooga Times* interview, March 17, 1935, that earlier in the year he found the painting, dingy and dust-covered, in a local attic, where it had been forgotten and neglected for possibly as long as forty years. LeBron, who also conserved paintings as a hobby, cleaned and restored the picture before putting it on display at the Edwards and LeBron showroom, where it remained for about a decade.

Goodwin was one of several American artists* in the period following the Civil War to the turn of the century who specialized in this variation on the still-life theme, the antecedents of which can be traced to the so-called "rack" and "game" paintings of seventeenth and eighteenth century Europe. Their manner was to depict ordinary but personally meaningful objects — often actual-sized for heightened veristic effect — positioned randomly on a vertical plane. The arrangement typically appears set at very close range; in fact, the shallower the pictorial depth, the more convincing the illusion. The rendering style is highly realistic, a technique that has come to be called *"trompe l'oeil,"* after the French expression meaning "fool the eye."

The point of this painterly deception, this fascination with textures and surface qualities, does not end solely in the achievement of incredibly true-to-life images. The artworks are in addition subjective narratives: nostalgic associations with the person or persons to whom the properties belonged or the fond recollection of an event (Goodwin's hunt, for

(color plate 9)

THE HUNTSMAN'S DOOR

Richard LaBarre Goodwin

c. 1890

oil on canvas

50½ x 30¼ inches

signed lower left

Gift of Mrs. Otto K. LeBron in memory of her husband, Otto K. LeBron

Provenance

Mr. and Mrs. Otto K. LeBron, Chattanooga, Tennessee.

(Continued on page 71)

example) or an esteemed and happier time. In a broader sense the paintings may celebrate the simple joys of rustic living or revere time-worn, yet time-honored, values.

Alfred Frankenstein, art historian and authority on American *trompe l'oeil* still-life painting, calls Goodwin (who also painted landscapes and portraits) "the master of the hunting cabin door." On the basis of considerable research, he believes the artist may have produced as many as a hundred such pictures; most, however, have been lost, and today only eighteen are known to exist. The Museum is indeed fortunate in having not just one of the surviving pieces, but one that is an excellent painting and a superb example of the artist's skill.

Goodwin was born in Albany, New York, in 1840. His father, Edwin Wyburn Goodwin, was an itinerant portraitist who over a span of fifteen years produced an astonishing number of paintings, in excess of eight hundred. The elder Goodwin died when Richard was only five, however, so that he was not a direct influence on his son's professional development. Young Goodwin probably studied with several undistinguished artists in New York City before declaring himself a practicing portrait painter at about age twenty. At the onset of the Civil War he enlisted with a regiment of New York volunteers and was shortly thereafter wounded at the first battle of Bull Run. Given a disability discharge, he soon resumed painting.

The artist never lived any one place very long. From temporary home bases at Ithaca, Seneca Falls, Clifton Springs, Penn Yan, Rochester, and Syracuse, he traveled widely through upstate New York for about twenty-five years. Like his father, he plied mainly the portrait craft, though he painted his first still lifes from the Syracuse studio in the early 1880s. He went west in the '90s, living for a while in Chicago, Colorado Springs, Los Angeles, San Francisco, and Portland, Oregon, before returning to Rochester, New York, in 1908. He had recently moved to Orange, New Jersey, when he died in 1910.

*The others: notably William Michael Harnett, John Frederick Peto, John Haberle, and J. D. Chalfant.

(Continued from page 70)

Publications

N. Key Hart, "Masterpiece Found in an Attic?" *The Chattanooga Sunday Times,* Magazine Section, March 17, 1935, p. 1.

Diana W. Suarez, *Bluff and the Magic Mansion, A Children's Guide to the Hunter Museum of Art,* Chattanooga: Hunter Museum of Art, 1980.

J. Francis Murphy (1853-1921)

THE GLORY OF EVENING
J. Francis Murphy
1888
oil on board
3½ x 5¼ inches
initialed lower right
Museum purchase

Provenance
Kennedy Galleries, Inc., New York, New York.

SUMMER TIME
J. Francis Murphy
1908
oil on canvas
24¼ x 36 inches
signed and dated lower right
Gift of William J. Flather, Jr.

Provenance

William J. Flather, Washington, D.C.
William J. Flather, Jr., Washington, D.C.

Exhibitions

Second Exhibition of Oil Paintings by Contemporary American Artists, Corcoran Gallery of Art, Washington, D.C., Dec. 8, 1908-Jan. 17, 1909.

Fall Fiesta Benefit, Montgomery Museum of Art, Montgomery, AL, Oct. 28-Nov. 5, 1961.

American Traditionalists of the Twentieth Century, Columbus Museum of Arts and Crafts, Columbus, GA, Feb. 15-March 17, 1963.

Publications

Second Exhibition of Oil Paintings by Contemporary American Artists, exhibition catalogue, Washington, D.C.: Corcoran Gallery of Art, 1908, no. 278.

By the mid-1870s, when J. Francis Murphy was embarking upon his career as a serious landscape artist, the Hudson River School painters, then in the so-called "third generation," were sharply declining in popularity. Outsized vistas by such figures as Frederic Church, Albert Bierstadt, and Thomas Moran — stressing objective detail, awesome grandeur, vast panorama, and the terrible beauty of raw, primitive nature — with some validity perhaps, came to be seen as artificial, overblown and melodramatic. What is more, rapid westward settlement in the post-Civil War years diminished the fascination and intrigue of the wilderness. Growing industrialization at the same time in numerous American cities made the Hudson River School artists' worshipful regard for the native land seem increasingly out-of-touch with contemporary reality. At a fit stage for challenging traditional landscape painting, susceptive American artists — particularly a large number studying in France — learned of two comparatively radical approaches, both of which advanced the idea that nature could be "interpreted" for its mellowness, potential subject feeling, and nuances of color, light and atmosphere. Childe Hassam, Theodore Robinson, and John H. Twachtman were among those who adopted impressionist theory and characteristic brushwork. Others, including Murphy, worked in a style more closely alligned to the poetic, *plein aire* Barbizon style painting of Jean Francois Millet, Theodore Rousseau, and Camille Corot. Though Murphy never studied abroad, he exuberantly employed stylistic devices reminiscent of Corot, whose work he highly regarded.

Both Murphy oil paintings in the Hunter Museum collection, *The Glory of Evening* of 1888, and *Summer Time* from 1908, reveal Corot landscape design tendencies: the broadly generalized field or pasture, a somewhat more carefully rendered clump of trees just off center, and a portion of the tree branches set out as quick linear wisps. Color too — the tawny golden cast of *Glory* . . . or the muted silvery greens of *Summer Time* — follows the purposely limited range favored by Corot and other Barbizon painters. American art historian Samuel Isham coined the word *tonalism* in 1905, to describe Murphy's reserved usage (as well as the late work of Twachtman, and certain paintings by George Inness, Homer Dodge Martin, William Morris Hunt, John LaFarge, and several others). An extreme variant of both luminism and impressionism, objects pictured in tonalist compositions appear semi-dissolved in light and closely keyed color. Detail is subordinate to a subtle pervading harmony, and the resultant works often impart a moody dreamlike character. Isham was writing in a specific instance about tonalist painter Dwight William Tyron, but his comments could as readily have applied to Murphy:

The color is kept within one milky, luminous tone that softens and transmutes whatever more violent tints may be beneath to something in harmony, though there is no monotony. It is not a messing together of warring colors into one solid monotone, but each is pure and distinct for all its delicacy.

Murphy was born in Oswego, New York, in 1853. From an early age he showed talent for drawing and painting; however, he had no formal art instruction. At age seventeen, he went to Chicago to take a job as an advertising signboard painter. The following year he returned east, settling near Orange, New Jersey, where he painted and supported himself by teaching. Four years later, 1875, he moved to New York City, and took a space at the Tenth Street Studio building. In another year, he exhibited for the first time at the National Academy of Design. He was elected an associate member of the Academy in 1885. About this time, he moved his lodging and studio to the Chelsea Hotel, which remained his "city" residence until his death in 1921. In 1887, the same year he was made full academician, he built a studio near Arkville, New York, where he devoted summers and falls to painting the surrounding Catskill Mountains. Murphy also achieved membership in the Salmagundi Club and the Society of American Artists.

George Inness (1825-1894)

NEAR MILTON
George Inness
1880
oil on panel
16¼ x 23¾ inches
signed and dated lower right
Gift of Mr. and Mrs. Scott L. Probasco, Jr.

Provenance

F. G. Lloyd
Rennie P. Schwerin
LeRoy Ireland
Dr. T. E. Hanley
Lake View Galleries, Lake View, New York
Douglas James & Co., Signal Mountain, Tennessee
Mr. and Mrs. Scott L. Probasco, Jr., Lookout Mountain, Tennessee

Exhibitions

Inness Memorial Exhibition, Fine Arts Building, New York, NY, Dec. 27, 1894.

Inness Executor's Sale, Fifth Avenue Art Gallery, New York, NY, Feb. 12-14, 1895.

George Inness Exhibition, John Levy Galleries, New York, NY, Feb.-March, 1947.

An American Collection, Hunter Museum of Art, Chattanooga, TN, Sept. 9-Oct. 15, 1978.

Flowers and Art, Dixon Gallery, Memphis, TN, April 7-15, 1984.

Publications

Inness Memorial Exhibition, exhibition catalogue, New York: Fine Arts Building, 1894, no. 187.

Inness Executor's Sale, catalogue, New York: Fifth Avenue Art Gallery, 1895, no. 147.
(Continued on page 74)

George Inness was one of the ablest and most prolific American nineteenth-century landscape painters. But while his stylistic formation was in the Hudson River School, in the course of his career he moved steadily away from its predominant objective and naturalistic tenets in favor of a subjective, freely brushed, diffused-image, tonalist approach that aptly demonstrated his immersion into metaphysics and spiritualism. Speaking chiefly of his later and more widely acclaimed work, Robert S. Mattison has noted: "Inness thought that landscape painting should result from a dialectic between the artist's personal feelings and experiences." Inness shares this mystic, visionary purpose with certain other artists of the period, notably Ralph A. Blakelock, Albert Pinkham Ryder, and George Fuller.

Born on a farm near Newburgh, New York, Inness was the sixth of thirteen children of Clarissa and John Inness, a Scottish immigrant who had successfully re-established himself as a grocer. The family soon moved to New York City and then on to Newark, New Jersey, where Inness spent most of his childhood. He was a sickly youth, suffering several undisclosed illnesses, of which one was probably epilepsy. He had little formal education and, to his father's initial consternation, virtually no interest in the grocery business. In his early teens he studied briefly with a little-known local artist named John Jesse Barker. About 1840 he went to New York to apprentice in the engraving firm of Sherman and Smith. While in the city he also took painting lessons with the French-émigré landscape artist, Regis Gignoux. In 1844, still not yet twenty years old, he began exhibiting regularly at the National Academy of Design and the American Art Union.

Six years later Inness married and undertook the first of several extended study trips to Europe. He worked two years in Italy, followed immediately by a second two-year stay in France, where he came to know and admire Barbizon School painting. He admitted to being especially taken with the work of Corot, Daubigny, and Rousseau. At about this time, as well, he arrived at a monumental conclusion that would bear upon all his subsequent work. "I had begun to see," he wrote, "that elabourateness in detail did not gain me meaning." Thus, in his painting, he grew progressively less interested in topographical accuracy and more concerned with mood and pictorial drama. Further, inspired almost certainly from his awareness of such important seventeenth-century Dutch landscapists as Jacob Van Ruisdael, Inness often painted the forces of nature in transition: approaching storms, the stirring contrast and interplay of sunlight against deep shadows of ominous dark clouds, or of dark trees silhouetted against billowing white thunderheads. This preoccupation is evidenced in *Near Milton*, painted of an area in southeastern New Hampshire the artist periodically visited on excursions to the White Mountains, this occasion in 1880. One sees, too, a favored motif of Inness and numerous other Hudson River School contemporaries: a lone figure, purposely diminutive by comparison to the surrounding land and sky, so as to suggest man's finiteness and absorbtion in the infinite vastness of Creation. Consistent with his striving for emotional meaning, the brushwork is deft and painterly.

After a second sojourn in France between 1856 and '59, Inness returned to America and settled at Medfield, Massachusetts, near Boston; then between 1864 and '70 he lived at Eagleswood, New Jersey, where significantly a friend and fellow artist, William Page, also resided. Page was an ardent believer in the teachings of eighteenth-century Swedish scientist, philosopher and mystic, Emmanuel Swedenborg. After 1866 he introduced these precepts to an interested and receptive Inness. (From his youth, Inness had felt uncomfortable and dissatisfied with the conservative Protestant church experiences of his upbringing.) It was a system of religious thinking he found intellectually palatable, and he soon was a committed follower.

Swedenborg contended, among other things, that the corporeal world one perceives with the physical senses is in reality a kind of parallel formation, a coextension of an ideal spiritual world that exists simultaneously in a different dimension. To know God and to know truth, therefore, is to transcend that dimension by metaphysical means, in the process achieving a state of consciousness where one can discern — again according to Swedenborg — a world characterized by greater lustre and less fixed or constant spatiality than that of the regular earthly domain. Abraham A. Davidson notes: "Inness' late landscapes look as though they could be snippets of that world." Speaking also of the late and most visionary of Inness' paintings, Nicholas Cikovsky has observed:

> Because Inness does not firmly anchor any object to the ground, spaces are, within limits, indefinite and extendable as they are in Swedenborg's vision. And if the colors of Inness' paintings do not equal the splendor and refulgence of those of the spiritual world, their glowing, lustrous quality is not inadequate approximation.

Exactly such a painting is *Rosy Morning* (color plate 10) finished in 1894, the last year of the artist's life. Judging by the southern loblolly pines pictured and by the similarity of the site to other Inness paintings with titles more descriptive of the locale, the scene is probably at Tarpon Springs, Florida, one of Inness' favored winter retreats. A lone enigmatic figure to the left, a single sailboat at mid-depth to the right and the greyed lavender, pinks, and greens impart a feeling of solitude and melancholy. At the same time, the viewer, as though longing for warmth, hope or divine radiance, is drawn beyond the partial obstruction of wraith-like trees to the rising sun just above the horizon.

(Continued from page 73)

George Inness Exhibition, exhibition catalogue, New York: John Levy Galleries, 1947, no. 16.

LeRoy Ireland, *The Works of George Inness*, Austin: University of Texas Press, 1965, pp. 226-227, no. 914.

Zane Probasco Brown, *An American Collection*, exhibition catalogue, Chattanooga: Hunter Museum of Art, 1978, no. 11.

Flowers and Art, exhibition catalogue, Memphis, TN: Dixon Gallery, 1984, no. 12.

(color plate 10)

ROSY MORNING

George Inness

1894

oil on canvas

30 x 45 inches

signed and dated lower left

Gift of the Joseph H. Davenport, Jr. family in memory of Laura Voigt and Joseph Howard Davenport

---

Provenance

Martin A. Ryerson, Chicago, Illinois
Thomas J. Watson, New York, New York
I.B.M. Corporation, New York, New York
Joseph H. Davenport, Jr., Lookout Mountain, Tennessee

Exhibitions

Inness Memorial Exhibition, Fine Arts Building, New York, NY, Dec. 27, 1894.

Inness Executor's Sale, Fifth Avenue Art Gallery, New York, NY, Feb. 12-14, 1895.

George Inness Centennial Exhibition, Buffalo Fine Arts Academy, Albright Art Gallery, Buffalo, NY, Oct.-Nov. 1925.

Royal Academy, Stockholm, Sweden, March-April, 1930.

Grand Central Galleries, New York, NY, Dec. 1947.

A Rare View of American Art: Selections from a Southeastern Collection, Hunter Museum of Art, Chattanooga, TN, Nov. 11-Dec. 16, 1979.

Publications

Inness Memorial Exhibition, exhibition catalogue, New York: Fine Arts Building, 1894, no. 4.

Inness Executor's Sale, exhibition catalogue, New York: Fifth Avenue Art Gallery, 1895, no. 78.

Pen and Brush, July, 1902, p. 193.

George Inness Centennial Exhibition, exhibition catalogue, Buffalo, NY: Albright Art Gallery, 1925, p. 18, no. 21.

(Continued on page 75)

Inness was elected an associate of the National Academy of Design in 1853 and elevated to full membership in 1868. In 1875, after a five-year stay in Italy and France during which he developed his mature "Swedenborgian" style, he returned to the United States, settling first in Boston, then New York City. In 1878 he moved to Montclair, New Jersey, where he painted many of his best-known canvasses and where, except for periods of extended travel, he would reside for the remainder of his life. Though some critics at the time faulted Inness because, in their judgment, he combined invention with observation to an excessive degree, his work was nonetheless widely acclaimed and collected, and he enjoyed a measure of financial success. He died in 1894 while on a vacation trip to Scotland. His only son, George, Jr., who was also a painter (whose less innovative and less competent landscapes are sometimes mistaken for his father's), published in 1917 an intimate and informative biography titled *Life, Art, and Letters of George Inness*.

(Continued from page 74)

Helen Gardner, *Art Through the Ages*, New York: Harcourt Brace & Co., 1926, p. 382, illus. plate 154 (A).

LeRoy Ireland, *The Works of George Inness*, Austin: University of Texas Press, 1965, pp. 396-397, illus. p. 396, no. 1507.

A Rare View of American Art: Selections from a Southeastern Collection, exhibition catalogue, Chattanooga: Hunter Museum of Art, 1979, no. 7.

Albert Pinkham Ryder (1847-1917)

That Albert Pinkham Ryder became one of the foremost mystic-visionary painters of the late nineteenth century is in no small measure due to a single event of his childhood. An infection following a vaccination left his eyes permanently hypersensitive and his vision impaired. Throughout his life he was especially bothered by bright lights. If he read or painted too long, his eyes grew inflamed. He had difficulty making out detail and perceiving depth. Because of his eyes, he ended his formal education with grammar school. Not surprisingly, he grew up quiet and introspective. By himself, and without benefit of regular instruction, he began painting. At first his experience was frustrating, as he recalled years later: "In my desire to be accurate I became lost in a maze of detail. Try as I would, my colors were not those of nature. My leaves were infinitely below the standard of a leaf, my finest strokes were coarse and crude." In time, he was struck by what must have seemed a revelation:

> *The old scene presented itself one day before my eyes, framed in an opening between two trees. It stood out like a painted canvas — the deep blue of a midday sky — a solitary tree, brilliant with the green of early summer, a foundation of brown earth and gnarled roots. There was no detail to vex the eye. Three solid masses of form and color — sky, foliage and earth — the whole bathed in an atmosphere of golden luminosity.*

He responded to the view ecstatically:

> *I threw my brushes aside; they were too small for the work at hand. I squeezed out big chunks of pure, moist color and taking my palette knife, I laid on blue, green, white and brown in great sweeping strokes. As I worked I saw that it was good and clean and strong. I saw nature springing into life upon my dead canvas. It was better than nature, for it was vibrating with the thrill of a new creation. Exultantly I painted until the sun sank below the horizon, then I raced around the fields like a colt let loose, and literally bellowed for joy.*

The episode was like a rapturous religious conversion. From that point on, as the artist's chief biographer, Lloyd Goodrich, states, Ryder's painting would be "not mere representation, but a creative language speaking directly to the senses through form, color, and tone." It became an apt vehicle for expressing reverie and subjective mood. In this respect Ryder descends from the early nineteenth-century romanticism of Thomas Cole and Washington Allston — as do his fellow mystic-visionary contemporaries: Elihu Vedder, Robert Loftin Newman, Elliott Daingerfield, Ralph Blakelock, and the late works of George Inness. But with Ryder particularly, subject and rendering style are intertwined; one proceeded from the other interchangeably, as emotional transport dictated the design. An artist should "strive to express his thought and not the surface of it," Ryder contended. "What avails a storm cloud accurate in form and color if the storm is not therein?" But for Ryder that "storm" need not be invested, as one might suppose, by impulsive, vigorous brushwork.

PLODDING HOMEWARD
(Also known as *Homeward Plodding*)
Albert Pinkham Ryder)
c. 1878
oil on canvas
11 x 16½ inches
Gift of Mr. and Mrs. Llewellyn Boyd

Provenance

Charles de Kay, New York, New York
Alexander Morton, New York, New York
Arther E. Egner, Newark, New Jersey
Babcock Galleries, New York, New York
T. E. Hanley, Bradford, Pennsylvania
Mr. and Mrs. Llewellyn Boyd, Chattanooga, Tennessee

Exhibitions

Fifth Annual Exhibition, Society of American Artists, New York, NY, 1882, no. 91.

Sale: American Art Association, January 29, 1919, no. 36.

Sale: Sotheby Parke Bernet, New York, NY, April 11, 1973, no. 42.

Publications

Henry Eckford (Charles de Kay), *Century Illustrated Monthly Magazine*. June, 1890, vol. 40, illus. p. 258.

Frederick F. Sherman, *Albert Pinkham Ryder*, 1920, nos. 45, 55.

Frederic Newlin Price, 1932, no. 136.

Lloyd Goodrich, *Albert P. Ryder*, New York: George Braziller, Inc., 1959, p. 14.

Important 18th, 19th and Early 20th Century American Paintings, Watercolors and Sculpture, auction catalogue, New York: Sotheby Parke Bernet, Inc., April 11, 1973, no. 42, illus.

Quite the contrary, he worked slowly, methodically, even tediously. "Art is long," he declared, going on to explain:

> The artist must buckle himself with infinite patience. His ears must be deaf to the clamor of insistant friends who would quicken his pace. His eyes must see naught but the vision beyond. He must await the season of fruitage without haste, without worldly ambition, without vexation of spirit. An inspiration is no more than a seed that must be planted and nourished. It gives growth as it grows with the artist, only as he watches and waits with his highest effort.

Ryder once remarked that he "pondered over" his paintings "with prayer and fasting, letting them ripen under the sunlight of the years that come and go." He is known to have worked on virtually all his canvases for greatly protracted periods—some pieces for ten or more years, applying layer upon layer of pigments and glazes. In the last decade and a half of his life he rarely started a new picture, but rather repainted earlier starts over and over. Consequently his career output totaled only about 165 paintings. Sadly, as his work came to be understood and accepted during his late years and after his death, popular demand brought forth many forgeries; approximately 800 are estimated to have been offered on the art market. Of American artists, Ryder is second only to Blakelock in the number of fakes produced.

Ryder unfortunately lacked sound technical knowledge. Bad enough that in constantly reworking the surface he pushed and extended his oil paints beyond their normal body and plasticity, he also frequently admixed unstable media such as candle wax, grease, and alcohol in seeking a particular depth of tone. He often painted wet into wet, applied faster-drying colors over slower-drying, or glazed and scumbled with varnish before the various layers of pigment below had completely dried and cured. As a result his paintings have severely cracked and turned darker with age, and most have needed comprehensive restoration.

Such technical faults are readily apparent in the Hunter Museum's *Plodding Homeward* (also known as *Homeward Plodding*) from the late 1870s. The multi-layered oil-paint surface is thoroughly subjected to what conservators call "traction crackle," and progressive darkening has reduced contrast between shapes. The silhouette image of a driver and horse-drawn cart, "plodding" from the left toward the setting sun, is barely distinguishable. As in all the artist's paintings, illumination of the scene is dim and ambiguous, what James Thomas Flexner calls Ryder's "crepuscular" light. Goodrich believes the subject and title undoubtedly derive from the closing lines of Thomas Gray's *Elegy in a*

Country Churchyard: "The plowman homeward plods his weary way, And leaves the world to darkness and to me." The artist was in his late twenties or early thirties when he worked on the picture, and it is representative of the early or "bucolic" phase of his career.

In the 1880s Ryder turned to more literary and imaginative themes, inspired by the Bible, classical mythology, Shakespeare, Byron, Tennyson, Poe, Melville, the poems of Emily Dickinson, even Wagner's music, which he often hummed as he painted. From childhood days in his birthplace, New Bedford, Massachusetts—then the chief whaling port in the world—he retained a lifelong fascination with the sea. A favorite topic among his later work was a lone boat sailing phantasmic, often heavy, moonlit waters.

Ryder was born in 1847. When he was twenty, he moved with his family from New Bedford to New York City, where he would reside for the rest of his life. He applied to the school of the National Academy of Design, but was initially turned down. He then studied independently with the naive-style portrait and religious-theme painter, William Edgar Marshall. The N.A.D. school finally admitted him in 1871, and he attended four terms. Largely in opposition to the Academy's conservative posture, Ryder was one of the twenty-two who founded the comparatively progressive Society of American Artists in 1877. Ironically, the S.A.A. merged with the N.A.D. in 1906. Shortly after, in that same year, Ryder was elected full academician. In 1913 he exhibited six paintings in the Armory Show.

Though he made four trips abroad—in 1877, '82, '87, and '96—Ryder remained essentially a tourist. He was little interested in European art. His greater pleasure, in fact, was not in the destinations, but rather the sea voyages to and from.

Perhaps because of an interview with the artist titled "Paragraphs from the Studio of a Recluse," published in the *Broadway Magazine* September 1905, some art historians have tended to exaggerate Ryder's reputation as an unsociable, hermitic loner. Though he never married, all his life he was devoted to a small group of friends. They knew him as a pleasant, good-humored dinner companion and raconteur. He enjoyed the company of children, and often played with those in his immediate Greenwich Village neighborhood. True, he was eccentric and entirely unworldly. Within his own apartment he was oblivious to creature comforts. In his last years, as strength and health gradually failed, he lived in miserable disorder, amidst waist-high trash—narrow paths connecting from the entry door to the stove (on which an oddments stew interminably simmered), to the easel, to the place on the floor where he slept atop old window shades or carpet scraps. A friend in those late years, Kahlil Gibran, the Lebanese-American mystic, writer, poet, and sometime artist, wrote of Ryder in 1915, two years before the latter's death:

> I found him on a cold day in a half-heated room in one of the most poor houses on 16th Street. He lives the life of a Diogeneus, a life so wreched (sic) and so unclean that it is hard for me to discribe (sic). But it is the only life he wants. He has money — all the money he needs — but he does not think of that. He is no longer on this planet. He is beyond his own dreams.

Probably Ryder would only have sighed and concurred. "The artist needs but a roof, a crust of bread and his easel," he declared, "and all the rest God gives him in abundance. He must live to paint and not paint to live."

Ralph Albert Blakelock (1847-1919)

So much has been written about Ralph Blakelock's personal misfortune that — as with Van Gogh — it is difficult to set his paintings apart and consider them with fair objectivity. The visionary and mystical style that characterizes his later and best known work has been seen by some writers as clear evidence of his troubled states of mind, as forerunners of the delusion and psychosis that resulted in his being confined at a sanatorium for most of the last twenty years of his life. Art critic J. N. Laurvik, writing in 1915, four years before the artist's death, found Blakelock "a tragic and solitary figure who, born out of his proper time and place, is ending his sad days in a madhouse." Even noted art historian Virgil Barker, thirty-five years later, called Blakelock's story "the bitterest known tragedy in the history of American painting." Such epithets now seem both exaggerated and melodramatic. Though the artist did periodically suffer bouts of schizophrenia, he was never as thoroughly demented as these accounts suggest. He was however totally exhausted, frustrated, and embittered by years of critical disinterest and neglect of his work. Nonetheless, he continued to sketch and paint and to play the piano (a favorite pastime, and he liked to improvise themes and variations) up to the time of his death at age seventy-two.

Blakelock was born, raised, and lived his adult life in New York City. He studied at the Free Academy (which later became City College) in 1864 and afterwards at the Cooper Union, where he learned the manner and theories of the Hudson River School. Like Bierstadt, T. R. Peale and other "Eastern" artists before him, he made an extensive two-year trek to the West during 1869-71. The awesome grandeur deeply impressed him; throughout his life he held a romantic, if not reverential, attachment to wilderness that is evident in nearly all his work.

In the mid-1870s Blakelock began to evolve from a factual to a more interpretive and introspective approach. In so doing he was quite in step with several of his important contemporaries. George Inness, Albert Pinkham Ryder, and John H. Twachtman, for example, each in his own way pointed a direction for American landscape painting away from the prevailing criterion of the preceding fifty years: that, to be true to divine creation, nature had to be represented in literal detail. Blakelock became one of the most subjective and most abstract painters of the new movement. And for his deeply personal expressions of mood, wonder, and transcendence, he also came to be spurned as too experimental, too unconventional for the established exhibition opportunities of that time. With increasing public disfavor, joined by the fact that he coped poorly with business matters, he fell into extreme financial difficulty, whereupon followed the strain of supporting his large family (Blakelock and his wife had nine children). Not surprisingly, circumstances took an emotional and physical toll.

Fond of the random pattern of nature and designs made by attrition for their inherent sensory visual appeal, Blakelock would transcribe such tactile effects to his canvases by methodically building up paint surfaces, frequently admixing bitumen and varnish for the rich color depth that resulted. (In many cases this method of materials handling has also resulted in a variety of conservation problems years later.) The masses of texture might at first be read as flat design with a certain density and substance; then slowly the surface resolves into convincing spatial illusion. One sees thus the artist's typical imagery in his mature style: a landscape in which the dark foliage of trees forms a lacy decorative pattern and through which can be seen distant woods, sky, and a sun or moon glowing silvery-green or mellow gold. The Hunter Museum's *Landscape with Moon* (color plate 11) aptly fits this description. Blakelock transformed the appearance of nature to evoke for the viewer the emotions and contemplations that a scene worked in him.

Ironically, before the artist's death critical interest in the work revived (but for no particular benefit or remuneration to himself or his family). Sad to say, too, as his painting came finally to be understood and appreciated — and as the sales improved dramatically — his style was blatantly counterfeited, yet offered as Blakelock original work. He remains today perhaps the most "forged" of American artists.

James Abbott McNeill Whistler (1834-1903)

Art historians on both sides of the Atlantic claim James Abbott McNeill Whistler as fellow countryman, and each side with reasonable justification. American critics point out that he was American-born, and though he spent much of his life as an expatriate, he remained nonetheless an American who simply happened to live elsewhere. In attitude as well, he was, as E.P. Richardson suggests, American in his "quick receptivity to new ideas, and in his cleverness in improvising upon them." English critics, on the other hand, note that Whistler left the United States at age twenty-one, never to return. His most famous paintings and etchings were produced in England. What is more, in 1884 he was elected to membership in the prestigious Royal Society of British Artists, and even was the organization's president from 1886 to '88. In truth, the sum of his career belongs to no one nation, except, as Richardson finally concludes, "the new cosmopolitan world of art that he helped to create."

(color plate 11)
LANDSCAPE WITH MOON
Ralph Albert Blakelock
c. 1885-1890
oil on canvas
20 x 30 inches
signed lower right
Gift of the Benwood
Foundation (by exchange)

Provenance
Private collection, New York, New York
Coe Kerr Galleries, Inc., New York, New York
Exhibitions
Ralph A. Blakelock, M. Knoedler & Co., New York, NY, March 3-31, 1973.

American Landscape Painting, Sewall Art Gallery, Rice University, Houston, TX, Feb. 18-March 31, 1976.

Whistler was born in Lowell, Massachusetts, in 1834. His father, George Washington Whistler, a retired army major and an engineer, in 1843 moved the family to Russia, where he had been retained by the government to oversee construction of the Moscow to St. Petersburg railway line, a six-year assignment. Young Whistler often visited the Hermitage Museum. He also took drawing and French lessons at the Imperial Academy of Science. (French was then the fashionable second language in Russia, and Whistler developed fluency.) Upon his father's death in 1849, the family returned to the United States. Two years later, Whistler, then seventeen, entered West Point (the father's alma mater). He studied there three years, including art classes with Robert W. Weir, but he never took to the military life. He was dismissed in 1854 for failing a chemistry course and for receiving more than the maximum allowable demerits.

That he wanted to become an artist, Whistler was then certain. In 1855 he sailed for France. He studied briefly in Paris with Charles Gabriel Gleyre, who was the teacher of Claude Monet, Pierre-Auguste Renoir, and Alfred Sisley, and he established friendships with painters Alphonse Legros and Henri Fantin-Latour. He also met Gustave Courbet, Edouard Manet, critic Theophile Gautier, and poet Charles Baudelaire. Whistler's earliest work in Paris was done in an objective-realist manner reflecting the strong influence of Courbet. A few years later he regretted having been so thoroughly seduced by realism. In a letter to Fantin-Latour he exclaimed: "It is because that damned realism made an immediate appeal to my painter's vanity, sneering at old traditions, cried aloud to me with the assurance of ignorance: 'Long live Nature!'" One may glimpse in this statement certain aspects of the artist's personality that often allienated others—his egotism, biting wit, and sardonic outlook. As his reputation as a painter grew, so also did his notoriety as an eccentric, non-conformist, flamboyant character.

In 1859 Whistler moved to London, settling in the motley and free-spirited Chelsea district (though he continued to make periodic trips to the continent). Very soon thereafter his work evolved to the style for which he is best known — an ethereal, tonal landscape imagery that emphasizes subjective feelings rather than objective details. Donelson F. Hoopes describes the effect as "nature seen through a veil." About 1860 Whistler had become interested in oriental art, with its typical decorative, flat patterning, refined pictorial activity, and understated rendering. Numerous paintings of the subsequent decade show persons clad in oriental costume or surrounded by oriental accouterments. It was also at this time that he sought to adapt to visual art Baudelaire's conviction that "poetry has no other end but itself." Whistler in turn declared that subject matter was of little consequence to painting; what really counted was *the way* a picture was painted, the essence of an art-for-art's-sake approach. "As music is the poetry of sound, so painting is the poetry of sight," he stated confidently, "and the subject matter has nothing to do with the harmony of sound or of color." To stress this point, he additionally began in the 1860s titling many of his paintings by color scheme—"Brown and Silver," "Blue and Gold," etc.—often in combination with the terms "arrangement," "symphony," and "nocturne," (then perhaps followed by the identification of the place or persons as a subtitle).

It was upon seeing one of the nocturne series, *Nocturne in Black and Gold: The Falling Rocket* (1875, Detroit Institute of Arts) displayed at London's Grovesnor Gallery in 1877 that critic John Ruskin was provoked to write: "I never expected to hear a coxcomb ask two hundred guineas for flinging a pot of paint in the public's face." Whistler sued Ruskin for libel. The artist won the suit after an arduous and highly publicized trial, but was awarded just one farthing in damages. The ordeal turned into a personal tragedy; litigation costs forced him to bankruptcy. With a commission from a London gallery to produce a series of etchings, he retreated to Venice, where he worked nearly a year. In 1880 he returned to England to publish the etchings and to rebuild his career.

Though Whistler earlier had several mistresses, he did not wed until age fifty-two, in 1886, the same year he became president of the Royal Society. The ten-year marriage was generally happy, and it was a time of considerable creative output. In 1890 he published a compilation from correspondence and essays, titled *The Gentle Art of Making Enemies*. Two years before, he had been elected an honorary member of the Royal Academy of Fine Arts in Munich, and in 1892 he was made an officer of the Legion d'Honneur in France. When his beloved Trixie died of cancer in 1896, Whistler was grief stricken. For about two years after, he traveled widely in Europe and North Africa. Shortly following his return to a temporary residence in Paris in 1898, he became a charter member and first president of the International Society of Sculptors, Painters, and Gravers.

(color plate 12)

GRAY AND GOLD — THE GOLDEN BAY

James Abbott McNeill Whistler

1900

oil on panel

5½ x 9¼ inches

signed lower right with butterfly monogram

Gift of Mr. and Mrs. Scott L. Probasco, Jr.

Provenance

Richard A. Canfield, New York, New York
Henry Clay Frick, New York, New York
Mrs. H. K. S. Williams, San Francisco, California
M. Knoedler & Co., New York, New York
Prew Savoy, Washington, D.C.
Norton Galleries, New York, New York
Newhouse Galleries, New York, New York
Thomas Agnew & Sons, London, England
Dr. and Mrs. Irving F. Burton, Huntington Woods, Michigan
Mr. and Mrs. Scott L. Probasco, Jr., Lookout Mountain, Tennessee

Exhibitions

Copley Society of Boston, Boston, MA, before 1904, no. 78.

Albright Art Gallery, Buffalo, NY, 1911, no. 6.

William Macbeth Gallery, New York, NY, April 1947, no. 3.

The *Dr. and Mrs. Irving F. Burton Collection of American Art*, Flint Institute of Arts, Flint, MI, Feb. 14-March 12, 1961, no. 18.

American Paintings and Drawings from Michigan Collections, The Detroit Institute of Arts, Detroit, MI, April 10-May 6, 1962.

Whistler: The Later Years, The University of Michigan Museum of Art, Ann Arbor, MI, Aug. 27-Oct. 8, 1978.

An American Collection, Hunter Museum of Art, Chattanooga, TN, Sept. 9-Oct. 15, 1978.

Notes, Harmonies and Nocturnes, Small Works by James McNeill Whistler, M. Knoedler & Co., Inc., New York, NY, Nov. 30-Dec. 27, 1984, no. 136.

Publications

Elizabeth Luther Cary, *The Works of James McNeill Whistler*, New York: Moffatt Yard, 1913, p. 168, no. 75.

Denys Sutton, *James McNeill Whistler: Paintings, Etchings, Pastels and Watercolors*, London: Phaidon, 1977, no. 119.

American Paintings and Drawings From Michigan Collections, exhibition catalogue, Detroit: The Detroit Institute of Arts, 1962, p. 7, no. 58.

Zane Probasco Brown, *An American Collection*, exhibition catalogue, Chattanooga: Hunter Museum of Art, 1978, no. 26.

(Continued on page 80)

Whistler painted *Gray and Gold: The Golden Bay* (color plate 12) in 1900, only three years before his death. The scene actually is at Dublin Bay in Ireland, where he had gone in August to visit close friends. Typical of his later landscape style, the rendering is mainly horizontal strips of alternating color in soft, creamy tones. From the placement of the small sailboat at right center, a sense of depth is imparted. Yet the study remains strongly two-dimensional, as pervading blue-greens in what is both sky and water appear equidistant from the viewer. For all its simplicity and quietude, lack of detail, reduced color intensity and contrast, and despite its small size (5½ x 9¼ inches), the painting conveys remarkable profundity and strength.

(Continued from page 79)

Whistler: The Later Years, exhibition catalogue, Ann Arbor, MI: The University of Michigan Museum of Art, 1978.

Margaret MacDonald, Hamish Miles, Robin Spencer and Andrew M. Young, *The Paintings of James McNeill Whistler*, New Haven, CT: Yale University Press, 1980, p. 358, no. 537.

Margaret F. MacDonald, *Notes*, *Harmonies and Nocturnes, Small Works by James McNeill Whistler*, New York: M. Knoedler & Co., Inc., 1984, illus. p. 93.

John LaFarge (1835-1910)

Cosmopolitan, intellectual, and complex, John LaFarge moved in a prominent social and cultural circle. He was a close personal friend of historian and philosopher Henry Adams, of William and Henry James, of statesman John Hay, and of numerous artists, including especially sculptor Augustus Saint-Gaudens and architect Henry Hobson Richardson. It was Richardson, in fact, who in 1876 provided LaFarge the project for which perhaps he is best known today, the elaborate interior decorating scheme for Boston's famed Trinity Church. Beyond that, LaFarge is recognized chiefly as a painter of still life, portrait, and landscape — with a particular fluency in watercolor. But he is also important for the late nineteenth century as a designer of murals and stained glass. He helped establish a popular taste for stained glass in domestic architecture. LaFarge's glass production was limited to windows for churches and homes, which may be the main reason the eminence of his work has been eclipsed by that of Louis Comfort Tiffany. Tiffany's total output was substantially greater, and his art nouveau creations extended to lamps, vases, and screens, as well as windows. It should be noted, however, that the greater body of Tiffany work *follows* LaFarge, well into the twentieth century.

SPRING and AUTUMN
John LaFarge
c. 1896
stained glass windows (pair)
43⅝ x 36 inches; 44⅛ x 36 inches
Gift of Mrs. Arthur Hays Sulzberger

(Continued on page 81)

LaFarge became interested in stained glass art on his first trip to Europe in 1856, when he had opportunity to visit many of the great medieval French and English cathedrals. (He also studied briefly at that time with Thomas Couture in Paris, and in London was impressed with work by the pre-Raphaelites.) His interest was rekindled on a second European sojourn in 1873, when he learned leading and other technical aspects of the craft. He perfected the process of making what was then called "pot metal" glass, that is, glass in which the coloring agent is blended while molten, and also the fusing of a color film to clear glass by heat. For optical mixture of hues and for varying degrees of opacity, he experimented with superimposing and laminating thin pieces of glass in two or more thicknesses. He further devised his own chemical or "batch" formula for producing an opalescent glass.

In 1874, Harvard University alumni from the class of 1844 offered LaFarge his first major stained glass commission, to design a large commemorative window for Memorial Hall at the campus in Cambridge, Massachusetts. The piece was completed, but never installed. In an interview years after, the artist contended that he was dissatisfied with the result, and elected to destory it. Other accounts, however, suggest that the class nullified the agreement because LaFarge excessively overran the available funds.

In designing four windows for the nave of Trinity Church two years later, LaFarge at last established his reputation as a stained-glass artist. Important commissions in the latter part of the century included windows for the homes of William Watts Sherman and Henry G. Marquand at Newport, Rhode Island, for English painter Sir Lawrence Alma-Tadema in London, and for Cornelius Vanderbilt in New York City. The two windows in the Hunter Museum collection have a circuitous history. They were originally installed in the dining room of the George Foster Peabody home in Lake George, New York, about 1896. (Peabody was a Boston financier and philanthropist.) Adolph Ochs, publisher of the *Chattanooga Times* and the *New York Times*, purchased the home from Peabody early in the twentieth century. The house was razed in 1940, five years after Mr. Ochs' death, but the windows were removed and reinstalled in the home of John B. Stapleton at Troy, New York. That house, too, was later sold and eventually razed. The windows were purchased by the Graham Gallery of New York City, which in turn sold them in 1978 to Mrs. Arthur Hays Sulzberger, daughter of Adolph Ochs. Later that same year, Mrs. Sulzberger donated them to the museum.

Helene Barbara Weinberg writes that LaFarge's stained-glass designs are characterized by "a sense of organic vitality, of action and atmosphere." That can fairly be applied to the Hunter pieces. For each window, one seems to be looking through a paired gothic-arched opening to a foliate design: respectively, a flowering tree branch to suggest *Spring*, and a grape vine for *Autumn*. To exemplify the seasons by relatively simple graphic "signs" may be an influence from LaFarge's 1886 visit to the Far East, where such poetic themes are favored topics of oriental artists. (Significantly, LaFarge was one of the first American artists to travel extensively in Japan.) The background field in various tones of blue was achieved in the artist's own opalescent glass invention.

Born in New York City in 1835, LaFarge grew up in a wealthy French emigré family. He received his earliest art instruction from his maternal grandfather, Binsse de Saint-Victor, a miniaturist. After graduating from Saint Mary's College in Maryland, he studied law. It was not until after the first European trip, and following a period of study in 1859 with an American painter, William Morris Hunt, that he decided to pursue art as a career. He came to be regarded in his own lifetime as one of the nation's greatest artists. He also wrote two books, *Considerations on Painting*, published in 1895, and *An Artist's Letters from Japan*, released in 1897. He died in Providence, Rhode Island, in 1910.

(Continued from page 80)

Provenance

George Foster Peabody, Bolton Landing, Lake George, New York
Adolph Ochs, Bolton Landing, Lake George, New York
John B. Stapleton, Troy, New York
Eugene Frost, Troy, New York
Graham Gallery, New York, New York
Mrs. Arthur Hays Sulzberger, New York, New York.

Mary Cassatt (1845-1926)

Mary Cassatt was born at Allegheny City, Pennsylvania (near Pittsburgh), in 1845. She was the daughter of a prominent businessman and spent much of her childhood in France and Germany. In 1858 her family moved to Philadelphia and two years later she commenced study at the Pennsylvania Academy of Fine Arts. After the Civil War she studied briefly in Paris with the official Salon painter, Charles Chaplin. In 1870, at the outbreak of the Franco-Prussian War, she returned to the United States, but was back in Europe two years later. As early as 1874 she became aware of a struggling group of French painters, then rejected by Salon juries, but who would eventually be called "impressionists." Cassatt understood their creative premise and developed an enthusiasm for their work. She became a close friend of Edgar Degas, who in 1877 invited her to join and exhibit with the group. (She subsequently also showed works in the major impressionist exhibits of 1879, '80, '81, and '86.) Undeniably her work was influenced by Degas and his marginally impressionist style; she never totally adopted the strict application of color theory and divisionist brushwork technique employed by the more doctrinaire impressionists like Monet and Pissarro.

In 1890, the same year the charming pastel *Baby Bill in Cap and Shift, Held by His Nurse* (color plate 13) is believed to have been drawn, Cassatt attended the great exhibit of Japanese printmaking at the École des Beaux-Arts. She was deeply impressed with the subtle abstract beauty she saw. Much of her work in the succeeding several years consequently took on a pronounced oriental effect: flat decorative patterning, carefully calculated asymmetry, and a delicate linear outlining of form. In fact, *Baby Bill* may well represent a pivotal piece in the artist's increasing comprehension of such design modes. While the sketch seems fresh and spontaneous, in keeping with the artist's developed impressionist manner, at the same time it manifests characteristics that suggest she had already assimilated some of the Japanese sense of rendering and pictorial arrangement. The dark-eyed, chubby infant is set out from the nurse and surrounding spaces by rather accentuated contour outlining. The swath of yellow-green along the right edge is an important element for balancing the composition, both in terms of its inherent visual weight and attraction and as a counterpoint, that is, as the hue complement to the warm pinkish glow of the two subjects' fleshtones. On the other hand, these same skin tones, in accord with typical impressionist color usage, are composed of various carefully juxtaposed shades — shadows of blue and green that impart unusual vibrancy.

The Hunter's piece, moreover, is a delightful example of the theme that most of Cassatt's best-known works express: the tender relationship between mother (or in the case of an upper-class household, the nurse) and child. It is an iconographic type, with considerable religious precedent and residual overtone.

Cassatt continued to draw and paint well into the twentieth century, though in the later 1880s her work gradually grew, as David W. Scott suggests, "drier in technique and less imaginative in concept." At the same time she began having problems with her eyesight. Her vision degenerated to a state of nearly total blindness over the last ten years of her life. She died in France in 1926.

Though she spent most of her professional life in Europe and was an admitted expatriate, Cassatt always considered herself fundamentally American in outlook and personality. As such, her importance as an American artist cannot be overlooked. She was the first American to become associated with the impressionist movement. What is more, she was the most avant-garde American *woman* artist of her era.

(color plate 13)

BABY BILL IN CAP AND SHIFT, HELD BY HIS NURSE
Mary Cassatt
c. 1890
pastel on paper
16⅞ x 15⅛ inches (sight)
signed lower left
Gift of the Benwood Foundation (by exchange)

Provenance

Private collection, Paris, France
Private collection, New York, New York
Douglas James & Co., Signal Mountain, Tennessee

Exhibitions

Mary Cassatt: Pastels and Color Prints, National Collection of Fine Arts, Washington, D.C., Jan. 23-May 26, 1978.

Fifty Years of French Painting: The Emergence of Modern Art, Birmingham Museum of Art, Birmingham, AL, Feb. 1-March 30, 1980.

The Art of Mary Cassatt, 1840-1929, American Federation of Arts, traveling exhibition to Tokyo and Nara, Japan, June 11-Aug. 23, 1981.

Publications

Mary Cassatt: Pastels and Color Prints, exhibition catalogue, Washington D.C.: National Collection of Fine Arts, 1978, no. 10.

Fifty Years of French Painting: The Emergence of Modern Art, exhibition catalogue, Birmingham, AL: Birmingham Museum of Art, 1980, no. 20.

Adelyn Dohme Breeskin, *Mary Cassatt, A Catalogue Raisonne of the Oils, Pastels, Watercolors and Drawings,* Washington, D.C.: Smithsonian Institution Press, 1970, p. 96, no. 182.

Adelyn Dohme Breeskin, *The Art of Mary Cassatt, 1840-1926,* exhibition catalogue, New York: American Federation of Arts, 1981, illus. p. 40, no. 22.

John Henry Twachtman (1853-1902)

BOATS AND RIVER
(Also known as *River And Bridge*)
John Henry Twachtman
c. 1890
oil on canvas
20¼ x 16¼ inches
signed bottom, left of center
Gift of the Benwood Foundation

Provenance

Babcock Galleries, New York, New York
Mr. and Mrs. Louis D. Cohen, New York, New York

Exhibitions

Frances and L.D. Cohen Collection, Norton Gallery and School of Art, West Palm Beach, FL, Feb. 23-March 17, 1968.

When John H. Twachtman died suddenly in 1902, a few days after his forty-ninth birthday, he was not greatly appreciated by the public or art patrons of his time. Though he was moderately well reviewed by critics and had occasionally won medals and prizes in significant competitions, throughout his career he had difficulty advancing his work. His friend and fellow artist Edward Simmons recalled once walking with an embittered Twachtman up and down New York's Fifth Avenue, visiting dealer after dealer in a futile attempt to sell one of Twachtman's landscapes for twenty-five dollars. Ironically, not long after his death, both private and institutional collectors enthusiastically began acquiring the work. Today his position in American art history is highly regarded. Donelson F. Hoopes calls Twachtman "without doubt the most lyrical exponent of the school of American impressionism." Oswaldo Rodriguez Rogue describes him as "probably the most individual of the American painters who studied in France and were influenced by impressionism." In his authoritative book, *American Impressionism*, Richard J. Boyle declares: "Twachtman was the most sensitive and unique of all the American impressionists. His painting was more searching, his style more personal; he understood abstraction, the essence of things."

Twachtman was born in 1853 in the German-American "Over-the-Rhine" district of Cincinnati. Only five years before, his mother and father (who at that time had not yet met) emigrated from Hannover, probably to escape the political oppression that followed the unsuccessful liberal revolution of 1848. Young Twachtman began his career at about age fourteen, painting floral ornament for the Breneman Brothers Window Shade Factory, where his father was also a decorative painter. The following year he commenced evening art classes at the Ohio Mechanics Institute, and continued until 1871, when he transferred to the McMicken School of Design (which later became the Art Academy of Cincinnati). There in 1874 he met and formed a strong friendship with painter Frank Duveneck, who had recently returned from an agreeable period of study at the Royal Academy in Munich. (By the 1870s Munich had displaced Düsseldorf as the leading art center of Germany.) In 1875 Duveneck asked Twachtman to join him on a return to Munich. Twachtman attended the academy two years, studying chiefly under Ludwig Loefftz, and at this stage his painting took on the dark tonality generally associated with the school. He returned to the United States in 1878, and that same year exhibited in New York at the inaugural showing by the Society of American Artists. He was elected a member of that association the next year. Between 1879 and '83 painting trips to Europe were annual events. In fall 1880 he taught at Duveneck's school in Florence, Italy. From there Duveneck and Twachtman traveled to Venice, where they met the American expatriate James McNeill Whistler, notorious following the well-publicized lawsuit against British critic John Ruskin. Whistler's characteristic painting, with its diffused images, soft colors, and delicate value contrasts, would have profound influence on Twachtman's work.

Between 1883 and '85 Twachtman studied at the Academie Julian in Paris under the conservative painters Gustave Boulanger and Jules Lefebvre, but he also came to admire the works of Monet, Pissarro, and other of the French impressionists. Twachtman's own style evolved as a modified and personal version of the varegated French impressionist mode, combined with — or perhaps more accurately subdued by — the restrained, mellow disposition of Whistler's "nocturnes" and "harmonies." The Hunter Museum's oil, *Boats and River* (also known as *River and Bridge*, c. 1890), for example, manifests typical impressionist paint handling, while the muted color and close tonal effect suggest Whistler's aesthetic. In fact, Twachtman's museful scene may remind one slightly of Whistler's *Nocturne: Blue and Gold – Old Battersea Bridge* (1872, Tate Gallery, London). Both paintings are essentially monochromatic with limited contrast, though Whistler's is at twilight or early evening. Both have similar topics. Whistler's bridge is closer to the viewer, is somewhat more sharply defined, and hovers higher above the horizon line, but in both pictures the heavy supporting pier or tower is off-center to the left, while the greater part of the roadbed extends to the right. Twachtman's bridge is the suspension type, however, and, as a clever and subtle design effect, the long catenary curve of the central spanning cable is repeated in the gentle perpendicular arc of smoke from the steamer in the lower foreground.

Twachtman returned permanently to the United States in 1885. After a brief stay in Cincinnati he moved to Branchville, Connecticut, where his friend J. Alden Weir lived close by. In 1889 he purchased a farm near Greenwich in southwestern Connecticut, near the New York state line. For the remainder of his life he divided his time between the farm and a Manhattan residence. He illustrated for *Scribner's* magazine regularly between 1888 and '93. From 1889 on, he taught at the Art Students League, and also at the Cooper Union from 1894. In 1897 Twachtman was one of the founders of the group called The Ten American Painters, impressionist-style artists who exhibited together in 1898 and annually thereafter for twenty years at the Durand Ruell Gallery. With Twachtman's untimely death after participating in the association for only five years, the members invited the notable William Merritt Chase to take his place.

Edward Moran (1829-1901)

The last decade or so of his life, that is, from about 1890 to 1901, Edward Moran painted a series of American historical marine subjects. The thirteen completed canvases eventually came to the collection of the United States Naval Academy Museum in Annapolis, Maryland. One of that number is the large (60" x 42") *Burning of the Frigate "Philadelphia" in the Harbor of Tripoli*. The painting, signed and dated 1897, depicts an event that actually took place nearly a century before. During the Tripolitan Wars (1801-1805), when American, British, Spanish, and French naval forces sought to eradicate the Barbary-pirate menace in the Mediterranean, the *Philadelphia* and its crew were captured and taken to Tripoli (today one of the capitals of Libya). Rather than let the vessel be appropriated by the enemy, the American high command determined that it should be destroyed. On February 16, 1804, a twenty-five year old officer named Stephen Decatur led a detachment stealthily into the harbor, boarded the ship and set it afire, then successfully escaped. News of the feat made

BURNING OF THE
PHILADELPHIA
Edward Moran
c. 1897
oil on canvas
20 x 16 inches
signed lower left
Gift of Mrs. Robert Toombs
Wright

Provenance
Helen H. Gardener, New York, New York
Margaret Peale Wright
Mrs. Robert Toombs Wright, Lookout
Mountain, Tennessee.

Decatur a national hero, and he was promptly elevated to captain. The *Philadelphia*, meanwhile, became a rallying cause for the duration of the conflict, which ended by treaty the following year.

The Hunter Museum's smaller (20 x 16 inches) *Burning of the "Philadelphia"* is doubtless a preliminary study for the Naval Academy piece. This is not to say, however, that the work is in the nature of an oil sketch or that it is inferior to the larger painting. Indeed, particularly in the rendering of the burning masts, the Hunter work is perhaps the more vivid, more dextrously handled, more convincing suggestion of the motion and intensity of the blaze.

In the *Burning of the "Philadelphia"*, Moran continued a specific romantic theme that was popular in the late eighteenth and early nineteenth centuries: the "disaster at sea" or "ship in peril." French painters Theodore Géricault and Eugene Delacroix, and the English J. M. W. Turner are among the better-known European artists who produced celebrated sea-disaster pictures. In America, John Singleton Copley's *Watson and the Shark* (1778, Museum of Fine Arts, Boston), Washington Allston's *The Rising of a Thunderstorm at Sea* (1804, M.F.A., Boston), Emmanuel Leutze's *Washington Crossing the Delaware* (1850, Metropolitan Museum of Art, New York), James Hamilton's *The Capture of the Serapis by John Paul Jones* (1854, Yale University Art Gallery), Martin Johnson Heade's *Coastal Scene with Sinking Ship* (1863, Shelburne Museum, Vermont), and Albert Bierstadt's *The Burning Ship* (1869, Shelburne) are additional examples of the same creative attitude. The aesthetic impulse was, in turn, largely generated by the widely read theses of two English philosophers. Edmund Burke, in his 1756 treatise on the nature of the "sublime," and Sir Uvalde Price's 1794 essay on the "picturesque" established the premise that compositional irregularity, vigorous brushwork, and dramatic lighting, along with emotionally perceived episodes — even to the extent of arousing fear or terror — all combine to incite from the viewer an optimally felt response.

Edward Moran was born at Bolton, Lancashire, England, in 1829. He was the older brother of photographer John Moran (1831-?), and of painters Thomas Moran (1837-1926) and Peter Moran (1841-1914). The family emigrated to the United States in 1844, settling in Maryland. In the mid 1850s, Edward studied in Philadelphia, with Paul Weber and the James Hamilton mentioned above, from whom he was probably first inspired to marine painting. By 1857 he was established as a professional artist in Philadelphia, and he became a member of the Pennsylvania Academy of the Fine Arts. In 1862 Edward and Thomas went to London, where they briefly attended the Royal Academy. While in England, both men saw and were openly impressed by the paintings of Turner. Moran moved to New York City in 1872, and, except for an extended stay in Paris in 1879 and '80, he reamined in New York until his death. He was elected an associate of the National Academy of Design in 1873.

Lilla Cabot Perry (1848-1933)

A STREAM BENEATH
POPLARS
Lilla Cabot Perry
c. 1890-1900
oil on canvas
25¾ x 32 inches
signed lower left
Gift of Mr. and Mrs. Stuart P. Feld

Provenance

Mr. and Mrs. Stuart P. Feld, New York, New York

Exhibitions

Lilla Cabot Perry, A Retrospective Exhibition, organized by Hirschl & Adler Galleries, Inc., New York, NY, circulating exhibition: Hirschl & Adler Galleries, Inc., New York, NY; Currier Gallery of Art, Manchester, NH; New Jersey State Museum, Trenton, NJ; Oct. 10, 1969-Jan. 11, 1970.

An Internatioal Episode: Millet, Monet and their North American Counterparts, organized by Dixon Gallery, Memphis, TN, circulating exhibition: Dixon Gallery, Memphis, TN; Terre Museum of American Art, Evanston, IL; Worcester Art Museum, Worcester, MA; Nov. 21, 1982-April 30, 1983.

Publications

Lilla Cabot Perry, A Retrospective Exhibition, exhibition catalogue, New York: Hirschl & Adler Galleries, Inc., 1969, no. 7.

Diana W. Suarez, *Bluff and the Magic Mansion, A Children's Guide to the Hunter Museum of Art*, Chattanooga: Hunter Museum of Art, 1980.

Laura L. Meixner, *An International Episode: Millet, Monet and their North American Counterparts*, Memphis, TN: Dixon Gallery of Art, 1983, illus. p. 133, fig. 31,; p. 166, p. 193, no. 57.

In recognition as an important American *woman* impressionist, Lilla Cabot Perry is perhaps second only to her contemporary, Mary Cassatt. And if her work seems to fall short of the more famous artist's compositional finesse, luminosity, and evocative mood, Perry's biographers are quick to point out that painting was far from her undivided life pursuit. Unlike Cassatt, who never married, Perry was a devoted wife and mother to her three daughters. What is more, she painted essentially for her own satisfaction, and though she was a strong advocate for impressionism generally, she was not an aggressive promoter of her own work. Significantly, she was also an accomplished poet, publishing her verse in four volumes. (Of special note, the third volume, released in 1898, was titled *Impressions*.)

The artist was born in Boston in 1848, and was a member of the socially prominent Lowell and Cabot families. In 1874 she married Thomas Sargent Perry, a scholar in eighteenth-century English literature, author, and teacher, who was himself from a distinguished family. He was the grand-nephew of Commodore Matthew C. Perry, who had opened Japan to American commercial and social exchange in 1853-54. It was not until a decade after the marriage that Mrs. Perry took her first professional art instruction at Boston's Cowles School under Dennis Bunker and Robert Vonnoh. Vonnoh, particularly, had studied in Paris only a year before, and had adopted a kind of early or pre-impressionist style in the manner of his teacher there, Jules Bastien-Lepage. Perry went on to study in Paris at the Julian and Colarossi Academies, and independently with Belgian impressionist Alfred Stevens. In the summer of 1889, the Perrys visited Giverny, a village in Normandy on the Seine River, northwest of Paris, where they met Claude Monet. Monet established few close relationships outside his family and took no students. Yet he was cordial to Perry and encouraged her in her work. Through Monet, Perry befriended painter Camille Pissarro, who also lived close by. Back in America that fall, Perry brought with her one of Monet's dazzling views at Etretat. She commented some time later: "When I took it home that autumn of 1889 (I think it was the first Monet ever seen in Boston), to my great astonishment, hardly anyone liked it, the one exception being John LaFarge." As an interesting aside, LaFarge was Perry's brother-in-law; and he decorated the drawing room of Perry's Marlborough Street home, a home that became a gathering place for artists and writers of the day. The Perrys spent the next ten summers at Giverny occupying the house immediately next door to Monet. Recalling her friendship, Perry wrote "Reminiscences of Claude Monet from 1889 to 1909," which was published in the *American Magazine of Art*, March 1927.

In 1898 Thomas Perry accepted a professorship in English literature at Keiogijiku College in Tokyo. During the three years the family lived in Japan, the artist painted more than eighty pictures of Japanese people and settings.

The Hunter Museum's oil, *A Stream Beneath Poplars*, though undated, was probably painted on one of the Giverny summers prior to the departure for Japan. Laura L. Meixner notes a similarity in format, composition, and technique between Perry's painting and John Leslie Breck's *The River Ept, Giverny*, which is dated 1886. A fellow Bostonian, Breck was one of the first Americans to go to Giverny (after studying at Munich and the Académie Julian in Paris). It cannot necessarily be concluded that he influenced her, or she him. But it is known that Perry admired Breck, and in subsequent years invited him to show his work at her Boston home.

Perry's style — especially when seen next to Breck and much other American impressionist painting — is comparatively calligraphic. She rarely made preparatory drawings or even oil sketches, preferring to work directly on canvas. As a result, she had a tendency to draw with the brush, often applying her pigment in long, thin traces, and allowing the canvas to remain visible between brush strokes. In *A Stream Beneath Poplars* the linear effect defines the tall grasses at the creek's edge, and in juxtaposition suggests tree trunks and branches.

In 1914 Perry was one of the founding members and the first secretary of the Guild of Boston Artists, a group that included Edmund C. Tarbell, Frank W. Benson, John J. Enneking, and Maurice B. Prendergast. Many of her late paintings were shown in guild exhibitions, including still bright, impressionist landscapes of the rolling hills around Hancock, New Hampshire. The Perrys had purchased a house at Hancock in 1903 that they used chiefly as a summer residence. In the last few years of the artist's life, she remained at Hancock year round, and it was there she died in February 1933. The Boston Art Club presented a memorial exhibition of her paintings the following October and November. For that occasion, fellow guild member Tarbell wrote: "No wonder that . . . Monet and Pissarro admired her work, for Mrs. Perry was a most beautiful and personal talent."

Childe Hassam (1859-1935)

The majority of American artists who adopted impressionism in the last decades of the nineteenth century had either studied formally in Paris, or Barbizon, or Giverny, or they had spent sufficient time there to absorb the movement's aesthetic principles. Yet in implementing those tenets, the Americans were inclined to be less doctrinaire in the application of impressionist light and color theory and characteristic brush technique. Consequently, some critics and art historians, the notable E. P. Richardson for example, find the American development generally more decorative than that of the French innovators (a natural evolution reflecting the tendency of second-generation practitioners to refine, but at the same time reduce, the boldness and experimental vigor of the original style to an ornamental idiom).

Art historians James Thomas Flexner and Donelson F. Hoopes separately have suggested that Frederick Childe Hassam, of all the American impressionists who studied in France, is probably closest in style and spirit to his sources. In visual result as well as title, the vibrant oil *French Tea Garden* (color plate 14) aptly demonstrates the artist's more European manner and compares favorably with similar domestic outdoor scenes by Monet. (In fact, Hassam has been called the "American Monet.") With typical impressionist nonchalance, a seated young woman appears to be sewing the hem of an indeterminable cloth. Before her, a small table is spread with teacups, utensils, and attendant paraphernalia. The scene is bathed in sunlight; colors dance in the shadows of the white table covering and the woman's dress. Behind, a veritable tapestry of pigment suggests lush greenery and flowering things, and just a whisper of breeze that makes it all shimmer. Despite its overt calm, the image is blithe and zestful. It was painted on the artist's third and final visit to Europe during the summer of 1910.

As Hassam grew older, his style tended to increasing delicacy, one might even say fussiness or prettiness. Richard J. Doyle unflatteringly calls the late painting "slack" and "easy." With no less deprecation, fellow American impressionist Theodore Robinson wrote of Hassam's late work: "After a certain astonishment of the cleverness of his painting of detail, one is struck by the superficiality, the glitter, and nothing beside 'the tinsel of art.'" Whether totally fair or not, one can see the gist of this criticism in such works as the 1921 oil, *Spring, the Dogwood Tree*. The frilly treatment of the foliage seems aptly suited to the subject, and the painting effectively imparts the sense of exuberance, warmth, and new growth associated with the season. The large house immediately behind the tree, however, is an ambiguous image, lost in the fidgety, unaccentuated brushwork and the lack of tonal contrast. One feels too that the small nude child in the center foreground is meaningful to the scene, but it almost succumbs to the lacy surroundings.

Hassam was born in Dorcester, Massachusetts, in 1859. He left high school to apprentice as an engraver and illustrator in Boston, at the same time taking lessons at the Boston Art Club under I. M. Gaugengigl. Later he also studied at the Lowell Institute. His illustrations were published in *Scribner's* and *Harper's* magazines and in several books. In 1883 he made his first extended tour of Europe. From 1886 to '89 he was again in Paris. He studied briefly at the Académie Julian with Gustave Boulanger and Jules Lefebvre, but his chief influence at that time came from the impressionists. By 1887 his works had begun to show impressionist effects.

After returning to the United States in 1889 Hassam settled in New York. His principal circle of artist friends were others with impressionist tendencies, including those with whom he formally associated in 1889 as the group called The Ten American Painters, which exhibited annually for twenty years thereafter at the Durand-Ruel Gallery in New York. Hassam also presented his work regularly, until his death in 1935, at shows of the Carnegie International, Pennsylvania Academy of the Fine Arts, and the National Academy of Design. He was elected an associate of the Academy in 1902 and elevated to full academician in 1906. He was also a member of the National Institute and the American Academy of Arts and Letters. In his long career he won thirty-five noteworthy prizes and awards, not the least of which was an invitation to participate in the 1913 New York Armory Show.

(color plate 14)

FRENCH TEA GARDEN
(Also known as *The Terre-Cuite Tea Set*)
Childe Hassam
1910
oil on canvas
35 x 40¼ inches
signed and dated lower right
Gift of the Benwood Foundation

Provenance

American Art Association, New York, New York
Stephen C. Clark, New York, New York
Victor Spark, New York, New York
Garfinkle Collection, New York, New York
Mr. and Mrs. Louis D. Cohen, New York, New York

Exhibitions

Exhibition of Pictures of Childe Hassam, Montross Gallery, New York, NY, Feb. 1- 14, 1911, no. 5.

Fifteenth Annual Exhibition, Museum of Art, Carnegie Institute, Pittsburgh, PA, April 27-June 30, 1911.

Panama-Pacific International Exhibition, San Francisco, CA, 1915, no. 3696.

Post-Exposition Exhibition, Panama-Pacific Exposition, San Francisco, CA, Jan. 1-May 1, 1916, no. 5558.

Paintings, Watercolors, Pastels and Etchings by Childe Hassam, City Art Museum of St. Louis, St. Louis, MO, May, 1917.

Masterpieces of Art, Catalogue of European and American Paintings, 1500-1900, New York World's Fair, May-Oct. 1940, no. 312.

American Bank & Trust Company, Fifth Avenue, New York, NY, Nov. 19-Dec. 19, 1969, no. 6.

Summer Exhibition, Norton Gallery of Art, West Palm Beach, FL, 1970.

Childe Hassam, 1859-1935, University of Arizona Museum of Art, Tucson, AZ, Feb. 5-March 5, 1972; Santa Barbara Museum of Art, Santa Barbara, CA, March 26-April 30, 1972.

American Impressionist Painters, Huntsville Museum of Art, Huntsville, AL, Dec. 1, 1978-Jan. 15, 1979.

American Impressionists, Smithsonian Institution Traveling Exhibition Service circulating exhibition: Musee de Petit Palaise, Paris, France; Staatliche Museen zu Berlin National Galerie, East Berlin, East Germany; The National Museum, Cracow, Poland; Art Museum of the Socialist Republic of Romania, Bucharest, Romania; National Art Gallery, Sofia, Bulgaria; March 30, 1982-Jan. 31, 1983.

(Continued on page 89)

SPRING, THE DOGWOOD TREE

Childe Hassam

1921

oil on canvas

43 x 46 inches

signed and dated lower right

Gift of the Benwood Foundation

Provenance

Collection of the artist
American Academy of Arts and Letters, New York, New York (by bequest)
E & A Milch, Inc., New York, New York
Private collection, Palm Beach, Florida
Mr. and Mrs. Louis D. Cohen, New York, New York

Exhibitions

Thirty-fifth Annual Exhibition of American Paintings and Sculpture, Art Institute of Chicago, Chicago, IL, Nov. 2-Dec. 10, 1922, no. 96.

An Exhibition of Modern American Paintings (From the Annual Exhibition of the Art Institute of Chicago), Minneapolis Institute of Arts, Minneapolis, MN, Dec. 20, 1922-Jan. 30, 1923.

International Exhibition, American Federation of Arts, Venice, Italy, Summer, 1924.

Ninth Exhibition of Contemporary American Oil Paintings, Corcoran Gallery of Art, Washington, D.C., Dec. 16, 1923-Jan. 20, 1924, no. 117.

Exhibition of Paintings by Childe Hassam, House of Durand-Ruel, New York, NY, 1926.

First Exhibition of Selected Paintings by American Artists, California Palace of the Legion of Honor, Lincoln Park, San Francisco, CA, Nov. 26, 1926-Jan. 30, 1927, no. 93.

Childe Hassam, Guild Hall, East Hampton, New York, NY, July 30-Aug. 16, 1967, no. 7.

Exhibition of American Paintings, American Bank and Trust Company, New York, NY, 1969, no. 6.

Childe Hassam, 1859-1935, University of Arizona Museum of Art, Tucson, AZ, Feb. 5-March 5, 1972; Santa Barbara Museum of Art, Santa Barbara, CA, March 26-April 30, 1972.

Master American Impressionists, Marietta/Cobb Fine Arts Center, Marietta, GA, Oct. 12-Nov. 29, 1983.

The Four Seasons, Columbus Museum of Arts and Sciences, Columbus, GA, March 17-May 20, 1984.

Publications

International Studio, March, 1922.

Bulletin of Minneapolis Institute of Arts, Vol. XII, No. 1, Jan. 1923.

Art Notes, The Milch Gallery, Spring, 1925, p. 18.

Art News, Milch Gallery advertisement, March 2, 1929, illus.

Childe Hassam, 1859-1935, exhibition catalogue, Tucson: University of Arizona, 1972, illus. p. 42, p. 142, no. 114.

The Four Seasons, exhibition catalogue, Columbus, GA: Columbus Museum of Arts and Sciences, 1984, p. 26.

(Continued from page 88)

Publications

Fifty American Pictures, New York: Montross Gallery, 1911, no. 252.

Fifteenth Annual Exhibition, exhibition catalogue, Pittsburgh: Carnegie Institute, 1911, illus. no. 116.

Nathaniel Pousette-Dart, *Childe Hassam*, New York: Frederick A. Stokes, Co., 1922, illus.

Childe Hassam, 1859-1935, exhibition catalogue, Tucson: University of Arizona Museum of Art, 1972, illus. on cover, illus. p. 38, p. 142, no. 80.

Donelson F. Hoopes, *Childe Hassam*, New York: Watson-Guptill Publications, 1979, p. 77, illus. p. 78, no. 28.

Diana W. Suarez, *Bluff and the Magic Mansion, A Children's Guide to the Hunter Museum of Art*, Chattanooga: Hunter Museum of Art, 1980.

"Diversity Colors the South's Art Collections." *Southern Living*, Jan. 1982, pp. 62-66, illus. p. 65.

Barbara Novak, *American Impressionists*, exhibition catalogue, Washington, D.C.: Smithsonian Institution, 1982, p. 96, no. 32.

Vivian Ruth Sawyer, "American Impressionist Paintings Make European Debut." *Antique Monthly*, March 1982, pp. 1A-8A, illus. p. 8A.

"Americans in Paris." *The Collector-Investor*, April, 1982, pp. 13-16, illus. p. 16.

Michael Brenson, "Innocence Abroad—American Impressionism on Tour." *The New York Times*, May 30, 1982, pp., D27-D28.

S. Dillon Ripley, "The View from the Castle." *Smithsonian*, June 1982, pp. 8-9, illus. p. 9.

Maurice Prendergast (1859-1924)

During the first quarter of the twentieth century, when Boston native Maurice Prendergast was producing what has since come to be his most highly regarded work, the majority of critics tended to see his art as radical, if not downright inept. One reviewer scoffingly described his painting as "an explosion in a color factory," while another even more derisively called it "unadulterated slop." There were a small few who at least acknowledged its pleasant ornamental effect, and an even smaller few understood that, in moving away from conventional nineteenth-century realism, Prendergast did so with sincere purpose and good result.

By contemporary European standards, of course, his painting did not seem remarkably innovative. Clearly his style was in large measure adapted from the modern movements he had encountered while a student in Paris between 1891 and '93. Though enrolled successively at the conservative Académies Colarossi and Julian, Prendergast marveled at the vivid light illusion of the impressionists who had been well-established and exhibiting since the early 1870s. He admired Whistler's subtle sense of abstract arrangement and the compositional structure of the postimpressionists — particularly Cézanne, Gauguin, and Seurat. He was intrigued by the color and mood of such symbolists as Bonnard, Denis, and Vollaton.

Evidence of these influences shows in the paintings he executed after his return to the United States. Working at that time chiefly in watercolor, his manner grew increasingly decorative and pattern-oriented, yet always controlled by a precise underlying draftsmanship. By 1897 his work had come to the attention of several prominent Boston collectors, including especially Mrs. Montgomery Sears, who in the following year financed for him a lengthy study trip to Italy. He found the intense daylight of the Mediterranean region — so different from either New England or northern Europe — manifestly stimulating. There too, significantly, he was fascinated upon seeing various paintings by the late fifteenth/early sixteenth-century Venetian masters (Gentile) Bellini and Carpaccio that depicted scenes of pagentry and festive procession at the Piazza San Marco. One sees this theme re-interpreted by Prendergast, virtually his favorite topic: people gathered in New York's Central Park or by the seaside at Ipswitch, Marblehead, or Gloucester, Massachusetts. The Hunter's *Gloucester Harbor* (color plate 15) is a fitting example.

After the Italian trip Prendergast also tended to compose his pictures with a more systematic integration of fore- and background elements, building the design on a distinct interlocking vertical-horizontal network. And, painting then as often in oils, he further devised a kind of buoyant "gum-ball" color swatch brushwork to achieve an effect similar to tapestry or mosaic. He was much more interested in the visual coherence of the whole than in sharp detail among its parts. Consequently, people in his scenes are usually faceless, suggesting ideal or universal types and unspecified times or occasions—a perpetual holiday. The overall quality is anecdotal and poetic.

In 1900 Prendergast was given his first major one-man show at the Art Institute of Chicago. Shortly thereafter he met and formed a strong friendship with the Ash Can School painter William Glackens, who in turn introduced him to other members of the Robert Henri circle. He thus became one of The Eight (the only one from outside New York City) who exhibited at the controversial Macbeth Gallery show in 1908. Rather like Davies and Lawson, he was affiliated more by temperament than by painting style, and he did not share the original group's concern for social commentary. The association continued beneficial in that Davies went on to be one of the chief organizers of the 1913 New York Armory Show and was instrumental in enabling Prendergast to participate. Prendergast moved to New York the following year. In 1917 he became a charter member of the Society of Independent Artists, which, patterned after a successful anti-academy group in France, was organized to promote and exhibit members' work.

Prendergast was a private person. He never taught or gave interviews, which leaves him a somewhat enigmatic study. Friends described him as decidedly un-bohemian, proper, and punctilious. Though deafness and failing health marked the last decade of his life, he continued to paint to the time of his death in 1924, at age sixty-five.

(color plate 15)

GLOUCESTER HARBOR

Maurice Prendergast

1918

oil on canvas

19⅝ x 26½ inches

signed lower left

Gift of the Benwood Foundation

Provenance

Mrs. Charles Prendergast, Westport, Connecticut

Robert Schoelkopf Gallery, New York, New York

Mr. and Mrs. Louis D. Cohen, New York, New York

Exhibitions

Frances and L. D. Cohen Collection, Norton Gallery and School of Art, West Palm Beach, FL, Feb. 23-March 17, 1968.

American Bank and Trust Company, New York, NY, Nov. 19-Dec. 19, 1969.

Publications

Frances and L. D. Cohen Collection, exhibition catalogue, West Palm Beach: Norton Gallery and School of Art, 1968, no. 20.

Diana W. Suarez, *Bluff and the Magic Mansion, A Children's Guide to the Hunter Museum of Art,* Chattanooga: Hunter Museum of Art, 1980.

Ernest Lawson *(1873-1939)*

The American painter Ernest Lawson was actually born in Halifax, Nova Scotia, Canada. In 1891, at age eighteen, he moved to New York City to attend the Art Students League. There he studied principally with J. Alden Weir and John H. Twachtman. Both teachers had worked earlier in France and had adopted the impressionist manner (and both eventually became members of the group called "The Ten," which E. P. Richardson has called "a kind of academy of American Impressionism"). Two years later Lawson enrolled at the Académie Julian in Paris. In 1895 he met the prominent French impressionist, Alfred Sisley, who further influenced his developing style.

On returning to the United States in 1898 Lawson settled again in New York where, curiously, he associated not with The Ten (whose members were divided between New York and Boston), but rather with the Robert Henri circle that included especially William Glackens, whom he had befriended in 1904. Still another friend of Glackens was Maurice Prendergast, an American who also painted in a variant impressionist style. Significantly, Prendergast and Lawson were the atypical pair invited to exhibit with Henri's "Ash Can" group at the Macbeth Gallery in 1908, the memorable show by The Eight. Lawson subsequently took part in two other major showings of non-traditional art that were eventful for the growth of modernism in this country—the Exhibition of Independent Artists in 1910 and the Armory Show in 1913.

In reaction to the dark, academic, studio painting of the mid-nineteenth century, the impressionists generally opted for the out-of-doors and the brilliance of nature. They declared that form and space are perceived essentially as colored light that is vibrating and changing constantly. To express this phenomenon, the artists devised a technique of applying paint in small brushstrokes, often with primary or secondary hues unmixed and juxtaposed so that the tones are blended in the viewer's eye at an appropriate distance. Contour outlining was avoided, and since the artists observed color even in shadows, browns and blacks were rarely used. The resulting mosaic of color dabs typically enhanced the surface pattern rather than the illusion of depth. Indeed, Lawson's work meets these criteria. His consistently impressionist style led critic James Huneker to extol the artist's "palette of crushed jewels."

The Hunter's *Old Tulip Tree, Long Island* (color plate 16) demonstrates just such a palette. It is optically vibrant and the broken-color impasto technique, rendered largely with a painter's knife, is inherently rhythmic. The bold, rippling tulip tree in the right foreground is shadowed in dark blue, and it in turn casts a blue shadow over the turf behind and green against the house near the picture's center. The tree thus appears almost to lay hold of the structure. Clearly this is the dominant motif; the activities of the farm people shown in the lower front are indistinct and inconsequential by comparison.

Lawson wanted his landscapes to express an inner mood, and he was himself often a moody and emotional person. He once wrote that he felt color should be employed to represent "the three major emotions in a man's life—anticipation, realization, and retrospection." It is not surprising that another of Lawson's close friends, Somerset Maugham, took him as the model for Frederick Lawson, the temperamental artist character in *Of Human Bondage*.

(color plate 16)

THE OLD TULIP TREE, LONG ISLAND
(Also known as *The Old Tulip Tree*)

Ernest Lawson

undated

oil on canvas

25¾ x 30⅝ inches

signed lower left

Gift of the Benwood Foundation

Provenance

Ferargil Collection, New York, New York
Mr. and Mrs. Louis D. Cohen, New York, New York

Exhibitions

Annual Exhibition, National Academy of Design, New York, NY, 1914.

Frances and L. D. Cohen Collection, Norton Gallery and School of Art, West Palm Beach, FL, Feb. 23-March 17, 1968.

Publications

Annual Exhibition, exhibition catalogue, New York: National Academy of Design, 1914, no. 257.

Diana W. Suarez, *Bluff and the Magic Mansion, A Children's Guide to the Hunter Museum*, Chattanooga: Hunter Museum of Art, 1980.

Edward Henry Potthast (1857-1927)

Initially prepared by study at conservative art schools, first in his native Cincinnati and later at Antwerp and Munich, Edward Henry Potthast had been working in a reserved, academic style more than a decade when in 1887 he began a second European stay, a seven-year period that was pivotal to his development. While living in Paris, he met and formed fast friendships with Robert Vonnoh and Roderick O'Conor, Americans living abroad and already painting in an impressionist mode. Potthast devised his own modified impressionist style from the influence of these friends and his exposure to the work of French impressionists. He embraced typical impressionist subject matter (the out-of-doors, leisure activity, informally arranged people and settings, spontaneity, bright palette, and light theory). However, instead of applying paints to canvas in the characteristic small dabs of broken color (for a shimmer or flicker effect), he continued the strong, full-brushed impasto he first learned at the Munich Academy—unfortunately with sometimes flat or chalky result.

Potthast is best known for his many scenes of surf and sandy beaches, where people relax or recreate happily in the bright sun. He returned to the subject so often that the unidentified writer of a brochure for Macbeth Galleries in the 1920s felt obliged to extenuate: "When a man paints a theme as well as Potthast paints seashore subjects, we forgive him for sticking to it to the exclusion of other subjects." The writer's implication that Potthast was a one-track artist was clearly uninformed; he *did* paint other topics, landscape chiefly, as the Hunter Museum's piece aptly verifies.

In the Far Northwest — Montana (color plate 17), though not dated, was probably painted about 1913, on a trip the artist made to the western United States and the province of Alberta, Canada. (In any case, the piece was shown publicly in 1914 at the Worcester [Massachusetts] Invitational Exhibition.) The view is of McDonald Lake and the surrounding timber and mountains in Glacier National Park, near the Canadian border. Compared to the high horizon line Potthast employed for most the beach pictures, here the horizon crosses the lower quarter of the composition. Consequently the viewer looks up to landscape elements that seem majestically tall. The design is built on a system of diagonals and overlapping planes that step the eye into deep space. Consistent with the artist's impressionist color usage, black is avoided altogether; shadowed areas are rich tones of green, blue, and violet. Small swatches of bright orange outcropping from the massive rock cliffs at right balance the larger triangle of reduced-intensity blue violet at left. Horizontal bands of green and blue-green, suggesting mirror-smooth water in the foreground, complete an orchestration of color harmonies that in turn speak subjectively of the organic balances and harmonies in nature.

Potthast was born into Cincinnati's large German-American community in 1857. (Near-contemporaries Frank Duveneck and John H. Twatchman came out of the same district, and both men later were frequent visitors in Potthast's home and studio.) As early as 1870, when he was just thirteen, he took classes at the McMicken School of Design. Two years later he began an apprenticeship with the Ehrgott Krebs lithography firm, though he resumed study at the McMicken School in 1874 and again from 1879 to '82. With fellow Cincinnati artists Charles Haider and Joseph Henry Sharp, he began the first of his European sojourns in fall 1882. He studied briefly in Antwerp with Charles Veriat, then three years in Munich under Nicholas Gysis and Ludwig Loefftz. Returning to Cincinnati in 1885, he enrolled for evening courses at the Museum School, where he studied with Thomas S. Noble, who had earlier been one of his teachers at McMicken.

After the eventful second European stay, mainly in Paris between 1887 and '94, Potthast returned again to Cincinnati. He moved to New York in 1896, and, except for his extensive travels, resided there the rest of his life. To support himself, he regularly did free-lance lithography for *Century* and *Scribner's* magazines. He was elected as associate of the National Academy of Design in 1899, and made full academician in 1906. He was also a member of the National Watercolor Society, and served as the organization's director in 1903.

(color plate 17)

IN THE FAR NORTHWEST — MONTANA

Edward Henry Potthast

c. 1913

oil on canvas

50 x 40 inches

signed lower right

Gift of Mr. and Mrs. Scott L. Probasco, Jr. and Mrs. Elizabeth L. Davenport

Provenance

Christian Zabriskie, New York, New York
Berry-Hill Galleries, New York, New York
Maurice Solo, Mamaroneck, New York
Private collection, Virginia Beach, Virginia
Douglas James, Ft. Pierce, Florida
Mr. and Mrs. Scott L. Probasco, Lookout Mountain, Tennessee

Exhibitions

Worchester International Exhibition, Worchester, MA, 1914.

Twenty-third Annual Exhibition of American Art, Cincinnati Art Museum, Cincinnati, OH, May 27-July 31, 1916, no. 46.

Building the West, Schlier Memorial Gallery, Denver Art Museum, Denver, CO, Oct. 9-Nov. 27, 1955.

American Painting 1900-1916, Birmingham Museum of Art, Birmingham, AL, Oct. 1-23, 1960, no. 21.

Publications

Sotheby Parke Bernet, Inc., Sale catalogue #2326, Jan. 27, 1965, no. 65.

Peggy and Harold Samuels, *The Illustrated Biographical Encyclopedia of Artists of the American West*, New York: Doubleday & Co., Inc., 1976, p. 378.

A particular distinction in November 1910, Potthast was one of five artists (the others were Thomas Moran, Elliott Daingerfield, Frederick Ballard Williams, and DeWitt Parshall) given a trip and commission by the Santa Fe Railroad to paint scenes of the Grand Canyon. Nina Spalding Stevens, then assistant director of the Toledo Art Museum, accompanied the party to Arizona. She wrote at length on the positive implications of corporate patronage to individual artists, noting specifically: "Never before had so large a group of serious artists made such a pilgrimage to the Far West with the avowed intention of studying a given point of their own country." Artworks produced as an outcome of the trip were assembled as a special exhibition that circulated to Chicago, Rochester, and New York.

Potthast was an exceedingly shy and self-deprecating person, an inexpedience to his career because he was averse to promote himself and his work, and to his personal life because he had few close friends and never married. When he died alone in his studio in March 1927, reportedly amidst several hundred finished and unfinished works, his only heirs were his brother's grown children. Insisting it was what their uncle would have wanted, the heirs destroyed everything in the studio that they considered not up to the artist's customary standard. As a result, little of the late work was left available when Cincinnati's Traxel Galleries mounted a memorial exhibition the following November. Arlene Jacobowitz, in her 1969 catalogue essay for an important Potthast exhibition held at Chapellier Galleries in New York, ponders resentfully: "One cannot help from wondering if posterity would agree with the decision of his heirs as to which works were 'sketches,' 'unfinished,' or 'inferior.'"

Color plate 9. Richard LaBarre Goodwin, *The Huntsman's Door*, c. 1890, oil on canvas, 50$\frac{1}{2}$ x 30$\frac{1}{4}$ inches. Gift of Mrs. Otto K. LeBron in memory of her husband, Otto K. LeBron. (See article, page 70.)

Color plate 10. George Inness, *Rosy Morning*, 1894, oil on canvas, 30 x 45 inches. Gift of the Joseph H. Davenport, Jr. family in memory of Laura Voigt and Joseph Howard Davenport. (See article, page 73.)

Color plate 11. Ralph A. Blakelock, *Landscape With Moon*, c. 1885-90, oil on canvas, 20 x 30 inches. Gift of the Benwood Foundation (by exchange). (See article, page 77.)

Color plate 12. James Abbott McNeill Whistler, *Gray and Gold – The Golden Bay*, 1900, oil on panel, 5½ x 9¼ inches. Gift of Mr. and Mrs. Scott L. Probasco, Jr. (See article, page 78.)

Color plate 13. Mary Cassatt, *Baby Bill in His Cap and Shift, Held by His Nurse*, c. 1890, pastel on paper, 16⅞ x 15⅛ inches. Gift of the Benwood Foundation (by exchange). (See article, page 82.)

Color plate 14. Childe Hassam, *French Tea Garden*, 1910, oil on canvas, 35 x 40¼ inches. Gift of the Benwood Foundation. (See article, page 88.)

Color plate 15. Maurice Prendergast, *Gloucester Harbor*, 1918, oil on canvas, 19⅝ x 26½ inches. Gift of the Benwood Foundation. (See article, page 90.)

Color plate 16. Ernest Lawson, *The Old Tulip Tree, Long Island*, undated, oil on canvas, 25¾ x 30⅝ inches. Gift of the Benwood Foundation. (See article, page 91.)

Color plate 17. Edward Henry Potthast, *In the Far Northwest — Montana*, c. 1913, oil on canvas, 50 x 40 inches. Gift of Mr. and Mrs. Scott L. Probasco, Jr. and Mrs. Elizabeth L. Davenport. (See article, page 92.)

Color plate 18. William Glackens, *Miss Olga D.*, 1910, oil on canvas, 32 x 26 inches. Gift of the Benwood Foundation. (See article, page 114.)

Color plate 19. Frank Weston Benson, *Lilies and Laurel in a Blue Vase*, 1929, oil on canvas, 30 x 25 inches. Gift of Mr. and Mrs. John T. Lupton. (See article, page 125.)

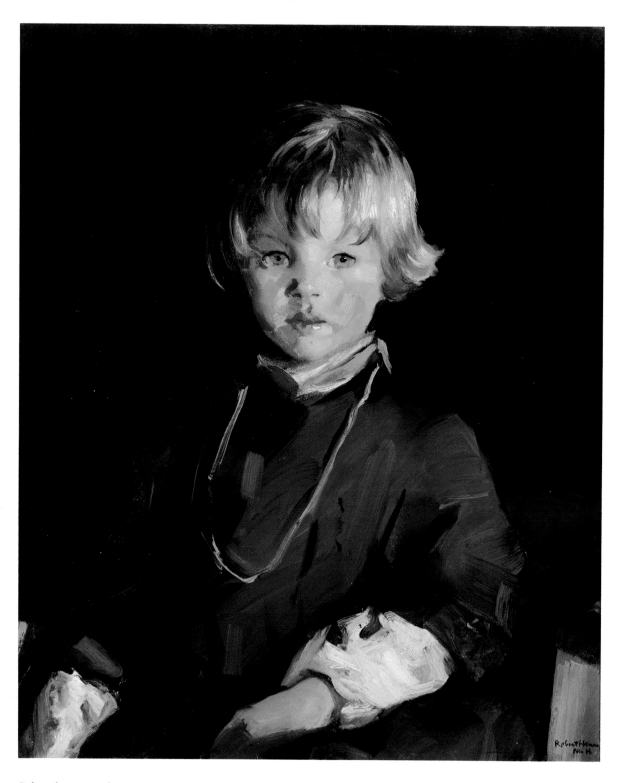

Color plate 20. Robert Henri, *Pet*, 1927, oil on canvas, 24 x 20 inches. Gift of the Benwood Foundation. (See article, page 125.)

Color plate 21. George Benjamin Luks, *Allen Street*, c. 1905, oil on canvas, 32 x 45 inches. Gift of Miss Inez Hyder. (See article, page 127.)

Color plate 22. Everett Shinn, *Actress in Red Before Mirror*, c. 1910, pastel on paper, 25½ x 14⅝ inches (sight). Gift of the Benwood Foundation. (See article, page 128.)

Color plate 23. William S. Horton, *Punch on the Beach at Broadstairs, England*, 1920, oil on canvas, 25⅜ x 30¾ inches. Gift of M. R. Schweitzer in memory of Robert L. Maclellan (by exchange). (See article, page 130.)

Color plate 24. Edward Hopper, *House and Boats*, c. 1923, watercolor on paper, 13½ x 19¾ inches (sight). Gift of the Benwood Foundation. (See article, page 131.)

The Modern Era: Formation and Transition

The independent "giants" Winslow Homer, Thomas Eakins, Albert Pinkham Ryder, and John Singer Sargent lived and continued working well into the twentieth century—as did the principal American impressionists: Childe Hassam, John H. Twatchman, Robert Reid, and others of "The Ten." But their styles were firmly rooted in the previous century. The early 1900s were "stand-pat" years for American art. John I. H. Baur notes: "Perhaps at no time has our art been more truly provincial or more intolerant of stylistic deviations." Painter Everett Shinn described the situation in more graphic and moribund terms. American art "had inherited a preceding drowsiness, and that virus of ease and artificiality produced in the non-resistant body a lowering of vitality and a state of staggering decrepitude." "Art galleries," he continued, "were more like funeral parlors wherein the cadavers were displayed in their sumptuous coffins."

It was a kind of doldrums, out of which American art took three courses of development. Many artists—indeed the largest number—including such technically competent figures as Kenyon Cox, Charles Hawthorne, Frank Vincent Dumond, and William McGregor Paxton, perpetuated or only slightly updated the status quo. Under the pervasive sway of the National Academy of Design, nineteenth-century academic modes—generally realistic in style and genteel in subject matter—were formally sanctioned. Lloyd Goodrich describes the gravity of the situation for artists:

> Almost the only way to get one's work before the public was in regular exhibitions of museums or artists' societies, dominated by conservative juries who excluded anything unorthodox, and awarded to their own kind the prizes so dear to the academic mind. Getting into one of these big shows was a major event in a young man's career; it meant the difference between artistic survival or failure.

For a 1907 N.A.D. show, the judges had rejected as too coarse, too unrefined, work by several artists who would soon after represent a second direction, a revolt against fashionable academic idealism. The following year these men exhibited together as The Eight at New York's Macbeth Gallery. Five of the group—Robert Henri, George Luks, William Glackens, Everett Shinn, and John Sloan—came to be identified as the Ash Can School. In reviving the vigorous brushwork and dramatic lighting of the earlier Munich manner, they were not innovative stylistically. But they jarred the prevailing sensibilities of their day with unconventional, often seamy views of urban life. Except for Henri, the Ash Can artists had formerly been newspaper illustrators. It is not surprising that "progressive painting should be in the hands of a group of newspaper-trained artist-journalists," Sam Hunter observes, noting further the thematic similarity of the artworks to the writings of such contemporaries as Steven Crane, Theodore Dreiser, Lincoln Steffens, Frank Harris, Jack London, and Upton Sinclair.

At about the same time, photographer Alfred Stieglitz had begun exhibiting European modern artists—cubists, fauves, expressionists—at his New York gallery, informally known as "291" (for 291 Fifth Avenue). He also provided show opportunities to numerous Americans who shared the creative spirit of the European avant-garde and would represent the third course, including Marsden Hartly, Arthur Dove, Alfred Maurer, and John Marin. American art was, as Goodrich says, "at a starting point for free creation, in which color, line, and design became a direct physical language." Cut off from "establishment" support, the new moderns organized their own autonomous exhibitions, the most notable of which were the Society of Independent Artists show in 1910 and the watershed event held in 1913 at New York's 69th Regiment Armory—the "scandal on 26th Street," the Armory Show. A large section of the latter exhibit introduced the principal French modern artists to a widespread, but mainly bewildered and shocked American public. Though conservative critic Royal Cortissoz denounced the French work as "a gospel of studied license and self assertion" fit only for "the rubbish heap," American art was profoundly infected. "When the anger and astonishment subsided," George Heard Hamilton explains, "a new situation had been created for the American artist. Whether or not the Armory Show made America safe for modernism, it showed him that he could venture as far as the Europeans had gone, and it eventually made possible a more sympathetic audience." Goodrich declares flatly: "No single event, before or since, has had such an influence on American art."

Conservatism held prevalent in the late teens and 1920s; still in the spirit of cultural and political internationalism that followed World War I, non-literal expression also flourished with artists like Max Weber, Patrick Henry Bruce, Joseph Stella, and Stuart Davis. Interestingly, a number of artists of the period devised a kind of hybrid style in which elements of abstract design and composition were bred with traditional American realism. The resulting effect—figurative, yet subject to non-representational design principles—is seen in the work of Charles Sheeler, Charles Demuth, Georgia O'Keeffe, Niles Spencer, Edward Hopper, and numerous others.

Progressive artists of the 1920s continued to produce into the '30s. But America's national mood changed in the wake of the stock market "crash" of 1929 and ensuing depression years. The country turned inward, economically, politically, socially, assuming an isolationist stance. During the long recovery, the government's Federal Art Project and Treasury Department programs sustained many artists through the leanest times. The chief object of the government's patronage was decorating post offices, court houses, and other civic buildings. Participating artists, therefore, were virtually obliged to consider themes of popular interest—local history, industrial development, native landscape—and to work in a representational style that the "average person" could understand and appreciate. Apart from government support, as Baur points out: "The suffering of those years turned increasing numbers of artists to the consideration of man as a social being and to specific problems of social relations which were not susceptible to abstract treatment." The '30s, then, saw the advance of socially meaningful art, under the heading "American scene," with an essentially nostalgic and rural wing represented by the "regionalists"—Grant Wood, Thomas Hart Benton, and John Steuart Curry, for example—and a political and urban wing with the "social realists"—including Reginald Marsh, Ben Shahn, and Philip Evergood, and seen as well in the photography of Louis Hine and Dorothea Lange. Again, such authors as Sherwood Anderson, John Steinbeck, Sinclair Lewis, and William Faulkner reveal a comparable trend in literature.

Although American art of the 1920s and '30s was predominantly realistic, abstract and non-figurative styles were not without potent advocacy. From its founding in 1929, the Museum of Modern Art in New York was (and is still) a singularly formidable proponent. Joshua C. Taylor notes: "Through its exhibitions and publications, and eventually through its extraordinary permanent collection, it molded the concepts of the modern tradition into a convincing historical design." The New York group American Abstract Artists was organized in 1936, and in '37 the Chicago Bauhaus was founded by former members of the distinguished German design school who had fled the Hitler regime. All of this, and more, in effect set the stage for the great outburst of abstract and expressionist art that would dominate contemporary movements after World War II.

American sculpture in the first half of the twentieth century developed in a pattern similar to painting, only even more conservative and slow-changing. Members of the National Sculpture Society, an organization spiritually akin to the N.A.D., retained the Beaux-Arts styles of the previous era. To a small number of native-born sculptors like Jo Davidson, Paul Manship, John Storrs, and Hugo Robus, modern would mean simplified or streamlined figurative work. The chief practitioners of more abstracted design were immigrants from Europe who brought the latest trends with them: Gaston Lachaise, Elie Nadelman, Jacques Lipchitz, William Zorach, and Alexander Archipenko, to name the best known. Meanwhile, two particularly imaginative Americans began producing a remarkably innovative body of work: Joseph Cornell and his box sculptures, and the witty wire figures and mobiles of Alexander Calder.

In architecture, revivalist styles—represented at the beginning of the century by the influential firm of McKim, Mead, and White—gradually gave way to design based on the structural integrity of the edifice. During the long transitional phase, historical references were often veneered over technologically advanced building art, as in the notable examples of Cass Gilbert's Woolworth Building in New York, from 1913, and Hood and Howells' gothicized Chicago Tribune Building in 1923. Skeletal structural-steel systems made possible "curtain" rather than load-bearing walls, which in turn made possible the skyscraper. Upward-soaring office buildings demanded design characteristics that would articulate strength, verticality, efficiency, and newness, not to mention corporate pride or one-upsmanship. At the same time, Frank Lloyd Wright—with his abhorance of the conventional box enclosure, his fondness for natural materials, colors, and textures, and his belief that structures should visually harmonize with their surroundings—devised the "prairie house," and dominated progressive domestic architecture (though he also designed many commercial and institutional buildings). In the '30s, Walter Gropius and Ludwig Meis van der Rohe, recently arrived from Germany, introduced the smooth, functional Bauhaus aesthetic, the beginnings of the International Style that would markedly affect American business and industrial architecture for more than two decades after World War II.

Arthur B. Davies (1862-1928)

JUNO AND THE THREE GRACES
Arthur B. Davies
1902
oil on canvas
16 x 20⅛ inches
signed and dated lower left
Museum purchase

Provenance

Mrs. Ronnie D. Owen, Brooklyn, New York
(daughter of the artist)
Mrs. Edward Langenbach, Canton, Ohio
Henry E. Sloan, Detroit Michigan
Count Louis Von Cseh, New York, New York
Jay C. Coe, Greensboro, North Carolina

Exhibitions

Canton Art Institute, Canton, Ohio, 1955.

Alumnae Show, University of North Carolina at
Greensboro, Greensboro, NC, 1965.

Reyn Gallery, Inc., New York, NY, 1980.

A.M. Adler Fine Arts, Inc., New York, NY, 1980.

Publications

Susan Dee Brotman, "The Image of Women in
the Work of Arthur Bowen Davis", unpub-
lished master's thesis, University of Chicago,
1983, pp. 22-23, illus, p. 60, no. 11.

Arthur B. Davies was one of the participating artists who exhibited as The Eight at New York's Macbeth Gallery in February 1908. But his work stands well apart from that of the other seven. It falls neither into the topic category of urban low-life favored by five of the members, the so-called "Ash Can" group (Robert Henri, George Luks, Everett Shinn, William Glackens, John Sloan), nor to the semi-impressionism of the remaining two (Ernest Lawson and Maurice Prendergast). The Eight was a tenuous association, to say the least. What the affiliates had in common was chiefly their progressive spirit and their opposition to—in several cases withdrawal from—the conservative National Academy of Design. Macbeth had already been Davies' dealer since 1886; it was convenient for him simply to join company with those others he had befriended, for mutual exhibit benefit.

From early in his career, Davies worked in a sensitive and decorative manner. He was fascinated by classical mythology, folk legends, mystic poetry, and nineteenth-century symbolism. On an independent European study tour in 1893, the artists with whose work he was most impressed were, mystics all, the English pre-Raphaelites, James McNeill Whistler, Arnold Bocklin, Ferdinand Hoedler, and Pierre Puvis de Chavannes. The following year, he was much impressed by a Puvis show he saw at the Durand-Ruel Gallery in New York. Not unlike Puvis, Davies' best-known imagery is typically set in an idyllic outdoor setting. Lithesome nudes, usually female, dance or move about gently. The season is mild, the time is twilight, so that tones are muted and edges softened. A diaphanous haze spreads over the scene. Titles often refer to poems or romantic stories.

Juno and the Three Graces, a small oil from 1902, aptly demonstrates the artist's characteristic style. The theme is mythological, the place pastoral, and the coloring predominantly reserved greens. At the same time, the painting may be singularly representative of an important event in his personal life. 1902 was also the year that Davies—two years separated from his wife—met Edna Potter, an artist who would be his mistress until his death twenty-five years later. Susan Dee Brotman notes in her 1983 master's thesis on Davies that the Juno character especially, but the other women depicted as well, are far from the languid, ethereal figures of earlier paintings. Juno is Edna. (Edna was, in fact, probably the physical model.) What is more, she is corporeal, buxom, and sensuous. Recalling that one of Juno's several storied aspects was as goddess of beginnings, Brotman further points out the appropriateness of this portrayal for the beginnings of the new relationship.

Davies was born in Utica, New York, in 1862, the fourth child of a Welsh-immigrant Methodist minister. At age fifteen, he took art lessons from landscape painter Dwight Williams of nearby Cazenovia. When the father accepted a pastorate in Chicago in 1878, Davies, then sixteen, attended the Chicago Academy of Design. He worked as an engineering draftsman in Mexico from 1880 to '82. Returning to Chicago, he studied at the School of the Art Institute between 1882 and '86. He then moved to New York City, where he supported himself by illustrating for *Century* magazine, while studying part-time at the Gotham Art School and the Art Students League. In 1892 he met and married Lucy Virginia Meriwether, a physician who maintained a successful medical practice at Congers, New York, about twenty-five miles north of Manhattan. The couple resided on a farm near Congers. Though he tried sincerely, Davies was no farmer, and soon he elected to stay weekdays in New York City, returning to the country only on weekends. Initially the marriage was happy. Two sons were born. By 1900 however they were estranged and living apart, though they never divorced. Two years later as mentioned above, Davies began his liaison with Edna Potter. In 1905 he and Edna were living together as Mr. and Mrs. David Owen in an apartment on East 52nd Street, and a daughter was born to them in 1912. Davies went to great lengths to keep his "second family" secret. Even his closest friends were not aware of it; nor was his wife until after his passing.

Following the showing with The Eight, Davies participated in the Exhibition of Independent Artists in 1910. It was the first large unrestricted, unjuried exhibition of progressive art in the United States; more than a hundred artists took part. It was enough of a sensation that one year later four artists—Walt Kuhn, Jerome Myers, Elmer MacRae, and Henry Fitch Taylor—met to plan a truly grand and international display of modern art. Shortly, nine others, including Davies, joined the originators, and adopted the name, American Association of Painters and Sculptors. Davies was elected president in 1912. Thereupon he assumed a major role in organizing what would eventually be the epochal Armory Show of 1913. Some artists whom he had alienated in the planning process sarcasticly referred to the exhibit as "Davies' party." Davies and Kuhn, on a prior trip abroad, chose most of the examples of European modernism that were subsequently shown.

After the Armory Show, Davies experimented in a cubist manner. About 1916 he turned his attention to etching and aquatint, and in 1922 and '23 he attempted color lithography. He suffered a heart attack in 1924 that thereafter curtailed his activity. While visiting Florence, Italy, with Edna and their daughter in 1928, he succumbed to a second attack. Only two years after his death, the Metropolitan Museum of Art mounted a large memorial retrospective.

William Glackens (1870-1938)

Who was the enigmatic "Miss Olga D"? . . . this dark-clothed woman sitting on a serpentine-back sofa, motionless and emotionless, near yet distant, with wistful countenance, wide-set eyes gazing blankly, lost in thought. Is the expression one of mystique, or merely boredom? More likely the latter, for the young lady in William Glackens' painting from 1910 (color plate 18) was probably no more to the artist than a suitable model, retained solely for the pose. Glackens kept a small notebook with the names, addresses, and brief comments about numerous available models ("Miss Mignon Fyella, 593 West 145th St. Has yellow dress"). While no reference to an Olga appears in the book, Ira Glackens, son of the artist and his chief biographer, still feels that she may be hidden on its pages. Responding to an inquiry from the museum on the subject's possible identity, he relates in a letter of November 27, 1975:

> I do not know who the lady was, . . . and the name might not even have been hers. Father was always prone to hire models who needed a job, and that is why so many of his canvases were of exceedingly plain females, though paintable.

Although the subject apparently is not some secret *femme fatale*, the painting is no less noteworthy in that it is one of the first products of a rather abrupt, and perhaps overdue stylistic change. For the decade and a half, preceding it, Glackens painted in an earthy, realist manner, suggestive of his close friend and mentor, Robert Henri. But about 1910 he began to respond to influences he had seen four years earlier on a trip to Spain and France: He met the great impressionist, Pierre Auguste Renoir, and the fauve master, Henri Matisse. One sees elements of both Renoir and Matisse in *Miss Olga D.* Renoir is the feathery brushstroke, fluid edges, and warm, rosy palette with colored shadows (especially the greenish flesh tones). One senses Matisse in the bold contrast of decorative patterns (the wallpaper print against the plumed hat), in the voluptuous, undulating contours, and graceful negative shapes. The same swelling curves of the sofa, same warm color scheme, comparable negative shapes, a similar pensive facial expression by the model (though the model is not Olga) — all may be seen in another significant Glackens painting of the same year, *Nude with Apple* (Brooklyn Museum).

Glackens was born in Philadelphia in 1870. He attended Central High School, where John Sloan was a classmate. With a keen eye and a natural gift for drawing, he landed a position as staff illustrator for the *Philadelphia Record* in 1891. The next year he moved to the rival *Press*, where Sloan was in the art department along with Everitt Shinn, and, after 1893, George Luks. At the same time, he took night classes under Thomas Anshutz at the Pennsylvania Academy of the Fine Arts. About 1894 Glackens met the magnetic Henri, who was then teaching at the Philadelphia School of Design for Women. The two men shared a studio later the same year. Then in the spring of 1895, Glackens, Henri, and another Philadelphia artist-friend, Elmer Schofield, traveled eighteen months through France, Holland, and Belgium. Henri was particularly impressed upon seeing the work of Franz Hals, Rembrandt, Diego Velásquez, Francisco Goya, and Edouard Manet, and he led in adapting for his own expressive ends the dark-toned, freely brushed method of those earlier Europeans. By the time the party returned to America in late 1896, Glackens was confirmed to the Henri approach.

Resettled in New York City, Glackens found that Shinn and Luks had transferred from Philadelphia. Luks, then with the *New York World*, gave him a job to create comic drawings for the paper's Sunday supplement. Shortly, Glackens also began illustrating for the *Herald*. Glackens and Luks shared a room and studio for several months, during which time Glackens is acknowledged for having provided Luks crucial encouragement to pursue painting seriously. In 1898 the national illustrated magazine, *McClure's*, sent Glackens to Cuba to cover events of the Spanish-American War. After the important 1906 European trip, and after having been elected an associate member of the National Academy of Design the same year (he was not raised to full membership until 1933), he concentrated more and more on painting. He gave up illustration altogether in 1914.

As one of the Henri circle, Glackens had six pictures in the showing by The Eight at New York's Macbeth Gallery in 1908. In 1910 he helped organize and participated in the first large no-prerequisite (only a modest entry fee), no-jury, no-prize show in the United States, the controversial Exhibition of Independent Artists. It was also in 1910 that Glackens was re-acquainted with an old high school friend, Dr. Albert C. Barnes, a wealthy manufacturer and the inventor of the antiseptic compound, Argyrol. Barnes heretofore had been a diletante art collector, acquiring little of note or value. But he wanted to improve his holdings significantly, and to that end sought Glackens' help. In February 1912, Barnes sent Glackens to Paris with a sizeable amount of money to buy for him whatever paintings he thought worthwhile. Glackens purchased twenty French modern works, including pieces by Cézanne and Renoir. Later Glackens counseled Barnes in buying paintings by each of The Eight. These two ventures established the nucleus of what would eventually become the esteemed Barnes Foundation Collection in Merion, Pennsylvania. Later in 1912 Glackens joined the planning group for the prodigious Armory Show, held in New York the following year. He served as chairman for the selection of American art, and, somewhat modestly, included only three of his own works in the exhibit.

(color plate 18)

MISS OLGA D.
Williams Glackens
1910
oil on canvas
32 x 26 inches
signed lower right
Gift of the Benwood
Foundation

Provenance

Estate of the artist
Joan and Lester Avnet
Margot Chanin
Whitney Museum of Art, New York, New York
Kraushaar Gallery, New York, New York
Samuel Shore, New York, New York
Mr. and Mrs. Louis D. Cohen, New York, New York

Exhibitions

Thirty-four Paintings from the Whitney Museum of American Art, circulating exhibition organized by the Museum of Modern Art, New York, NY: Abilene Museum of Fine Arts, Abilene, TX; Hackley Art Gallery, Meskegon, MI; Art Institute of Zanesville, Zanesville, OH; Tucson Fine Arts Assoc., Tucson, AZ; Lauren Rogers Library and Art Museum, Laurel, MS; Louisiana State Exhibit Museum, Shreveport, LA; J. B. Speed Art Museum, Louisville, KY; and Miami Beach Public Library and Art Center, Miami Beach, FL; Oct. 6, 1952-June 29, 1953.

Tenth Anniversary Show, Des Moines Art Center, Des Moines, IA, June 1-July 20, 1958.

William Glackens Retrospective, Carpenter Art Galleries, Dartmouth College, Hanover, NH, May 15-June 30, 1960.

The Art of William Glackens, Fort Wayne Art Institute, Fort Wayne, IN, March 16-April 13, 1969.

American Bank and Trust Company, New York, NY, Nov. 19-Dec. 19, 1969.

Publications

Dwight Kirsch, *Tenth Anniversary Show,* exhibition catalogue, Des Moines: Des Moines Art Center, 1958.

In 1916 Glackens was a founding member and the first president of the Society of Independent Artists. Throughout his New York years, he taught periodically at the Art Students League. After 1925 the artist and his wife divided their time between America and Europe. Abroad, he resided mainly in France, a country he very much loved. In the mid 1930s, his health gradually deteriorated. While visiting in the Westport, Connecticut, home of long-time friends, artist Charles Prendergast (brother of Maurice) and his wife, in May 1938, Glackens died suddenly of a cerebral hemorrhage. He was sixty-eight.

John Sloan (1871-1951)

FIFTH AVENUE CRITICS
John Sloan
1905
etching
image: 4½ x 6¾ inches
signed and dated in plate
lower left and
signed lower right
Gift of Douglas James

Provenance
Douglas James & Co., Signal Mountain, Tennessee.

John Sloan's *Fifth Avenue Critics* from 1905 is one of thirteen plates in a series of etchings called "New York City Life" that the artist produced in the first year after moving to Manhattan from his native Philadelphia. Sloan was enthralled by the multifarious activity and by the great numbers and types of people on the streets or in the shops of that largest American city. It accorded his definition of "life," "real life," life as it is lived by the vast majority, the unvarnished life that merits societal concern through pictorial commentary. "An artist is the product of life," Sloan maintained, "a social creature . . . a spectator of life . . . The artist is interested in life the way God is interested in the universe." Assessing Sloan's broader career achievement, Lloyd Goodrich advances the same theme: "His art had that quality of being a direct product of the common life, absolutely authentic and unsweetened, that has marked the finest genre of all times." With a gift for narrative, developed in his early professional years as a newspaper and book illustrator, and with a flair for humor, Sloan could subtly poke fun at those persons, objects, or situations he thought derisible. Jonathan Greenberg observes: "No scene in the human comedy was too helpless for his optimism, no gesture too refined for his satire."

Of the two preening dowagers at left in *Fifth Avenue Critics*, Sloan wrote: "These were typical of the fashionable ladies who used to drive up and down the avenue about four o'clock of an afternoon, showing themselves and criticizing others." Their faces reveal a smug, disdainful expression. One woman absent-mindedly twiddles her gloved fingers. The other affectedly holds her lorgnette ready on the remote possibility something or someone will arrest her attention. The women in their finery are effectively set out in relatively light tones against the rich, dark, cross-hatched lines that become the darks of carriage and background.

Sloan, well known as a painter, was virtually self-taught in printmaking. His interest in graphic arts began about 1888 when, at age seventeen, he dropped out of high school to help support his family. He took a job at a book store that happened also to deal in fine prints. Shortly, he read and began to apply the lessons from Philip G. Hamerton's *The Etcher's Handbook*. At the same time he studied prints by great European masters: Rembrandt, Albrecht Dürer, Francisco Goya, and William Hogarth. (Sloan would later be called the "American Hogarth.") He was further influenced by the pictorial wit of two Englishmen, John Leech and Charles Keene, whose lampooning illustrations on the morals and manners of Victorian London society appeared in the waggish magazine, *Punch*.

Sloan was born in Lock Haven, Pennsylvania, in 1871, and reared in Philadelphia. After his stint with the bookseller, he joined the art department of the *Inquirer* in 1891, and transferred to the *Press* in '95. He also attended the Pennsylvania Academy of the Fine Arts, studying chiefly with Thomas Anshutz. In time, however, he concluded that the school's regimen was too structured. With former high school friend William Glackens, he met George Luks and Everitt Shinn at Robert Henri's studio. That circle, and in particular Henri's compelling theories about art, he found much to his liking. Later he would acknowledge Henri as his "father in art." In New York City Sloan participated with the re-established Henri group in the exhibit of The Eight at Macbeth Gallery in 1908. He took part in the Independent Artists' show in 1910, and submitted two paintings and five etchings for the historic Armory show in 1913.

Sincerely disturbed by perceived injustice, inequality, unequal opportunity, and economic hardship, Sloan was — to borrow Greenberg's designation — an "earnest socialist." He was an active member of the American Socialist Party from 1910 to 1916, during which period he regularly contributed cartoons and drawings to three socialist newspapers: *The Call*, *The Coming Nation*, and *The Masses*. Over a policy dispute with the editors of *The Masses*, he resigned both the paper and the party, though he retained his basic political beliefs. From 1916 to 1938, Sloan taught at the Art Students League. A popular instructor, his more recognized students included Alexander Calder, David Smith, Reginald Marsh, Adolph Gottlieb, and Barnett Newman. In 1918 he was elected president of the Society of Independent Artists, a capacity in which, remarkably, he served until 1944. After about 1925 Sloan moved away from the social-realist, Ash-Can approach in favor of more design-oriented studio problems, experimenting with colors, textures, and abstracted shapes.

On a trip to the Southwest in 1919, Sloan and his wife Dolly discovered Santa Fe, New Mexico. Taken with the scenic beauty of the place and fascinated with the prevalent Hispanic and Indian cultures, the artist returned every summer but one until his death in 1951. (Dolly died in 1943. After that the trips were with his second wife, Helen Farr, a former student who co-authored with Sloan the book *Gist of Art*, published in 1938.) He had wanted to retire full-time to Santa Fe, but the community's high altitude (7,000 feet) stressed his heart. They settled instead at Hanover, New Hampshire, where less than a year later Sloan died of heart failure during surgery for an operable tumor. He was eighty.

George Bellows (1882-1925)

ELSIE, EMMA AND
MARJORIE
George Bellows
1921
lithograph
image: 9⅜ x 12⅛ inches
signed lower right
Gift of the Art Study Club in
memory of Anna C. Turner

Provenance
Kennedy Galleries, Inc., New York, New York.

Painter and printmaker George Bellows is probably most associated in the public mind with his intense prize-fight pictures, particularly the vigorously brushed, savagely dramatic oils: *A Stag at Sharkey's* (1907, Cleveland Museum of Art), and *Both Members of This Club* (1909, National Gallery of Art), as well as the somewhat more restrained *Dempsey and Firpo* (1924, Whitney Museum of American Art). These and other works—landscapes, city-street views, nudes, and portraits—reflect the earthy, forthright, vigorous approach of Robert Henri and John Sloan, under whom Bellows studied at the New York School of Art from 1904 to 1906. Henri's dictum ". . . every evidence of research is worthy of the artist" is essentially restated in Bellows' lengthier "The ideal artist is he who knows everything, feels everything, experiences everything, and retains his experience in a spirit of wonder and feeds upon it with creative lust."

Partly because Bellows was nearly a generation younger than his illustrious teachers, and was rightly seen as their protégé, art historians have tended to regard him as a second-wave twentieth-century urban realist. Alexander Eliot, for example, calls Bellows "the greatest alumnus of the old Ash Can School," as though the bulk of his work followed awhile afterward. In truth, his production was contemporary with that of the group's "senior" members (including also George Luks, William Glackens, and Everett Shinn). What is more, owing to Bellows' untimely early death, all of the Ash Can artists outlived him. Incidentally, Bellows would have been totally unfamiliar with the Ash Can designation; it was not applied until nine years after his death, when Holger Cahill and Alfred H. Barr, Jr. first coined the term for a 1934 publication.

Bellows' interest in lithography began in late 1915 or early 1916. Greatly admiring the etchings of his friend Sloan, he experimented briefly with that intaglio process. But the medium adapted poorly to his skill and temperament, as Charles H. Morgan explains: "Drawing with a metal stylus through a film of wax onto a metal plate that then allowed acid to finalize the design posed too many mechanical and slow steps to suit Bellows' aggressive personality." For a lithograph, on the other hand, one draws directly onto the printing stone with a rich black crayon; it is more direct, more personal. Once embarked, Bellows pursued printmaking with characteristic drive. He bought his own press and six lithograph stones—costly items, then or now. All the while still painting, he produced nearly two hundred images and about eight thousand impressions. "They vary greatly in quality," Suzanne Boorsch observes with critical honesty, but she adds: ". . . the best ones rank with master prints of all time." Bellows was especially prolific in 1921, when he completed fifty-nine images, including *Elsie, Emma, and Marjorie*, in the remarkably small edition of sixteen. The three women are elegantly posed on a chair and sofa in the parlor of the artist's home at 146 East 19th Street, Manhattan. (The same room and furnishings are seen in numerous other Bellows prints.) Elsie, at left, is Elsie Speicher, wife of artist Eugene Speicher. Appearing lost in her own thoughts is Bellows' wife, Emma, at center. Marjorie Henri, wife of Bellows' close friend and mentor, Robert Henri, with her head tipped down and inclining slightly to the viewer's left, completes the main threesome. In the upper-left background one sees the husbands, doubtless conversing about art. The men are more summarily rendered, but are nonetheless recognizable likenesses: the balding Bellows, dark-haired Speicher, and Henri, with thin moustache and hair falling over the forehead. Boorsch feels that such domestic scenes and portraits are among Bellows' freshest and most vital lithographic work. "The better he knew the sitter, the better the portrait was," she writes. "Those of his family or close friends are the finest."

Bellows was born in Columbus, Ohio, in 1882. His devout Methodist parents chose his middle name, Wesley, in honor of John and Charles Wesley, the founders of Methodism, and they earnestly hoped their only son would study for the ministry after high school. But young Bellows liked to draw; he illustrated for his school paper and successfully submitted cartoons to the city newspaper. He also excelled as an athlete, which enabled him to enroll at Ohio State University, where he played baseball and basketball. At the end of his junior year, however, he decided to work seriously toward a career in art. That, in turn, prompted his move to study in New York. Following upon wide acclaim for his early paintings, including the first two boxing pictures, he was elected an associate of the National Academy of Design in 1909; at age twenty-six, he was the youngest member in the organization's history. He achieved full standing just four years later. In 1910 he was invited to instruct life drawing and composition classes at the Art Students League. He taught there in the 1910-11 school year and again from 1917 to '19. Between 1912 and '19 he also taught at the Ferrer Center in New York, where his students included William Gropper and Moses Soyer.

Bellows was a principal organizer of the 1913 New York Armory Show, to which he submitted fourteen of his own paintings. In 1916 he was a founder of the Society of Independent Artists. He was sympathetic to the Socialist cause, and between 1912 and '17 regularly contributed illustrations to the party's journal, *The Masses* (for which John Sloan was art editor until 1916). From early in his career, Bellows had obviously been interested in compositional order and balance through the careful disposition of shapes, lines, angles, and patterns in a system of effects stabilized by other effects in opposition. By 1916, therefore, he was a ready disciple for Jay Hambridge and his recently published design theories of "dynamic symmetry"—to the detriment of Bellows' subsequent work, many art historians feel. Hambridge propounded a strict and complicated set of formulas—basing pictorial arrangement as a substructure of squares, rectangles, and triangles—mathematically calculated to bring about a sense of force and counterforce. In practice, Bellows' result seems contrived, stiff, and awkward—poses with arms and legs conspicuously positioned, one feels, only to accommodate prerequisite angles.

In 1925 Bellows died of peritonitis following emergency surgery for a ruptured appendix. He was forty-two. Later that same year, the Metropolitan Museum of Art mounted the *Memorial Exhibition of the Work of George Bellows*, and the year following the Albright-Knox Art Gallery presented a similar show in Buffalo, New York. Both exhibitions paid tribute to an artist whose work was "indigenously American," reminding spectators that Bellows never went abroad and was little influenced by European modernism. David W. Scott summarized: "He was so completely representative of the American spirit of his day—restless, vigorous, pragmatic, humorous, adventurous, healthy, assertive, inclined to bravura."

James Earle Fraser (1876-1953)

END OF THE TRAIL
James Earle Fraser
1918 (cast in 1968), 5/24
Cast from original plaster model by the Modern Art Foundary of Long Island under supervision of Syracuse University
bronze
34 x 30⅜ x 10 inches
signed on base proper right side
Museum purchase

Provenance
Kennedy Galleries, Inc., New York, New York
Publications
Diana W. Suarez, *Bluff and the Magic Mansion, A Children's Guide to the Hunter Museum of Art,* Chattanooga: Hunter Museum of Art, 1980.

At the outset it should be noted that the Hunter Museum's nearly three-foot-high bronze by James Earle Fraser, *End of the Trail,* is a posthumous casting authorized by Syracuse University in 1968, fifteen years after the artist's death. The university had acquired the contents of Fraser's studio in 1967, including the original plaster model of 1918, from which this casting was done as part of a limited edition of twenty-four. Fraser had made several plaster versions of the subject in different sizes that also have been used for casting multiples in bronze. A singular life-sized bronze was commissioned in 1929 for a park in Waupun, Wisconsin. However, the largest and most famous *End of the Trail,* a sixteen-foot tall (excluding spear) plaster work, never made it to bronze, though there was at one time a plan to do so. The outsized statue was created in 1915 for prominent display in the Court of Palms at the Pacific-Panama Exposition in San Francisco. Fraser's ultimate aim was to do a casting after the fair closed, and to place the more durable bronze on a promontory overlooking the ocean at Pacific Palisades, California—the ocean being literally the end, the farthest the disenfranchised Indian could migrate. Unfortunately, America's entry into World War I interrupted the project. The grand piece instead went to storage with other sculptural items from the exposition. Eventually it was sold for $400 and transported to a shelter at a park in Visalia, California. There it remained until the mid-1960s, when it was purchased by the National Cowboy Hall of Fame and Western Heritage Center in Oklahoma City, where it is now on permanent exhibit.

By the early years of the twentieth century, "the Indian was no longer the feared heathen savage but the heroic, ill-fated warrior of the plains," writes sculpture historian Wayne Craven. "Belatedly the white man began to sympathize with the Indian's plight and romanticizing him as America's 'noble savage'." *End of the Trail* epitomizes these rather guilt-generated sensibilities, but Fraser's expression was borne as well of direct encounters with Indians on the frontier. Ten years of his childhood, from ages four to fourteen, he lived in the Dakota Territory. His father, a civil engineer and builder for the Chicago, Milwaukee, and St. Paul Railroad, worked with crews extending the train lines westward into the Sioux prairielands. Traveling the range, the family lived out of a boxcar the first six months. They settled finally into a rustic house on a ranch near the town of Mitchell. Young Fraser regularly saw the stoic Indians at close range. Later he was profoundly troubled, as he explained to J. Walker McSpadden in 1924:

> I was oppressed with sadness, the tragedy of it all. The Sioux around us had ceased to go upon the warpath, and were being pushed farther and farther back. They were not permitted to go off their own reservations, even to hunt; and remember, their fathers and their fathers' fathers had hunted all over those broad plains, and considered them their own. Occasionally they would break loose and chase some small game across somebody's homestead, and then what a furor there was! The Indians were loose again! They would be herded back into their corrals like so much cattle, and really treated very little better . . . And how proud those redmen were, despite the indignities they suffered.

Fraser was doubtless also inspired to Western-theme subjects by the numerous sculptures of cowboys and Indians he had seen in 1893 at the Chicago World Columbian Exposition. And a still more specific influence for *End of the Trail* was probably a moving passage written in 1890 by Marion Manville Pope:

> The trail is lost, the path is hid and winds that blow from out the ages sweep me on to that chill borderland when Time's spent sands engulf lost peoples and lost trails.

Indeed, as the horse's tail and mane ripple in the direction being traveled, one senses the wind slowly pushing the lone brave, in Fraser's mind, to the end of the continent. The slumped-over rider (for whose likeness Seneca chief John Big Tree posed), head feathers falling forward, the drooping angle of the spear, the downcast animal with closed eyes and unsteady footing—all tell of the subject's exhaustion and utter helplessness. Yet in engendering sentiment, the artist converts defeat and humiliation into a study of long-suffering virtue. The depiction conveys what Adeline Adams in 1923 called "moral earnestness," one of the chief characteristics of the Beaux-Arts classical style that dominated American sculpture in the late-nineteenth and early-twentieth centuries.

Fraser was born in Winona, Minnesota, in 1876. After those childhood years in what is today South Dakota, he attended secondary schools in Minneapolis. At age eighteen he enrolled at the School of the Art Institute of Chicago, where he became a studio assistant to sculptor Richard W. Bock. In 1898 he went to Paris and attended successively the École des Beaux-Arts, Académie Julian, and Académie Colorossi. On the merits of his student work, prominent American sculptor Augustus Saint-Gaudens invited him to join as assistant in the former's Paris studio from 1898 to 1900 and New Hampshire studio from 1900 to 1902. Fraser then established his own studio in New York City, after which he was never wanting for work. Martin H. Bush affirms: ". . . he may well have received more commissions to create monumental public sculpture than any artist of his time." Among his most famous pieces are four busts of Theodore Roosevelt; the earliest, from 1906, is now in the Senate corridor of the Capitol in Washington. Fraser is also highly regarded as a designer of coins and commemorative medals. Assuredly the most famous is the "buffalo" or "Indian head" nickel, minted in 1913. In terms of indigenous subject, it is widely recognized as the first distinctively American coin. At the end of World War I, he designed the Victory Medal, awarded by the United States government to nearly five million armed service personnel as well as non-military participants in the war effort. Numismatics aside, however, *End of the Trail* remained Fraser's most notable achievement. When he died in 1953, the *New York Times* obituary judged it the best-known sculptural image in America.

Malvina Hoffman (1887-1966)

FIDELIA LAMSON HOFFMAN
Malvina Hoffman
1918
marble
16½ x 9½ x 7¾ inches
Gift of Mrs. Arthur Hays
Sulzberger

Provenance

Malvina Hoffman Properties (Estate of the artist)
FAR Gallery, New York, New York

Exhibitions

Malvina Hoffman, FAR Gallery, New York, NY, April 22-May 24, 1980.

Publications

Malvina Hoffman, exhibition catalogue, New York: FAR Gallery, 1980, no. 34.

Malvina Hoffman was born into a culturally prominent family in 1887. Her father, an accomplished musician and a piano soloist with the New York Philharmonic Orchestra, encouraged his family to develop a keen interest in the arts. As a girl, Hoffman early exhibited a talent for drawing and painting, and when she was only fourteen years old she enrolled at the Women's School of Applied Design. In her teens she also attended the Art Students League and the Vetlin School, where she studied painting with John White Alexander and sculpture with Herbert Adams and George Gray Barnard.

While visiting in the Manhattan home of a long-time family friend, Mrs. John Simpson, in 1909, Hoffman saw a collection of pieces by the great French sculptor Auguste Rodin, who was then still actively working. Deeply moved by Rodin's strong, emotionally expressive style, she resolved soon thereafter to travel to Paris, meet the master, and apprentice in his studio if he would accept her. The meeting took place a few months later. Rodin was favorably impressed with examples of her work (and perhaps also with her fluency in the French language and remarkable knowledge of its literature and poetry), and he invited her to remain as a student and assistant. For a year she applied herself to the strenuous regimen and high standard that Rodin demanded of his pupils. She developed technical facility and an increased proficiency in correct anatomical rendering. Moreover, as Janis Connor, curator of the Malvina Hoffman Estate, has written: "From Rodin, Hoffman acquired a sense of spirit, a somewhat romantic concept about the process of modeling a face or figure and infusing it with dramatic power."

For the most part Hoffman did not succumb to the often-typical disciple's emulation of a compelling teacher's style. A few of her works, however, do reflect Rodin's influence, the most notable of which probably is the 1918 marble portrait bust of *Fidelia Lamson Hoffman*, the artist's mother. The head and hands appear to emerge from the rough uncut portion of the stone, and the piece compares to such similarly conceived Rodin marbles as *Thought* (1886-89) and *Madame Rodin* (1898). All three works manifest a pensive quality, as though the subjects are caught in reverie. And all three visually impart the idea of formation out of formlessness, of bringing forth vital substance out of a void. There is the further subjective implication of order prevailing against obscurity or reason against confusion.

Chiefly through contacts first made in France, Hoffman knew the friendship of numerous artists, performers, and intellectuals, including Anna Pavlova, Vaslav Nijinsky, and Ignace Paderewski. She did portrait sculptures of each of these, which are among her finest work. But she is probably best known for an extensive commission she was granted in 1930 by Chicago's Field Museum of Natural History. Over a period of five years (which included an around-the-world tour to study various native peoples and their environments) she modeled more than one hundred works, full figures and heads, to represent the earth's racial and ethnic types. The project can still be viewed at the museum's Hall of Man, but it seems more an ambitious exercise in anthropological documentation than creative art. Nonetheless, it was an extraordinary venture, and it greatly advanced her reputation.

Hoffman was the author of two autobiographies and a textbook on sculpture techniques. She held memberships in the National Academy of Design, National Sculpture Society, and American Institute of Arts and Letters, from each of which she at one time was awarded prizes. And she received five honorary degrees — Smith, Mt. Holyoke, and Bates colleges, University of Rochester, and Northwestern University. She died in New York City in 1966.

Harriet Whitney Frishmuth (1880-1980)

Though she produced commemorative, portrait, and monumental pieces, sculptor Harriet Whitney Frishmuth (who, by the way, detested the word "sculptress") is probably best known for exuberant, lithe, usually nude female figures whose vigorous movement, one feels, is suspended but an instant. Stylistically, her mature work indicates an important transition between the Beaux-Arts classicism that had dominated American sculpture from the end of the Civil War well into the twentieth century (seen in the work of Augustus Saint-Gaudens, Daniel Chester French, J.Q.A. Ward, and Frederick MacMonnies, among the better known) and what Joshua C. Taylor calls the "design conscious," streamlining mode of the 1920s, '30s, and '40s (represented by such significant sculptors as Paul Manship, Elie Nadelman, Gaston Lachaise, and Hugo Robus). It was a transition from heroic realism to a linear and smooth-flowing manner that, while still representational, ventured onto the creative provisos of early twentieth-century modernism—much as progressive painters already had been doing for a decade.

Change in style was accompanied by a shift in basic purpose: from monumental public statuary that embodied lofty virtue, noble idealization, and "moral earnestness"— to borrow critic Adeline Adams' term from 1923—to a more personal, decorative art that stimulates both eye and imagination. Noting that the newer-style sculpture seemed better suited to private residences and grounds, Daniel Robbins categorized the work "garden ornaments." Indeed, Frishmuth's *Crest of the Wave,* a bronze from 1926, is aptly fitted for such an installation. Narrow conduits emerge from the mouths of the several fish at the foot of the piece to propel gentle streams of real water in the originally intended fountain operation.

Crest of the Wave, obviously, is not a literal depiction of swelling sea water. The dancing nude figure atop scant wavelets is rather a personification of the vital force and seeming individuality of the surge. She is a latter-day nymph, descended from the sprightly maidens of Greek and Roman mythology who were believed to inhabit and to animate various forces of nature. In grounding such themes in the symbolisms of antiquity, Frishmuth and many other American artists of the nineteenth and early-twentieth centuries also devised a legitimate and respectable way to portray the nude in a society that predominantly saw the unclothed human body as shameful or lewd. Taylor explains

CREST OF THE WAVE
Harriet Whitney Frishmuth
1926
bronze
66 x 16 x 15 inches
signed on back of base
Gift of Mr. and Mrs. Cartter
Lupton

Provenance

Mr. and Mrs. Cartter Lupton, Chattanooga,
Tennessee.

how nudity "posed a problem for Americans since there was still a certain amount of resistance to nakedness at home (it was associated with the immoral French.) The solution was allegory, which everyone could recognize as not dealing with the real world. So painters and sculptors alike created a whole population of nude or scantily clad virtues and personifications."

Frishmuth's model for *Crest of the Wave* and, by her own estimate, "ninety percent of the decorative figures I have made" was a French dancer named Desha, who was performing in New York City at the time. Desha had been posing regularly for the artist since 1916. Eventually she married and returned to France. As late as 1970, she was still teaching dance in Paris. In addition to her slender and supple physique, she brought strength, stamina, and concentration to modeling. "She could take exactly the same pose from one day to another with no variation" Frishmuth recounted, "especially valuable to me in creating dancing figures."

Frishmuth was born in Philadelphia in 1880. She attended private schools there, as well as in Paris and Dresden. In 1900 she studied briefly under Auguste Rodin and, also in Paris, with Henri-Desire Gauquier and Jean-Antoine Injalbert. She went on to work two years as an assistant for Cuno von Euchritz in Berlin. On returning to the United States she enrolled at the Art Students League, where her sculpture instructors were Hermon A. MacNeil and Gutzon Borglum. After a year at the League, she established a studio in New York City. In 1929 she was elected to full membership in the National Academy of Design. Following World War II she moved to Southbury, Connecticut, where in 1953 she sustained an arm injury that forced her retirement from active work. She was ninety-nine when she died in a nursing home at nearby Waterbury on New Year's Day 1980.

Frank Weston Benson (1862-1951)

Frank Weston Benson was born in Salem, Massachusetts, in 1862. When he was nineteen he enrolled at the Boston Museum School where he studied mainly with Otto Grundmann, an artist trained in the Dutch tradition who taught by the tedious though necessarily disciplined practice of drawing from plaster casts. That same year, 1881, Edmund C. Tarbell also entered the School. The two artists formed a personal and professional friendship that endured their entire lives (Tarbell died in 1938). Both left for Paris in 1883 to attend the Académie Julian, where again instruction was typically in the dry, academic manner of their teachers: Gustave Boulanger, Jules Lefebvre, and William Dannat. Both artists came to admire the work of the impressionists. Both returned to the United States in 1886. And three years later both were teaching at their alma mater, the Museum School. Tarbell in fact was named head of the painting department upon the unexpected death of Grundmann in 1890.

Tarbell was a compelling personality and persuasive teacher. His painterly yet subdued Boston School manner affected students and colleagues alike, to the extent that many, including Benson, were popularly called "Tarbellites." Benson began moving away from Tarbell's influence about 1912, following what must at the time have seemed an unfortunate circumstance, but in the long run proved advantageous for his individual development. Over an administrative dispute with the trustees of the Museum School, Tarbell and Benson resigned. From that point each went his own creative direction. Benson seriously took up etching, a medium in which he was largely self-taught. His wildlife-subject prints grew tremendously popular and as a result became a major part of his production after 1915. His painting of what might be designated the post-Tarbellite period changed as well, showing a brighter palette and an easier, even more fluid brushwork than before. The Hunter's *Lilies and Laurel in a Blue Vase* (color plate 19) from 1929 is an excellent example of this later progress.

Notably, Benson was one of The Ten American Painters (more familiarly known simply as The Ten), the association that in 1898 withdrew from the Society of American Artists in order to exhibit together their works in the impressionist style, and that continued to show annually at the Durand-Ruel Gallery through 1906, and at the Montross Gallery until 1917. Benson was elected an associate of the National Academy of Design in 1903 and elevated to full membership in 1905. He was a founding member of the Guild of Boston Artists in 1914 and served as the group's president in 1915-16. In his long career he won thirty significant awards or medals. The last surviving member of The Ten, when he died in 1951 he was widely recognized and respected.

(color plate 19)

LILIES AND LAUREL IN A BLUE VASE

Frank Weston Benson

1929

oil on canvas

30 x 25 inches

signed and dated lower left

Gift of Mr. and Mrs. John T. Lupton

Provenance

Collection of the artist
Jacob J. Bogart, New York, New York
Joel Bogart, New York, New York.

Robert Henri (1865-1929)

In the early twentieth century, five determined young painters "bunched together like the fingers and thumb of a fist," to relate Alexander Eliot's graphic analogy, and "struck a mighty blow for artistic freedom of worship, and pushed American art into the quickened tempo of the modern age." The group was called variously the "New York Realists," the "Black Gang" (because of the considerable use of that color in their paintings), and the "Ash Can School." Stylistically their work had much in common with the earnest human dramas of such earlier European masters as Rembrandt, Frans Hals, Diego Velásquez, and Francisco Goya. Their subject matter, on the other hand, was contemporary, even controversially so. Earthy views of urban America — of the poor, the have-nots, the immigrants, the low-life — shocked the genteel estheticism that had dominated late nineteenth-century American taste in the visual arts. The eldest and acknowledged leader of the "Gang" was the articulate and philosophical Robert Henri. (The other four were George Luks, William Glackens, Everett Shinn, and John Sloan, each of whose work is discussed elsewhere in this catalogue.)

Henri is recognized as much perhaps for his effective teaching and bold advocacy as for his painting. His widely read book, *The Art Spirit* (which is actually a collection of lectures and criticisms taken down and edited by student Margery Ryerson, published in 1923), reveals the fundamental thrust of his persuasive instruction, the following excerpts to wit:

WOMAN IN PINK ON BEACH
Robert Henri
1893
oil on canvas
18 x 24 inches
signed and dated lower left
Gift of the Benwood
Foundation

Provenance

Frank Reed Whiteside
David David, Inc., Philadelphia, Pennsylvania
Hirschl & Adler Galleries, Inc., New York, New
York
Mr. and Mrs. Louis D. Cohen, New York, New
York

Exhibitions

American Paintings for Public and Private Collectors, Hirschl & Adler Galleries, Inc., New York,
NY, Dec. 26, 1967-Jan. 13, 1968.

Frances and L. D. Cohen Collection, Norton
Gallery and School of Art, West Palm Beach, FL,
Feb. 23-March 17, 1968.

American Bank and Trust Company, New York,
NY, Nov. 19-Dec. 19, 1969.

Robert Henri, Painter, Delaware Art Museum,
circulating exhibit: Delaware Art Museum,
Wilmington, DE; Pennsylvania State University
Museum of Art, University Park, PA; Cincinnati
Art Museum, Cincinnati, OH; Phoenix Art
Museum, Phoenix, AZ; and the Corcoran Gallery of Art, Washington, D.C.; May 4, 1984-June
9, 1985.

Publications

Frances and L. D. Cohen Collection, exhibition
catalogue, West Palm Beach, FL: Norton Gallery and School of Art, 1968, no. 13.

Bernard B. Perlman, *Robert Henri, Painter,*
Wilmington, DE: Delaware Art Museum, 1984,
p. 25, no. 3.

*All art that is worthwhile is a record of intense life, and each individual artist's work
is a record of his special effort, search and findings.*

*The first prerequisite of the artist is that he . . . have guts— without the attributes
of the fighter, he can expect little or no success with an uninterested public.*

*Work quickly . . . Don't stop for anything but the essential . . . Keep the flow
going . . . it's the spirit of the thing that counts.*

That spirit, that sense of immediacy and vitality, is seen in Henri's mature style after
about 1895, and is particularly evident in his portraits of children, a favorite topic. "If one has
a love of children as human beings and realizes the greatness that is in them," Henri wrote,
"no better subjects for painting can be found." And again: "In the faces of children I have
seen a look of wisdom and of kindness expressed with such ease and such certainty that I
know it was the expression of the whole race." "Feel the dignity of a child," Henri
admonished. "Do not feel superior to him, for you are not."

The Hunter Museum's *Pet* (color plate 20), an excellent example of Henri's smaller
child-portrait work, was painted in July 1927, according to the artist's personal records, and
was probably completed in one or two sittings. It was originally titled after the subject's
identity, *Wee Annie Lavelle,* but the nickname "pet" was entered above the title in the artist's
record book by Henri's sister-in-law sometime after his death. The blond, blue-eyed,
rosy-cheeked Annie was one of Henri's many child friends who lived near the house in
County Mayo, Ireland, where he summered in his later years.

The artist was born Robert Henry Cozad at Cincinnati, Ohio, in 1865. In 1873 his father, a
professional gambler, moved the family to the frontier of western Nebraska, and there
founded the town of Cozad. Young Robert lived in the new community until 1882, when his
father, in self-defense, shot a man to death in a gambling argument. Though exonerated by
law enforcement officials, the father and family, fearing reprisals from the deceased's
relatives, fled. They went first to Denver, then, sometime the following year, to Atlantic City.
With the move east, the several family members, still fearing for their safety, adopted new
names. Eighteen-year old Robert, by then realizing he wanted to pursue art as a career,
elected to affect a French mode. He dropped the last name altogether, and converted the
"y" in his middle name to "i" (though he always pronounced it as the Americanized
Hen-rye).

(color plate 20)
PET
(Also known as *Wee Annie
Lavelle*)
Robert Henri
1927
oil on canvas
24 x 20 inches
signed lower right
inscribed lower right:
"M. H."
Gift of the Benwood
Foundation

(Continued on page 127)

126

In 1886 Henri enrolled at the Pennsylvania Academy of the Fine Arts, where he studied mainly with Thomas Anshutz. Two years later he went to Paris to attend the Académie Julian, and in 1891 he was admitted to the more competitive École des Beaux Arts. He returned to the United States later in '91, and re-enrolled at the Pennsylvania Academy to study with American impressionist Robert Vonnoh. Henri's painting of the early to mid-1890s demonstrates his impressionist phase. *Woman in Pink on Beach*, an apt example from 1893, shows the characteristic impressionist preoccupation with the bright, airy out-of-doors, casually disposed subject, fleeting notion of time, and small-stroke, patchy brushwork and flecks of pigment. As the woman holds the brim of her hat against a seemingly brisk coastal breeze, the viewer senses the restless atmosphere and the transitory moment. The scene was posed near Avalon, New Jersey, where the artist sketched and painted for about a month.

Henri had begun his professional teaching in 1892 at the Philadelphia School of Design for Women, but in '95 he returned to Europe. Gradually he embraced the darker-tonal, broadly brushed style for which he would become known. After visiting Spain in 1900, he settled in New York City, and soon was teaching at William Merritt Chase's New York School of Art. In 1906 he was elected to full membership in the National Academy of Design. Despite subsequent disagreements with the Academy over exhibition policies that he strongly believed were inadequate, he never completely forsook that venerable association. The most celebrated dispute resulted in his bolting to display his work as one of The Eight at Macbeth Gallery in 1908. And though he was not one of the more avant-garde element, Henri participated in the Armory Show of 1913.

From 1915 to 1928, nearly the end of his life, Henri taught at the Art Students League. He also operated his own Henri School of Art concurrently between 1909 and 1912. The 1917 edition of *Who's Who in American Art* listed more than one hundred figures who had studied under Henri, chief among which included George Bellows, Leon Kroll, Eugene Speicher, Rockwell Kent, and Edward Hopper.

Henri succumbed to cancer in July 1929. The *Index of Twentieth Century Artists*, compiled by the College Art Association of America, lists Henri's work as having been shown in 365 major exhibitions between 1892 and his death — an average of nearly ten per year. As Rowland Elzia has noted: "These figures bear witness not only to Henri's industry and organization, but also to his immense popularity as an artist." In 1931, less than two years after his passing, the Metropolitan Museum of Art presented the significant retrospective: *Robert Henri Memorial Exhibition*.

(Continued from page 126)

Provenance

Estate of Robert Henri
Organ collection, New York, New York
Hirschl & Adler Galleries, Inc., New York, New York
Frank and Flora Winton, Birmingham, Michigan
Mr. and Mrs. Louis D. Cohen, New York, New York

Exhibitions

American Paintings and Drawings from Michigan Collections, The Detroit Institute of Arts, Detroit, MI, April 10-May 6, 1962.

Frances and L. D. Cohen Collection, Norton Gallery and School of Art, West Palm Beach, FL, Feb. 23-March 17, 1968.

ACA Galleries, New York, New York, Nov.-Dec. 1977.

Publications

American Paintings and Drawings from Michigan Collections, exhibition catalogue, Detroit: The Detroit Institute of Arts, 1962, p. 9, no. 115.

Frances and L. D. Cohen Collection, exhibition catalogue, West Palm Beach, FL: Norton Gallery and School of Art, 1968, no. 12.

George Benjamin Luks (1867-1933)

"Technique did you say! Say listen you — it's in you or it isn't. Who taught Shakespeare technique? or Rembrandt? Guts! Guts! Life! Life! That's my technique." George Luks' emphatic if not blustery response to a question of his painting method also gives an indication of the artist's effusive but often contentious personal nature. Gregarious, cocky, outrageously funny — or just plain outrageous — the salty Luks was, as friend and fellow painter Everitt Shinn remarked, "a great talker and a fascinating liar." He enjoyed diverting a willing audience with stories of his younger days as a prize fighter, competing under alias "Chicago Whitey — Terror of the Windy City." Yet, no evidence exists that he ever boxed or, for that matter, had ever been to Chicago. His listeners doubtless knew it, but delighted in his stories just the same. Luks was a heavy drinker, and when drunk his conviviality gave way to meanness. He frequently became belligerent and unruly, and was given to brawling. When he was found dead below the tracks of an elevated railway the morning after a barroom row, his friends concluded that he had finally picked one fight too many.

Still, in outlook and temperament, Luks was aptly fitted for his role as a member of the Ash Can group. Like Robert Henri, to whose circle he was first attracted in Philadelphia in 1894, Luks was interested not in recording precise detail, surface corporeality, or aesthetic niceties, but rather in the *personalities* of his subjects and the *feel* of their life-circumstance. Subjects and situations in turn were the more intriguing and picturesque if they represented the urban poor, working classes, immigrants, and ethnic groups (in many cases, of course, all one and the same). Again, like Henri, Luks rendered quickly, summarily, in a painterly mode — adapting also his earlier skills as a news illustrator — to capture the vitality and immediacy of the scene.

Allen Street (color plate 21) was precisely the type of city neighborhood Luks and his fellow Ash Can School colleagues found appealing. A place on Manhattan's Lower East Side, it bustled with the commotion of vendors selling food, utensils, furniture, rugs, yard goods, and second-hand wares — from carts, open-air stalls, store-fronts, and second-story walk-up shops. (Similar districts can still be seen in some parts of New York City.) Characteristically, Luks subordinated color in favor of what he felt was a more dramatic result through light and dark contrast. His brushwork was in broad, relatively flat strokes, developing simple planes, and only slight modeling. The effect is reminiscent of the painting of Franz Hals, which he greatly admired; of Edouard Manet, whose recognition and influence at the time, on both sides of the Atlantic, was considerable; and, once more, of Robert Henri, whose bearing upon Luks' development, both thematically and stylistically, is evident — though Luks would not likely have admitted it. He openly disliked being in Henri's shadow. *Allen Street*, while undated, was probably painted about 1905, or at about the same time he completed other important street views, the similar *Hester Street* (1905, Brooklyn Museum) and *Cochetti's Fish Market* (1903, private collection).

Luks was born in 1867 at Williamsport, Pennsylvania, and he grew up in that coal mining territory. His father, a physician, and his mother were both amateur painters. When he was sixteen, he performed briefly with a vaudeville company in Philadelphia. The following year, 1864, he attended the Pennsylvania Academy of the Fine Arts, studying mainly with Thomas Anshutz, whom he would later say was the best teacher he ever had. Luks' activity between 1884 and '94 is uncertain, made additionally unclear by his penchant for exaggeration and concoction. He was in Europe most of the decade, but no evidence substantiates his claim that he had attended art schools in Düsseldorf, Munich, Paris, and London.

In 1894, the same year he met Henri, Luks joined the art staff of the *Philadelphia Press*. The rival *Evening Bulletin* sent him the following year to cover the Spanish-American War, though he never actually observed any action. His illustrations were done at a favorite bar after hearing soldiers' stories and other new accounts from the front. Upon his return to the United States in 1896 he joined the *New York World*. William Glackens and Everitt Shinn, former Philadelphia friends and future Ash Can cohorts, also joined the *World* in 1897. It was Glackens who most encouraged Luks to resume painting, and Luks at one time roomed with Shinn. Luks was one of the participating artists in the exhibition of The Eight at Macbeth Gallery in 1908, and his work was included in the Armory Show of 1913. He taught at the Art Students League and intermittently conducted private classes. Though his drinking was frequently a problem, he was a good teacher, as devoted students would attest. Probably his best known students were Philip Evergood and Reginald Marsh.

The often acerbic Guy Pene du Bois, writing in *Artists Say the Silliest Things*, published in 1940 (seven years after Luks' death), describes Luks as brilliant, but also as a windbag and a fool. For Luks' art, du Bois had high regard: "When he painted a great picture, and they are surprisingly many in view of his hit or miss way of work, it held the richness and dignity and strength of a full-blooded man, an intimate and real achievement."

(color plate 21)
ALLEN STREET
George Benjamin Luks
c. 1905
oil on canvas
32 x 45 inches
signed lower right
Gift of Miss Inez Hyder

Provenance
Collection of the artist
George B. Luks Estate
The Milch Galleries, New York, New York

Exhibitions
Fall Fiesta Benefit, Montgomery Museum of Fine Arts, Montgomery, AL, Oct. 28-Nov. 5, 1961.

American Traditionalists of the Twentieth Century, Columbus Museum of Arts and Crafts, Columbus, GA, Feb. 15-March 17, 1963.

Museum Masterpieces, Mobile Art Gallery, Mobile, AL, Oct. 30-Dec. 12, 1964.

George Luks, Paintings and Drawings, 1889-1931, Munson-Williams-Proctor Institute, Utica, NY, April 1-May 20, 1973.

Publications
Joseph S. Trovato, *George Luks, Paintings and Drawings, 1889-1931*, exhibition catalogue, Utica, NY: Munson-Williams-Proctor Institute, 1973, p. 22, no. 16.

Irwin Unger, *American History*, Grade 11, Vol. 2, Lexington: Ginn and Company, 1974.

Everett Shinn *(1876-1953)*

Everett Shinn was part of the circle of resurgent realists led by Robert Henri. He was in fact the youngest of The Eight who exhibited at Macbeth Gallery in 1908, and he is generally regarded a key member of the Ash Can School. Yet of the coterie, he was the least "Ash Can" in creative spirit and topic interest. True, he produced the obligatory street scenes, river and bridge views, and glimpses of urban low life — but his real element was among the well-to-do, the cultivated elite, the smart set. Mahonri Sharp Young writes: "He was the only one of the group who felt the attraction of pretty actresses, great ladies, and rich men. He was dazzled by the rich just as he was dazzled by women and the theater." Shinn himself stated, somewhat defensively: "I was often accused of being a snob. Not at all. It's just the uptown life with all its glitter was more good looking; the people made pictures. And the clothes then — the movement, the satins, women's skirts and men's coats, and the sweep of furs and swish of wild boas, oh Lord!" As Young additionally points out, Shinn "was the only one of The Eight who *did* glamorize" the people and places recorded in his work.

Shinn's infatuation with the theatre went beyond his attending performances or using stage sets and theatre people as subjects for drawing and painting. In his studio at 112 Waverly Street, New York, he built a small stage, complete with proscenium and crimson curtains, with seating for an audience of fifty-five. There, between 1900 and 1912, he regularly acted in original shows with a company of friends he called the Waverly Street Players. Biographer Edith Shazo notes: "Shinn did everything: he was the playwright, director, and producer. He made the scenery, did the casting." Shinn actually wrote thirty-five plays, melodramas, and movie scenarios. While most are trite and long forgotten, his best-known vehicle, *Hazel Weston, or, More Sinned Against Than Usual*, played in seven languages for a quarter of a century. But what is probably his most memorable character line comes from the less successful *Lucy Moore, The Prune-Hater's Daughter*, wherein the crestfallen heroine cries at the dastardly adversary: "Oh, you prune, you've been my ruin!"

As further indication of Shinn's close involvement with the performing arts, in 1907 he employed a rococo-revival style to decorate the interior of his friend David Belasco's Stuyvesant Theatre in New York. Between 1917 and 1923 he also worked successively as art director for three movie companies: Samuel Goldwyn's first Goldwyn Pictures, Inspiration Pictures, and William Randolph Hearst's Cosmopolitan Pictures. Best remembered films for which Shinn designed sets and properties include: *Polly of the Circus* (for Goldwyn), *The Bright Shawl* (Inspiration), and *Jamie Meredith* (Cosmopolitan).

Unfortunately, as a serious fine artist, Shinn was inconsistent. He produced much mediocre work, a consequence, some critics feel, of overly diverse interests. Milton W. Brown, for one, finds: "Shinn was a man of many talents, and it was perhaps just this virtuosity which was his artistic undoing." Despite a small number of adept canvases, Shinn was the weakest of the Ash Can painters. Observing a characteristic Shinn mannerism, Barbara Rose states bluntly: "He uses a gay sprinkling of highlights to disguise what is essentially superficial technique." It would be kinder to say a rapid or sketchy or notational technique, and in that respect it was better suited to pastel, the medium by which he achieved his most competent and effective result. He was particularly fond of Edgar Degas' pastel work, both for rendering skill and for certain pieces that depict theatre or dance activity. Brown, fittingly, though with probable disparaging intent, calls Shinn "a minor echo of Degas."

The Hunter Museum's pastel, *Actress in Red Before Mirror*, from c. 1910, (color plate 22) is Shinn at his best technique and favorite subject type. The attractive female performer is primping, one senses, shortly before the call to go on stage. Her figure is reflected in the full-length mirror, as is the curious, less distinct image of another woman a short distance away. As reflected, the second woman would have to be standing perpendicularly outside the picture space, to the viewer's right. The dark-garbed woman thus is the spectator's friend or consort, and it is partly because of her presence that the viewer is drawn psychically into the scene as a companion visitor to the dressing room. Interestingly, Degas was one of several French artists, including also Edouard Manet and Berthe Morisot, who had earlier found mirror reflection a novel and technically challenging visual effect, featuring it in a number of their impressionist works. Assuredly, Shinn was prompted to the motif by such examples.

Shinn was born to a Quaker family in the small southern New Jersey community of Woodstown; he was the youngest of eight children. As a boy he showed precocious ability both in art and in mechanics. At age fifteen he designed and built a working steam engine. Later the same year, 1891, he went to Philadelphia, where he enrolled in mechanical drawing classes and shop training at Spring Garden Institute. Just two years later, the seventeen-year-old took a position as illustrator with the *Philadelphia Press*, where he first met George Luks, William Glackens, John Sloan, and through that association, Robert Henri. Shinn also began classes in 1893 with Thomas Anshutz at the Pennsylvania Academy of the Fine Arts. In 1897 he moved to New York (the first of the Henri circle so to transfer) to work for the *World* and the *Herald*. He turned to magazine illustration in 1899, and eventually did commissions for the widely circulated *Harper's Weekly*.

(color plate 22)

ACTRESS IN RED BEFORE MIRROR

Everett Shinn

c. 1910

pastel on paper

25½ x 14⅝ inches

Gift of the Benwood Foundation

Provenance

Estate of Everett Shinn
Graham Gallery, New York, New York
Mr. and Mrs. Louis D. Cohen, New York, New York

Exhibitions

American Bank & Trust Company, New York, NY, Nov. 19-Dec. 19, 1969, no. 17.

Graphics on Paper, 1900-1940, Huntsville Museum of Art, Huntsville, AL, Jan. 29-April 22, 1984.

Publications

Diana W. Suarez, *Bluff and the Magic Mansion, A Children's Guide to the Hunter Museum of Art*, Chattanooga: Hunter Museum of Art, 1980.

A 1901 trip to Paris brought him initial contact with the theatre and with impressionism. Upon his return he took the Waverly Street studio. During the 1906-07 school year, he taught at the Art Students League. Like all the other members of The Eight, Shinn was invited to submit pieces for the 1913 Armory Show. Perhaps not fully anticipating its significance, he declined. Author Theodore Dreiser modeled the bohemian artist-character Eugene Witla in the 1915 novel, *The Genius*, after Shinn, his real-life, gregarious and fun-loving friend. Shinn was elected to full membership in the National Academy of Design in 1943. Less successful in his personal life, he was married and divorced four times. The last surviving member of The Eight, he died in New York in 1953, at age seventy-six.

William S. Horton (1865-1936)

Though usually identified as an impressionist in art-historical and critical reviews, William S. Horton might more appropriately have been called a postimpressionist—if the term had been applied to American art as it was to certain European, mainly French production by such figures as Paul Cézanne, Vincent van Gogh, and Paul Gauguin. Perhaps because American impressionist painters worked well into the twentieth century—through and past the height of French impressionism; or because prominent independent realists—Thomas Eakins, Winslow Homer, John Singer Sargent, to name the better known—dominated American art at the end of the nineteenth century; or because the Ash Can School commanded the critics' attention in the early twentieth century: whatever the reason, postimpressionism never realized distinctive status in the United States. Surprisingly, the designation was first coined, not in France, but in England, when Roger Fry arranged an exhibition for winter 1910-11 that he titled *Manet and the Post Impressionists*.

On the face of it, the term means little but that the artists involved apparently moved on from impressionism to new ways of painting. Impressionism emphasized tone, atmospheric color, and the play or reflection of light from the surfaces of objects depicted; characteristically paint was applied in small dabs, so as to impart a shimmering, radiant effect. The postimpressionists found such results contrived and insubstantial; they opted for a return to form and volume, structured composition, more deliberate, though often expressive, brushwork, and a greater stress on the importance of subject—features evident in Horton's *Punch on the Beach at Broadstairs, England*, an oil from 1920 (color plate 23).

Broadstairs is a small resort town, especially popular with day-trippers and week-enders, on the Kent coast about seventy miles east of London. Charles Dickens described it as "one of the freest and freshest little places in the world." From a house on Harbour Street he wrote part of the novel *Barnaby Rudge*. Horton painted, albeit animatedly, tangible shapes in strong hues to record a festive outing. The figures in the crowd and the systematic repetition of same-color swatches lead the eye upward and inward, arriving at the image of the entertainer who has captured the people's attention, a clown with his puppet, Punch. (Punch, incidentally, a stock wise-cracking character, as in the *Punch and Judy* show, was originally introduced to England in the mid-seventeenth century by itinerant Italian puppeteers; the name was shortened from Punchinello.)

The pictorial arrangement is subtle and complex. A near-vertical axis is implied by the file of figures, beginning in the foreground with the girl in the dotted green outfit, ascending through other figures to the clown's conical hat. In turn, the tip of the hat breaks the horizon line, while the complementary-colored pinkish-orange clown's face intersects the blue-green shoreline. This rather precise convergence of horizontal and vertical also draws the viewer to a focal point. Then, too, by observing the backs of so many in the scene, the viewer may psychically project into the moment, becoming another member of the crowd. The artist personally enjoyed such gatherings, as the painting aptly demonstrates, and he painted numerous other pictures of group outdoor recreation. "His style, like his subject matter, conveys the vigor of human beings alive to their fingertips," writes Nicholas Fox Weber. "Strong staccato lines, bold compositions and explosive colors reflect the artist's sheer physical energy and appetite for vision. Horton balanced enthusiasm with discipline, considerable technical skill, and much visual imagination."

(color plate 23)

PUNCH ON THE BEACH AT BROADSTAIRS, ENGLAND (Also known as *The Beach at Broadstairs – Punch Amid The Trippers*, and *Broadstairs, England*)

William S. Horton

1920

oil on canvas

25⅜ x 30¾ inches

signed and dated lower left

Gift of M.R. Schweitzer in memory of Robert L. Maclellan (by exchange)

Provenance

W. Gray Horton (son of the artist)
Kennedy Galleries, Inc., New York, New York
Mr. and Mrs. Scott L. Probasco, Jr., Lookout Mountain, Tennessee
Douglas James & Co., Signal Mountain, Tennessee

Exhibitions

William S. Horton, American Impressionist, M. Knoedler & Co., New York, NY, May 3-June 9, 1974.

Publications

Nicholas Fox Weber and Deedee Wigmore, *William S. Horton, American Impressionist*, exhibition catalogue, New York: M. Knoedler & Co., Inc., 1974, no. 13.

Horton was born in Grand Rapids, Michigan, in 1865. When he was five, he moved with his family to Lisbon, North Dakota. Because he could draw well, at age fourteen he was conducting introductory art classes in his small home town. Horton's father thought art an unseemly occupation, and he tried to thwart his son's advancement. The predicament grew to an intolerable strain when the elder Horton destroyed the young artist's paintings and threw away his oils and brushes. Determined to study art, he left home at age seventeen, and was promptly disinherited. He went first to Chicago, where he attended the School of the Art Institute. When he was twenty, he went on to New York. There he took courses at the National Academy of Design and Art Students League, all along supporting himself by working part time as an illustrator. He married in 1892. The following year the couple made an extended tour to Europe. The artist returned with his wife to Europe in 1895, and began a two-year study with Benjamin Constant at the Académie Julian in Paris.

Horton remained in Paris the next thirty-five years (designation as a postimpressionist may not be so improbable after all), though he traveled regularly and widely about the continent. He exhibited in the Salon des Independents shows of 1901 and 1908, and Salon d'Automne shows of the same years. He became a personal friend of impressionist Claude Monet and fauve Andre Derain. Horton was back in the United States, living in New York from 1927 to 1932. Curiously, his paintings of the period, mostly Manhattan townscapes, are more impressionist in style. When his wife died in '32, Horton was disconsolate. Seeking to get over the loss, he made world trips in 1933, '34, and '35. He died in London in 1936. In 1939, the Galerie Charpentier in Paris presented a major retrospective of his work, including paintings, drawings, and pastels—450 items. Reviewing the show, Louis Vauxelles, one of the foremost French critics of the time, named Horton to a select group of artists he called "intrepid voyagers," an association that includes Gauguin and Matisse.

Edward Hopper (1882-1967)

Edward Hopper was not unfamiliar with the new currents in European and American art of the early twentieth century. From 1900 to 1906 he studied at the New York School of Art, chiefly with Robert Henri; he also exhibited his classroom work with other Henri students. And on three occasions between 1906 and 1910 he studied abroad, mainly in Paris, where he essayed the then-recent modes of European experimental painting. Though he was enthralled by impressionist light and intrigued by cubist composition, it is otherwise apparent that he little regarded the ascending styles of international modernism. Like other American artists such as Charles Sheeler, Ralston Crawford, Niles Spencer, and Guy Pene de Bois, Hopper felt the need to adapt the design merits of formal abstraction to the traditional American bent for no-nonsense factual reporting. An oft-quoted Hopper statement well summarizes his credo: "Instead of subjectivity, a new objectivity; instead of abstraction, a reaffirmation of representation and specific subject matter; instead of internationalism, an art based on the American scene."

This is not to say, however, that because Hopper painted "realistically" his work should be pigeonholed with that of his similarly "realistic" contemporaries—the social realists (like Reginald Marsh and Raphael Soyer) or the regionalists (Thomas Hart Benton, Grant Wood, and others), styles that are by comparison highly narrative and illustrational. Though based on familiar recognizable images, Hopper's paintings are introspective, quietly symbolic, laconic, psychologically penetrating, often spare in their pictorial components. Rather than the brashness and hyperactivity of American life, Hopper was interested in its other side: its banality, loneliness, detachment, and dull routine. In many of his best-known canvasses, *Hotel Room* (1931), *New York Movie* (1939) and *Nighthawks* (1942), for example, the one, one, two, or few people depicted are characteristically isolated, pensive, humorless.

(color plate 24)

HOUSE AND BOATS
(Also known as *Seaside House*)
Edward Hopper
c. 1923
watercolor on paper
13⅞ x 20 inches
signed lower right
Gift of the Benwood Foundation

Provenance

Estate of the artist
Josephine N. Hopper (the artist's wife), New York, New York
Whitney Museum of American Art, New York, New York
Mr. and Mrs. Louis D. Cohen, New York, New York

Exhibitions

Graphics on Paper, 1900-1940, Huntsville Museum of Art, Huntsville, AL, Jan. 29-April 22, 1984.

Architectural studies and unpeopled city views also constitute a large segment of Hopper's painting. The inherent structural geometry of buildings appealed to his sense of design order and dynamics. Typically his compositions are "built" on a sub-pattern of rectangles, strong horizontals, verticals, and diagonals, reinforced by a system of alternating tonal values — imparting a feeling of control and stability. Hopper's lighting, too, a distinctive feature of his work, tends to be pure and bold, sometimes analytic and severe. Smooth cast shadows are often an integral aspect of the design. While people may not appear in many of the architectural scenes, as with all his painting, the potential human drama is ever implied. In looking at such paintings as *Manhattan Bridge Loop* (1928), *House by the Railroad* (1928), and *Early Sunday Morning* (1932), one senses profound solitude and nostalgia. One wants to ask: "Why is the place deserted?" "Why are the windows shuttered or empty?" "Where have the people gone?" "Who were they?" "Why did they go?" "Will they return?" The Hunter Museum's *House and Boats* (color plate 24) fits well into this chapter of production. It is thought to have been painted at Gloucester, Massachusetts, about 1923, one of the periods when the artist was working extensively in watercolor. True to the conventional aquarelle technique, the painting is more loosely arranged and freely brushed than his oils. Still, it aptly demonstrates the essential ingredients of his architectural mode: strong geometry, bold lighting, starkness, clearly defined forms. And one does indeed wonder about the people who may inhabit this seaside dwelling. The nearby boats suggest they may be within. Are they perhaps reclusive? Confined?

Hopper was born in Nyack, New York, in 1882. After his study in New York and Europe, he achieved early success in being invited to exhibit at the Society of Independent Artists show in 1910 and at the Armory Show in 1913. It was also in 1913 that Hopper took a studio at 3 Washington Square North in New York City, a space he maintained until his death in 1967. The first twelve years he was there, however, to support himself he worked largely as a commercial illustrator. Though his art was regularly reproduced in *Sunday Magazine*, *Adventure*, and *Scribner's*, he disparaged the necessity to do commissioned work. Recalling his chagrin at having to solicit assignments from publishers, he commented years later: "Sometimes I'd walk around the block a couple of times before I'd go in, wanting the job for the money, and at the same time hoping to hell I wouldn't get the lousy thing."

After more than a decade's hiatus following the Armory Show achievement, Hopper's painting career began to prosper again in 1924, when the Rehn Gallery presented a showing of his watercolors. Every piece in the exhibit sold, including probably *House and Boats*. That same year he married Josephine "Jo" Verstille, a painter who had also studied with Henri. The Hoppers summered at South Truro, on Cape Cod, Massachusetts, in 1931 and '32. After a successful retrospective show at the Museum of Modern Art in 1933, he built a studio at South Truro, where he and Jo returned nearly every summer.

Never forgetting that earlier in his career the National Academy of Design had declined to show his work, he turned down membership in that organization when associate status was extended to him in 1932. On the other hand, there was a form of recognition he *did* relish: He was one of just four artists chosen to represent the United States in the internationally prestigious Venice Biennale exhibition of 1952.

Through his sixty years as an active painter, Hopper remained fundamentally true to his stated credo. His style changed only slightly and — doubtless to his ultimate benefit — he reacted little, if at all, to the various revolutionary "isms" that captivated American comtemporary art during his lifetime. Guy Pene du Bois, a close friend of the artist, fittingly assessed his accomplishment and significance:

> Hopper is an artist who will make many artists of the past or present seem trivial. He will make them seem too talkative or too wasteful. He will make many of the "great" moderns seem like funny little reciters of fairy tales. He will be shown in any comparison as a serious man, without patience for trivialities, capable of reaching majesty.

Harold Cash (1895-1977)

D'A-LAL
Harold Cash
1929
bronze
65 x 15 x 12½ inches
Museum purchase with funds supplied in part by the National Endowment for the Arts, a Federal agency

Provenance

From the collection of the artist

Exhibitions

Galerie de la Renaissance, Paris, France, Feb. 1-14, 1930.

Forty-six Artists Under Thirty-five from America and Europe, Museum of Modern Art, New York, NY, April, 1930.

Weyhe Gallery, New York, NY, 1931.

Richmond Academy of Arts, Richmond, VA, April 22-May 14, 1933.

Rockefeller Center, New York, NY, Feb.-March, 1937.

Sculpture Show, Philadelphia Museum, Fairmont Park, Philadelphia, PA, Aug.-Oct. 1940.

Publications

"Young Painters and Sculptors at Modern Museum." *The Art News*, April 19, 1930, pp. 3-6.

"Nudes & Lovers Brim Philadelphia Museum in Biggest Sculpture Show." *Life*, Aug. 12, 1940, pp. 54-55, illus. p. 54.

Holger Cahill and Alfred H. Barr, Jr., *Art in America in Modern Times*, New York: Reynal and Hitchcock, 1934, p. 62.

As of this writing, the Hunter Museum has few pieces of sculpture from the first third of the twentieth century. Those several items, however, demonstrate remarkably well the gradual progress of American sculptors toward modernism: the Rodin-esque romanticism of Malvina Hoffman (see p. 122), to the Beaux-Art classicism of James Earle Fraser (p. 120), on to Harriett Whitney Frishmuth's "design-conscious" garden ornaments (p. 123), proceeding to Chattanooga native Harold Cash's reserved, unglamorized, compendious portrait busts or studies of the human figure. None of these artists would have been thought avant-garde by European standards, where cubism, futurism, constructivism, and free-form abstraction had noteworthy sculptural proponents (Pablo Picasso, Henri Matisse, Jacob Epstein, Umberto Boccioni, Constantin Brancusi, Ossip Zadkine, to name a few). Nor did American sculptors keep pace with such modern American painter-contemporaries as Arthur Dove, Marsden Hartley, John Marin, and Georgia O'Keeffe.

Until the early 1940s, public taste and patronage in America dictated a course for sculpture still tied mainly to the commemorative heroics or lofty moralizations of nineteenth-century academicism. The most experimental American sculptors of the time were either immigrants from Europe who brought the latest modern trends with them (for example, Elie Nadelman from Poland, Gaston Lachaise from France, William Zorach from Lithuania) or natives who had studied abroad (Jo Davidson, John Storrs, Paul Manship, Hugo Robus). Even these, upon their arrival or return to the United States, tempered their invention to accommodate the prevailing American preference for true-to-life images. Wayne Craven puts the situation in perspective: "The key to the new sculpture in America, therefore, is the theory of simplification and abstraction of natural form, which represents a far more moderate approach than that taken by European art during the period."

By American norms, then, Harold Cash was progressive. Though his mature work is highly representational, it also manifests the artist's editing eye. Subjects are stylized, detail reduced. He was attentive to the balance of masses, the play of reflected light over surfaces, and the nicety of shapes in the "negative" areas that surround or are enclosed by solid form. Cash shared with other progressive sculptors a new-found regard for the essential working characteristics of materials—to the extent that it became an operative aesthetic. His work visually intimates the process of fabrication, the subtle trace of carving or modeling. Even cast pieces, as an unidentified New York critic observed, show "almost a vermicular patterning that imparts vigor and vivacity to the bronze, and eliminates the overfinished quality that polished metal often displays."

The Hunter's standing female nude, *D'A-lal,* aptly demonstrates the tactile bronze surface of which the critic spoke. Rather than as hard, shiny, and cold, the figure conveys the female body as warm and sensuous. Yet the young woman is neither exceedingly voluptuous nor idealized. She is, in fact, curiously remote. Her face is expressionless, the eyes blank. From the front, her stance is immobile and symmetrically balanced, and one senses the tedium of the long studio pose.* Seen from the side, however, the figure at once suggests an internal energy not apparent from directly in front or directly behind. Commenting on the piece in the April 19, 1930, issue of *Art News* magazine, an unnamed writer observed: "The head and torso of the full-length figure of *D'A-lal* are buoyant and vigorous, but modeled with astonishing subtlety, and, though the legs seem lifeless in comparison, they serve to accept the vivid animation of the body. The girl's body is arched like a drawn bow, with the chest thrust forward and head proudly held."

That same writer's larger purpose was reviewing an exhibition at the Museum of Modern Art titled "Forty-six Artists Under Thirty-five from America and Europe." Cash received the highest praise of any sculptor in the show: "One man in particular lifts the group to unexpected levels and if for no other reason than that his work is included, the exhibition is a real success." Cash was living in Paris at the time of the exhibition, and it was there that *D'A-lal* was executed and cast the year before, 1929. The model was a black dancer from Martinique, who was also a popular—by some accounts, notorious—character in Parisian café society.

Cash was born in Chattanooga in 1895. His father James A. Cash, was a city commissioner of public utilities. After graduating from Baylor School, young Cash attended the University of Virginia, where in 1919 he completed a bachelor's degree in interior design. With a scholarship award he went on to study at the School of Fine and Applied Art in New York from 1919 to 1926. All along he supplemented his income working as an interior decorator for Wannamaker's stores. From 1926 to '28 he attended the Beaux Art Institute of Design. He moved to Paris in 1928, and with the aid of two prestigious Guggenheim fellowships, in 1930 and '31, he was able to remain through 1932. It was an important four-year phase in his development. He became aware of the full-bodied human figure studies of prominent sculptors Aristide Maillol (1861-1944) and Charles Despiau (1874-1946). Stylistically and technically their strong influence is evident in *D'A-lal* and other pieces Cash produced during the European stay. Upon his return to America he established a home and studio in New York's Greenwich Village, but he also spent part of each year at his family's Wildwood, Georgia, farm, about ten miles southwest of Chattanooga. After 1963 he resided permanently at the farm until his death in 1977.

*Cash's sculpture is related to what in painting is called the "studio picture." For a more complete explanation see the Jules Pascin article on page 136.

Walt Kuhn (1877-1949)

Walt Kuhn was born October 27, 1877 in Brooklyn, New York. Philip Rhys Adams, director emeritus of the Cincinnati Art Museum and author of an in-depth book on Kuhn, believes that the artist's "early exposure to the romantic and seamy side of seafaring life" witnessed at the Brooklyn docks and shipyards aroused a lifelong interest in strong, forceful subject types. And the late Mitchell Wilder, former director of the Amon Carter Museum, described his close friend Kuhn as a "roustabout," a tough guy himself who admired and respected toughness in others. This quality is perhaps best demonstrated in the artist's well-known paintings of circus performers. He chose to depict not the big "stars" but rather

THE RIDER
Walt Kuhn
1924
oil on canvas
50⅛ x 33⅜ inches
signed and dated lower left
Gift of the Benwood
Foundation

Provenance

Estate of Walt Kuhn
Walter Maynard Gallery, New York, New York
Mr. and Mrs. Louis D. Cohen, New York, New
York

Exhibitions

Walt Kuhn Retrospective Exhibit, University of
Arizona, Tucson, AZ, Feb. 6-March 31, 1966.

Loch Haven Art Center, Orlando, FL, Jan. 15-
Feb. 15, 1969, no. 40.

Publications

Walt Kuhn Retrospective Exhibit, exhibition
catalogue, Tucson: University of Arizona, 1966,
p. 17.

Diana W. Suarez, *Bluff and the Magic Mansion,
A Children's Guide to the Hunter Museum of Art*,
Chattanooga: Hunter Museum of Art, 1980.

acrobats, clowns, chorus girls, and various unsung artisans of the trade. He presented them not in the action or glamour of their respective events, but as though caught between acts or after the performance. They are not gaudy or happily extroverted showpeople, but severe protagonists in human dramas where workaday cares, pent-up emotions, and personal tragedies are but partially concealed by the costumes and grease paint.

For the majority of paintings in the circus-performer series, Kuhn pictured a single figure, posed frontally and immobile, theatrically lighted, boldly outlined and set against a nondescript, dark background. Art historian David W. Scott adds: "The forms were simplified, flattened, but brusquely modeled by sharp, dark accents. Colors and textures were strident, the mood intense—even disturbing." These descriptions aptly fit the Hunter's oil, *The Rider*, which is uncomplicated in design and execution, yet forceful in the subject's profound concentration.

Kuhn arrived at his prevailing subject motif after a remarkable series of interconnecting circumstances. At age sixteen he began classes at the Brooklyn Polytechnic Institute and by the time he was twenty he had opened a bicycle shop. This in turn led to his becoming interested in bicycle racing. Shortly he was competing at county fairs, where he encountered carnival and amusement park types with whom he made friends and from whom he derived indelible impressions. Meanwhile, he showed a natural talent for drawing and humorous illustration. In 1899, at age twenty-three, he journeyed west, where for two years he found work as a cartoonist for the *San Francisco Wasp*. As he grew progressively more devoted to his art, he realized that he needed instruction. From 1901 to 1903 he studied in Europe, first at the Académie Colarossi in Paris and later the Royal Academy in Munich. He absorbed the contemporary art movements of that day so that his own work evolved over the next two decades through several changes in style: from impressionism, then synthetic cubism, on to an expressionist manner akin to the fauves, arriving finally at a comparatively formalist approach that recalls the works of Cézanne, Rouault, and Derain.

Though never actually counted among their numbers, Kuhn associated with the group of painters called The Eight or Ash Can School. At the same time he was one of four artists who began planning in 1911 what two years later would be a singularly important event in the development of modern art in America, the 1913 Armory Show in New York City, at which many major European avant-garde artists were first exhibited in this country. In fact it was Kuhn and fellow artist Arthur B. Davies who selected most of the European pieces.

That Kuhn was a man of diverse interests, great energy, and enormous drive is well demonstrated by his substantial involvement in the Armory Show. It is also evidenced by the fact that through nearly all of his professional life he simultaneously carried on two different artistic careers. In the teens, that time of greatest growth and transition in his painting, he also regularly submitted cartoons to such popular magazines as *Puck*, *Judge*, *New York Sunday Sun*, *New York World*, and the old *Life*. In the twenties his career was divided about equally between painting, and designing sets and costumes — even directing — plays and musical reviews. During the thirties and forties he was a prolific painter, but he also worked extensively as a design consultant to the Union Pacific Railroad.

As early as 1946 Kuhn's family and friends began to observe signs that the artist's life of strenuous activity and extreme dedication to his work might be exacting a toll. With the ascendency of abstract expressionism following World War II he was unhappy with the contemporary art scene, and with dealers and critics. Eventually he grew bitter and disillusioned, while his behavior became irrational and dangerous. He suffered a nervous breakdown and, on Thanksgiving Day in 1948, he was committed to a psychiatric hospital in White Plains, New York. He died there July 13, 1949, concluding a career that biographer Adams has called "one of the major artistic achievements of the first half of the twentieth century."

Jules Pascin (1885-1930)

Escaping strife-torn Europe at the time of the First World War, Jules Pascin spent only six years of his life self-exiled in the United States. But he can properly be considered an American artist, if not for his legitimate claim, having taken citizenship within a year of his arrival, then more especially because he produced much of his best painting during the period, and because he had direct and considerable influence on certain American artists who knew him and his work: principally Alexander Brook, Emil Ganso, Bernard Karfoil, and Charles Demuth.

As had perhaps no artist in America before him, Pascin painted what Milton W. Brown has defined as the "studio picture." With European antecedents as far back as Jan Vermeer in the seventeenth century, later French painters—including Gustave Courbet, Pierre Auguste Renoir, Edgar Degas, Henri de Toulouse-Lautrec, Henri Matisse—devised something quite different from the genre interior, portrait, conversation group, or still life. "The studio picture in its modern form had its origins in the nineteenth century as one reflection of the artists' increasing isolation from normal social relationships," writes Brown, who continues:

> It is only in the twentieth century that the studio became the limit of artistic life and that the paraphernalia of the studio became a major subject matter of art. Studio life gave way to studio objects — the model, the guitar, the vase, the apple, the bottle . . . One might even say that the basic concept of "significant form" is nothing but a philosophical rationalization of the disenfranchisement of the artist.

PORTRAIT D'UNE JEUNE
FILLE ASSISE
Jules Pascin
undated
oil and pencil on canvas
32 x 25¾ inches
signed top right
Gift of the Benwood
Foundation

Provenance

Mr. and Mrs. Louis D. Cohen, New York, New
York

Exhibitions

Frances and L. D. Cohen Collection, Norton
Gallery and School of Art, West Palm Beach, FL,
Feb. 23-March 17, 1968.

Pascin's preferred studio object was the seated female model, sometimes shown nude or nearly nude, sometimes scantily clothed. The Hunter Museum's *Portrait d'une jeune fille assise* (Portrait of a Young Seated Girl), though undated, is one of approximately 500 such studies the artist is known to have painted from about 1912 until his death eighteen years later. As critic Ronny Cohen has noted, Pascin converted a "nominal subject" into a "meditative image." The young women are posed simply, often inelegantly, with neither coquetry nor preoccupation in silly dalliances, without primping or adorning. Their expressions are blasé, eyes stare languidly. Often the faces are heavily rouged, a frank intimation that the subjects usually were strumpets or café girls the artist met on his frequent visits to brothels or bohemian gathering places. "Like Toulouse-Lautrec," Brown compares, "Pascin was interested in the demi-monde of prostitution . . . He could transform a scrawny and undernourished whore into a vision of fragile and flowerlike delicacy." Ilya Ehrenberg, an expatriate Russian journalist and novelist who lived in Paris during the '20s and '30s, saw profound tragedy rather than eroticism in Pascin's work. In contrast to Brown, Ehrenberg saw the models as chubby, and spoke of "all these short-legged, plump girls with hurt eyes" who "look like broken dolls."

Pascin's composition and distinct rendering style evoke a pensive mood, an almost surreal presence. Alfred Werner has written of the artist's skilled and subtle draftsmanship and his "unusual gift for capturing the three-dimensional world in a thin, wiry, economical line." It is a "drawn" line that, even in painting, is clearly evident. Much inspired by Cézanne's patchy watercolors, Pascin applied his oils in thin watercolor-like washes, here filling in between lines, there blurring or softening a contour, elsewhere building up filmy intangible shapes through gradations of tone. Colors are played in melancholy reserve—

grayed, faded, dulled. The light source illuminating the scene is ambiguous. "To increase the aura of unreality, bodies are often foreshortened, almost thrust at the beholder," Werner continues, "and there is only a minimum of orthodox perspective, of an attempt to render space." The moment conveyed is dreamlike and ethereal.

Pascin was born Julius Pincas at Vidin, Bulgaria, in 1885. He lived a portion of his teen years in Vienna, where he received his earliest formal art instruction, and in Munich, where, having already developed prodigious drawing ability, he regularly submitted cartoons to the elite German art nouveau periodical, *Simplicissimus*. When he was twenty, in 1905, he emigrated to Paris. Soon he changed his name to the Gallicized Jules Pascin. Enthusiastically he moved in the circle of the French postimpressionist and fauve painters. In 1912, the same year that Pascin settled into his familiar young-woman figurative mode, American artists Arthur B. Davies and Walt Kuhn were in Europe inviting participation in the forthcoming Armory Show. They selected twelve Pascin paintings for display at the monumental New York exhibit the following year. It was perhaps this singular involvement that induced Pascin to come to the United States in 1914 for the duration of the war. He went back to France on an American passport in 1920. Except for a brief portion of 1927-28, when he made a return visit to New York, he lived the remainder of his life in Paris. By 1930, years of heavy drinking and dissipation left Pascin severely ill, suffering advanced cirrhosis of the liver. Werner relates Pascin's appearance as "pasty skin, sunken eyes, white hair," and looking "years older" than his actual forty-five. Dissatisfied with recent work, physically burnt out, and emotionally despondent, he took his own life in his Montmartre studio.

Oscar Bluemner (1867-1938)

By the time German-born Oscar Bluemner emigrated to the United States in 1892, the twenty-five year old artist had already studied architecture, started a professional practice, and designed a theatre and two post offices in his native country. In America he continued his architectural career for another two decades. He was, in fact, one of the designers of pre-fabricated units for the World Columbian Exposition of 1893 in Chicago, and in 1902 he won the commission to design the Borough Court House for the Bronx, New York. But he also had all the while a strong interest in drawing and painting. When he was nineteen he participated in a portrait exhibition, and he made many fine sketches and watercolors of the German landscape.

Except for periodic work and study in New York, Boston, and Hartford, Bluemner lived in Chicago until 1900. He then settled permanently in the East, first in New York City and then in neighboring New Jersey. In 1910 he met noted photographer Alfred Stieglitz and began frequenting his "291" Gallery in Manhattan, which showed many of the most avant-garde European and American artists of the period. Excited on seeing the latest trends in art, Bluemner soon produced his first oil paintings. At the same time, he grew increasingly uninterested in architectural work. He abandoned architecture altogether in 1912 to pursue painting full time. That year he also traveled again to Europe, where he enthusiastically visited galleries and museums throughout France, Italy, and Germany. He admitted to being impressed by the work he saw of the individual artists Cézanne and Van Gogh and by the several figures who constitute the Orphists and futurists — particularly for their use of intense and exotic color. Bluemner returned to the United States in the fall of 1912; he submitted five paintings to the famous Armory Show in 1913 and he was given a one-man exhibition at "291" in 1915.

Judith Zilczer, the curator at the Hirshhorn Museum who organized that institution's important 1979-80 Bluemner retrospective, calls the artist's mature style "color expressionism." Indeed his landscapes of the late teens, twenties, and thirties assume the bold palette of the Orphists or the German Expressionists, and aptly manifest the independent abstract function of color: psychological association, temperature, relative strength, optical vibration, advancing or receding spatial properties. At the same time his preference for simplified shapes, monumental groupings, and tightly structured compositions doubtless reflects his architectural background. The Hunter's *Form and Light, Motif in West New Jersey (Beattiestown)* (color plate 25) of 1914 shows all these characteristics and further demonstrates how the artist liked to weld the components of his pictures together by the rhythmic repetition of

(color plate 25)

FORM AND LIGHT, MOTIF IN WEST NEW JERSEY (BEATTIESTOWN)

Oscar Bluemner

1914

oil on canvas

30 x 40⅛ inches

signed lower left

Gift of the Benwood Foundation

Provenance

The estate of the artist

James Graham and Sons Gallery, New York, New York

Mr. and Mrs. Louis D. Cohen, New York, New York

Exhibitions

The American Scene, 1900-1970, Indiana University Art Museum, Bloomington, IN, April 6-May 7, 1970.

Publications

The American Scene, 1900-1970, exhibition catalogue, Bloomington, IN: Indiana University Art Museum, 1970, no. 43.

shapes and contours (swatches of sunlight streaming across the ground, branches of trees, roofline diagonals, etc.) to achieve an effect of sequential ordering in a carefully calculated depth of field.

Bluemner's career was brought to an abrupt end in 1935 when he was severely injured in an automobile accident. Then sixty-seven years old, he never fully recovered, and he was never able to resume painting. Sadly, he committed suicide three years later. Sadly, too, in his lifetime he never knew the critical recognition he has since been accorded. His work helped define the upward striving impetus of American modernism in the pubescent years immediately before and after the Armory Show. He was a pivotal figure in the advancement of abstract art and is now, of course, especially regarded for his effective use of color. As curator Zilczer has noted: "In his preoccupation with color and emotive symbolism, Bluemner created a highly personal style and esthetic of color expressionism."

Alfred H. Maurer (1868-1932)

STILL LIFE WITH MUFFINS
Alfred H. Maurer
c. 1929-1930
oil on board
18¼ x 21¾ inches
signed top right
Gift of Ione and Hudson D. Walker

Provenance

Ione and Hudson D. Walker, Forest Hills, New York

Exhibitions

Fall Fiesta Benefit, Montgomery Museum of Fine Arts, Montgomery, AL, Oct. 28-Nov. 5, 1961.

Meridian Museum of Art, Meridian, MS, Oct.-Nov., 1970.

The viewer would be correct in noting a strong similarity between Alfred H. Maurer's *Still Life with Muffins*, an oil on panel from 1929-30, and certain synthetic cubist still lifes from ten to fifteen years earlier by Pablo Picasso, Georges Braque, and Juan Gris. Maurer was one of the first of only a few American painters (including also Marsden Hartley, Max Weber, and Arthur Dove) who experimented in the second and third decades of the twentieth century with the then revolutionary pictorial concept. Robert Rosenblum calls cubism "one of the major transformations in Western art," going on to explain:

> As revolutionary as the discoveries of Einstein or Freud, the discoveries of cubism controverted principles that had prevailed for centuries. For the traditional distinction between solid form and the space around it, cubism substituted a radically new fusion of mass and void. In place of earlier perspective systems that deter-

139

mined the precise location of discrete objects in illusory depth, cubism offered an unstable structure of dismembered planes in indeterminate spatial positions. Instead of assuming that the work of art was an illusion of a reality that lay beyond it, cubism proposed that the work of art was itself a reality that represented the very process by which nature is transformed into art. In the new world of cubism, no fact of vision remained absolute.

Cubism derives in part from Paul Cézanne's contention in the late nineteenth century that *all* forms, natural or man-made, can, and for clarity and coherence should be, reduced to an inherent geometry. Cubist artists took the proposition an additional step by reordering perceived geometric components into imaginative new combinations and contexts. Thus the approach is as much *con*ceptual as *per*ceptual. Rather than one static, topographical view, the "idea" or sundry physical and subjective characteristics of an object might be better communicated through simultaneous multiple views, overlapping and interpenetrating forms, or by abstracted, expressively modified images. Maurer painted *Still Life with Muffins* by yet another aesthetic hypothesis: Jay Hambridge's principles of pictorial arrangement, "dynamic symmetry," wherein mathematically based formulas determine the positioning of squares, rectangles, and triangles, so as to lay a skeletal substructure on which the composition is built. Hambridge theorized that applying his systems generates an intrinsic sense of visual push and pull, of force and counterforce. Indeed, the carefully set out angles and diagonals of Maurer's still life seem to invest a subtle energy in an otherwise inert and pedestrian grouping of objects.

Maurer rarely dated his paintings; consequently one cannot establish with certainty when he began producing cubist-style pictures. According to friends, it was about 1927. And such work was first reviewed by the New York press in 1928. The artist continued in the style on and off until his death four years later. The late paintings, usually done on hardboard panels, typically are the product of tedious scrubbing, scraping, and re-painting. Still, as Barbara Rose observes, "the ultimate result is often quite fresh."

Maurer encountered European modernism while he resided in Paris from November 1897 to August 1914 (except for a portion of 1901-02, when he visited his family in New York City). Initially he had gone abroad to attend the famed Académie Julian, but finding the French academism that dominated the school too conservative for his tastes, after a brief period of study he withdrew to work independently. From 1898 to about 1905 he painted in a tonal manner, similar to the late romanticism of James McNeill Whistler. Accordingly, his favorite subjects were fashionably dressed women, full-length figure, informally posed, both seated and standing. In 1904 he met Gertrude and Leo Stein, and, as is mentioned in the *Autobiography of Alice B. Toklas*, became a regular visitor in their Paris home. They in turn introduced Maurer to their circle of avant-garde intellectuals, writers, and artists— not the least of whom was Henri Matisse. Maurer never studied under Matisse, as has sometimes been reported, but the fauve master had profound influence upon his painting for the remaining nine years of the stay in Europe. Differences in Maurer's style were apparent by 1906, as he painted landscapes, figures, and still lifes in characteristic fauve raw color and impulsive brushwork. By 1909 *New York Sun* critic James Huneker had dubbed Maurer "Knight of the Burning Pestle."

Largely through close friend Arthur Dove, Maurer was one of several Americans in Paris introduced to photographer and art dealer Alfred Stieglitz, whose gallery at 291 Fifth Avenue in New York City (often referred to simply as "291") was the first in the United States regularly to show works by the European and American moderns. Stieglitz was, in fact, the first to exhibit not just Dove and Maurer, but also Marsden Hartley, John Marin, and Max Weber. Participating in "291" shows in 1909 and 1910 led to Maurer's submitting four fauve-style paintings to the Armory Show in 1913.

The following year, at the onset of World War I, Maurer reluctantly came home to New York. But with every intention of returning to France after the conflict, he kept his Paris studio until 1925. (Eventually the artworks left there—hundreds of items, estimated at half his life's production—were sold to recover back payments of rent.) To his consternation and displeasure, he was never able to go back. His disposition changed markedly. Sculptor Mahonri Sharp Young, who knew Maurer on both sides of the Atlantic, comments: "During his early days in Paris, until 1914, Maurer was an exceptionally cheerful fellow. Something happened to his life, which may not even have had anything to do with his art, and for the rest of his life in New York this pioneering abstractionist was an unhappy recluse." By some accounts that "something" was despair over a love interest left behind. In any case, his depression was compounded by his finding it necessary to live at home with parents. His authoritarian father, Louis Maurer, a successful genre painter and lithographer for Currier and Ives, openly detested the son's modern work. Though introverted and reticent, especially since the return from France, Maurer resisted his father's disdainful criticism and imperious manner. Nonetheless, Peter Pollack believes that Maurer may actually have been sustained by the very contentiousness of the relationship. When the father died at age one hundred in 1932, Maurer was severely grieved. Totally despondent, he took his own life two weeks later.

Maurer was born in New York City in 1868. He dropped out of school at age sixteen to work in the family's lithographic firm, Heppenheimer and Maurer. The same year he began classes with Edgar Ward at the National Academy of Design. He was nearly thirty before he left for the long stay in Paris. After "291" ceased operation in 1917, Maurer was virtually forgotten until 1924, when E. Weyhe rediscovered the work and showed it in his New York gallery. Even so, Maurer remained little recognized in his later years. "Maurer is an enigma in American art," wrote his first biographer, Elizabeth McCausland, "loved by old friends and connoisseurs, but with no general acceptance by artist, critic, and public. His obscurity is puzzling." In a review for a Hartley and Maurer two-man exhibit presented in 1950 at the Bertha Schaefer Gallery in New York, Hans Hofmann offered a touching assessment:

> Maurer is a painter of enormous stature. His vision of the reality of painting drove him to leave behind the success that accompanied his earlier work. This is the tragedy and glory of every great man; he must follow an inner urge of deeper purpose, which may destroy him in order that the work may live.

Reginald Marsh (1898-1954)

Reginald Marsh was born in Paris in 1898. His American parents, Fred and Alice Marsh, were painters. The family came home to the United States two years later, and young Marsh grew up in New Jersey. He attended Yale University and there began his career as an artist, serving as editor and cartoonist for *The Yale Record*. Upon graduation in 1920 he was employed as an illustrator for *Vanity Fair* and the *New York Daily News*. In 1925 he joined the staff of the *New Yorker* magazine, but left shortly thereafter to travel and study abroad. He returned to New York in 1926 and enrolled in the Art Students League, where he studied with Joan Sloan, George Luks, Boardman Robinson, and Kenneth Hayes Miller. It was Miller, in fact, who encouraged Marsh to follow up on an impulse he brought back from Europe, to adapt the design and technique of certain old masters (Marsh admitted to being particularly impressed with Rubens and Delacroix) to the raw pictorial potential of his immediate contemporary surroundings.

To Marsh, that potential was indeed truly and often raw. He once remarked: "Well-bred people are no fun to paint." His favorite subjects consequently were people caught up in what to most would seem the unsavory aspects of ultra-urban life: Bowery derelicts, the burlesque theatre, dance halls, the public beach, the subway or the congested subway station. Certainly the element of social criticism is an integral feature of Marsh's imagery, and though he is identified as a social realist, and was, as Oliver Larkin calls him, "a parlor socialist," he was not otherwise radical or politically motivated. He was satisfied in letting his art be the extent of his political statement.

In the Hunter Museum's *Subway-14th Street* of 1930 (color plate 26), the weighty, massive, dark ceiling of the station is accentuated by a series of long, parallel, near-horizontals that comprise the overhead beams. The relatively low sight line augments this same feeling. The sense of enclosure is heavy and oppressive. The walking strides of the various characters in the scene establish a pattern of diagonals that enhances the perceived motion and scurry. Periodic blotches of bright color — chiefly the greens, reds, and light blues of women's outfits — further provide a kind of raucous vitality appropriate to the situation and useful in relieving an otherwise dingy setting. One interesting fellow in the center-left foreground momentarily arrests the staccato movement as he reads the latest flap in a sensationalist tabloid. Overall, though, the people seem to move determinedly,

(color plate 26)
SUBWAY — 14TH STREET
Reginald Marsh
1930
egg tempera on canvas,
mounted on masonite
36 x 48 inches
signed and dated lower right
Gift of the Benwood
Foundation

Provenance

Frank Rehn Gallery, New York, New York
John Clancy, New York, New York
Mrs. Marilyn Goodman, New York, New York
Mr. and Mrs. Louis D. Cohen, New York, New York

Exhibitions

Reginald Marsh Retrospective: East Side, West Side, All Around the Town, University of Arizona Museum of Art, Tucson, AZ, March 9-April 6, 1969.

Reginald Marsh: A Retrospective Exhibition, organized by the Newport Harbor Art Museum, circulating exhibition: Newport Harbor Art Museum, Newport Beach, CA; Des Moines Art

(Continued on page 142)

impervious to one another, preoccupied with their own concerns, and each one alone in the crowd.

In the early 1930s, Marsh did numerous depictions of New York's popular Gaiety Burlesque. Therefore the Hunter's painting, which identifies that troupe in its title, though undated was probably finished between 1930 and '33. "The burlesque show is a very sad commentary on the state of the poor man," the artist professed. "It is the only entertainment, the only presentation of sex that he can afford. As for painting it, the whole thing is extremely pictorial. You get a woman in the spotlight, the gilt architecture of the place, plenty of humanity. Everything is nice and intimate, not spread out and remote as in a regular theater." For this particular performance Marsh puts the viewer in the midst of the all-male audience. The other show spectators in the foreground are quite close by, as though seated immediately adjacent. Their gazes are fixed upon the stage, except for one grinning character in the lower left who looks back over his shoulder. His eyes catch ours. He seems to recognize us and acknowledges our just coming into the parquet.

Both paintings are highly narrative, which is no doubt a ramification of Marsh's early years as a story illustrator. And both paintings are in the artist's preferred medium, egg tempera, which, because it dries quickly and cannot readily be re-worked, was particularly well-suited to his essentially linear approach. Marsh was rather more a draftsman than a total painter; he "drew" with a brush, building up forms with graphic skill. He tended moreover to keep his paint translucent. Highlights are usually achieved by the gesso ground showing through thinly painted glazes. "This linear brushwork," observes Marsh biographer Lloyd Goodrich, "has a sureness and refinement that give it a beauty of its own, and that make his temperas repay close study."

Marsh taught drawing and painting at the Art Students League in the summers of 1935, '36, '39, '40, and '41. In 1942 he began to teach there in the regular school year as well, and did so for the rest of his life (except for summer 1946, when for six weeks he was a visiting instructor at Mills College in California). He was vice president of the League in 1933-34. He was elected an associate of the National Academy of Design in 1937 and made full academician in 1943. In 1946 he was elected to the American Academy and Institute of Arts and

(Continued on page 159)

(Continued from page 141)

Center, Des Moines, IA; Fort Worth Art Center Museum, Fort Worth, TX; University Art Museum, The University of Texas, Austin, TX; Nov., 1972-May, 1973.

Publications

"Paintings in the 20's." *American Heritage*, August, 1968, p. 8.

Reginald Marsh Retrospective: East Side, West Side, All Around the Town, exhibition catalogue, Tucson: University of Arizona, 1969, no. 3.

Lloyd Goodrich, *Reginald Marsh*, New York: Harry Abrams, Inc., 1972, p. 46.

Matthew Baigell, *The American Scene*, New York: Praeger Publishers, Inc., 1974, p. 148, illus. pp. 158-159, no. 88.

Thomas W. Garver, *Reginald Marsh. A Retrospective Exhibition*, exhibition catalogue, Newport Beach, CA: Newport Beach Harbor Art Museum, 1972, no. 2.

Diana W. Suarez, *Bluff and the Magic Mansion, A Children's Guide to the Hunter Museum of Art*, Chattanooga: Hunter Museum of Art, 1980.

Marilyn Serman and others, *Reading Literature, Grade 9*, Evanston: McDougal, Littell and Co., 1984, illus. p. 525.

(GAIETY) BURLESQUE
(Also known as *Irving Place Burlesque*)

Reginald Marsh

c. 1930-1933

egg tempera on canvas, mounted on masonite

36 x 48 inches

Gift of the Benwood Foundation

Provenance

Frank Rehn, New York, New York
John Clancy, New York, New York
Mr. and Mrs. Louis D. Cohen, New York, New York

Exhibitions

Frances and L. D. Cohen Collection, Norton Gallery and School of Art, West Palm Beach, FL, Feb. 23-March 17, 1968.

Loch Haven Art Center Museum, Orlando, FL, Jan. 15-Feb. 15, 1969, no. 8.

Reginald Marsh Retrospective: East Side, West Side, All Around the Town, University of Arizona Museum of Art, Tucson, AZ, March 9-April 6, 1969.

Publications

Frances and L. D. Cohen Collection, exhibition catalogue, West Palm Beach, FL: Norton Gallery and School of Art, 1968, no. 17.

Reginald Marsh Retrospective: East Side, West Side, All Around the Town, exhibition catalogue, Tucson: University of Arizona, 1969, p. 15, no. 1.

Color plate 25. Oscar Bluemner, *Form and Light, Motif in West New Jersey (Beattiestown)*, c. 1914, oil on canvas, 30 x 40⅛ inches. Gift of the Benwood Foundation. (See article, page 138.)

Color plate 26. Reginald Marsh, *Subway – 14th Street*, 1930, egg tempera on canvas, mounted on masonite, 36 x 48 inches. Gift of the Benwood Foundation. (See article, page 141.)

Color plate 27. Guy Pene du Bois, *Shopper in a Red Hat*, 1939, oil on canvas, 30⅛ x 25 inches. Gift of the Benwood Foundation. (See article, page 159.)

Color plate 28. Milton Avery, *Young Girl in Blue*, 1939, oil on canvas, 33 x 26 inches. Gift of Mr. and Mrs. Roy R. Neuberger. (See article, page 173.)

Color plate 29. Thomas Hart Benton, *The Wreck of the Ole '97*, 1943, egg tempera on gessoed masonite, 28½ x 44½ inches (sight). Gift of the Benwood Foundation. (See article, page 178.)

Color plate 30. Jacob Lawrence, *The Apartment*, 1943, gouache on paper, 21 x 28½ inches. Museum purchase with funds provided by the Benwood Foundation and the 1982 Collectors' Group. (See article, page 179.)

Color plate 31. Charles E. Burchfield, *Gateway to September*, 1946-56, watercolor on paper, 42½ x 56 inches. Gift of the Benwood Foundation. (See article, page 180.)

Color plate 32. George L. K. Morris, *Arizona Altar*, 1949, oil and pencil on unprimed cotton, 53 x 40½ inches. Gift of Ruth S. Holmberg. (See article, page 186.)

Color plate 33. Hans Hofmann, *Scintillating Blue 38-30*, 1956, oil on canvas, 38 x 30 inches. Museum purchase with funds provided by Ruth S. and A. William Holmberg, Mr. and Mrs. Olan Mills, II, Mr. and Mrs. Scott L. Probasco, Jr., and Mr. and Mrs. Phil B. Whitaker. (See article, page 189.)

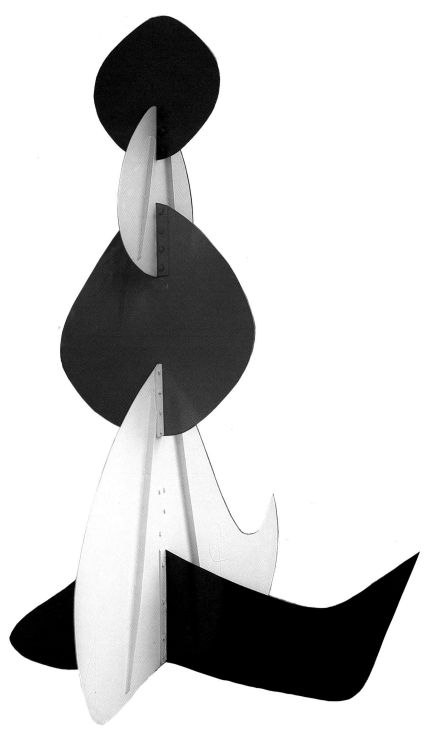

Color plate 34. Alexander Calder, *Pregnant Whale*, 1963, painted steel plate, 126½ x 105 x 88 inches. Gift of the Benwood Foundation (by exchange). (See article, page 193.)

Color plate 35. Lawrence Poons, *Sunnyside Switch*, 1963, acrylic on canvas, 80 x 80 inches.
Gift of the Museum Purchase Fund Collection, established by Gloria Vanderbilt, under the
auspices of the American Federation of Arts. (See article, page 194.)

Color plate 36. Willem de Kooning, *Untitled 1969*, 1969, oil on paper, mounted on board, 41⅜ x 30⅛ inches. Museum purchase with funds provided by the Benwood Foundation, Mr. and Mrs. Joseph H. Davenport, Jr., Mr. and Mrs. Scott L. Probasco, Jr., and Mr. and Mrs. Phil B. Whitaker. (See article, page 208.)

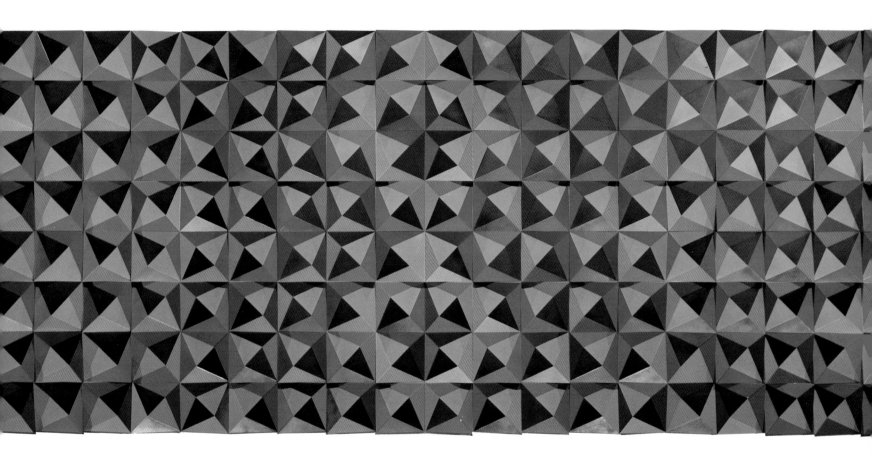

Color plate 37. Doris Leeper, *Modular Wall Relief in Eight Colors*, 1972-74, enamel on polyester and fiberglass, 120 x 300 x 4 inches (assembled). Museum commission. (See article, page 216.)

Color plate 38. Robert Rauschenberg, *Opal Reunion*, 1976, mixed media combine, six panels, 84 x 158 x 36 inches. Gift of the Benwood Foundation, Mr. and Mrs. Joseph H. Davenport, Jr., Ruth S. and A. William Holmberg, and Mr. and Mrs. Olan Mills, II. (See article, page 229.)

Color plate 39. Paul Jenkins, *Phenomena Royal Violet Visitation*, 1977, acrylic on canvas, 55 x 169 inches. Gift of Ruth S. and A. William Holmberg. (See article, page 234.)

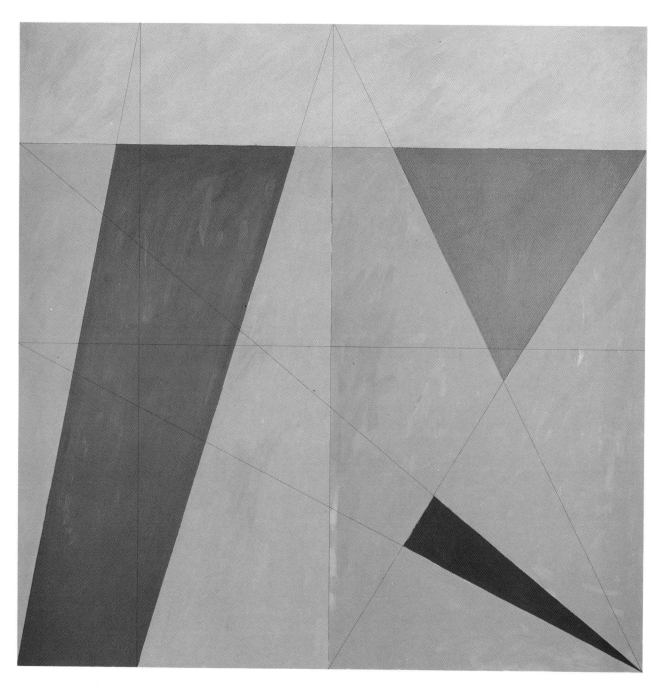

Color plate 40. Jack Tworkov, *Q3-78-#3*, 1978, oil on canvas, 54 x 54 inches. Museum purchase with funds provided by the Benwood Foundation and the 1983 Collectors' Group. (See article, page 240.)

(Continued from page 142)
Letters. He was also a member of the Society of American Graphic Artists. In June 1954 he was appointed art editor of the *Encyclopedia Britannica*, but a month later he died of a heart attack in Dorset, Vermont. He was fifty-six.

Guy Pene du Bois *(1884-1958)*

CENTRAL PARK
Guy Pene du Bois
c. 1940
pastel and oil on paper
15 x 21 inches (sight)
signed lower right
Gift of the Benwood
Foundation

Provenance

Private collection, New York, New York
Kennedy Galleries, Inc., New York, New York
Mrs. Marilyn Goodman, Palm Beach, Florida
Mr. and Mrs. Louis D. Cohen, New York, New York

Exhibitions

Frances and L. D. Cohen Collection, Norton Gallery and School of Art, West Palm Beach, FL, Feb. 23-March 17, 1968.

Publications

The Kennedy Quarterly, March 1967, Vol. VII, No. 1, p. 75.

Frances and L. D. Cohen Collection, exhibition catalogue, West Palm Beach, FL: Norton Gallery and School of Art, 1968, no. 4.

Despite his rather exotic French name and the opinion of numerous art critics that his mature work has a decided French cast, Guy Pene du Bois was thoroughly American. He was born in Brooklyn, New York, in 1884. His ancestry, however, was indeed French, tracing its roots in this country back to 1738 New Orleans.

Dropping out of high school at age fifteen, du Bois in 1899 became the youngest person enrolled in William Merritt Chase's New York School of Art. Over a period of six years he studied there with Chase and with Kenneth Hayes Miller, Carroll Beckwith, Frank V. DuMond, and Robert Henri. Then, in 1905, he studied in Paris under Alexandre Steinlin. Shortly upon his return to the United States the following year, his father, Henri Pene du Bois, died. The elder du Bois had been a literary and music critic for the *New York American*. The articulate and well-read son succeeded to the position. Painting less often (though he did exhibit at the Armory Show in 1913), du Bois stayed with the *American* seven years. He then transferred to the *Tribune*, where he was named assistant to the noted critic Royal Cortissoz. In another year he had moved on to become chief art critic for the *New York Post*. Simultaneously, from 1913 to 1920, he was editor for the magazine *Arts and Decoration*.

In the early '20s du Bois resumed painting seriously, but the real turning point in his growth as an artist occurred between 1924 and 1930 when he returned to France to study and work. His earlier painting was related to the Ash Can School, with its interest in the vigor and picturesqueness of city low life. During the European stay he gradually developed his personal view of contemporary society. Milton W. Brown contends that he was strongly influenced by the satirizing approach of such nineteenth-century French artists as Honore Daumier, Paul Gavarni, Constantin Guys, and Jean-Louis Forain. Drawing too upon his New York experience as newspaper reporter, critic, and urban-scene painter, he forged his own satirical genre style. Accordingly, his pictures usually show two or three figures frozen in motion. They seem like mannequins in their cylindrical shapes, affected expressions, and inane superficialities. They seem cold and detached; rarely do they appear happy or content. They are mild caricatures of the pompous, over-fed, pseudo-chic, and pseudo-sophisticated types the artist had seen in real life—particularly among the "social climbers." In his autobiography, however, (published in 1944 and provocatively titled *Artists Say the Silliest Things*), du Bois more sympathetically declares: "People are not really so bad. Indeed what they pretend to be is often worse than what they are."

Technically du Bois' treatment is broad, his volumes ample, forms simplified. Like Cézanne, he held that the artist's task is to disentangle the complexities of a scene and to make the actual shapes, colors, spaces, and rhythms plain and intelligible to the eye. In achieving such design order, his paintings are invested with a certain quietude and monumentality.

Of the two pieces in the Hunter Museum collection, *Shopper in a Red Hat*, a 1939 oil, (color plate 27), is more typical of his characteristic mannequin-figure style. The adult subjects seem hard and even a little cynical, while the child appears lost in reverie. By comparison, *Central Park*, drawn in pastel in 1940, is more casual. This is in part because of the inherently softer medium and in part because of the salubrious subject matter. Interestingly, each of the four (or five if one includes the small dog) principal figures to the left side of the picture strides on the left foot. The axis of their bodies, therefore, inclines slightly left of perpendicular. That axis is repeated in the row of trees at the mid to rear ground. In counterpoint, the body axis of the long line of seated figures — especially the pattern of legs—inclines to the right, establishing an effective foil and a subtle dynamism for the composition. Otherwise the various people are indistinct and their identities need not concern the viewer. There is a certain universality to the scene. It could just as well be a European park as an American, or just as well a midwestern city as New York.

Du Bois was a member of the National Academy of Design, having been elected an associate in 1937 and full academician in 1940. He was also a member of the American Academy and National Institute of Arts and Letters. He taught at the Art Students League from 1920 to '24, '30 to '32, and '35 and '36. He died in Boston in 1958.

Andrew Wyeth (b. 1917)

Andrew Wyeth had just turned twenty years old when he painted the remarkably facile *Lobster-Man*, one of a series of watercolors produced in Maine in 1937, and exhibited later that same year in the young artist's first one-man show at New York's Macbeth Gallery. The show was an extraordinary success. Every piece promptly sold, and the work was favorably reviewed in the press. An unidentified correspondent for the October 23, 1937, issue of *Art News* magazine declared: "These are very breezy arresting papers, indicating a talent which intrigues one's interest, partly because they exhibit so able a technician, but partly for the freshness of the artist's approach." A critic, also unnamed, for the January 1938 issue of *Art in America* commented: "For a youth of twenty to appear upon the horizon of American art today with a series of watercolors that take one back to the work of Winslow Homer and do not suffer an eclipse from the comparison is something those who care for our native art must find highly encouraging." The likening to Homer was apt. Wyeth himself has admitted that at the time: "I loved the works of Winslow Homer, his watercolors, which I studied intently so I could assimilate his various watercolor techniques."

Wyeth's early, wet-brush watercolor style was a departure from—if not reaction to—the strict regimen of careful drawing, perspective problem, anatomical study, light-and-shadow modeling of form that had been meted by his father and only principal teacher, noted illustrator N. C. Wyeth. And though he was sufficiently heartened by public response to continue producing in the Homer mode until 1942, soon after the Macbeth show Wyeth began to question the direction he had taken: "So I returned to Chadds Ford," he recounted to Thomas Hoving in a 1976 interview, "pleased but then in a while a bit disturbed, because I felt the work was still too free, too deft, too popular, perhaps still too undisciplined. My anxieties led me to get more into the thing, into realism

(color plate 27)

SHOPPER IN A RED HAT
Guy Pene du Bois
1939
oil on canvas
30⅛ x 25 inches
signed and dated lower right
Gift of the Benwood
Foundation

Provenance

Estate of Guy Pene du Bois
Graham Gallery, New York, New York
Mr. and Mrs. Louis D. Cohen, New York, New York

Exhibitions

Frances and L. D. Cohen Collection, Norton Gallery and School of Art, West Palm Beach, FL, Feb. 23-March 17, 1968.

Publications

Frances and L. D. Cohen Collection, exhibtion catalogue, West Palm Beach, FL: Norton Gallery and School of Art, 1968, no. 5.

160

THE LOBSTER-MAN
(Also known as *The Lobster Fisherman*)
Andrew Wyeth
1937
watercolor
21½ x 29 inches (sight)
signed lower right
Gift of the Benwood Foundation

Provenance

B. H. Emmett
Ambassador and Mrs. J. William Middendorf, III, New York, New York
Kennedy Galleries, Inc., New York, New York
Mr. and Mrs. Louis D. Cohen, New York, New York

Exhibitions

First Exhibition, Watercolors by Andrew Wyeth, Macbeth Gallery, New York, NY, Oct. 19-Nov. 1, 1937.

Masters of American Watercolor, State Council on the Arts and American Federation of Arts, New York, NY, Jan. 1962-Jan. 1963, no. 35.

Paintings by Andrew Wyeth, San Jose Museum of Art, San Jose, CA, Nov. 17, 1979-Jan. 9, 1980.

Andrew Wyeth in Southern Collections, Greenville County Museum of Art, Greenville, SC, Feb. 1-March 31, 1978.

Publications

First Exhibition, Watercolors by Andrew Wyeth, exhibition catalogue, New York: Macbeth Gallery, 1937, illus. on cover, no. 2.

"The Watercolors of Andrew Wyeth." *Art in America,* Jan. 1938, illus. p. 37, p. 41.

Paintings by Andrew Wyeth, exhibition catalogue, San Jose: San Jose Museum of Art, 1980.

. . ." By the mid '40s he had devised the tight, detailed, veristic style for which he shortly became one of the most widely known and respected American artists.

To persons unfamiliar with or suspicious of abstract art, Wyeth's acutely true-to-life rendering—coupled to stark genre subject matter—champions "old values" and "traditional ways." One should not conclude, however, that his works are mere snapshots in paint. Colors, tones, and textures are purposely employed, and compositions carefully arranged, to impart certain moods or intuitive feelings. John Wilmerding writes: "Mistakenly admired for the apparent photographic literalness in his temperas and drybrush watercolors, he had rather sought an economy of design often approaching abstraction, expressive angles of vision, selective focusing of detail, and intimation of psychological presences . . ." "In the world of art today," Wyeth exclaimed to Richard Meryman in a 1965 interview, "I'm so conservative I'm radical . . . I honestly consider myself an abstractionist."

Often Wyeth depicts a solitary human figure playing out a quiet, dignified, personal drama. One senses the subject's prevailing against exasperation, boredom, weariness, pain, handicap, or loneliness. Wanda M. Corn finds an explanation for such preoccupation in the artist's roots and upbringing:

> Andrew Wyeth belongs to the generation that grew up between the world wars. Born in 1917, his baby years were colored by reminiscences of the horrors and heroism of the First World War. He was a teenager during the great Depression. Just as he reached adulthood and maturity, the whole world was swept into another tragic war. This basic chronology suggests that his was a generation brought up on the milk of harsh human realities. To be developing as an artist in the late 1930s and early 1940s meant coming of age in a time of bleakness. Not surprisingly, artists of this particular generation tended to turn inward and became introspective in their expression.

One sees Wyeth's exposition on the indomitable human spirit even in the early *Lobster-Man*, as all alone the obscure fisherman meets the challenge of a difficult task in a formidable and potentially dangerous surrounding. A strong pattern of diagonals—the boat, oars, and shadows of the water in the foreground—augments for the viewer a physical awareness of the small craft's pitching on the choppy sea.

A lifelong resident of Chadds Ford, Pennsylvania, his birthplace, the "world" Wyeth had recorded is limited chiefly to the land and people of the Brandywine Valley district in that rural southeastern part of the state, or to the spare environs of his summer home at the small town of Cushing, on the Maine coast. Wyeth was elected to full membership in the National Academy of Design in 1945. He is also a member of the American Watercolor Society and the American Academy and Institute of Arts and Letters. In 1963 President John F. Kennedy awarded him the prestigious Presidential Medal of Freedom, and in 1970, during the term of President Richard M. Nixon, he was honored by a special showing of his work at the White House.

William McGregor Paxton (1869-1941)

HARRY P. MEIKLEHAM
William McGregor Paxton
1937
oil on canvas
40¼ x 35¼ inches
signed and dated lower left
On loan from Monticello, Thomas Jefferson Memorial Foundation, Inc., Charlottesville, VA

Provenance
Commissioned by Pepperell Manufacturing Co., Dalton, Georgia
Thomas Jefferson Memorial Museum, Monticello, Virginia

Publications
Clyde W. Jolley, "Thomas Jefferson's Great-great Grandson was a Great Man in Lindale." *Georgia Life*, Winter 1976, pp. 36-37, illus. p. 37.

The stout, rather severe gentleman in William McGregor Paxton's three-quarter-length seated portrait is Harry P. Meikleham, who for thirty years was manager of the Peperell (today West Point-Peperell) Manufacturing Company mill in Lindale, Georgia. The sixty-five-year-old subject sat for the portrait in 1937, just six months before he was stricken by a fatal heart attack. Georgia historian Clyde W. Jolley called Meikleham "a man with a tender heart beneath a gruff exterior" (an outward appearance that Paxton seems aptly to have recorded). For his dynamic—if not sometimes autocratic—leadership in organizing and supporting local civic, fraternal, benevolent, and religious activities, friends and fellow townspeople affectionately addressed him as "the Captain," or more simply, "Cap'n." Jolley elaborates further:

Captain Meikleham never stopped trying to improve the quality of life in Lindale. Childless in two marriages, he looked upon everyone in the community as his personal responsibility. He organized a number of societies and secret orders including the Masons, Oddfellows, Redmen, Pocahontas, and Rebekkahs. He organized the Red Cross, which, in 1919, boasted 900 members. He organized a burial society that forever banished the necessity for "passing the hat" to take care of the last rights of mill employees. His Lindale band became one of the best musical outfits in the state. For the youth he started the Boy Scouts, and built a clubhouse complete with a heated swimming pool and basketball courts and outfitted throughout with athletic equipment. He established baseball, basketball, and track teams. He always presented Bibles to graduates of the Vacation Bible Schools that were held in all the churches.

Born in New York City in 1872, Meikleham grew up in the home of his grandparents in Alexandria, Virginia. His grandmother, Septimia Randolph Meikleham, was, as the given name suggests, the seventh daughter of Martha Jefferson Randolph, daughter of Thomas Jefferson. Meikleham was particularly proud of his Jeffersonian heritage, and upon his death he was buried in the family cemetery at Monticello.

The artist, Paxton, was one of a loose-knit association identified as the Boston School, active in the late nineteenth and first quarter of the twentieth century. Other members included Abbott Thayer, Frank W. Benson, Thomas Wilmer Dewing, and Edmund C. Tarbell. Most, like Paxton, had an extensive portrait trade, though some members of the group (not including Paxton) also produced impressionist-style paintings and exhibited together with The Ten. The distinguishing achievement of the Boston School was in depicting sumptuous interiors—parlors, music rooms, studies—with fashionable young women who serenely converse, or read, or examine a flower or piece of decorative art, or are purely lost in thought. In short, it was a genteel, sociable art, suited to the gracious homes of patrons in Back Bay or on Beacon Hill. It was suited as well for the transplanting of the Salon and academic painting that many Americans had absorbed while studying abroad.

Paxton's "chamber pictures" are additionally distinctive in two respects: First, the cool single light source, rich furnishings and clothing, and porcelain-faced women—often shown from the side and in profile—reveal the direct influence of seventeenth-century Dutch master Jan Vermeer, whose work Paxton much admired. Second, Paxton experimented with an effect he believed would more naturally represent "binocular" rather than "monocular" vision. He would render the main figure or center of interest in conventional contour. But for surrounding or distant objects in the same composition he painted blurred double edges, lines, and highlights in close juxtaposition, so as to simulate the actual ocular phenomenon.

Born in Baltimore, Maryland, in 1869, Paxton moved with his family the following year to Newton, Massachusetts, where he spent his childhood and youth. At age eighteen he began a two-year period of study with Dennis Miller Bunker at Boston's Cowles School of Art. In 1889 he entered the prestigious École des Beaux-Arts in Paris. He remained four years, studying mainly with Jean-Léon Gérôme, but he came also to know and esteem the work of Jules Bastien-Lepage and Pierre Puvis de Chavannes. He returned to Boston in 1893, and established a studio (initially shared with his friend, painter Joseph R. DeCamp). The mainstay of his livelihood was then, and continued to be, portraiture. With droll frankness, Paxton admitted in an undated paper:

I am by profession a portraitist — and what success has come to me is chiefly as a painter of bank presidents. In no branch of the arts have whiskers played so important a part . . . Perhaps I should here confess that I was never very good at mouths and the smooth face exposed my weakness. However, since the moustache has returned I note that my business has picked up a bit.

Between 1906 and '13 Paxton was an instructor in drawing at the Boston Museum School. He enjoyed teaching and was popular with his students. He was elected an associate member of the National Academy of Design in 1917, and raised to full academician in 1928. Despite his outspoken belief that the organization in the '30s forfeited its standards by admitting unqualified (which to Paxton was to say "modern") artists, he continued to exhibit regularly in academy shows until 1941, the year of his death.

Edward Weston *(1886-1958)*

DUNES, OCEANO, 1936
Edward Weston
print, c. 1977
(printed by Cole Weston, the artist's son)
gelatin silver print photograph
7½ x 9½ inches
Museum purchase

Provenance
Cole Weston, Carmel, California.

The American photographer Edward Weston loved the stark, dramatic beauty of the sand dunes at Oceano in California. He shot hundreds of pictures at the site — from different vantage points, at different times of day, under varying qualities of light, and with constantly changing configurations of the wind-blown sand. Several of these studies were printed as finished works. The example in the Hunter Museum collection (printed by Cole Weston, the artist's son, from a 1936 negative) is perhaps the best known.

Essentially, the picture's effectiveness is in its abstraction: the rippling alternation of light and dark bands in the foreground, changing direction with the landscape at mid-depth, showing an intensified but more irregular shadow pattern that suggests eerie human-like figures trudging along from left to right; the dynamic diagonal sweeps; the theatrically bold light striking the dune at upper right contrasted at once with a black serpentine ribbon, and the overall tactile richness. The scene thus has been endowed with a character and meaning that goes beyond subject matter or simple place recognition. It is additionally a sharing of the artist's personal vision: his sensitivity to form, light, aesthetic arrangement, and subjective mood.

Because of this rather art-for-art's-sake approach, with its strong emphasis upon design, critics have called Weston's style "pure" or "straight" photography. It is demonstrated not only in the result, but also in his characteristic method for taking a picture. Weston's own writing in this regard—virtually like a poem—is quite revealing:

> *I start with no preconceived idea — discovery excites me to focus — then redis-covery through the lens — final form of presentation seen on ground glass, the finished print previsioned complete in every detail of texture, movement, propor-tion, before exposure the shutter's release automatically and finally fixes my conception, allowing no after manipulation — the ultimate end, the print, is but a duplication of all that I saw and felt through my camera.*

Therefore accidental effects, cropping or trimming the final image, and darkroom artifice, either on the negative or in the printing and developing processes, would be to Weston a severe compromise of creative integrity.

Weston was born in Highland Park, Illinois, in 1886. He began his career about 1910 as a portrait photographer in Glendale, California. From 1914 to 1917 he worked in a romanticized, soft-focus style for which he won numerous awards. But in the early 1920s he gravitated toward his more formal, purified realist approach. In 1922 he met Alfred Steiglitz, Paul Strand, and other prominent artist-photographers in New York. The following year he began a three-year stay in Mexico, where he met and was undoubtedly influenced by the great muralists Diego Rivera, Jose Clemente Orozco, and David Alfaro Siqueiros. He returned to the United States in 1927 and established a studio in Carmel. In 1932 he was a co-founder of the "f/64" group of West Coast photographers, which also included Ansel Adams, Willard Van Dyke, Imogene Cunningham, and another of the artist's sons, Brett.

Significantly, in 1931 Weston became the first photographer ever to be awarded a Guggenheim Fellowship, with a grant to do studies of California and the West. In 1941 he received a commission to photo-illustrate a special issue of Walt Whitman's *Leaves of Grass*; his pictures for the project, taken in the southern and eastern states, probably brought him his greatest popular acclaim. In recognition of four decades of pioneering work in his medium, the Museum of Modern Art presented a major Weston retrospective in 1946.

Weston was stricken with Parkinson's Disease in 1948, which increasingly curtailed his work. His health deteriorated steadily until his death on New Year's Day 1958. Besides his photography, Weston left a considerable legacy in his "Daybooks," diary-journals of both his professional and personal life, compiled and edited by Nancy Newhall and published after his death. They remain widely read by photographers and students in the history of photography.

John Marin (1870-1953)

"The most consistently strong and productive original artist in America was John Marin," declared E. P. Richardson, "the dominant figure of the twenties, who lived long enough to become the patriarch of American painters and to produce some of his finest work in his fifth decade of painting." In his early years as a serious artist, Marin methodically assimilated stylistic influences that are apparent in the highly personal vision and characteristic technical facility of his mature work: the arbitrary color of the fauves, implied kinetics of futurism, fractured imagery of cubism, illusionistic space, economy and airiness of traditional Oriental painting, and more specifically, the reserved tinted watercolors of Paul Cézanne (an exhibition of which he had seen in 1911 at Alfred Stieglitz' "291" gallery in New York City). Rather than imitation, however, Marin's style is an amalgam; it was innovative enough in its time that John I. H. Baur was prompted to write: "There is no close echo in his work of the defined European movements. He stands as a pioneer of a distinctly American modernism."

With particular purpose for his painting, Marin would studiously observe a natural or man-made setting and intuitively discern the basic physio-dynamics that regulate the position and movement of objects. "As my body exerts downward pressure on the floor," he remarked, "the floor in turn exerts an upward pressure on my body." And again, somewhat more poetically: "While these powers are at work pushing, pulling, sideways, downwards, upwards, I can hear the sound of their strife and there is great music being played." To transcribe such impulses into visual form, he devised an architectonic method of composition, featuring bold, straight "force lines" coursing obliquely and breaking the vista into transparent, intersecting planes—usually enframing the central image. Those planes, moreover, operate like the "tormentor" curtains or wing flats on a stage, simultaneously reiterating the two-dimensionality of the paper or canvas while setting the scene in depth.

CITY MOVEMENT, DOWNTOWN MANHATTAN #2

John Marin

1936

watercolor and ink on paper

25⅜ x 20⅝ inches (sight)

signed and dated lower right

Gift of the Benwood
Foundation

Provenance

The Downtown Gallery, New York, New York
Mr. and Mrs. Lawrence A. Fleischman, Detroit
Michigan
Kennedy Galleries, Inc., New York, New York
Mr. and Mrs. Louis D. Cohen, New York, New
York

Exhibitions

*American Painting, 1760-1960, A Selection of
Paintings from the Collection of Mr. and Mrs.
Lawrence A. Fleischman, Detroit*, Milwaukee Art
Center, Milwaukee, WI, March 3-April 3, 1960.

Small Paintings of Large Import, Pennsylvania
Academy of the Fine Arts, Philadelphia, PA,
Nov. 24-Dec. 3, 1964.

*Past and Present, Two Hundred Years of Ameri-
can Painting, Part Two, Nineteenth and Twentieth Centuries*, Kennedy Galleries, Inc., New
York, NY, Oct. 3-31, 1966.

*Frances and L. D. Cohen Collection, Norton Gal-
lery and School of Art*, West Palm Beach, FL,
Feb. 23-March 17, 1968.

Publications

*American Painting, 1760-1960, A Selection of
Paintings from the Collectoin of Mr. and Mrs.
Lawrence A. Fleischman, Detroit*, exhibition
catalogue, Milwaukee: Milwaukee Art Center,
1960, p. 103.

Small Paintings of Large Import, exhibition
catalogue, Philadelphia: Pennsylvania
Academy of the Fine Arts, 1964, no. 32.

*Past and Present, Two Hundred Years of Ameri-
can Painting*, exhibition catalogue, New York:
Kennedy Galleries, Inc., 1966, no. 236.

Frances and L.D. Cohen Collection, exhibition
catalogue, West Palm Beach, FL: Norton Gallery and School of Art, 1968, no. 16.

The Kennedy Quarterly, New York: Kennedy
Galleries, Inc., Oct. 1966, p. 251.

Sheldon Reich, *John Marin: A Stylistic Analysis
and Catalog Raisonne, Part II*, Tucson: The University of Arizona Press, 1970, p. 678, no. 36.10.

Often Marin stopped short of painting to the picture edge so that the image takes on an added sense of lightness and buoyancy. Though objects rendered are recognizable, the artist typically employed a whimsical, abbreviated brush technique to simplify forms and to generate a feeling of spontaneity and energy. "It's like golf," he quipped. "The fewer strokes I can take, the better the picture." Early in his career, he found the water-color medium particularly adaptable to his sure yet vigorous creative approach. He painted in oils from time to time, but many critics find the results comparatively turgid.

New York City's massive buildings, congestion, and bustle fascinated Marin. "You cannot create a work of art unless the things you behold respond to something within you," he wrote to Stieglitz in 1913. "Therefore if these buildings move me, they too must have life. Thus the whole city is alive; buildings, people all are alive." The artist could well have been speaking of the Hunter Museum's watercolor: *City Movement, Downtown Manhattan, No. 2* (but for the fact that it was painted thirteen years later). The several structures animatedly lead the eye into depth, and an alternation of light and dark tones adds an element of meter to the progress. Meanwhile the visual flow reverses as the teeming wash of color, which summarily suggests a crowd of pedestrians, issues forth individual figures at closer range.

The painting is part of a larger body of works; Marin biographer Sheldon Reich explains: "In 1936 he executed a series of large, complicated watercolor paintings of New York City, emphasizing the transformation of buildings into intersecting angular planes and the schematized rendition of people on the streets." Reich continues (recounting *New York Sun* critic Ralph Flint's initial observation in January 1937): "In these he made use of an ink line, apparently drawn with a pen, which imparted to the painting a look distinct from that given by the pencil, charcoal, and painted line preferred by Marin up to this time." Reich's catalogue raisonné lists 2,987 paintings. Most are titled simply, according to place identification. But, interestingly, the artist included the word "movement" in titles for 159 works, including fourteen as "Street Movement" and seven "City Movement."

Marin was born in Rutherford, New Jersey, in 1870. His mother died when he was two weeks old. The father traveled extensively in business, so that the boy was reared by his maternal grandparents and two maiden aunts at Weehawken, New Jersey, directly west across the Hudson River from Manhattan. Young Marin had many opportunities to visit the city and its many galleries, art museums, and other cultural institutions. When he was eighteen, he painted his first watercolors in an impressionist manner, emulating the style he had doubtless seen at numerous exhibitions. He had no formal training then, but at about the same time he began a year's study in architecture at Stevens Institute of Technology in close-by Hoboken. Afterward he worked almost a decade as an architectural draftsman in New York. He was nearly thirty before he elected to pursue a career in painting. In 1899 he enrolled at the Pennsylvania Academy of the Fine Arts, where he studied two years, chiefly with Thomas Aushutz and Hugh Breckenridge. He also studied briefly under Frank Vincent Dumond at the Art Students League early in 1905.

The following September he left for a five-year stay in Europe. He traveled widely in the summers, but worked the remaining months of the year in Paris. Moving in an avant-garde circle, Marin became aware of the major modern trends of the period. Nonetheless, and rather surprisingly, at that time he developed his own style more in the tonal manner of James McNeill Whistler. In 1908 he met painter and photographer Edward Steichen. Steichen was so taken with Marin's delicate watercolors that he sent examples of the work back to Stieglitz in New York. Steiglitz enthusiastically concurred, and gave Marin his first one-man show at the "291" gallery in March 1901. Marin, still in Europe meanwhile, had also shown at the Salon des Independents and Salon d'Automne. He returned to the United States in 1911, established a studio in New York, and exhibited a second time at "291." He contributed ten watercolors to the important Armory Show in 1913, including several city views that are among his earliest experiments with the schematic force lines—the modified cubist effect that would come to typify his best-known work.

1936 was an especially eventful year for Marin: he began the cityscape series of which the Hunter's painting is a part; exhibited at Stieglitz' newest gallery, An American Place; and was given a significant retrospective at the Museum of Modern Art. Marin—who by his speech, mannerisms, and personal appearance gave the impression of a lean, crusty Yankee—loved the land, coast, and islands of Maine. Better than half his paintings are of Maine locations. In 1933 he purchased property for a summer residence at Cape Slit. He died there in 1953, at age eighty-two.

Philip Evergood (1901-1973)

Probably no painting currently on display in the Hunter Museum generates more visitor comment and, for that matter, more indignation than Philip Evergood's seamy *Love on the Beach*. Rather contrary to the title, the concept of "love" is presented only in its basest sense and the picture overall is far from "lovely." The design is cluttered, forms exaggerated nearly to the grotesque, perspective distorted, and the rendering technique unrefined. These apparent faults however were part of the artist's calculated effort to produce a scene so agitating that the viewer cannot just look casually, but must react, and in so doing be compelled to consider certain underlying issues. Kendall Taylor has noted: "Neutrality is as impossible for the observer of Philip Evergood's art as it was for its creator."

LOVE ON THE BEACH
Philip Evergood
1937
oil on canvas
30¼ x 37¼ inches
signed lower left
Gift of the Benwood
Foundation

Provenance

Collection of the artist
Mr. and Mrs. Louis D. Cohen, New York, New
York

Exhibitions

Frances and L. D. Cohen Collection, Norton
Gallery and School of Art, West Palm Beach, FL,
Feb. 23-March 17, 1968.

New York Cultural Center, Huntington, NY,
Feb.-March, 1969.

Philip Evergood Retrospective, Gallery of Modern Art, 1969, no. 10.

Publications

Frances and L. D. Cohen Collection, exhibition
catalogue, West Palm Beach, FL: Norton Gallery and School of Art, 1968, no. 9.

Subjectively then, *Love on the Beach* is a cynical study of shallow human relationships, wanton pleasures, and tawdry existence. Intimations of sexual indulgence are numerous. The three couples cavort or embrace licentiously. The spread-leg positioning by several of the figures is additionally suggestive, while the grappling crabs in the mid-foreground are a not-too-subtle allusion to the contracted parasites associated with promiscuity and uncleanliness. Dominant lines and shapes of the composition — including the strangely angular seashore — draw the eye to the center, where the principal characters are superimposed at the hips (hence the erogenous parts) in a visually tight, gnarled knot. Even the litter-strewn sand reinforces the general feeling of shabbiness.

Evergood was born Philip Howard Blashki in New York City in 1901. (His father, a Polish immigrant by way of Australia, changed the family name to Evergood, which was an Anglicization of Immergut, his mother's — i.e. Philip's grandmother's — maiden name.) He was raised and educated in England, attending Eton, Cambridge University, and London's Slade School of Art. At age twenty-two he returned to the United States and promptly enrolled at the Art Students League, where he studied two years, principally with William von Schlegell and George Luks. Subsequently, he also attended Stanley William Hayter's well-known graphic arts school in New York, Atelier 17. In the late twenties he went again to Europe to study at the Académie Julian in Paris.

On his second homecoming Evergood found an America reeling from the Great Depression. He was aghast at the poverty and the physical or emotional distress he witnessed, and his painting style changed accordingly. Though tempered by fantasy, wry humor, and an obscure personal symbolism, social criticism characterizes what today is regarded as his most significant work. Typical themes include political oppression, racial discrimination, coarse life among the urban poor, and, as in the case of *Love on the Beach*, the mundane amusements of people uninspired or oblivious to nobler pursuits. Interestingly, Reginald Marsh, a "social realist" and a contemporary with whom Evergood is often compared, painted similar studies of the teeming masses at the beach.

Tragically, Evergood died in a fire at his Connecticut home in 1973. One of his biographers, John I. H. Baur, fittingly summarized his personality and career:

He had to weep or laugh in life with the same intensity that he wept or laughed on canvas. And he had to translate the emotions of life into the very different language of art with the utmost immediacy of feeling. Despite the fact that he painted many hasty and even some downright bad canvases, he never painted a dull or conventional one.

Marsden Hartley (1877-1943)

Marsden Hartley was a pioneer in the early struggles of modern art in the United States. He was one of the first Americans before World War I to understand and sympathize with the European avant-garde, and one of the first to experiment in a fully abstract mode. Though his career can be divided into clearly defined stylistic periods, his work is consistently infused with strong emotional content and personal mysticism, a result of his lifelong search for spiritual values.

The product of a lonely and insecure childhood, Hartley grew up in a lower working-class home in the factory town of Lewiston, Maine, where he was born in 1877. He was the youngest of nine children, only five of whom survived to adulthood. His mother died when he was eight. When his father, Thomas Hartley, remarried four years later, young Marsden was left with an older sister and her husband in Auburn, Maine, while the rest of the family moved to Cleveland, Ohio. What he took as abandonment haunted Hartley for years to come. "I had a childhood vast with terror and surprise," he wrote in 1921. "If it is true that one forgets what one wishes to forget, then I have reason for not remembering the major part of those days." He lived a reflective and moody adolescence and was given to flights of imagination. Like the character Laura in Tennessee Williams' *Glass Menagerie*, he often escaped to a world of precious things, in his case, beautiful natural objects. But it was a diversion that undoubtedly sharpened his eye and his appreciation for shape, texture, and color.

Required to contribute to the sister's family income, Hartley unwillingly dropped out of school at age fifteen to work for a shoe manufacturer. By the following year, 1893, he had set aside enough to enable him to rejoin the others in Cleveland. Once there, he took painting lessons from John Semon and Cullen Yates. He also attended the Cleveland School of Art, where a drawing instructor named Nina Waldeck gave him a copy of Ralph Waldo Emerson's *Essays*, which he would later call the "greatest book" of his life. Emerson's belief that all nature embodies a divine spirit gave Hartley a rationale for his own mystical philosophy. After one semester at the Cleveland School, trustee Anne Walworth provided the artist a small stipend to study in New York. In 1899 he enrolled at William Merritt Chase's school, but transferred the next year to the less expensive National Academy of Design, where he continued through 1904. Initially he worked in an academic-realistic style, then in a quasi-impressionist manner, moving on to a postimpressionist enigmatic landscape style reminiscent of Albert Pinkham Ryder. Hartley met Ryder in 1909 and was recurrently influenced by his work.

It was in 1909 too that Hartley was introduced to Alfred Steiglitz, who only two months after their initial meeting gave him his first one-man show at the Photo Secession Gallery, more commonly known as "291." The following year Hartley exhibited with a group called the Younger American Painters, and in 1913 he submitted two oils and six drawings for the Armory Show. With Stieglitz' help and that of friend and fellow painter, Arthur B. Davies, Hartley went to Europe in 1912. He met Gertrude Stein and members of her circle in Paris, and Franz Marc and Wassily Kandinsky in Munich. Accordingly, his painting passed through Cézanne-esque, cubist, fauve, and expressionist phases. World War I forced Hartley's return to the United States. But in 1921 he went back to Europe and, except for intermittent trips home, he remained most of the decade of the '20s either in Berlin, Paris, or southern France. Upon his return to America in 1930, he began dividing time between New York, the Franconia Valley of New Hampshire, and Gloucester, Massachusetts. Especially at Gloucester he renewed his appreciation for the rugged New England coast and the lives of its commensurately rugged people.

CHANTIES TO THE NORTH
Marsden Hartley
1938-1939
oil on board
28¼ x 22⅜ inches
initialed lower right
Gift of the Benwood
Foundation

Provenance

Adelaide Kuntz, Bronxville, New York
Frances Malek, New York, New York
Paul Rosenberg & Co., New York, New York
William Zierler, Inc., New York, New York
Mr. and Mrs. Louis D. Cohen, New York, New York

Exhibitions

Marsden Hartley – 25th One Man Show, Hudson Walker Gallery, New York, NY, March 6-April 8, 1939.

The Animal Kingdom in Modern Art, traveling exhibition circulated by the Museum of Modern Art, New York, NY: Vassar College, Poughkeepsie, NY; Art Institute of Zanesville, Zanesville, OH; University of Virginia, Charlottesville, VA; College of William and Mary, Williamsburg, VA; University of Texas, Austin, TX; Wilmington Society of Fine Arts, Wilmington, DE; Nov. 1, 1942-Aug. 1, 1943.

Knoedler & Company, New York, NY, Jan. 9-27, 1968.

American Bank and Trust Co., New York, NY, Nov. 19-Dec. 19, 1969.

The American Scene, 1900-1970, Indiana University Art Museum, Bloomington, IN, April 6-May 17, 1970.

Animal in Art, Tennessee Fine Arts Center, Cheekwood, Nashville, TN, June 11-Sept. 17, 1978.

Publications

The American Scene, 1900-1970, exhibition catalogue, Bloomington, IN: Indiana University Art Museum, 1970, no. 31.

Hartley was awarded a Guggenheim Fellowship to work in Mexico from 1932 to '33. Back in New York during the height of the Depression, he could not afford to pay the warehouse bill for more than a hundred paintings and drawings he had put in storage. Seeing no other alternative, he went to the vault where the pieces were kept and, in a fit of desperation, destroyed the entire lot. Loath after that to remain in the city, he sold other paintings in his studio for much lower than his customary prices, until he had sufficient funds to book passage for Bermuda. There he remained through the summer, living in a shabby rental house. In the fall he sailed for Nova Scotia, which earlier had been recommended by his friend, Canadian novelist Pierre Coalfleet, as an inexpensive alternative to Gloucester. Visiting first at Lunnenberg, then Blue Rocks, Hartley finally settled at the small offshore island of Eastern Points, where he found room and board with the simple, pious, and dignified Francis Mason family. The Masons had two young adult sons living at home, Alty and Donny, to whom the artist was particularly attracted and they to him. (Hartley and the two brothers were homosexuals, and, by all accounts, the ensuing relationships were both active and sincere.) When Alty, Donny and a third youth, a cousin, drowned in a boating accident September 1936, Hartley was devastated and was again driven to an extended period of anguish and depression.

Responding to the tragedy, Hartley returned to his native Maine in 1937 and commenced a number of symbolic portrait and figure studies, including especially the similar works, both poignantly titled *Fishermen's Last Supper* (private collections), that feature likenesses of Alty, Donny, and other members of the Mason family. He also painted a series of blunt, somber land and seascapes with "north" or "northern" in the title, his personal reference to Nova Scotia. In *Chanties to the North* of 1938-39 the two principal stocky bird forms may be a plaintive allusion to the lost men. Alike bird types appear in another painting of the period, *Give Us This Day* (1938, Fine Arts Work Center, Provincetown, Massachusetts), specifically about which Barbara Haskell has commented: "Hartley uses an allegorical mode to invoke a relgious faith and an acceptance of the natural cycle of which the death of three boys is a part."

Biographers usually mark Hartley's late period as beginning with the aftershock of the drowning incident. Besides the symbolic and northern themes, the artist also painted blocky, powerful studies of the Maine coast, all in a structured expressionist style that again seems reminiscent of Cézanne, though further influenced by the abstract rigidity and primitivism of Georges Rouault, to whose religious pictures Hartley was drawn at this time. In the late '30s Hartley's health and vision began to deteriorate. By 1941 he had almost ceased painting, but turned his attention to writing verse and discourses on his theories about art. He spent the last two years of his life at Corea, Maine, residing with Forest and Katie Young, an elderly couple who were virtually his only close friends at the end. He died of heart failure in a hospital at nearby Ellsworth in 1943, at age sixty-six.

Arshile Gorky (1904-1948)

Arshile Gorky is an important *transitional* figure in the history of American modern art. Barbara Rose has noted that whether he was "the last of the surrealists or the first of the abstract expressionists has not yet been resolved." Then, advancing her own conclusion, "The answer is that he was both . . . Gorky was the first to synthesize abstract painterliness with surrealist motifs." One does indeed see intensely personal fantasies with Gorky's mature work, paintings with almost, but not quite, suggestions of human and animal body parts — fleshy masses, attenuated membranes, viscera, sexual organs. The images seem sensual, yet insidious and tormented. The artist devised a highly individual iconography of symbols and ideas that graphically reveal his often troubled states of mind and circumstance.

Gorky's surrealist roots lie not with the acute focus, realist styles of Salvador Dalí or Yves Tanguy, but rather with the biomorphic, semi-abstract modes of Joan Miró, André Breton, André Masson, and Matta (Roberto Matta Echaurren). Of these, all but Miró had emigrated from Nazi-beleaguered Europe to the United States in the late 1930s and early '40s. Gorky came to know and befriend each. He learned from them the surrealist creative principle of "automatism," the subjugation of conscious thought in order to give a freer flow to subconscious ideas and feelings (a valid and accepted psychoanalytic approach ever since Freud). Impulse, improvisation, and free association are integral to its proper application. The articulate and philosophical Breton urged Gorky to interpret the world as a system of cryptic ideograms, beset by what he called "hybrids," and defined as "the resultants provoked in an observer contemplating a natural spectacle and a flux of childhood and other memories."

Such "hybrid" creatures appear in the Hunter's small (by abstract-expressionist norms) Gorky oil, *In the Garden*, painted between 1938 and '41. One can make out in the figure or figures to the left a leg and a hoof, perhaps the contour of buttocks and shoulder, a profile face that menaces a female figure to the right of center. That second being in turn may be resisting with an outstretched thrust, and seems by the indefinite flutter of legs below to be moving away. Her most distinguishing feature otherwise is a pair of sharply outlined and brightly colored breasts. The breast motif may have held particular significance, if not a fetish, for the artist at this time. In a wonderfully descriptive writing, Gorky recalled a vivid

IN THE GARDEN
Arshile Gorky
1938-1941
oil on canvas
16 x 20 inches
Museum purchase with funds
provided by the Benwood
Foundation and the 1984
Collectors' Group

Provenance

Estate of Arshile Gorky
Harold Diamond, New York, New York
Allan Stone Gallery, New York, New York
London Arts Group, Detroit, Michigan
Philip T. Warren

Exhibitions

Metropolitan Museum and Arts Center,
Miami, FL, Aug.-Nov. 1978.

Publications

Harry Rand, *Arshile Gorky: The Implications of
Symbols,* Montclair: Allanheld & Schram, 1980,
p. 78, illus. p. 80, no. 5-8.

impression from his childhood in Armenia. Not far from his family's house was a lovely natural setting that local people called the Garden of Wish Fulfillment. Within stood a large "blue rock half buried in the black earth, and often I had seen my mother and other village women opening their bosoms and taking their soft and dependent breasts in their hand to rub them on the rock." According to the folklore, the women would thereby know enhanced desirability and fertility. Gorky also proceeded to recollect an enormous poplar in the garden, the "Holy Tree" on which the townspeople would propitiatingly attach strips of their clothing. The word for poplar in Armenian is *sosi*, and despite the change in Gorky's spelling, it is the reference for at least four paintings done between 1941 and '43, all titled *Garden in Sochi*. The "garden" of the museum's painting is almost certainly the same garden. With reasonable probability, therefore, the piece can be identified as a prologue to the notable *Sochi* series.

Early in his career, Gorky progressed through numerous eclecticisms. Meyer Shapiro recounts his development "from what seemed a servile imitation of other painters." "For almost twenty years," Schapiro continues, "he produced obviously derived pictures, versions of Cézanne, Picasso, Léger, Miró, Kandinsky, and others, and suddenly he flowered as an imaginative artist." *In the Garden* is significant to that flowering; it is one of the earliest experiments in the artist's new-found surrealist-abstract style.

Gorky was born Vosdanig Manoog Adoian in 1904 at Khorkom, a Christian community in Turkish Armenia. To avoid conscription into the Turkish army, his father fled with his family into Russian Armenia in 1908. Following the Soviet revolution in 1917, many Armenians, including the Adoians, were dispossessed, and became itinerant refugees. After living in poverty several months, the father and two older children, both daughters, departed for America in 1918. Gorky, his mother, and younger sister remained behind to await the father's establishing himself and eventually sending for them. Meanwhile, looking for better prospects, they moved about constantly. Sadly, the mother died of starvation in March 1919. With the help of family friends, the two orphans made their way to Istanbul, where they stayed about six months, until boat passage money from their father arrived. Gorky, a month short of his fifteenth birthday, and sister arrived at Ellis Island in March 1920.

The Adoians initially settled at Providence, Rhode Island, where Gorky attended Technical High School. Between 1922 and '24 he was in Boston, where first he attended as a student and shortly afterward taught at the New School of Design. He moved to New York City in 1925, the same year he elected to change his name. According to biographer Harry Rand, he took Gorky not, as has often been suggested, because of his admiration for Russian author Maxim Gorky (even though the artist sometimes facetiously maintained he was the writer's cousin), but rather because it was more celebrity in the U.S. at that time to be a Russian exile than a Near-Eastern immigrant. Of greater purpose, the word *gorky* in Russian means "the bitter one." Arshile is a variant of Achilles. Thus, as Rand explains, "his chosen name suggests the 'bitter Achilles' of the *Iliad*, whose wrath kept him from battle until a new wrath impelled him to act."

In 1925 Gorky also enrolled at the Grand Central School of Art, and, repeating the Boston pattern, he taught at the school from later in '25 until 1931. About 1933 he began a friendship with Willem de Kooning; the two shared a studio several years in the late '30s. De Kooning has always spoken magnanimously of his debt to Gorky, though in truth Gorky's appropriation from de Kooning—the gestural, action-painting method—is at least comensurate. Gorky worked with the Public Works of Art Project in 1933 and '34, and the Federal Arts Project from 1935 to '41. Under the second agency he completed the "aviation" murals for Newark Airport in 1936 and the similar "Flight" murals for the Aviation Building at the 1939 New York World's Fair. Both commissions were done in a geometric semi-abstract manner, reminiscent of Stuart Davis, who had also been a close friend since the late '20s. Gorky became an American citizen in 1939. With genuine patriotic commitment, he taught military camouflage at Grand Central School in 1942.

Gorky's years immediately following World War II were marked by a sequence of tragic personal misfortunes. In January 1946 the studio adjacent to a home he had recently purchased in Sherman, Connecticut, burned; with it, twenty-seven paintings were destroyed. Only three weeks later, he was diagnosed as having cancer. Following urgent surgery, the prognosis was favorable; still, his mental state began to deteriorate. His marriage, already pained for some months, grew further troubled. Eventually his wife left, taking as well their two children, whom he adored. To an Armenian man, it was an especially shameful outcome, compounded by the wife's subsequent liaison with his friend and fellow artist, Matta. In February 1946 Gorky's father died. Four months later, the artist was seriously injured in an automobile accident from which he never satisfactorily recovered. Upon his release from the hospital, he found his right arm and hand impaired. Increasingly despondent, Gorky hanged himself in a woodshed near his home in Sherman on July 21, 1948.

Milton Avery (1885-1965)

Milton Avery has been described as a gentle, quiet, unassuming man who disliked publicity, cared little for talking about himself or his work, affiliated with no groups, and championed no issues or causes — save for his painting, to which he was thoroughly committed. His only apparent "act of vanity," as Robert Hughes politely puts it, was subtracting eight years from his actual age so he would not seem "too old" to young art student Sally Michel, whom he had met in 1924, fallen in love with, courted, and married two years later. He perpetuated the erroneous birthdate for the remainder of his life. The deception was uncovered when Whitney Museum curator Barbara Haskell was studying the artist's life in preparation for that institution's monumental 1982 retrospective exhibition.

The Averys had just one child, a daughter whom they named March, born in 1931. She is the subject of both Avery paintings in the Hunter Museum collection. The earlier and more realistic *Young Girl in Blue* (color plate 28) of 1939 was painted when the dark-eyed March would have been between six and seven years old, though she appears slightly younger perhaps. It is a charming and wistful study in subdued tones of predominantly grey, umber, and, of course, blue. *March by the Sea* was painted six years later when Avery's style had evolved to the bold, simplified, geometric compositions that characterize his mature and better known work. Obviously it is of little consequence that the viewer recognize the figure as the artist's daughter.

(color plate 28)
YOUNG GIRL IN BLUE
Milton Avery
1939
oil on canvas
33 x 26 inches
signed lower right
Gift of Mr. and Mrs. Roy R. Neuberger

Provenance
Valentine Gallery, New York, New York
Mr. and Mrs. Roy R. Neuberger, New York, New York.

MARCH BY THE SEA
Milton Avery
1945
oil on canvas
28 x 36⅛ inches
signed and dated lower left
Gift of the Benwood
Foundation

Provenance

Mrs. Sally Avery
Rudolph Galleries, Coral Gables, Florida
Mr. and Mrs. Louis D. Cohen, New York, New
York

Exhibitions

Frances and L. D. Cohen Collection, Norton
Gallery and School of Art, West Palm Beach, FL,
Feb. 23-March 17, 1968.

American Bank and Trust Company, New York,
NY, Nov. 19-Dec. 19, 1969.

Publications

Frances and L.D. Cohen Collection, exhibition
catalogue, West Palm Beach, FL: Norton Gallery and School of Art, 1968, no. 1.

Both works reveal Avery's debt to earlier movements in European expressionism, especially the fauves and Henri Matisse, with whom he is often compared. In a statement that might readily be taken as by Matisse, Avery explained:

> I try to construct a picture in which shapes, spaces, colors form a set of unique relationships, independent of any subject matter. At the same time I try to capture and translate the excitement and emotion aroused in me by the impact with the original idea.

Like Matisse, Avery's work always involves recognizable — though highly abstracted — objects, decorative compositional arrangement, and carefully balanced color. Yet typically his designs are, by comparison, reduced even further. Essential shapes and large fields of flat, delicately modulated tonalities result in what Dore Ashton calls his "grandeur of sparsely designed surfaces."

Avery was born in 1885 in Altmar, New York, where he lived till his early teens, when the family moved to Hartford, Connecticut. He studied intermittently over a period of twenty years at the Connecticut League of Artists and the Art Society of Hartford, at the same time holding jobs variously in business, manufacturing, and construction. In 1925, at age forty, he moved to New York, chiefly to be near his future wife. It was not until then that he pursued his career as an artist full time. Recognition came very slowly. Critics tended to see his work as always out-of-step with the current avant-garde. He was not like the regionalists and social realists of the '30s, even less like the "gesture" abstractionists of the '40s and '50s. He had his first major retrospective show at the Baltimore Museum of Art in 1952. The Whitney Museum presented an updated retrospective in 1960. Avery's last years were marked by failing and debilitating health. He suffered serious heart attacks in 1949 and 1960; from the latter he never fully recovered. He was hospitalized the final nine months of his life and died January 3, 1965. At the memorial service four days later his longtime close friend Mark Rothko spoke in fond tribute:

> There have been several others in our generation who have celebrated the world around them, but none with that inevitability where the poetry penetrated every pore of the canvas to the very last touch of the brush. For Avery was a great poet-inventor who had invented sonorities never seen nor heard before. From these we have learned much and will learn more for a long time to come.

174

Ansel Adams (1902-1984)

MOONRISE, HERNANDEZ,
NEW MEXICO, 1941

Ansel Adams

1941

gelatin silver print
photograph

image: 15 x 19½ inches

signed on mat lower right

Gift of Dr. and Mrs. Bruce E.
Dahrling, II

Provenance

King Dexter, San Francisco, California
Dr. and Mrs. Bruce E. Dahrling, II, Lookout
Mountain, Tennessee.

Ansel Adams' dramatic black-and-white images are related stylistically to what critics and art historians have called "straight" photography. A reaction to commemorative, narrative, illustrational picture taking, "straight" photographs, as a primary aim, impress the viewer with the sheer beauty of form and tone; people, objects, or the scenes photographed become vehicles to that end rather than ends to themselves. As Beaumont Newhall explains:

> They are photographic abstractions, for in them form is abstracted from its illustrative significance. Yet paradoxically the spectator is not for an instant left unaware of what has been photographed. With the shock of recognition he realizes almost at once that the form which delights his eye is significant, and he marvels that such beauty can be discovered in what is commonplace.

Of course Adams often directed his lens to the far-from-commonplace, expecially his well-known studies of Yosemite and other Western American landmarks. But whether the photograph is mountain scenery, a grove of trees, a detail of vegetation or architectural ornament, or a still-life arrangement of utilitarian things, Adams takes the viewer to an enhanced awareness of essential abstract form and the visual relation of forms one to another.

"You don't take a photograph, you make it," Adams insisted. He painstakingly endeavored to visualize the finished photo print while framing the potential image in the ground glass viewfinding plate of the large format camera, making most pertinent decisions—film type, composition, lighting, aperture, time of exposure, focus, depth-of-field—before releasing the shutter. Unlike his friend Edward Weston who, in a comparatively "purist" approach, would then simply develop the film and print the result, Adams had no aversion to experimenting with darkroom procedures: manipulating papers, emulsions, exposures, developing and printing chemicals, to modify the final printed effect. Of particular importance, he devised for black-and-white photography a step-interval system of notation by which the infinite gradation of tones in nature is reduced to ten zones, much as the range of an octave in music is divided by intervals of pitch into the notes of a scale. Zone 0 is black; IX is white. The eight steps in between modulate from dark gray to light gray. Thereby a kind of simplification and order is measured out to an otherwise unrestrained diversity of shades. In considering the luminescence of a subject as it appears on the ground glass of the camera, and again in the darkroom after making the exposure, Adams employed the system to prescribe necessary contrast, and to control the light and dark compositional pattern. In a sense, he would "play" calculated intervals of principal tone, as a pianist might play a harmonic chord.

Analogy to musical effect is not inappropriate. Adams seriously studied piano much of his youth and early adulthood. Patrick Sarver believes that musical training bore unmistakably upon Adams' subsequent development of a photographic style, "for it gave him a sense of discipline and aesthetics and an appreciation for the perfection that only long hours of practice can bring." Adams himself admitted: "I can look at a fine photograph and sometimes I can hear music, not in a sentimental sense, but structurally. I don't try to do it; it just sometimes comes. It's a synesthetic reaction." As for his own preference in classical music, he declared: "I've always liked heroic music. I can't stand Debussy and Ravel. I like Beethoven, Bach, Chopin, Scriabin—anything architectural and big has much more appeal to me." Correspondingly, Adams also found the monumental and grand in nature especially appealing as subject for photography. Thomas F. Barrow continues the musical idiom in speaking of Adams' "Wagnerian visual approach," while noting the photographer's fondness for majestic rock formations, towering storm clouds, and polyphonic woodland grottoes.

Barrow easily could be alluding to the three Adams pieces in the Hunter Museum collection, two of which are illustrated here. *Moonrise, Hernandez, New Mexico*, from 1941, is probably the best-known and most popular of Adams' images. The stark contrast of dark sky, more than half the picture area, punctuated by a near full moon slightly left of center, over streaming bands of white clouds parallel to and against the horizon—all combine as the scene's most compelling effect. (From the same negative, incidentally, Adams has also printed versions in which the sky is lighter, and an earlier time of day suggested.) Snow-covered low mountains in the distance create an alternation of light-and-dark peaked shapes that is similarly repeated in roofs and wall planes of dwellings in the small Hispanic community at mid-depth. Quietude pervades, as the place is devoid of visible human activity. A monolithic adobe church, seen at left from apse end, balances the larger mountains at far right. Though a subjective statement may not have been Adams' intent, the church speaks of the solid faith of people who built the simple structure in that semi-arid land—some of whom are doubtless buried in the cemetery close by. Crosses and grave markers that dot the yard stand conspicuously crisp and white, reflecting late afternoon or setting sun. A highly tactile field of sagebrush in the foreground separates viewer from village and adds to the feeling of remoteness. Much changed today, Hernandez is near the larger town of Española, about twenty-five miles north of Santa Fe.

Three years later Adams made *Mount Williamson, Sierra Nevada, from Manzanar, California*. A field of massive boulders, over which light plays and reveals nuances of texture and tone, leads the eye steadily to an awe-inspiring mountain backdrop. Prodigious clouds array the peaks, while a shaft of sunlight beams diagonally from upper right to near the center of the composition at the horizon line, giving focal effect and a romantic sense of supernatural presence. To achieve the remarkably even progression of rock shapes receding in depth, "I made this photograph from a platform on top of my car," Adams informs. "The camera was pointed slightly down, and the elevated camera position provided a greater overlook of the foreground than would have been possible from ground level."

Adams was born in San Francisco in 1902. Anticipating a career as a professional pianist, at age eighteen he began study with Frederick Zech. But four years earlier his father had taken him on his first visit to Yosemite National Park. He packed along a Kodak Brownie box camera. The experience was the genesis of both his interest in photography and his love of and concern for the natural environment. A member of the Sierra Club all his adult life, and a director of the organization from 1934 to '71, Adams was a strong, often vocal advocate for conservation and preservation of wilderness. Though he made his first serious pictures of Yosemite and High Sierra subjects in 1927, and subsequently published a portfolio, he did

MOUNT WILLIAMSON,
SIERRA NEVADA, FROM
MANZANAR, CALIFORNIA,
1944
Ansel Adams
1944
gelatin silver print
photograph
image: 15⅜ x 18¼ inches
signed on mat lower right
Gift of Dr. and Mrs. Bruce E.
Dahrling, II

Provenance

King Dexter, San Francisco, California
Dr. and Mrs. Bruce E. Dahrling, II, Lookout
Mountain, Tennessee.

not elect photography as a life pursuit until 1930. In that year he met Paul Strand, a "straight" photographer with whose work he was deeply impressed. Though he was unaware of it at first, Adams also renewed and extended the tradition of nineteenth- and early twentieth-century American landscape photographers Timothy H. O'Sullivan, Carleton E. Watkins, William Bell, and William Henry Jackson.

In 1932, Adams joined with Weston, Imogen Cunningham, Willard Van Dyke, and others to found the association of like-minded creative photographers called Group f/64 (so named from the lens aperture that achieves great depth of focus). Alfred Stieglitz gave him his first one-man show three years later at An American Place, in New York City. Especially in the 1930s, but continuing into the '70s, Adams did commercial photography, a fact he never tried to minimize despite considerable negative criticism. Instead, he allowed that it helped him perfect the technical aspects of his craft. In turn, Adams was an effective teacher; he wrote books on aesthetics and techniques of photography, and in workshops at Yosemite or his studio in Carmel, California, he personally taught an estimated 4,500 students. In 1979, the Museum of Modern Art presented a major retrospective: "Ansel Adams and the West." Reviewing the show, *Time* magazine's Robert Hughes observed: ". . . his photographs of lakes, boulders, aspens, and beetling crags have come to look like icons, the cult images of America's vestigial pantheism." After photographing that America for sixty years, Adams died in 1984.

Exactly one year later, April 22, 1985, the Federal Board of Geographic Names officially designated a previously unnamed, 11,750-foot peak in the Sierra Nevada range Mt. Ansel Adams. The steep and craggy mountain rises above the Lyell Fork of the Merced River on the southeastern boundary of Adams' beloved Yosemite Park. Interestingly, so naming the peak was first proposed by a group of environmentalists in 1934 to recognize the photographer's dedicated service to the Sierra Club. Government policy, however, (as it similarly applies to stamps, coins, and currency) prohibits naming geographic features after living people.

Thomas Hart Benton (1889-1975)

Thomas Hart Benton was born in Neosho, Missouri, in 1889. He was the son of a Missouri U.S. Congressman and the grandnephew of a U.S. Senator. It is not surprising that from such a background he would early develop an interest in American politics, history, folklore, and what might be called "common experience" — concerns that invest all of his best-known paintings and that have identified him with the regionalist movement. Benton, however, did not care to be known as a regional painter, because he felt his work transcended the values of any one locale and that Americans, no matter what area of the country they inhabited, could relate to his message. Nonetheless, Benton's characteristic imagery is decidedly rural and midwestern. *The Wreck of the Ole '97* (color plate 29), for example, appears set in the gently rolling pastures and cornfields of the prairie heartland. Yet the theme was inspired by events that happened in the far distant and different terrain of Virginia. In 1893 a Southern Railway train, running out of control down a steep grade on the line between Lynchburg and Danville, jumped track, causing a spectacular accident in which thirteen people died. Romanticized accounts of the disaster soon came to be heard in the Blue Ridge high country, propounding the intense contest between man and powerful machine. Some variations suggested that the engineer, angered or bereft of love, deliberately sped to his death. At first the stories were continued by oral tradition. Then innumerable unknown authors reduced the narrative to verses for ballads that were sung to standard folk melodies. One of these lyrics, adapted to the tune of "The Ship that Never Returned" and now titled *The Wreck of the Old Ninety-Seven*, was recorded in 1923 by a nasal-voiced Virginia folksinger named Henry Witter, and again the following year by Vernon Dalhart, one of the most popular country recording stars of the period. That Benton drew upon this story is quite evident, but clearly he transported it to the territory he knew best.

The placement of objects and figures in Benton's scene is carefully composed so as to augment the sense of drama in the impending catastrophe. The system of diagonals on which the design is built leads the eye toward the center, emphasizing the instant of derailment and the potential danger for the approaching wagon and its riders. The long attenuated shapes of the cornstalks, clouds, and smoke add an eerie animation. As an optical rather than actual weight, the smoke moreover presses down ominously against the startled horse and driver.

Benton's earliest formal art instruction was at age eighteen at the Corcoran Gallery School in Washington, D.C. Later that same year, 1907, he also attended the School of the Art Institute of Chicago, but he disliked the heavy regimentation then of drawing from plaster casts. The next year he left for Paris to study at the Académie Julian. He remained there three years, all the while growing increasingly aware of postimpressionism, cubism, and other European contemporary art movements. His own work of this period followed in several of the prevailing modern tendencies. Unfortunately most of his early paintings were destroyed in a fire at his Neosho home in 1917.

In 1918 Benton was working as a draftsman at the Norfolk Naval Base. At about this time he rejected European and other modern influences, returning to realism and a more narrative style. Modernist principles hereafter would be applied only to the extent of his pictorial composition and to his expressive ends through purposeful distortion of form.

Benton settled in New York in 1923 to teach at the Art Students League. In 1935 he returned to his native Missouri to teach and direct the Kansas City Art Institute. He continued to reside in Kansas City until his death in 1975 at age eighty-five. Today Benton is probably best remembered for his important large mural commissions at the New School for Social Research in New York (1930), the Missouri State Capitol in Jefferson City (1936), the Harry S. Truman Library in Independence, Missouri (1959-62), and the Country Music Hall of Fame and Museum in Nashville (1974-75).

(color plate 29)

THE WRECK OF THE OLE '97

Thomas Hart Benton

1943

egg tempera on gessoed masonite

28½ x 44½ inches (sight)

signed and dated lower left

Gift of the Benwood Foundation

Provenance

Kennedy Galleries, Inc., New York, New York

Mr. and Mrs. Norman Goodman, Great Neck, New York

Mr. and Mrs. Louis D. Cohen, New York, New York

Exhibitions

Graham Gallery, New York, NY, Oct. 1968.

American Bank and Trust Company, New York, NY, Nov. 19-Dec. 19, 1969, no. 2.

Publications

Kansas Quarterly, Spring, 1969, p. 124.

Matthew Baigell, *Thomas Hart Benton,* New York: Harry N. Abrams, Inc., 1975, illus. p. 138, no. 100.

Diana W. Suarez, *Bluff and the Magic Mansion, A Children's Guide to the Hunter Museum of Art,* Chattanooga: Hunter Museum of Art, 1980.

Jacob Lawrence (b. 1917)

In the highly segregated American society of the 1940s, Jacob Lawrence was the first contemporary black artist to realize widespread critical acceptance in the white-dominated art world. This may be, in part, because his work addresses the longing of peoples everywhere to achieve dignity and better their condition. At the same time, as Milton W. Brown suggests: "He was the first wholly authentic voice of the black experience in the plastic arts. From the beginning his art was not only about blacks, but represented them honestly without idealization, sentimentality, or caricature." With the motivation of a social realist, Lawrence has depicted the situation of American blacks from the earliest time of their removal from Africa, through the period of slavery, to the struggles in the twentieth-century urban ghetto. Accordingly, he has often produced narrative works for particular series, as for example: *Great Figures in Black History, Migration of the Negro, Life in Harlem*, and the *Builders* (that is, working-class people at menial jobs).

Yet Lawrence is no mere illustrator. "I rely on composition," he wrote in 1960, "which to me is the essence of creative painting." Continuing in the pioneer modernist tradition of such artists as Arthur G. Dove, Marsden Hartley, John Marin, Ben Shahn, and Charles Burchfield, he works in a style that fuses realism with abstract design. His art is characterized by vivid color — typically the unmodeled primaries of red, yellow, and blue; stong, flat pattern; simplified shapes in what often appear as cut out figures; and the frequent use of masks or mask-like faces. His pictures express feeling with the intensity of primitive or folk art.

The Hunter Museum's decorative gouache, *The Apartment*, (color plate 30) is from the *Harlem* series, done in 1943. A solitary black woman stands near the middle of a furnished room. She is enigmatic, in that her face is turned completely away from the viewer toward the mirror on the back wall. (It may appear at first glance that the face is in profile silhouette, but close examination reveals the back of the head.) The accoutrements of the scene suggest that the "apartment" is essentially this room only; it is a combined sitting, dining, and sleeping space. A few bright, even gaudy appointments cheer an otherwise drab interior, and one senses that these objects — especially the big brass bed that inclines gently toward the figure — are the subject's treasured possessions. Perspective is dislocated in favor of patterned design, with the result that the articles seem suspended in a surreal or dreamlike vision. Especially conspicuous large swirls in the hanging at upper right give the impression of eyes, and perhaps even nose and mouth — strange company for a person all alone.

Lawrence was born in Atlantic City, New Jersey, in 1917. He spent his early childhood years in Easton, Pennsylvania, where his father was a coal miner. When he was thirteen, his family moved to New York City's Harlem. He attended the Utopia Children's House for two years and then took his first art instruction at the Harlem Workshop under the noted black artist Charles Alston. In 1937 he won a scholarship to the American Artists School, which he attended for two years. He taught at Black Mountain College in 1946, the Pratt Institute from 1956 to '71, and the Art Students League simultaneously from 1967 to '69. Since 1971 he has lived in Seattle, where he has been professor of art at the University of Washington. He is a member of the Artists Equity Association, and was its president in 1957. He was elected a member of the National Institute of Arts and Letters in 1965, and in 1971 was named an associate member of the National Academy of Design, and raised to full academician in 1977. He is also a member of the Black Academy of Arts and Letters. In 1970 the National Association for the Advancement of Colored People awarded Lawrence its coveted Spingarn Medal; he was the first artist to be so honored.

(color plate 30)
THE APARTMENT
Jacob Lawrence
1943
gouache on paper
21¼ x 29¼ inches
signed and dated bottom, right of center

Provenance
Downtown Gallery
Mother of Dorothy Dodge
Dorothy Dodge
Daphne Dodge (Hunter)
Terry Dintenfass, Inc.,
New York, New York

Publications
William T. Henning, Jr., *Recent Acquisitions*, Chattanooga: Hunter Museum of Art, 1982
Avis Berman, "Jacob Lawrence and the Making of Americans." *ARTnews*, February, 1984, pp. 78-86, Illus. p. 81

Charles E. Burchfield (1893-1967)

DECEMBER SUN
Charles E. Burchfield
1940
watercolor on paper
36 x 53 inches
signed with monogram and
dated lower left
Gift of the Benwood
Foundation

Provenance

John Clancy, New York, New York
Rehn Gallery, New York, New York
William Zierler Gallery, New York, New York
Mr. and Mrs. Richard M. Cohen, Great Neck,
New York
Mr. and Mrs. Louis D. Cohen, New York, New
York

Exhibitions

*The Nature of Charles Burchfield: A Memorial
Exhibition,* Munson-Williams-Proctor Institute
Museum of Art, Utica, N.Y., April 9,-May 31,
1970.

*The Four Seasons, American Landscape Paint-
ings,* Columbus Museum of Arts and Sciences,
Columbus, GA, March 17-May 20, 1984.

Publications

Joseph S. Trovato, *Charles Burchfield,
Catalogue of Paintings in Public and Private Col-
lections,* Utica, NY: Munson-Williams-Proctor
Institute Museum of Art, 1970, p. 190, no. 940.

Anne Russell King, *The Four Seasons, American
Landscape Paintings,* exhibition catalogue,
Columbus, GA: Columbus Museum of Arts
and Sciences, 1984, illus. p. 21, p. 28.

Charles E. Burchfield was one of the most imaginative and creative artists of his generation. Yet he developed almost totally isolated from the main currents of twentieth century European and American art. He was in many ways a solitary genius who evolved an idiosyncratic style that verged on tendencies as diverse as realism, surrealism, romanticism, expressionism, and abstraction. His work submits to no one of these inclinations exclusively, but is instead a composite, the stronger for its hybrid vigor.

More than anything, Burchfield was a visionary who saw all things in nature as possessing a dynamic character approaching personification. As he explained in a 1961 essay:

> An artist must paint not what he sees in Nature, but what is there. To do so he must invent symbols, which, if properly used, make his work seem even more real than what is in front of him.

It is curious to note the capitalization above of the N in nature. For Burchfield, nature was indeed a proper noun, something (or more accurately an infinite assortment of things) imbued with personality and intelligence. In his painting, therefore, he sought to evoke the vital presence of what he beheld. To this rather animistic end he devised decorative and purposefully exaggerated images to convey his highly subjective interpretations. Thus he effectively generated a sense of living force in his depictions of wind, clouds, rain, temperatures, sounds, times-of-day, seasonal change — not to mention the more obvious and often anthropomorphic flora and fauna.

To achieve his special effects, Burchfield employed a variety of technical devices. Agitated brushwork might suggest a form pulsating or impelled to motion; rapid repetition of a contour line seen beyond the object illustrated could imply vibration or sonorous waves; in some pictures a fuzzy yellowish band of light surrounds a form as though the configuration were emitting electrical radiation. Burchfield's preferred medium was watercolor, but he often built up his paint so heavily that it takes on the visual density of oil. Frequently, too, he would join pieces of paper together, in some cases simply to provide a larger surface and in others to combine image components from different projects into a single new concept. His execution was vigorous; one can sense the intensity with which he must have worked.

(color plate 31)

GATEWAY TO SEPTEMBER
Charles E. Burchfield
1946-1956
watercolor on paper
signed with monogram center
left and lower left
Gift of the Benwood
Foundation

(Continued on page 181)

Burchfield's career can be divided into three main phases: an early period, roughly 1915-1918, in which he painted nostalgic fantasies from his childhood; a middle period, about 1918-1943, his most "regionalist" work, in which he recorded the dreariness and seclusion of certain small towns in the American midwest and northeast; a final period, roughly 1943 until his death in 1967, for which he returned to fanciful and rhapsodic response to nature, but usually with a brighter palette and more romantic approach than before.

The Hunter Museum has in its collection five very fine Burchfield watercolors, three of which are illustrated in this catalogue. *December Sun* of 1940 is typical of the main body of work from the middle period. A lonely, isolated town, peopleless and austere, stands mute and somber just beyond a field of growth recently suspended by the change of season. In marked contrast is *Gateway to September* (color plate 31), which was begun six years later, well into the third period. According to the artist, the scene was inspired by an experience at a spot ten miles south of Hamburg, New York. The foliage and insect forms put forth an almost menacing presence, as if an ancient shaman or wizard called upon the assorted spirits residing within. Most viewers see a grotesque face in the dominant tree shape to the right as the trunk hollow becomes an open mouth and the wings of the oversized moth suggest eyes. At left center an irregular portal, ringed by a yellow electric charge, presents a perhaps dangerous route of escape to the more tranquil place in the distance. *Pioneer Evening* is from late in the artist's life. It was begun in 1961 and completed in 1966, the year before his death. The large crackling campfire in the foreground is psychologically disturbing, in part because the people who built it also deserted it. It casts warm yet ghostly light on the objects it strikes. And as small reddish particles lift above the blaze, a strong simile

(Continued from page 180)

Provenance

Frank Rehn Gallery, New York, New York
Mr. and Mrs. George J. Perutz, Dallas, Texas
Mr. and Mrs. Louis D. Cohen, New York, New York

Exhibitions

Charles Burchfield, Recent Paintings, Upton Hall Gallery, State University College at Buffalo, Buffalo, NY, April 24-May 19, 1963.

The Nature of Charles Burchfield: A Memorial Exhibition, Munson-Williams-Proctor Institute Museum of Art, Utica, NY, April 9-May 31, 1970.

Publications

Charles Burchfield, Recent Paintings/Early Watercolors, exhibition catalogue, Buffalo, NY: Albright-Knox Art Gallery, 1963, no. 15.

Joseph S. Travoto, *Charles Burchfield, Catalogue of Paintings in Public and Private Collections,* Utica, NY: Munson-Williams-Proctor Institute, 1970, p. 264, illus. p. 265, no. 1142.

PIONEER EVENING
Charles E. Burchfield
1961-1966
watercolor on paper
49 x 55 inches
signed with monogram and dated lower left
Gift of the Benwood Foundation

Provenance

Mr. and Mrs. John Clancy, New York, New York
Frank K.M. Rehn Gallery, New York, New York
Mr. and Mrs. Norman Goodman, Great Neck, New York
Mr. and Mrs. Louis D.Cohen, New York, New York

Exhibitions

Charles Burchfield, Frank Rehn Gallery, New York, NY, Oct. 3-29, 1966.

Dedication, The Charles Burchfield Center, Buffalo State University College, Buffalo, NY, Dec. 3, 1966-Jan. 29, 1967.

The Nature of Charles Burchfield: A Memorial Exhibition, Munson-Williams-Proctor Institute Art Museum, Utica, NY, April 19-May 31, 1970.

Publications

Joseph S. Trovato, *Charles Burchfield, Catalogue of Paintings in Public and Private Collections,* Utica, NY: Munson-Williams-Proctor Institute Museum of Art, 1970, p. 314, no. 1330.

comes to mind from the Old Testament Book of Job: "Yet man is born into trouble as the sparks fly upward." Though not actually aflame, the trees at mid ground symbolically represent, by the shape of their upward lifting branches, the ongoing spirit of the fire. Overhead the sky is alive with phantom creatures, undulating bird-like clouds in the upper left, the stark profiles of some sort of primordial beings that surround the mysteriously encircled moon.

Burchfield was born in Astabula Harbor, Ohio, in 1893. After the death of his father in 1898, the family moved to nearby Salem, Ohio, where he attended elementary and secondary schools, and where he very early showed a flair for drawing. But as a youth he was desperately shy and went through long periods of gloom and loneliness. At such times he found solace in exploring nature. After working in a metal fabricating plant for a year, he had earned enough money to enroll in 1912 at the Cleveland School of Art, where he studied mainly with Henry Keller. In 1916 he received a scholarship to the National Academy of Design, but he was unhappy there and stayed in New York only two months. Returning to Salem, he produced his first significant watercolors. He served in the U.S. Army between July 1918 and January 1919, after which he went to Salem. In 1921 he took a position as a wallpaper designer with the firm of N. H. Birge and Sons in Buffalo, New York. All the while he was actively painting. He remained with Birge until 1929 when the prominent New York dealer Frank Rehn agreed to represent him. From that point on he devoted full time to his art.

Burchfield married Bertha L. Kenreich in 1922. They subsequently had five children. In 1925 the family moved to the Buffalo suburb of Gardenville, where they lived until the artist's death. He was elected to the National Institute of Arts and Letters in 1943. In the 1950s, mostly during the summers, he taught at the University of Minnesota, Art Institute of Buffalo, University of Buffalo, and Ohio University.

The Modern Era: Post World War II Decades

Even for astute, well-informed observers, following the progress of American art since World War II can be confounding. "Isms," movements, counter-movements, variations, vogues, and fads seem to come and go with increasing rapidity. Art historian Marshall B. Davidson notes: "Developments and changes that were formerly wrought over several decades, at least, now take place in a matter of seasons, and what the mass media hail as the latest trend one week, may be obsolete the next." Indeed, the mass media—along with the nationwide growth of sophisticated art communities and the evolution of modern-leaning college and university art departments—are in great measure responsible for the swift spread of ideas and experiences. But as later-twentieth-century people have come to "consume" information, entertainment, and fashions (not to mention goods and natural resources) at an accelerated pace, so do styles satiate and quickly pall. Creative persons are continually challenged to explore and experiment.

Ironically, for all of humankind's cultural sharing—in the physical sciences, behavioral sciences, education, as well as the arts and humanities—the troublesome fact remains that, on a global scale, social, political, economic, and environmental problems evade solution. The post-war decades have seen enormous upheaval and collective apprehension, distress that is reflected in much American art. "It was primarily as a result of the cataclysmic events surrounding World War II," Davidson continues, "that artists began to revise their fundamental precepts and devise new approaches to their work that would express the distortion and anarchism of the age." Similarly, John Wilmerding reflects: "The explosion of the atomic bomb in 1945 marked a turning point in modern history; for the first time the human race possessed the ability to destroy itself totally. Man's affairs seemed to assume a heroic and tragic scale. Not surprisingly, so did the art of the period." And in a kind of apologia for abstract expressionism (a term first coined by critic Clement Greenberg), the dominant modern movement of the late '40s and '50s, former Metropolitan Museum of Art curator Robert Beverly Hale declares:

> If our art seems violent, it is because we have perpetrated more violence than any other generation. If it deals with weird dreams, it is because we have opened the caverns of the mind and let such phantoms loose. If it is filled with broken shapes, it is because we have watched the order of our fathers break and fall to pieces at our feet. We have seen in our century the development of fantastic scientific paraphernalia — and much ill will. We live in fear of some monstrous event which will bring, at best, a curious and distorted future; at worst, annihilation. The artist is in part a prophet. We should not complain if the shadows that have lately haunted us have for some time been visible upon his canvas.

Audacious, raw, impulsive, certainly anti-realistic—abstract expressionism enabled American art, as University of Illinois professor Robert M. Sokol explains, "to shuck its affected provinciality and its feelings of inferiority to contemporary European movements." While post-war European societies rebuilt and re-ordered, America (where the homeland was not physically hurt in the conflict) rode abstract expressionism to leadership on the international art scene. To be honest, however, the American avant-garde had been infused with the creative energy of those European moderns who emigrated to escape totalitarianism, a long list that includes: Josef Albers, André Breton, Marcel Duchamp, Max Ernst, Arshile Gorky, Hans Hofmann, Fernand Léger, Laszlo Moholy-Nagy, Piet Mondrian, and Yves Tanguy. "The fact that good European moderns are now here is very important," stated pioneer abstract expressionist Jackson Pollock in 1944, "for they bring with them an understanding of the problems of modern painting. I am particularly impressed with their concept of art being the Unconscious."

Greatly influenced by the "automatism" of surrealism, the abstract expressionists—Hofmann, Pollock, as well as Willem de Kooning, Franz Kline, Robert Motherwell, Sam Francis, sculptors Ibram Lassaw, David Hare, David Smith, and many others—emphasized the spontaneous *action* of creating (hence critic Harold Rosenberg's alternate designation: "action painting"). Much as a dancer may interpret the essentially abstract sound of music with equally abstract body movement, an abstract expressionist employs "pure," non-objective (with few exceptions) visual arrangements of color, line, shape, and texture to represent only his or her sense of design, the actual process of composition and fabrication, and subjective feelings at the time of producing a given piece.

By the late 1950s, a younger group of modern artists—believing abstract expressionism had sufficiently made its statement and that, in any case, its original vigor was long spent—sought new directions that were deliberately anti-expressionist. A small number, including Robert Rauschenberg and Jasper Johns, explored collage, found-object sculpture or assemblage, and neo-dada inventions. "And it was at this precise moment," Calvin Tomkins points out, "by one of those historical quirks that seem inevitable, that Marcel Duchamp re-emerged from the shadows of the New York art scene." The seventy-two-year-old dada master—whom de Kooning called "a one-man art movement"—was living in Manhattan in 1959, when French critic Robert Lebel published, in Paris, a book on Duchamp's career. It was read enthusiastically on both sides of the Atlantic, and Duchamp was "re-discovered." His work figured prominently in an influential Museum of Modern Art exhibit in 1961. Significantly, the show focused attention on the use of junk and found materials, and demonstrated the aesthetic possibilities of "things" one would ordinarily think of as non-art.

A second wave of reaction in the '60s, led by Andy Warhol, Roy Lichtenstein, Richard Lindner, and others, propounded a counter to abstract expressionism in images of popular culture—comic strips, advertising, package design, mass-produced utilitarian objects. Sometimes humorous, other times irreverent or downright grim, pop art, as it was called, addressed the chief preoccupations of a ravenously consuming American society—food, sex, and the automobile.

Meanwhile, a third group of reactionary artists faulted abstract expressionism for excessive emotional outpouring and undisciplined technique. The solution was a total about-face; they expunged their work of any evidence of materials manipulation (in painting: bravura brushwork, deliberate spattering, dripping for semi-accidental effect; in sculpture: obvious direct modeling, carving, assembling, typically resulting in strong textural contrasts) in favor of a smooth, ethereal—some would say dehumanized, or mechanized—reductive abstract object that is sublimely anti-expressionist. The same Clement Greenberg in 1961 bestowed the umbrella title "post-painterly abstraction," though the several variations, or sub-headings, are probably better known: "minimalism," "hard edge," "op," and "color field." Such earlier, less "gestural" abstract expressionists as Clyfford Still and Mark Rothko can be seen as stylistic progenitors for the post-painterly Barnett Newman, Ellsworth Kelly, Frank Stella, Gene Davis, Kenneth Noland, Jules Olitski, and Helen Frankenthaler, among many, as well as sculptors Larry Bell, Donald Judd, Robert Morris, Tony Smith, and others.

Little wonder that Tomkins would call the 1960s "a visual Tower of Babel." But it was no less so in the '70s. Again the emerging avant-garde pulled in opposite directions. Some artists, appalled by what they saw as unwarranted influence of art dealers—what Tomkins calls the "commercially tainted existence of art," and Sokol refers to as the "profiteering of collectors"—set out to devise works that were uncollectible, or, at least, not so readily suited to commercial exploitation. The result, which certain critics have labeled "post-studio" art, was either a de-emphasis of the physical object (as in the case of "conceptual art," performance art, self-destructive art, or forms involving transitory materials such as smoke, light beams, reflections, etc.) or enlargement of the physical object to scale much beyond what can be adequately displayed in parlor or museum (environmental art, earthworks). Sol LeWitt and Lawrence Weiner are among the better-known conceptual artists; Christo and Robert Smithson have created enormous outdoor "enhancements" of buildings or landscape settings.

At virtually the same time, remarkably, painters Richard Estes, Ralph Goings, Robert Bechtle, Philip Pearlstein, Chuck Close, Robert Cottingham, and numerous others, along with sculptors Duane Hanson and John D'Andrea, advanced the antithesis of non-art art—a revival of realism, identified variously as new realism, photo-realism, super-realism. These artists present images in acute focus and detail, "out-camera-ing" the camera, far out-doing the wax-museum figure. Some of the group have revived pop art's tongue-in-cheek look at glitzy commercialism—gaudy storefronts, packages, automobiles. Some borrow the advertising artists' technique of using projectors to throw a photographic image to paper or canvas, where it can be meticulously traced. All seem to view their worlds with cool, detached, un-romantic eyes. Moreover, one is struck by these artists' keen sensitivity to shape, pattern and design; at the most trompe-l'oeil illusionistic, the pieces can be astonishingly abstract.

Though trends of the '70s persist, the decade of the '80s, to this writing, has been marked by one conspicuous new development. Julian Schnabel, David Salle, Gary Stephan, Jean Michel Basquait, and Mike Glier are among a wave of younger artists who propound a harsh new kind of expressionism. (The trend is, in fact, being called neo-expressionism.) Much of the work may strike the spectator as warmed-over '60s-period Rauschenberg or de Kooning. Some of it seems a glorification of that anti-social, anti-establishment visual shout from the ghetto or bario—graffiti. Characteristically, the work is scruffy and crude, with brutal, slashing paint gestures and grotesque distortions of form, as though deliberately intended to challenge conventional felicity and refined taste. And it does. Much of the production, as Sam Hunter interprets, is an "apocalyptic art," revealing "profound anxiety," "a sense of social malaise," or, more objectively, "desolate vistas of a post-atomic universe." It is, in short, a disturbing, pessimistic vision of the world and its future. Curiously, certain abstract-expressionist impulses are being restated.

While abstract expressionism dominated contemporary American painting and sculpture in the late '40s and '50s, the prevailing modern architectural mode was its aesthetic contradiction: the orderly, strict-modular, sheer, rectangular design systems of the International Style. Introduced before the War by German émigrés Walter Gropius and Ludwig Meis van der Rohe, the style remained pre-eminent for business and large office structures through and beyond the time of the two men's death in 1967. Variations are built to the present day. But, as in the fine arts, reaction set in by the 1960s. Such inventive architect-designers as Louis I. Kahn, Eero Saarinen, and I. M. Pei led, as Frederick Koeper describes, "a major shift in contemporary architecture toward geometrical order and the celebration of the wall after many decades of ascendancy of the metal skeleton." Indeed, walls once again become massive elements to contrast surfaces of glass, and, particularly in reinforced concrete structures, curved planes and continuous "skins" or "shells" are part of the architect's more recent technical vocabulary. Some forms of architectural expression in the '80s—the work of Robert Venturi, Richard Meier, and Michael Graves, for example—are highly sculptural and decorative, with artfully integrated ornament, albeit of stylized or abstract design. A signal comparison of nomenclature for certain concurrent movements in painting and sculpture, much architecture of the '70s and '80s is critically identified as "post-modern."

George L. K. Morris (1905-1975)

George L. K. Morris was one of a small number of American artists* who worked extensively in the cubist idiom, a style that evolved in France during the early twentieth century with such artists as Pablo Picasso, Georges Braque, and Juan Gris. In its time, cubism was a revolutionary way of interpreting the visual world, an invention of pictorial design that had grown in part out of Paul Cézanne's deduction in the late nineteenth century that all forms, even natural configurations, can be characterized by an inherent geometry. The cubists took this premise a step further, imaginatively reordering the perceived geometric elements into novel combinations and contexts. But in many ways the approach was more intellectual than perceptual. For example, the cubists' typical use of multiple, overlapping or interpenetrating images of the same object in a single composition was intended to express the "idea" or the manifold physical and subjective aspects of the object — rather than one static, topographical view.

Thus in *Arizona Altar* (color plate 32) the fractured ceremonial mask-form at the upper center seems to look simultaneously — and warily — front, left, and right. And it is attached to a fragmented body that again appears both frontal and profile. The image, probably based on the Southwest Indians' Kachina doll, becomes mystically disembodied in the process. Or perhaps it can be read as dismembered by the cross of Christianity, both by the small motifs at the center and top of the canvas and by the strong diagonals that cross through and behind the doll figure. Linear baroque curves, candelabra, and parted curtain play above and contrast the angular center, implying once more that an older spiritual method has been subjugated to an intervening faith.

Morris was born in New York City in 1905. After graduating from Yale University in 1928, he attended the Art Students League for one year, then went to Paris, where he studied with the cubists Fernand Leger and Amadee Ozenfant. At that time he also visited the homes and studios of the other major cubist painters. Back in New York in 1930, he established his own studio and in the same year founded and edited *The Miscellany*, a bi-monthly cultural publication. His writing achievements are, in fact, noteworthy. In college he was editor of the *Yale Literary Magazine*, and from 1933 through '36 he edited the *Bulletin* of the Museum of Modern Art. In 1936 Morris was a co-founder of American Abstract Artists, an association established for the promotion and exhibition of members' work; he served as the group's president from 1948 to '50. He had numerous one-man shows before his death in 1975, and his paintings are now in many important institutional collections.

Morris holds a significant place in the history of modernism in the country. He developed the cubist aesthetic further than most other American artists of his generation, while successfully incorporating images of American life and lore into his abstract pictorial concept.

*The most notable others were Max Weber, Joseph Stella, Lionel Feininger, Stuart Davis, and the "Orphists" Morgan Russell and Stanton MacDonald-Wright.

(color plate 32)

ARIZONA ALTAR
George L. K. Morris
1949
oil and pencil on unprimed cotton
53 x 40½ inches
signed lower right
Gift of Ruth S. Holmberg

Provenance

From the collection of the artist through Hirschl & Adler Galleries, Inc., New York, New York

Exhibitions

George L. K. Morris, A Retrospective Exhibition of Paintings and Sculpture, 1930-1964, Corcoran Gallery of Art, Washington, D.C., May 1-30, 1965.

George L. K. Morris Retrospective, Montclair Art Museum, Montclair, N.J., Feb. 7-March 21, 1971.

George L. K. Morris, A Retrospective Exhibition, Hirschl & Adler Galleries, Inc., New York, NY, Oct. 5-30, 1971.

George L. K. Morris, A Retrospective Exhibition, organized by Hirschl & Adler Galleries, Inc., New York, NY, circulating exhibition: Hunter Museum of Art, Chattanooga, TN; Gibbes Art Gallery, Charleston, SC; Arkansas Arts Center, Little Rock, AR; Museum of Arts and Sciences, Daytona Beach, FL; Tennessee Botanical Gardens and Fine Arts Center, Cheekwood, Nashville, TN; Oct., 1972-May, 1973.

Visitors to Arizona: 1846 to the Present, Phoenix Art Museum, Phoenix, AZ, Sept. 6-Oct. 12, 1980; Tucson Museum of Art, Tucson, AZ; Oct. 15-Nov. 30, 1980.

Publications

George L. K. Morris, A Retrospective Exhibition of Paintings and Sculpture, 1930-1964, exhibition catalogue, Washington, D.C.: Corcoran Gallery of Art, 1965, p. 19, no. 34.

James K. Ballinger and Andrea D. Rubinstein, *Visitors to Arizona, 1846 to the Present*, exhibition catalogue, Phoenix: Phoenix Art Museum, 1980, p. 166, no. 97.

Patricia Janis Broder, *The American West, The Modern Vision*, Boston: Little, Brown & Co., 1984, illus. p. 125, p. 127.

Leonard Baskin (b. 1922)

MAN OF PEACE
Leonard Baskin
1952
woodcut on paper
image: 59½ x 30¾ inches
signed lower right
Museum purchase with funds supplied in part by the National Endowment for the Arts, a Federal agency

---

Provenance
Levine and Levine Graphics, New York, New York

Exhibitions
Contemporary Prints from the Collection of the Hunter Museum of Art, Dulin Gallery of Art, Knoxville, TN, Jan. 2-8, 1981.

The successful sculptor, painter, and printmaker Leonard Baskin has been fittingly called a *romantic humanist*. The great majority of his works, regardless of medium, feature a lone male figure who is partly the artist's own alter ego and partly a universal human type or "Everyman," much in the sense of that woeful hero from the medieval morality play bearing the same title. This persona, in whatever guise or character role, variously encounters the ultimate issues that confound his—and by extension, humankind's—very existence: aspiration, apprehension, corruption and inhumanity, physical and emotional suffering, fear of life continuing, fear of dying, the question of immortality. Yet even though Baskin's man may seem brooding and tormented, one senses in him also irrepressible dignity, grace, and inner strength. The *Man of Peace* is just such a person, what Baskin describes as "anxiety-ridden man, imprisoned in his ungainly self." Restrained by barbed wire and holding up to view a dead fowl that is perhaps symbolic of lost livelihood or earthly possessions, he is nonetheless firmly anchored, as the planting of his muscular legs suggests, and as his eyes engage the viewer, resolute in serene pride.

For the tenor of his imagery Baskin acknowledges the influence of German Expressionism and particularly the work of Ernst Barlach and Käthe Kollwitz. Technically he is indebted to Japanese calligraphy and printmaking art. The woodcut technique employed for *Man of Peace* is remarkable for its potential size. Baskin has commented: "Of all the graphic media, the woodcut alone holds the possibility of images conceived and realized in monumental scale. Only in the woodcut can vast areas of black be rich and splendid. No matter how wide the span, the black remains pure and terrible."

Baskin was born in New Brunswick, New Jersey, in 1922. His father, a rabbi, moved the family to Brooklyn when he was seven. He studied at New York University, Yale University, and the New School for Social Research, from which he received a B.A. degree in 1949. He also studied in Paris and Florence. Since 1953 he has taught at Smith College in Northampton, Massachusetts.

George Cress (b. 1921)

BROKEN LIGHT
George A. Cress
1953
oil on canvas
36 x 18¼ inches
signed lower right
Museum purchase

Provenance
From the collection of the artist.

Though George Cress has periodically applied his vigorous semi-abstract style to still life and interior views, by far the greater body of his work is landscape—especially that inspired by the Appalachian region, with its characteristic terrain and nuances of color, light, and mood. Obviously he is interested not in a veristic recording of every rock, tree, or cloud, but rather in the essences of a scene, perceived both as intuitive or felt response and as dynamic structural design.

One senses order and architectonics in Cress' work, though his manner is neither tightly rendered, hard-edge, nor geometric. One senses impulse and spirited regard for subject, though his technique is neither highly gestural nor dependent upon the action painters' semi-accidental effects through flow, drip, or spatter. Cress' style might best be described as *lyric* abstraction. His approach is subjective; he is interested in the poetry— the visual appeal of shapes and their relationships one to another, in the sensuous resonances of tone and hue, and in agreeable color harmonies. Controlled yet nimbly brushed areas build into a play of angles and planes, of thrust and counterthrust. In its striking balance between representation and abstraction, formalism and expressionism, intellection and emotion, Cress' style proceeds from such important early to mid-twentieth-century American moderns as John Marin, Lionel Feininger, Loren MacIver, and Jimmy Ernst.

The Hunter Museum's Cress oil from 1953, *Broken Light*, by its very title suggests the artist's deliberate "fracturing" of the image à la cubism, in the interest of visual invention, pattern, and design. "The work of many landscape painters looks as if it had been laboriously traced on a pane of glass set between the artist and scene," writes Alexander Eliot as a lead into a statement about John Marin. If in the ensuing comment "Cress" were substituted for "Marin," the observation would be just as valid. Hence: "*Cress* broke the glass and let daylight and fresh air flood in." In *Broken Light*, the view is set in depth by a series of flat, angular, superimposed and overlapping planes. Strong vertical stylized tree trunks to the left and right foreground frame a cluster of trees at middle distance. The trunks and limbs, in turn, operate as a kind of lattice on which swatches of color have been hung, and the composition thereby assembled. The colors themselves are mainly muted earth tones, punctuated by a few brighter accents in warm yellows and burnt oranges. Some of the shapes are picked out by brisk outlining—lines that follow more the rhythm of the composition than corporeal landscape contours. Nature's forms and colors are translated into a dynamic interaction of visual elements on two-dimensional painted surface.

Cress was born in Anniston, Alabama, in 1921. He attended Emory University from 1938 to '39, then went on to complete a B.F.A. in 1942 and an M.F.A. in 1949 from the University of Georgia, where he studied with Carl Holty, Jean Charlot, and the particularly influential Lamar Dodd. Rick Stewart, Curator of American Art at the Dallas Museum of Fine Arts, identifies Cress as "a member of the first generation of artists to rise to prominence within the Southern art educational system." Stewart was writing in the exhibition catalogue for *Painting in the South*, an important historical and contemporary survey—organized and circulated by the Virginia Museum in 1984—in which a Cress work was selected for showing. Significantly, he was the only Chattanooga-area artist included.

Following graduation, Cress taught at The University of Tennessee, Knoxville, from 1949 to '51. In the fall of 1951 he came to the University of Chattanooga (since 1969, The University of Tennessee at Chattanooga) to head the school's then two-person art department. He remained department head thirty-two years, through the 1983-84 academic year, seeing his faculty increase to fourteen and the greatly enlarged department facility ensconced in a new Fine Arts Building that opened in 1981. Though retired from administrative responsibilities, he continues teaching as Guerry Professor of Art, the first person appointed to that distinguished endowed position.

Hans Hofmann (1880-1966)

For Hans Hofmann, a leading figure of the abstract expressionist group, the optimum creative expression was endeavoring to translate inner states of mind or emotion into "pure" non-objective design. Just as a composer of music imparts mood and feeling through abstract audio sensations (volume, meter, harmony, dissonance, the tone and coloring of various instruments), so also should the visual artist be able to communicate personal sensibilities through the very handling of the chosen medium, and in selection and arrangement of lines, shapes, colors, and texture for their potential inherent psychological associations. The artwork does not *represent* corporeal things or scenes, but *presents* an abstract of the artist's disposition, at the time the piece was executed at least, along with a demonstration of technical facility and sense of composition. Rather than just "looking at" or "reading" a non-representational work, one is invited to project psychically into it, so as to "experience" the visual phenomena much as a listener is transported by music.

In Hofmann's work, heavy paint is applied boldly; color is ebullient. The viewer senses the artist's energy and intense absorption in a creative process that is simultaneously improvisational and methodical. One gesture or color seems to have motivated another, and still another, until the work was systematically brought to completion. The sum effect is explosive, yet held in a dynamic equilibrium. Hofmann described what he wanted to do pictorially in terms of force and counterforce. Barbara Rose explains:

> According to Hofmann, the essence of painting was the balancing out of certain types of pictorial tensions caused by spatial pushing and pulling at the picture plane, created by color and form relationship. Downgrading the purely intellectual and theoretical in favor of the intuitive and sensuous, Hofmann stressed the instinctual and the spontaneous.

The Hunter Museum's robust oil, (color plate 33) *Scintillating Blue 38-30* (the numbers allude to the size of the painting in inches), is characteristically turbulent. Yet the eye takes the composition in a calculated pattern, moving on the staccato repetition of color and the organized network of diagonals.

Hofmann was born at Weissenburg, Germany, in 1880. As a youth he studied music, mathematics, and science in Munich. Remarkably, at age sixteen, and until he was eighteen, he served as assistant of public works for the state of Bavaria. In 1903 he went to Paris to pursue technological studies, but instead enrolled at the École de la Grand Chaumiére. Matisse was attending the school at the same time. Soon he became a close friend of orphist Robert Delaunay, and he met Braque and Picasso. His style evolved rapidly, from meticulously rendered portraits and figure studies to still lifes and landscapes, first in a cubist manner, then in the freer and more colorful mode of the fauves. By the early 1940s, he arrived at a non-objective style that combined the compositional precepts of cubism and the vitality and coloristic expression of the fauves. Interestingly, he also experimented at that time with "drip and run" paint application — several years before Jackson Pollock appropriated a similar technique.

Hofmann also had a gift for effective teaching. He returned to Munich in 1915 and opened his first art school. One of his students there, Worth Rider, went on to become a professor of art at the University of California, Berkeley. Rider invited Hofmann to teach at the Berkeley summer session in 1930, and again the following summer. Hofmann moved permanently to the United States in 1932, and he became a citizen in '41. In 1932 and '33, he taught at the Art Students League in New York City. In '34 he opened the Hans Hofmann School of Fine Arts on Manhattan's 8th Street. Later he established a popular summer extension at Provincetown, Massachusetts. At his schools he introduced the most advanced concepts of European painting. Clement Greenberg noted that from Hofmann "you could learn more about Matisse's color . . . than from Matisse himself." Burgoyne Diller, Helen Frankenthaler, Lee Krasner, and Louise Nevelson are among his better-known students.

Because Hofmann was twenty to thirty years older than most of the generation of artists who emerged as the American avant-garde in the decades just before and just after World War II, he became a kind of patriarch to them. Truly, as both practicing artist and teacher, he had a profound influence on modern art in the United States for more than thirty years. He ceased teaching in 1958, but continued painting until shortly before his death in 1966.

(color plate 33)

SCINTILLATING BLUE 38-30
Hans Hofmann
1956
oil on canvas
38 x 30 inches
signed and dated lower right
Museum purchase with funds provided by Ruth S. and A. William Holmberg, Mr. and Mrs. Olan Mills, II, Mr. and Mrs. Scott L. Probasco, Jr. and Mr. and Mrs. Phil B. Whitaker

Provenance

Collection of the artist
Kootz Gallery, New York, New York
Private collection, New Jersey

Exhibitions

American Paintings: 1945-57, The Minneapolis Institute of Arts, Minneapolis, MN, June-Aug. 1956, no. 64.

Leon Golub (b. 1922)

Chicago-born Leon Golub is one of several prominent contemporary artists who in the mid-1950s bolted from the prevailing non-objective mode of abstract expressionism in favor of a brutal and coarse figurative style. Retaining the large scale, violent brush stroke, and agitated paint surface characteristic of abstract expressionism, Golub has created grotesque human forms that individually are psychologically disturbing characters and, when shown interacting in numbers of two or more, are contenders in powerfully moving, yet abstruse dramas. In the mid-and-late '50s, he painted a series of what he called "monster heads," which represent "mutations of thwarted feelings." The Hunter's *Head XXV* of 1959, an excellent example from the series, reveals not the countenance of a specific person, but

HEAD XXV
Leon Golub
1959
lacquer on canvas
48 x 38 inches
signed bottom, right of center
Museum purchase with funds provided by the Benwood Foundation and the 1983 Collectors' Group

Provenance

Private collection, New York, New York
Susan Caldwell Gallery, Inc., New York, New York

Publications

William T. Henning, Jr., *Recent Acquistions*, Chattanooga: Hunter Museum of Art, 1983.

Carolyn Mitchell, "The Hunter Museum, A Showcase for Modern American Art in Chattanooga." *Southern Accents*, May-June, 1984, p. 124.

rather a type. It is a being encrusted or attrited, depending upon one's point of view, by the deleterious effects of oppression, exploitation, and defeat. The facial expression is nonplused and stupified, yet the intense eyes seem to blaze with pent-up feeling. Golub wants his images to express indignation, anguish, and suffering, but without resorting to obvious propagandistic clichés. Speaking more specifically on a source of inspiration for the heads, the artist reveals:

> In the late '50s I used to go to see Roman and Greek sculpture and in many of my paintings I stole from Greek sculpture. That is to say I took a figure and imitated it. I tried to give it a contemporary flair, but I also wanted those who knew these sculptures, particularly the late pieces, to recognize them and make a connection from the condition of the original sculpture and the contemporary situation. I thought I found a kind of urban stress and violence and vulnerability in these sculptures which was equivalent to the kind of urban stress I was interested in in my own time.

From the preceding commentary one should not be surprised to learn that Golub has studied art history extensively. In fact he earned a B.A. degree in that discipline from the University of Chicago in 1942. He also received a B.F.A. in studio art in 1949 and an M.F.A. the following year, both degrees from the School of the Art Institute of Chicago. In the intervening years he had taught at Northwestern, Indiana, Temple, and Rutgers universities, though he is now working independently and lives in New York City. From his student days to the present, Golub has been a political activist, not only through the intended message of his art, but also by organizing and participating in events for "progressive" causes. While attending the Art Institute he was a force behind *Momentum*, an exhibits program developed as an alternative to the officially sanctioned Institute annuals. In the 1960s he was involved variously with the Artists and Writers Protest Group, the Committee for Artistic Freedom, Los Angeles Peace Tower, and the Angry Arts Week.

Sincere in his political and humanistic convictions, Golub has endeavored through his art to generate a consciousness about what he perceives to be the evils and injustices of modern times. For more than twenty years his painting has been something of an anomaly, existing outside the mainstream of American contemporary art — fashions dominated by the restrained aesthetics of pop art, op, minimal abstraction, color field painting, and the new realism. With the turn in the 1980s to what has been tentatively called neo-expressionism, Golub's seemingly raw visual statements have taken on a newly comprehended validity.

David Park (1911-1960)

BOY - GIRL
David Park
1959
oil on canvas
50 x 58 inches
Museum purchase with funds provided by the Benwood Foundation and the 1983 Collectors' Group

Provenance

From the collection of the artist through Hirschl & Adler, Modern Gallery, New York, New York

Exhibitions

David Park: A Retrospective Exhibition, Maxwell Galleries, Ltd, San Francisco, CA, Aug. 14-Sept. 26, 1970.

David Park Retrospective, The Oakland Museum, Oakland, CA, Dec. 9-Jan. 22, 1978.

The Figurative Mode: Bay Area Painting, 1956-1966, Grey Art Gallery and Study Center, New York University, New York, NY; Newport Harbor Art Museum, Newport Harbor, CA; March 27-Sept. 15, 1984.

Publications

William T. Henning, Jr., *Recent Acquisitions,* Chattanooga: Hunter Museum of Art, 1983.

Christopher Knight and Paul Mills, *The Figurative Mode: Bay Area Painting, 1956-1966,* exhibition catalogue, New York: Grey Art Gallery and Study Center, 1984, p. 51.

David Park was the first, the senior member, and the leader of a movement that came to be called the "California" or Bay Area figurative painters. Centered about San Francisco, Oakland, and Berkeley, it was at its height from the mid-1950s to the mid-'60s. Principal exponents also included Elmer Bischoff, Paul Wonner, Nathan Oliveira, and Richard Diebenkorn. In fact, Diebenkorn, who had been a student under Park and was later his faculty colleague at the California School of Fine Arts, at first derided Park when, in 1949, he abruptly abandoned abstract expressionism, exclaiming, "My God, what's happened to David!"

The decisive way Park "converted" was in great measure what alarmed Diebenkorn. All at once Park destroyed — actually carted to the city dump — every nonobjective-style piece still in his possession from the preceding four year's production. "Those paintings never, even vaguely, approximated any achievement of my aims," he remarked afterwards. What *did* fulfill his aims he put forth on another occasion:

I saw that if I would accept subjects, I could paint with more absorption, with a certain enthusiasm for the subject which would allow some of the aesthetic qualities such as color and composition to evolve more naturally. With subjects, the difference is that I feel a natural development rather than a formal, self conscious one. As a person, I have nothing in common with someone like Mondrian – he was an inventor, I am not; I love things, and my forms come more easily out of a less deliberate kind of invention.

Nonetheless, certain abstract expressionist tendencies—broad and vigorous brushwork, intense and not necessarily true-to-life color, ambiguous spatial organization, and shape-oriented composition — continued into Park's figurative style of the '50s. As in *Boy-Girl* of 1959, abstracted human forms — a nude male left and forward, a female right of center and back slightly — are placed within a unified color field. They are rendered in heavy impasto and partially outlined in black. Characteristically, the faces are enigmatic blank masks with dark blobs or streaks of paint to suggest coarse features. The overall sensation is one of stark, compelling immediacy. Gauging Park's work generally, Carl Belz has written:

The figure provides a starting point, a vehicle to sustain concentration – absorption as Park said – but the best paintings never stop with the figure, never become flaccid around the edges or in the interstices between the figures. Their surfaces are everywhere alive, their parts fully integrated, which means Park grasped on its highest level the modernist imperative that a successful painting must be seen first and last as a painting.

The stylistic similarity of Park's painting from the '50s to the violent, painterly canvasses of Europeans Karl Schmidt-Rottluff, Ernst Ludwig Kirchner, and Emile Nölde, mainly from the decade 1905-1915, has been observed by several art historians, including H. H. Arnason, who says, "Of all the California figurative painters, Park is perhaps closest to the earlier tradition of German Expressionism." The same could be said, probably to an even greater degree, of Park's painting of the mid-1930s, an expressionist-figurative mode. The artist's late work, therefore, was in many ways a personal revival.

Park was born in Boston in 1911, but moved with his family to southern California at age seventeen. He never finished high school, never attended college. Though he studied at the Otis Art Institute in Los Angeles for one year, he was essentially self-taught. In 1930 he married and moved to San Francisco, where he worked as a laborer by day and pursued his art by night. At that time he also completed a mural project for the W.P.A. Returning to Boston in 1936, he taught at the Windsor School until 1941. At the onset of World War II, he went back to California, settling permanently at Berkeley. He worked in a factory for three years. Then in 1944 he began teaching evening-school classes for the California School of Fine Arts (now the San Francisco Art Institute). Shortly he advanced to a full-time day instructor, and remained with the school until 1952. He also taught at the University of California at Berkeley from 1955 until his death from cancer in 1960, only a year after he completed *Boy-Girl*.

Alexander Calder (1898-1976)

A decade or more after American painters had begun to explore modern idioms, most American sculptors were still turning out provincial and generally uninspired work in an academic, Beaux Arts classical style. But between the two world wars, with the arrival of such important emigré progressive sculptors as William Zorach, Jacques Lipchitz (both from Lithuania), Gaston Lachaise (from France), Chiam Gross (Austria), Jose de Creeft (Spain), Eli Nadelman (Poland) and Alexander Archipenko (Russia), American sculpture was steered in the direction of modern technology and materials. New forms were devised—variously streamlined, mechanistic, or abstract—that seemed to represent contemporary society more graphically than traditional figurative work chiseled in wood or stone, or cast in bronze. Noting at the same time the European origins of these and other avant-garde people, many young Americans went to study abroad. It was an oddly reciprocal pattern that would be the groundwork upon which modern American sculpture developed.

Alexander Calder was one of the first native-born Americans to find aspects of European modernism adaptable to his own Yankee ingenuity. Studying in Paris between 1926 and '33, he became aware of dada, surrealism, formal abstraction, and other contemporary movements. He was especially intrigued by the ostensibly disparate fantasy world of Joan Miro and by constructivism, a style that originated mainly in pre-revolutionary Russia, involving—as the term implies—architectonic means of fabrication, as well as novel concepts of space, motion, and time. A visit to Mondrian's studio in 1930 prompted Calder to say of the *de Stijl* master's strict vertical-horizontal, "pure" abstract paintings: "I thought at the time how fine it would be if everything there moved." Rosalind E. Krauss suggests: "Out of the hypothetical situation that Calder fantasized in Mondrian's studio, the mobile was born."

Mobile was the name first applied by Marcel Duchamp to Calder's delicately balanced inventions of suspended wire and flat, aerodynamic, petal-like shapes that are propelled by air currents to ever changing designs. The mobile was the first venture into what has been called *kinetic* sculpture, and it is the art form for which Calder is probably best known.

Calder also created *stabiles*, a word coined by Swiss artist Hans Arp, to describe large stationary sculptures of cut out and painted sheet metal components, bolted together in freestanding compositions. The Hunter Museum's stout and colorful stabile, done in 1963, reveals a sophisticated humor and light-heartedness that typifies much of his work. Seeing a potential analogy in the rotund, biomorphic shapes and the fin-like lower supporting members, Calder whimsically titled the piece *Pregnant Whale* (color plate 34).

Calder was born at Lawnton (now part of Philadelphia), Pennsylvania, in 1898. His father and grandfather were notable American sculptors, and his mother was a professional portrait painter. For the father's health, the family moved west in 1906, living in Arizona and southern California before settling in northern California at Berkeley. After graduating from high school in 1919, he decided to study engineering. He attended the Stevens Institute of Technology in Hoboken, New Jersey, where he earned high marks and in 1923 completed a degree. While still at Stevens, he took drawing classes in night school, nearby across the Hudson in New York City. After finishing the engineering program he went on to the Art Students League, where, over a three-year span, he studied with Kenneth Hayes Miller, John Sloan, Boardman Robinson, Guy Pene du Bois, and Thomas Hart Benton. He then left for that eventful stay in Paris. Returning to the United States in 1934, Calder purchased a home and built a studio at Roxbury, Connecticut, where, except for periodic visits to a second home in Sache, France, he lived the remainder of his life.

Though Calder is most recognized for his mobiles and stabiles, he also produced paintings, jewelry, tapestries, rugs, stage sets, wood sculpture, wire sculpture, and ingenious household objects. A multi-faceted talent, he was truly, as Daniel Mendelowitz declares, "one of the most original and refreshing artists of the twentieth century." Also acknowledging that fact, the Whitney Museum of American Art in 1976 named Calder its Bicentennial artist and mounted a major retrospective exhibition of his work. A few weeks after the opening, Calder died in New York at age seventy-eight.

Lawrence Poons (b. 1937)

Lawrence Poons (who went professionally as Larry Poons until 1982) painted the Hunter Museum's deceptively ingenious, visually afferent *Sunnyside Switch* (color plate 35) in 1963. It is one of his earliest in a series of acrylic works that would identify him with the movement eventually called optical or "op" art. Poons, Richard Anuszkiewicz, Kenneth Noland, and Julian Stanczak were among the first Americans who in the mid '70s experimented with what might be termed "devices" of pure design and color to sensitize and play tricks on the eyes: vibrating color combinations, perspective dislocations, moiré-like patterns, illusory distortions of form caused by alternating positive and negative designs, reversible images and other traditional optical illusions.

(color plate 34)

PREGNANT WHALE
Alexander Calder
1963
painted steel plate
126½ x 105 x 88 inches
initialed and dated on lower unit
Gift of the Benwood Foundation (by exchange)

Provenance

Collection of the artist
Perls Gallery, New York, New York
Mrs. Julius Epstein, Northfield, Illinois
Private collection, New York, New York
Douglas James & Co., Signal Mountain, Tennessee

Exhibitions

New York Painting and Sculpture: 1940-1970, Metropolitan Museum of Art, New York, NY, Oct. 18, 1969-Feb. 1, 1970.

Publications

Marshall B. Davidson, *The Artists' America*, New York: Heritage Publishing Co., Inc., 1973, p. 394.

Henry Geldzahler, *New York Painting and Sculpture: 1940-1970*, exhibition catalogue, New York: E. P. Dutton & Co. and the Metropolitan Museum of Art, 1969, p. 42, illus. p. 67, no. 21.

Op was in part a reaction against abstract expressionism, the style that had dominated American contemporary art since the mid 1940s. Op artists, as well as those in the '70s who advanced "pop," "minimal," "color-field abstraction," and realist assemblage (Robert Rauschenberg, Jasper Johns, and Larry Rivers, for example) felt that abstract expressionism had languished, that it had degenerated into the production of cliché mannerisms. Op, more particularly, was further influenced by twentieth-century scientific research in perceptual psychology, ocular physiology, and the neural systems affecting retinal behavior. Poons and the other American op practitioners built on previous experiments in kinetic illusion by several prominent European artists: the work of Frenchman August Herbin in the 1930s, German-American Josef Albers' carefully controlled studies of simultaneous color contrast in the '50s and '60s, Hungarian-born Victor Vasarely's vivid geometric abstractions of the 1950s (his theories on color perception were published in 1955), and British painter Bridget Riley's complex linear designs, which appear to warp and distend the picture surface.

Poons has also acknowledged another influence not usually associated with op, the "boogie-woogie" paintings that Piet Mondrian produced in the United States the two years before his death in 1944. One senses a Mondrian-esque ordered rectangular system in *Sunnyside Switch*, as a kind of invisible structure seems to hold Poons' dot motifs suspended on a diagonal grid over the continuous color plane. Poons used the term "surface tension" to denote the quality of tautness, yet compositional tractability, that results. But the principal visual effect that distinguishes Poons' work is generated by the "device" of photogenes—more commonly known as afterimages. If one stares intensely at the picture surface, focusing on one of the dots for fifteen to twenty seconds, the cones—light and color receptors in the retina of the eye—over-stimulate and remain stimulated for a short period, even after the actual gaze ceases. Thus the cones continue to send image impulses to the brain (though in a complementary hue), and the viewer will "see" dots that are not really there. Moreover, if the viewer extends looking at the painting, with any movement of the eyes, the afterimage dots will seem to jump accordingly. And as certain of Poons' dots are eliptical, rather than round, and placed on a diagonal axis, those afterimage dots will take on "direction" and will appear to streak across the canvas. A whole new design phenomenon thereby plays over the original composition; though inasmuch as individuals have differing ocular sensitivities and view the total composition with different eye-movement patterns, no two people experience or "see" exactly the same result.

Nearly all Poons' op paintings are large, similar in size to the eighty-inch square Hunter piece. The spectator's full field of vision is thereby enveloped, enabling one more readily to project both optically and psychically into the work. The reader of this catalogue is at a disadvantage if only viewing *Sunnyside Switch* in the comparatively diminutive illustration that accompanies the article, and in such scale the afterimage effect does not occur.

Poons was born to American parents in Tokyo, Japan, in 1937; he came with his family to the U.S. the following year. Originally he had wanted to be a musician. Before taking up painting, he studied from 1955 to '57 at the New England Conservatory of Music, where modern composer John Cage expounded his theories and methods of random composition. In 1958 Poons attended the School of the Boston Museum of Fine Arts. He first achieved national recognition in 1965 when he exhibited at the major op show, *The Responsive Eye*, at the Museum of Modern Art. (The show's organizer, William Seitz, then called the trend "perceptual abstraction.") Poons' op phase was relatively short-lived, only from 1963 to '66. Between 1966 and '68 he continued to employ the eliptical dot motif, but with softer color combinations, feathery edges, and in irregular patterns. In the late '60s he moved on to a dense, expressionistic, highly tactile surface in which close color harmonies and subtle variations in rich thickets of paint convey the abstract design. Poons taught at the Art Students League from 1966 through 1970, and he was visiting lecturer at the New York Studio School between 1967 and '72. At this writing, he still maintains his home and studio in New York City.

(color plate 35)

SUNNYSIDE SWITCH
Lawrence Poons
1963
acrylic on canvas
80 x 80 inches

Gift of the Museum Purchase Fund Collection, established by Gloria Vanderbilt, under the auspices of the American Federation of Arts

Provenance

From the collection of the artist through the American Federation of Arts Museum Purchase Fund lottery

Exhibitions

Contemporary Selections, 1971, Birmingham Museum of Art, Birmingham, AL, Jan. 24-Feb. 20, 1971.

Richard Anuszkiewicz (b. 1930)

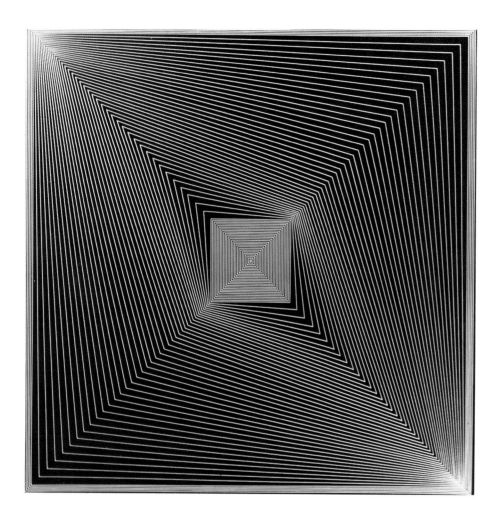

INFLEXIONAL II
Richard Anuszkiewicz
1966
acrylic on masonite
36 x 36 inches
signed and dated on reverse
Gift of the artist

Provenance
From the collection of the artist
Publications
Karl Lunde, *Anuszkiewicz*, New York: Harry N.
Abrams, Inc., 1977, no. 157.
Diana W. Suarez, *Bluff and the Magic Mansion,
A Children's Guide to the Hunter Museum of Art*,
Chattanooga: Hunter Museum of Art, 1980.

Richard Anuszkiewicz' (pronounced An-na-SKAY-vitz) bold geometric painting, *Inflexional II,* is an example of the style for which the term "optical" or "op art" came to be applied in the mid-1960s. Like "pop art," with which it is concurrent, op was a reaction against abstract expressionism, the movement that had dominated the contemporary art scene since the end of the Second World War. Many artists, conservative and modern alike, felt that the impulsive, emotional, semi-accidental, self-indulgent displays of the Action Painters (one of abstract expressionism's alternate handles) had played out, and that it was time for new direction. The artists who would ultimately be identified with op contended that, as an end complete in itself, art could just as legitimately explore the ways certain "pure" non-objective visible phenomena sensitize the eyes. Consequently, images that might evoke symbolic recognition, association from memory, empathy, or narrative contemplation—the antithesis of "pure" visual statement—should give way to forms devoid as possible of personal expression or subjective interpretation.

Mondrian and his *de Stijl* colleagues in Europe propounded much the same thesis sixty years ago. Op however takes on an added dimension from events that have transpired in the ensuing years: increasing mechanization and computerization of industrial society, and scientific studies in perceptual psychology, ocular physiology, retinal behavior, and the neural processes of sight. The French painter Auguste Herbin, as early as the 1930s, and the Hungarian-born Victor Vasarely, in the 1950s, had produced kinetic illusions by employing flat, intense color and geometric shapes in abstract compositions that appear to warp or distend the surface. Vasarely's theories on color perception, published in 1955, had profound effect on Anuszkiewicz, Larry Poons, Kenneth Noland, and other Americans who have subsequently experimented with "pure" optical devices.

Op is essentially an art of visual devices, such as mathematically organized, usually symmetrical patterns, moiré-like designs, reversible images, inversions of perceived depth, juxtaposition of vivid complementary hues, and rapidly alternating positive and negative bands. It is all calculated to make the eyes play tricks, perhaps to see vibrations, afterimages, colors not actually painted, or the sensation of movement.

These are some of the impressions viewers may take from acutely studying *Inflexional II* (unfairly experienced here in the comparatively small reproduction accompanying this article). Though the work is black and white, many people report seeing faint colors shifting fleetingly about the surface. Others see the system of diagonals as guidelines in two point perspective, which causes the square at the center to seem in one instant receding and in another coming forward. Some view the central configuration as the top of a four-sided pyramid. In short, the eyes are unable to hold the design as static or inert. The surface is instead agitated, pulsating, dynamic. It is as Anuszkiewicz sought, declaring: "What I am doing now is using a hard-edge system to produce a soft-edge result." Or as John Gruen has suggested, "The effect is like putting your finger in an electric socket."

The artist was born to Polish immigrant parents and raised in Erie, Pennsylvania. He earned a B.F.A. degree from the Cleveland Institute of Art in 1953. His painting at that time seems derivative of Charles Burchfield or Edward Hopper. The following fall he began graduate study at Yale University, where he came under the strong personality and persuasive teaching of the former Bauhaus color theorist Josef Albers. From this point, Anuszkiewicz' style moved in the direction that would lead eventually to op. After completing his M.F.A. degree at Yale in 1955, Anuszkiewicz attended Kent State University, where he received a second bachelor's degree, in education, the following year. He then moved to New York City, but did not achieve significant recognition until 1965 when he participated in a major exhibition of what was then called "perceptual abstraction." The show, titled *The Responsive Eye*, was organized by William Seitz for the Museum of Modern Art. He has taught at the Cooper Union in New York and has been artist-in-residence at Dartmouth College, University of Wisconsin, and Cornell University. Today he maintains his home and studio in Englewood, New Jersey.

Mauricio Lasansky (b. 1914)

Mauricio Lasansky is one of America's foremost living printmakers. He was born (to Lithuanian immigrant parents) in 1914 at Buenos Aires, Argentina. There as a youth he studied painting, sculpture, and engraving at the Superior School of Fine Arts. When he was only twenty-two he became director of the Free Fine Arts School in the provincial city of Córdoba. He had already received nearly a score of important art awards in Argentina by 1943 when he was given a one-man retrospective show at Buenos Aires' prominent Jalleria Muller. Later that same year he came to the United States under a Guggenheim fellowship. In New York he joined Stanley William Hayter's "Atelier 17," a graphic arts workshop that—while not discouraging technical virtuosity and precise draftsmanship—put great emphasis on pictorial innovation and media experimentation. Two of Lasansky's fellow students at the time were Marc Chagall and Jackson Pollock.

In 1945 Lasansky was invited to establish a printmaking department for the School of Art at the University of Iowa. He moved his wife and children permanently to the United States and a few years later became an American citizen. He remained on the Iowa faculty from that time. From nearly forty years of teaching, approximately 150 of his students have gone on to professorships or heads of print departments at colleges and universities across America and abroad. What is more, since arrival in this country Lasansky has received well over a hundred awards and prizes. He has had nearly as many one-man shows, and his work has been acquired by more than a hundred museums and public collections in Europe, Australia, South America, and the United States.

AMANA GIRL IN BLACK
WINTER COAT
Mauricio Lasansky
1967
intaglio, 15/70
47⅛ x 21⅝ inches
signed on mat, lower right
Museum purchase with funds
supplied in part by the
National Endowment for the
Arts, a Federal agency

Provenance
Private collection, Washington, D.C.
Tahir Galleries, New Orleans, Louisiana.

Lasansky employed six different plates to achieve the multi-colored, highly tactile, finely detailed, and remarkably large (nearly four by two feet) intaglio print, *Amana Girl in Black Winter Coat* from 1967. The subject is a member of the German-American religious society of the several Amana villages in east-central Iowa. While not to be confused with the Amish, the community is Protestant and conservative. The members' traditional garb (when worn, which no longer is every day) and personal grooming can be striking in its austerity; it presents a mood and bearing that appealed to Lasansky.

The girl is shown seated on a chair, in profile to the left. Her legs and feet seem disproportionately small, as though Lasansky was deliberately imitating a common tendency of primitive and folk artists—preoccupied with face, hands, and other focal points—to miscalculate the remaining space, finding it necessary therefore to shorten the lower extremities to fit the composition. The naive effect is often surprisingly charming. The profile head of a sad but trusty dog (a motif that the artist also used in three earlier works) enters the picture from the right, at the girl's shoulder. At nearly the same level on the opposite side appears what is probably the most curious and enigmatic element of the scene, a photo-engraved reproduction of Albrecht Durer's 1515 woodblock study of a rhinoceros. The intent of this image is perhaps several-fold. It may allude to the Amana's

German origins, or the pachyderm, per se, to the staunch toughness of the Amana people. It may represent Lasansky's own awareness and homage to the old-master printmaker. Or, on a lighter plane, the rhino may simply be a droll face-off to the dog.

Like Rembrandt, Francisco Goya, and Pablo Picasso, whose graphic work he admires, Lasansky achieves both a design fullness and depth of content rarely equaled in intaglio printmaking approaching even the inherent expressive capacity of oils or acrylics. As Michael Danoff, director of the Akron Art Museum, has fittingly observed:

> *Certainly some of the traditional prejudices against prints — that they are small or that they lack color — do not apply to Lasansky's often lifesized and richly colored impressions. For some critics, prints will never be as cherished and worthy of concentrated attention as paintings, simply because they exist in more than one impression. But this is quibbling when one realizes that Lasansky found his way to give prints the same emotional weight and impact found in the major paintings of his generation.*

Paul Caponigro (b. 1932)

Paul Caponigro's photographic image of a spectral herd of deer dashing right to left across the entire width of the horizontal composition was "an accident," according to the photographer, "or rather, a gift of my willingness to deal with a low light situation." He goes on to explain how the opportunity to make the photograph came about:

> *I'd heard about this group of white deer on an estate and was intrigued by the idea that they were white and in a herd. I called the owner and he gave me permission to work on the grounds. The deer were difficult to approach because they were scattered and constantly moving. I asked the owner to corral them at one end of a large field and, when I was ready, shoo them my direction. I saw the stand of trees in the photograph and decided to set up opposite them at the other end of the field. There I'd be out of the way and the deer wouldn't see me. I was so far away that, to bring the trees back to me, I had to use a long lens. My meter reading wouldn't allow me a fast enough shutter speed to stop the deer in motion. When the owner corraled enough deer, I said "ready," and he waved his hat. Sure enough, they spread themselves out in the way they appear in the photo. I was amazed they didn't clump up here and there. When I processed the negative I saw the blur. I thought, my God,*

(Continued on page 202)

RUNNING WHITE DEER,
WICKLOW COUNTY,
IRELAND, 1967
Paul Caponigro
1967
gelatin silver print photograph
5¼ x 13½ inches
signed on mat, lower right
Museum purchase

Provenance
From the collection of the artist.

Color plate 41. Jack Beal, *The Painting Lesson*, 1980-81, oil on canvas, 84 x 96 inches. Gift of Mr. and Mrs. John T. Lupton. (See article, page 243.)

Color plate 42. Janet Fish, *Orange Lamp and Oranges*, 1982, oil on canvas, 65⅞ x 50 inches. Museum purchase with funds provided by the Benwood Foundation and the 1982 Collectors' Group. (See article, page 257.)

(Continued from page 199)

this ghostly effect is more wonderful than the sharper focus I'd hoped for. In the printing, I cropped part of the trees and the foreground that were unnecessary. If the picture works better cropped, I do it.

Caponigro continues the tradition of "straight" or "form-for-form's-sake" imagery advanced by Alfred Stieglitz, Edward Weston, Paul Strand, and Ansel Adams, to name several of the best known. For these artists, the inherent abstraction of the objects or scenes depicted—the formal relation of shapes, tones, and patterns one to another—is of prime importance. Straight photographers can, of course, be impelled to swift action when happening upon a visual prospect they think worth taking. More typically, however, they carefully, even methodically "previsualize" the finished print in the camera's view finder or ground-glass plate before releasing the shutter. Caponigro has generally brought a greater degree of improvisation to the procedure; he has put greater trust in fortuity and intuition. As he discloses:

Of all my photographs, the ones that have the most meaning to me are those I was moved to make from a certain vantage point, at a certain moment and no other, and for which I did not draw on my abilities to fabricate a picture, composition-wise or otherwise. You might say I was taken in. Who or what takes one to a vantage point or moves one at a certain moment is a mystery to me.

To the formal abstract beauty of straight photography, Caponigro has sought to add a dimension of subjective response, not for the viewer's outward sentimental reaction to what is pictured, but rather for an awareness of inner feeling. The distinguished photographer Minor White, with whom Caponigro studied in 1957-58, advanced Alfred Stiegltiz' principle of *equivalents*. Stiegltiz coined the term in the early twentieth century to characterize his belief that a photographic image can function as symbol or metaphor, that it can be imbued with emotional significance or meaning personal to the photographer. White took the notion a step further, calling the photograph a "mirage" and the camera a "metamorphosing machine." Photography historian Beaumont Newhall adds that the equivalent is "something both rooted in subject and yet beyond it; surface appearance, though of secondary importance, is essential, and the photograph must be transformed into a new event to be interpreted or read." Caponigro, then, is not only concerned for the immediately recognizable in his art, but is as well captivated by—to borrow photographer and Caponigro-contemporary Paul Sommer's poetic summation—"that which hovers on a boundary of what can be seen and what can only be felt and imagined."

Caponigro was born in Boston in 1932. He developed an interest in photography while in high school. He was also accomplished at piano, however, and he elected to enter the Boston University College of Music. After a year's study, during which he gradually realized his preference for photography as a creative outlet, he took an apprenticeship in a commercial photography studio. He was drafted into the Army in 1953, but was fortunate to have been stationed in San Francisco, where concurrently he was able to study with Benjamin Chin (an Ansel Adams disciple) at the California School of Fine Arts. Following his military discharge in 1955, he returned to Boston and established a free-lance studio. In 1966 Caponigro received a Guggenheim fellowship for "Photographic Studies of Ireland's Ancient Monuments." It was while working at the commission in '67 that he digressed to make the *Running Dear*. Also in 1967, Aperture published an important monograph on Caponigro and his work. In 1968 he was recognized with a one-man show at New York's Museum of Modern Art. He taught at New York University from 1967 to '70, and at Yale in 1970-71. He has also conducted workshops at Princeton and St. Lawrence Universities, and Goddard College. In 1971 he received a special grant from the National Endowment for the Arts. Since 1973 Caponigro has lived in Santa Fe, New Mexico.

Jim Collins (b. 1934)

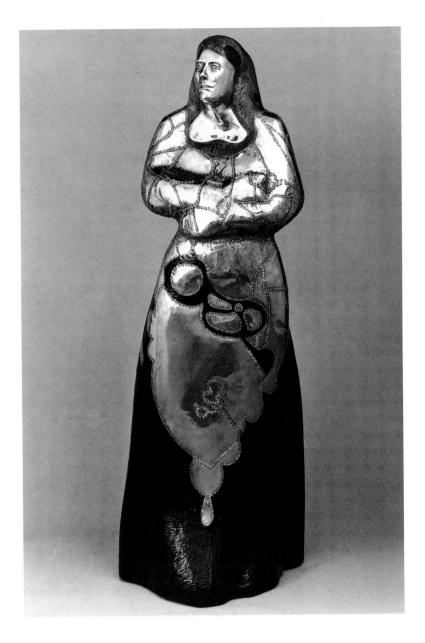

CEDAR BREEZE
Jim Collins
1969-1972
cedar, copper, cast brass, paint
45 x 16½ x 16 inches
signed on back near bottom of figure
Museum purchase

Provenance
From the collection of the artist.

The Hunter Museum's *Cedar Breeze* is one in a series of ingenious sculpted works that artist Jim Collins produced by elaborating the vague suggestion of a human form in the natural shape of a tree-trunk section. Interestingly, a number of the other pieces also include "breeze" as part of the title. Stretching the imagination, one might think of breeze not just as moving air current, but also as its action upon that which it encounters—how flags unfurl, sails swell, kites fly, clouds billow, foliage bends. Proceeding to yet another flight of fancy, one might visualize a figure standing into the wind or, even more specifically, a ship's figurehead cutting the air as the vessel drives forward. In turn the figure is swept by breezes rolling by, blowing the garment accordingly. That at least is how woodcarvers in the past often represented those distinctive, usually female, personages that adorned the prows of larger sailing ships. And it is the figurehead image, Collins readily admits, that inspired his "breeze" sculptures.

(Continued on page 206)

203

Color plate 43. Paul Wonner, *Dutch Still Life with Art Books and Field Guide to Western Birds*, 1982, acrylic on canvas, 72 x 50 inches. Museum purchase with funds provided by the Benwood Foundation and the 1983 Collectors' Group. (See article, page 258.)

Color plate 44. Miriam Schapiro, *In Her Own Image*, 1983, acrylic and fabric on canvas, 60 x 100 inches. Museum purchase with funds provided by the Benwood Foundation and the 1983 Collectors' Group. (See article, page 259.)

(Continued from page 203)

With its forward-leaning posture, arms bent and held close to the body as if bracing against the air stream, and overall smooth, undulating contours, *Cedar Breeze* seems particularly derived from the ship's figurehead prototype. The sculpture evolved over a three-year period. Begun in 1969, it was initially presented as wood only, finished to a stage that echoes the traditional craftsman's chisel-carved stroke. But in '72 Collins decided to embellish certain portions of the piece with a decorative overlay of brass and copper sheetings, thin and malleable enough to be cut easily and shaped around the wood configuration beneath. Closely spaced, round-head brass nails secure the plating in a stitchlike effect. The brass facemask is chased to delineate features, while the natural cedar, varnished to enhance its reddish tone, remains exposed as the subject's hair. Though a freely designed pattern, the metal covering descends from the bodice, both front and back, in such a way as to suggest, semi-abstractly, the draped-apron or gathered-flounce overskirt that fashionable European and American women wore in the 1870s (and that, incidentally, was often captured by figurehead carvers of the time). To set off the metal covering, Collins painted the lower portion of the sculpture, the exposed wood that corresponds to the underskirt, in black.

Cedar Breeze conveys an air of seriousness. But Collins is probably better known for works—paintings and drawings as well as sculpture—that impart humor. His "Watcher" theme pieces, for example, including the painted steel plate *Weather Watcher* from 1978 and the *Paper Watcher*, an embossed, handmade rag-paper piece from 1980 in the Hunter collection (not illustrated), depict the same mildly amusing character—a side-silhouette image of a seated, arm-crossed, leg-crossed, male figure wearing a conspicuous billed cap. From found and scrap materials the artist has also created tongue-in-cheek figures, whirligigs, weathervanes, and nonsense machines. "When I make a funny piece of sculpture, I expect people to laugh at it," Collins states with characteristic frankness. "I can't see any reason why humor and beauty can't be combined. And I can't see any reason why something that is intrinsically funny won't last."

Collins is a native of Huntington, West Virginia, where he was born in 1934 and where he attended Marshall University, completing a B.A. degree in art education in 1956. He earned an M.A. at the University of Michigan in 1961, and an M.F.A. in sculpture from Ohio University in 1965. The following year he joined the art department faculty of The University of Tennessee at Chattanooga. He remained through the 1982-83 academic year, rising to the rank of associate professor. He now works independently and resides in Ripley, Ohio. Collins is a member of the Southern Association of Sculptors, and served as the organization's president in 1970-71. He was also editor-compiler for the two-volume biographical index, *Women Artists in America, Eighteenth Century to the Present*, published in 1973 and '75.

Jasper Johns (b. 1930)

Jasper Johns is, along with Robert Rauschenberg, one of the most daring and influential artists who pointed American contemporary art away from abstract expressionism during the late 1950s. It is not inappropriate here to link Johns and Rauschenberg together. The two artists were especially close friends from about 1955 to 1962. They shared a studio and were each other's first audience and critic. For a while in the early '60s, they were so mutually interactive that their work of the period shows remarkable similarity (a situation not unlike the association of Braque and Picasso in Paris from about 1907 to 1914). Both Johns and Rauschenberg reintroduced recognizable objects and signs, though in an unexpectedly audacious and, in the opinion of many critics, decidedly un-aesthetic way. Both have been reviewed variously as makers of recycled dada conundrums, as proto-pop artists, as forerunners of conceptual art and, even recently, as antecedents for the neo-expressionism of the 1980s.

Yet the two men's individual personalities and their creative approaches could hardly be more different. Rauschenberg is gregarious and brash, and his art is experimental, improvisational, and heterogeneous. Johns is private, shy, and introspective; his work is laconic, paradoxical, and deliberately abstruse. "Johns is responsive to the ambiguity and disturbance latent in all sign-systems," writes Lawrence Alloway, "and has intensified this awareness until it is the main subject of his work."

Johns is probably best known for three controversial series of paintings begun in the mid 1950s: American flags (in an assortment of color combinations), targets, and sets of numerals. All are rendered frontally and without depth. The images are at once familiar, according the artist's declared purpose to start with "things the mind already knows." But on continued study, the viewer becomes aware of subtle surface embellishment, of the tactile richness inherent in John's chosen medium of the time, encaustic, of an interplay of brush technique and overlaid design. Johns augmented an essentially stock and idle format, providing a divergent visual effect with new evocative possibilities. Nicholas Callas describes the resultant works as "vehicles for delayed reading." For sheer irony, the artist later fashioned pieces with planned contradictions of visual and verbal information, such as a broad area painted red, but stenciled over with yellow letters spelling "blue." Some Johns canvases have mundane objects attached, such as kitchen utensils, brooms, cut-out letters, and rulers — often with the implication that these "devices" have pushed around the paint. Like Marcel Duchamp, whom he greatly admired, Johns makes art of things ordinarily seen as "non-art." He admonishes the viewer to reflect on what constitutes art, and to note that art is not necessarily prettyness or even beauty (whatever beauty is?).

The Hunter Museum's untitled, black-ink-on-vellum, three-section work from 1969 is a variation on an earlier and considerably larger (six-by-fourteen-foot) multicolored, paneled, oil and mixed-media piece, also untitled, now in the Stedelijk Museum in Amsterdam. It demonstrates several Johns-ian conventions. The ink handling approximates the variable density of the encaustic, what Max Kozloff aptly calls "vivification of paint . . . a sentient substance, layered with the fauna of emblems, signs, and words . . . a nervous emulsion." It is a precarious visual journey, best taken at a steady and deliberate pace. In route through dark interstices, the viewer will encounter shades (in the ghostly sense) of certain favored motifs: stenciled letters, hand-silhouettes, the ruler and the arched swipe it makes when used as a scraper, and at the right edge, the innocuous broom. The triptych format recalls devotional religious objects; by subliminal association, the viewer is predisposed to advance in a spiritual, or at least contemplative attitude.

Johns was born in Augusta, Georgia, in 1930, but he spent most of his childhood in Allendale and Columbia, South Carolina. To please his mother and stepfather, he says, he attended the University of South Carolina for a year and a half. Then, after a stint in the Army, he went to New York City in 1949. He was working in a bookstore and pursuing art in his free time when he first met Rauschenberg in 1954. Through Rauschenberg he also met dance choreographer Merce Cunningham and modern composer John Cage, both of whose aesthetic theories he studied carefully. The prominent dealer, Leo Castelli, in 1957 provided Johns his first one-man exhibition, which the press gave mixed reviews. The following year his work was selected for showing at the prestigious Venice Biennale, and again in 1964. In 1977, the Whitney Museum of American Art organized a major retrospective exhibition that showed graphically John's creative achievement and the surprisingly wide range of his exploration.

UNTITLED (Triptych)
Jasper Johns
1969
ink on synthetic vellum
20¾ x 56¼ inches (sight)
Gift of the Benwood
Foundation

Provenance

Beyeler Gallery, Basel, Switzerland
Jan Krugier Gallery, Geneva, Switzerland
Thomas Newman, New York, New York
Heath Gallery, Inc., Atlanta, Georgia.

Willem de Kooning (b. 1904)

The abstract expressionist painters subscribe to the tenet that brushwork, color, and form can function alone as powerfully expressive visual communication — without the necessity of depicting tangible things. Characteristic work by such important artists of the movement as Jackson Pollock, Hans Hofmann, Arshile Gorky, Franz Kline, Robert Motherwell, Clyfford Still, and many others is totally non-representational. Willem de Kooning, too, has produced a large body of non-objective work. But the pictorial theme on which his recognition is largely based involves human form, or perhaps more accurately, suggestions of human-like creatures with grossly distorted anatomical parts that seem to coalesce from the turbulent abstract design. Dore Ashton notes that de Kooning's style is a return to the figure all right — but with a vengeance!

Specifically, the topic is *woman*. With the exception of one amazingly biting caricature, titled *Marilyn Monroe* (1954, Neuberger Museum, State University of New York at Purchase), the women are not actual individuals, but rather monstrous subject types that by their very unseemliness both shock and captivate. De Kooning's paint is applied with emotional intensity, one might even say ferocity. The figure is set out in slashing strokes, as if struggling to assume an identity while yet held in ill-defined surroundings. Environment and anatomy flow ambiguously one into the other. In the artist's words, it is a purposeful "no-environment." Barbara Rose describes the effect as "a metaphor for the dislocated space in which the flux of modern life takes place."

To build on an already repugnant image, de Kooning's females often show a sinister toothy grin, wide glaring eyes, bovine chest, heavy hips, and spindly arms and legs. By his preoccupation with such unattractiveness, de Kooning would have the viewer reflect: When American society in particular makes a fetish of youth and surface good looks, when all-American girl idealism superabounds, when pretty cover-girl models look out from every magazine stand, when stunning young women beseige the consumer in advertising all manner of goods and services, when people are excessively concerned with sex appeal and sexual contact, with pinups and centerfolds, derrieres and bosoms — the artist sardonically jars the viewer back to the reality that not all women fit the ideal prototype, that "beauty is but skin deep," "all is vanity," that many women are unattractive, both in appearance and temperament; some women are crass, some even masculine. (Equivalent negative observations, of course, could be made about men.) De Kooning's women are a lampoon of shallow cosmetics and fallacious values.

De Kooning's best-known woman paintings were done between 1950 and '55. The Hunter Museum's untitled 1969 oil (color plate 36) is from a separate series that was begun in 1965 and continued to '71. Typical of the works from this later period, the figure is looser and more abstract, the color is cleaner and more delicate, often in warm fleshy pastel tones. In the upper center a calligraphic red-orange suggests both hair and a heavily lipsticked mouth. Raw pink and muted green similarly delineate pendulous breasts. Other jagged shapes faintly suggest shoulder, arms, torso.

De Kooning was born in Rotterdam, Holland, in 1904. At age twelve, he was admitted to the Rotterdam Academy of Fine Arts and Techniques, where he continued study till age twenty. Strict academic classes stressed the development of drawing skills and mastery of conventional artists' materials, traditional crafts such as carpentry, and a knowledge of art history. Between 1924 and '26, he also attended the Académie Royale des Beaux-Arts in Brussels and the Van Schelling Design School in Antwerp. In 1926 he emigrated to the United States as a stowaway aboard ship. Initially he settled at Hoboken, New Jersey, where he supported himself by sign painting and house painting. He moved to New York City the following year. Soon he was befriended by artists John Graham and Arshile Gorky. He shared a studio with Gorky in the 1930s. In 1935 he worked on the W.P.A. Federal Arts Project, but was asked to resign when government authorities learned he was not then an American citizen. (He did not achieve citizenship until 1962.) His early work in the United States was a stylized figure painting, much in the manner of Giacometti, and later of Picasso. Most work to the time of World War II has either disappeared or been destroyed. The gradual development of an abstract style began in the late '30s.

(color plate 36)

UNTITLED 1969

Willem de Kooning

1969

oil on paper, mounted on board

41⅜ x 30⅛ inches

signed lower left

Museum purchase with funds provided by the Benwood Foundation, Mr. and Mrs. Joseph H. Davenport, Jr., Mr. and Mrs. Scott L. Probasco, Jr., and Mr. and Mrs. Phil B. Whitaker

Provenance

Collection of the artist
Private collection, New York, New York
Heath Gallery, Inc., Atlanta, Georgia.

In 1948 de Kooning taught at Black Mountain College in North Carolina. At the invitation of Josef Albers, then head of the art school, he taught at Yale University the fall term of the 1950-51 academic year. His work was twice included in the prestigious Venice Biennale exhibition, 1954 and '56. President Lyndon B. Johnson presented de Kooning the Freedom Award Medal in 1964 for his contribution to American art. The year before, he moved from Manhattan to East Hampton, Long Island, New York, where he still maintains a studio.

Roger Minick (b. 1944)

TWO CHAIRS
(From the *Hills of Home: The Rural Ozarks of Arkansas* series)
Roger Minick
1972
gelatin silver print photograph
10⅝ x 13¾ inches
signed and dated on mat, lower right
Gift of the artist

Provenance
From the collection of the artist.

In contrast to the "straight" photographers whose chief interest is the abstract beauty of shapes, tones, textures, and the visual relationships of these elements in composition, Roger Minick strives for pictorial expression of subjective mood or feeling. This is not to say that he is unaware or unconcerned for design and arrangement, but his photographs must also relate some degree of story content or inner experience. *Two Chairs*, for example, a strangely moving image from a larger series called *Hills of Home: the Rural Ozarks of Arkansas*, shows the rustic porch of a frame dwelling, on which two ladderback, rush-seated chairs stand conspicuously idle. The chairs are stark, dark, near-silhouettes. One wonders who and where are the people who usually sit here. In fact, the owners of the property, Agnes and Harrison Pierce, were Minick's friends. Joyce Minick, the photographer's wife, recalls fondly:

> The Pierce home is much like others in the Ozarks — square and wooden with two front doors and a front porch with a pair of ladderback chairs where a person can sit and talk, read the local news, or simply look out across the trees and witness the cycles of the seasons . . . In many ways the Pierces lived like the original settlers in the Ozarks — the white settlers who came into this virgin country and homesteaded after the Louisiana Purchase. Many came from the southern Appalachians.

Joyce Minick goes on to reveal that, after being together in this same home for fifty years, the couple was separated by Mr. Pierce's death the January before the photograph was made in spring 1972. The image poignantly declares that those pleasant hours shared on the porch are stilled and gone forever. One senses that the straight chair on the right was customarily taken by Mr. Pierce. The road behind flows gently into it—or could it be read as *away from* the chair, symbolically illustrating the "departure" of the person who sat there? Curiously, the curvature of the road tracks is repeated in the rockers of Mrs. Pierce's chair at left. That the chairback pattern repeats, though in tonal reverse, in the stiles and rails of the screen door, is another obvious design connection. But it also creates a psychological correspondence between door and chair, suggesting perhaps that the widow will presently come out of the house, take her chair, and rock alone.

The *Hills of Home* series was begun in 1970, when Minick, then twenty-six-years-old and recently graduated from the University of California at Berkeley, felt a compelling urge to photograph in the region of northwestern Arkansas that had been his childhood home until age twelve. Though he had lived the fourteen-year interim in the Los Angeles area and at Berkeley, he retained a deep admiration for the simple and rugged Ozark backcountry people, and a respect for their harsh subsistence—without electricity, phones, or indoor plumbing, where the men plow the fields with a team of horses or mules, where women cook over woodburning stoves. It seemed to Minick a fascinating anachronism, a stoic nineteenth-century lifestyle in comfortable, technological mid-twentieth-century America. In 1972, the same year *Two Chairs* was made, Minick received a Guggenheim Foundation fellowship to enable him to complete what would be a four-year project. And in 1975, the set of eighty images was published by Scrimshaw Press, with a text by the photographer's native-Arkansan father, Bob Minick, and additional drawn engravings by Leonard Sussman.

Minick, who was born in Ramona, Oklahoma, in 1944, began studying photography about 1964, while a student at Berkeley (though his B.A. degree was earned in history). Between 1966 and '69 he undertook his first major pictorial series at California's Sacramento-San Jauquin River delta. It resulted in a book titled *Delta West*, published by Scrimshaw in '69. The Institute of Graphic Arts named the book to its list of "fifty best for 1970." After the *Hills of Home* project that followed, Minick began in 1975 what is probably his best-known series, *Southland*, in this instance alluding to southern California. It is a novel recording of the area's vast urban sprawl, as seen through windshields and rear-view mirrors of cars and trucks. "After taking up the 35mm one day," he explains, "I found myself photographing, almost as a lark, from inside the automobile. I realized immediately how much our conception and sensitivity to the world around us is shaped by the tinted-wrap-around windshield."

In 1977 Minick received a grant from the National Endowment for the Arts to photo-document the lifestyles of Mexican-Americans. Under the sponsorship of the Mexican-American Legal Defense Educational Fund, he was one of six photographers commissioned for the two-year project. Minick has also taught for University of Californian Extension, the Ansel Adams Yosemite Workshop, and the Volcano Art Center in Hawaii.

Hans Godo Fräbel (b. 1941)

Hans Godo Fräbel was twenty-four when he arrived in the United States in 1965, but he had already been certified a master glass craftsman in his native Germany. He had served a traditional European apprenticeship three years, and the five years following had been spent producing precision glass instruments and implements for hospital, laboratory, school, and industrial use. It was as a scientific glassworker, actually, that he was brought to the employ of Georgia Institute of Technology in Atlanta. However, having also taken evening classes in drawing and oil painting in Germany, he saw promise in adapting his skills to creative art. As an avocation, he had been fashioning decorative items in a wide variety of conventional, yet stylized motifs: floral, bird, animal, and human. The work met with such immediate success in Atlanta that friends and patrons urged him to pursue art full time. He enrolled for additional courses at Emory and Georgia State universities. Then in 1968 he established a studio and gallery from which continuously he has made, displayed, and sold his craft. Evidence of his increasing popularity, he opened a second gallery at Peachtree Center in 1976.

CROWDED
Hans Godo Fräbel
1970
blown borosylicate crystal
19½ x 6 x 5½ inches
initialed bottom of one rod
Gift of the artist

Provenance
From the collection of the artist.

Though Fräbel's representational work is his mainstay and livelihood, he has as well produced non-objective, geometrically-ordered pieces that are more in the nature of sculpture than object d'art, and are perhaps his most original and effective works. Removed from the necessity of imitating flora and fauna, the abstracts provide an enhanced awareness of the design phenomena inherent to glass through transparency, translucency, reflection and refraction of light, bending and diffusion of color and shadow, and the distortion of things seen within the medium. What is more, the design is ever changing, depending upon surroundings, lighting, and the viewer's own aspect.

In the Hunter Museum's *Crowded* of 1970, thirteen irregularly spaced vertical, columnar units, all equal in diameter, rise from a square-topped wood base. The length of each cylinder varies, so that the eye is led progressively upward to the tallest individual unit. Even-sized spheres, about twice the cylinder width, sit knob-like atop each column — a nice enough design even if it had been executed in wood, metal, or other opaque material. But what makes the sculpture different and remarkable, of course, is the visual action of the glass. Attenuated lines and swatches of color perform according to the contour and density of the component, particularly as the rods and spheres may happen to overlap. Again, as the lighting, environment, or observer's position changes, so is the design modulated accordingly.

Fräbel's glass is neither blown nor are molds or forms employed. No two pieces are ever exactly alike. His technique is the time-honored, though largely European discipline called "lampworking," whereby molten glass, held over an open flame or "lamp" (burning at about 1800 degrees fahrenheit) is shaped with elementary hand tools. He uses a special formula borosilicate glass that, compared to lead crystal, has exceptionally malleable working characteristics and substantially greater strength. Moreover, by resubjecting to the lamp, damaged sections can be readily repaired.

The artist was born in Jena, East Germany, in 1941. In 1948 he fled with his parents and two brothers to Mainz, West Germany, where his father, a glassblower, followed the recently removed Jena Glass Works. It was with this same company that Fräbel began his apprenticeship at age fourteen. Today he supervises apprentices of his own. Since 1978 the prestigious Rhode Island School of Design, by arrangement, sends one student annually to work in the Fräbel studio for an extended period. In addition, Fräbel personally selects apprentice glassworkers who apply from other European and American colleges, retaining up to five at a time.

Hughie Lee-Smith (b. 1915)

CONFRONTATION
Hughie Lee-Smith
c. 1970
oil on canvas
33 x 36 inches
signed lower right
Gift of the National Academy of Design, H. W. Ranger Fund

Provenance
National Academy of Design, H. W. Ranger Fund, New York, New York.

Hughie Lee-Smith is one of America's foremost contemporary black artists. But one would not necessarily know his race nor at once recognize his essentially "black" message on first viewing *Confrontation*, a scene in which the principal characters are two white girls. In numerous other of his characteristic dream-world pictures Lee-Smith has featured white actors as often — if not more often — than blacks. This may be his way of inducing white spectators, the more likely to identify with whites in his pictures, to experience empathically the feelings of isolation, loneliness, and futility that many blacks know as part of their *actual* day-to-day existence.

The "confrontation" here is not between the girls, who seem barely cognizant of one another, but rather between them and their situation. As youths, the two figures represent those whose prime-of-life is ahead and to whom the expectation of life's normal benefits should be a natural course. Instead they appear alienated, from each other to be sure, but more importantly from the strange, unreal, or better perhaps, surreal environment. Like a theatre stage property, the ruin of brick and stucco wall at mid-ground speaks of neglect, decay, and passage of time — a grim reminder of the delapidation one can readily find in the poorest urban neighborhoods. In a more symbolic sense the wall alludes to barriers, constraint, and frustration.

For counterpoint and irony the artist has placed with the figures in the near-ground ostensibly festive elements: slender staffs and a hoop festooned with ribbons of frosty pink and green. Yet even these seem meager and transitory. The long cast shadows, a favorite device of such surrealists as Dali and DeChirico, reinforce the notion that day is ending and, figuratively, time is running out. On the other hand, these same attenuated shadows strain to the left, to the edge of the scene and beyond, as if reaching out to the unknown. A spacious, inviting seacoast in the distance beyond the ruin may be a glimpse of that unknown. It is like a harbor from which ships of liberation and hope might set sail.

Lee-Smith was born in Eustis, Florida, but his family moved north when he was a boy, settling in Cleveland, Ohio. There he studied at the Karamu House, a regionally well-known center for black artists and performers, and later at the Cleveland School of Art. He transferred to Wayne State University in Detroit where he completed a B.S. degree in art education. He continued to live and work in Detroit until 1969, when he accepted a two-year appointment as artist-in-residence at Howard University in Washington, D.C. Since 1972 he has taught at the Art Students League in New York.

In 1975 Lee-Smith was one of the artists featured in the Whitney Museum's important exhibit, *An American Dream World: Romantic Realism 1930-1955*; accordingly, since that time he has generally been categorized a "romantic-realist."

Brett Weston (b. 1911)

As the photographer-son of a famous photographer, Brett Weston's work unavoidably has been compared to that of his father Edward. But it is not a comparison that Brett finds troublesome. When asked by Robert Holmes, in a 1980 interview for *Darkroom* magazine, if he was ever intimidated at being his father's son or by his father's reputation, Weston replied sharply: "I was never. He was a great companion and a marvelous parent." When queried by Holmes more pointedly if he felt, as some critics feel, that his photography rivals or even excels that of his father, he retorted: "Nobody will ever surpass Edward Weston in his own special thing. I'm not concerned about surpassing anybody, only myself."

The comparison is relevant, too, because, as Brett Weston readily admits, his father did subtly influence his developing photographic style "without being a teacher, without proselytizing." Still, Edward was his son's mentor and only instructor. Brett took his first photographs at age twelve under his father's guidance. When he was fourteen, his father gave him his first camera—not the Kodak or Brownie that most beginning photographers use, but a 4 x 5 Graflex, a multiple-setting, precision instrument that would offer great advantage to one learning the craft. "He gave me the fundamentals," Brett says of his father, "but he left me alone. I had to make it or break it on my own." Make it he did, and he progressed rapidly. Photography historian Nancy Newhall would later write: "He became a photographer as naturally as breathing." And Edward Weston wrote in his Daybook on November 5, 1926: "He's doing better work at fourteen than I did at thirty." The following year Brett exhibited twenty photographs alongside his father's at the University of California, Berkeley. In 1928 the Jake Zeitlin Gallery in Los Angeles gave young Weston his first one-man show. Of special note, in 1929 the Deutsche Werkbund, in its day probably the most progressive art society in Europe, selected twenty of Brett's photographs to be shown

CANAL, NETHERLANDS, 1971
Brett Weston
print, 1972
gelatin silver print photograph
18 x 14¼ inches (sight)
signed and dated on mat,
lower right
Museum purchase

Provenance
From the collection of the artist.

in the influential exhibit, *Film und Foto*, in Stuttgart, Germany. Brett was not yet eighteen years old.

The M. H. DeYoung Memorial Museum in San Francisco gave a twenty-year-old Brett Weston his first major *retrospective* show in 1932. And the avant-garde photography association called Group f64 (which Edward Weston had helped found with Ansel Adams, Willard Van Dyke, and Imogen Cunningham) also showed Brett's work in its exhibition at the DeYoung later in '32. Typical of the "straight" or form-for-its-own-sake design aesthetic that f64 members advocated, Brett's style has always been marked by a strong sense of abstract beauty in tonalities, shapes, and textures. Merle Armitage writes in his important book *Brett Weston Photographs*, published by Aperture in 1956—significantly, at the height of the abstract expressionist movement in painting:

> *Focusing his camera on his elected mise-en-scène – a tidepool, a piece of splintered glass, the eroded bark of a tree, a wind-swept sand dune or other secrets of nature – Brett produces an abstract result which should provide the key to persons who have as yet found the work of non-objective painters an unknown and alien world. For here are the patterns, the arrangements, the designs and the evocations sought by the finest abstract painters, captured perfectly intact, and presented with the brilliance and the pristine quality which only photography can command.*

214

"Straight" highly abstracted, bold-pattern images constitute one of two categories of production that critic and photography historian Beaumont Newhall has observed in Brett Weston's work.* The other reveals the artist's fondness for landscape—wistful, meditative, poetically interpreted landscape—that, as Newhall perceives, "fairly involve the spectator in space, and depend upon the subject." The Hunter Museum's sensitive *Canal, Netherlands*, from 1971, is such an image. The scene is set in depth, implementing a type of one-point perspective (that is, an apparent single vanishing point on the horizon at center), made particularly noticeable by the gradual diminution of the trees as they recede. One is further drawn to the light that seemingly emanates from the distant mist. At the same time, the view remains remarkably abstract and rhythmically ordered. The line of the water's edge at left forms a graceful reverse S curve, at right a strong, straight diagonal. Both lines visually carry forth with edges suggested in the density of overlapping tree limbs above. Those same upper tree branches and their reflections in the canal weave inherently rich, tactile shapes. As photography—focus, depth of field, contrast, alternating patterns of light and dark, nuance, mood—the image is an underplayed tour-de-force.

Weston has worked mainly with large-format view cameras, both 8 x 10 and 11 x 14 sizes, though since 1969 he has also frequently used a 2¼ inch single-lens Rolleiflex. He knows well the capability of his lenses and printing papers, so that in technical matters he relies on intuitive judgment. He never employs a light meter, for example, nor does he find need to utilize the zone contrast notation system popularized by Ansel Adams.

The second of Edward Weston's four sons, Brett was born in Los Angeles in 1911. After his early critical recognition in photography, he lived variously in Glendale, Santa Barbara, San Francisco, and Carmel, California. He served with the Army during World War II, though he had infrequent opportunity to avail his photographic talents until near the end of the war, when an understanding superior officer assigned him to the Signal Corps. In 1947 he received a Guggenheim Foundation grant to photograph along the East Coast, and in 1973 he was awarded a grant from the National Endowment for the Arts to photograph Alaska. Weston has rarely resorted to commercial work; since the mid 1940s he has been able to sell his prints at sufficient prices and in sufficient numbers to support his modest lifestyle. "I was willing to live simply and economically," he told Robert Holmes, "and still do." Since 1948 he has lived near Carmel, successively in two houses he built himself.

*The Hunter Museum has in its collection an example of Weston's more abstract direction, titled: A Temple Facade, Japan, 1970 (not illustrated).

Kenneth Snelson (b. 1927)

My concern is with nature in its more fundamental aspect: the patterns of physical forces in space. I try to reveal these patterns in my sculpture as directly as possible with linear material under tension and compression.

In two straightforward, declarative sentences, Kenneth Snelson gives a succinct yet vivid explanation for the premise of his creative work. His sculptures are indeed "force diagrams"—abstract compositions that visually express resistance to gravity, cantilevering, counterbalancing, and stabilized energy. For a typical Snelson structure, aluminum cables are tensed from the end-cap component of one aluminum or stainless steel tube to another. The tubes thus become elements of compression, and the resultant configuration is a network of interlocking triangles and tetrahedrons. The aesthetic feature is the actual design. A system of diagonal lines imparts a feeling of dynamism, yet the total arrangement seems contained and methodically disposed. Intersecting lines become angles that augment the sense of impulse by their contrasting directions. Multiple intersections generate areas of optical density. This periodic intensification of the pattern presents a series of focal points, a purposeful design emphasis that facilitates the eye's encompassing the piece in a systematic and rhythmic way. The linear pattern also shapes and articulates space, both within and immediately surrounding the structure.

The Hunter Museum's sculpture, titled *V-X II*, is one of Snelson's more tightly composed works. Stainless-steel tubes, inclining to the right at about a forty-five degree angle, appear to move around a central axis. They are suspended, of course, by an intricate

V-X II

Kenneth Snelson

1973-1974

stainless steel, 1/3

97 inches high x 161 inches diameter

Museum commission with funds supplied in part by the National Endowment for the Arts, a Federal agency

Provenance

Hunter Museum commission

Exhibitions

The American Eight, Hope College, Holland, MI, April 1-July 15, 1982.

weaving of tensed cables. There is considerable sense of centripetal force, enhanced in part by the system of diagonals and in part by the hyperbolic curve formed by the continuing coordinates of the orbiting diagonal tubes. The work gives the slight impression of an encircling concave plane.

Snelson was born in 1927 at Pendleton, Oregon. He attended the University of Oregon, Chicago Institute of Design, the Atelier Fernand Leger in Paris, and Black Mountain College in North Carolina, where he studied with Josef Albers and Buckminster Fuller. From Fuller he learned the geodesic principles that have had a pronounced impact upon his art. He lives in New York City.

Doris Leeper (b. 1929)

Close friends affectionately call her "Doc"—a reference to Doris Leeper's early intention to become a physician and her two years of study in the premedical program at Duke University. Curiously, it was a professor's commending the aesthetic quality of her laboratory illustrations that first prompted her to think of a career in the visual arts. She switched majors her junior year, and went on to graduate from Duke in 1951 with an A.B. degree in art history. Leslie Judd Ahlander, former curator of contemporary art at the Ringling Museum in Sarasota, Florida, feels that Leeper's clean, incisive, analytic approach to design and fabrication is at least partly attributable to her pre-med training.

Leeper's mature style is an amalgamation of several modern idioms: the seeming simplicity of hard-edge minimal abstraction, the organizational method of conceptual art, and the illusory kinetics of op. Technics, serial reproduction of unit parts, slick, bright packaging, hard utilitarian finish—all design features of twentieth-century commercial and industrial society—are expressed in Leeper's work. Francis Martin, Jr., art critic for the *Orlando Sentinal-Star*, elaborates:

In some ways, Leeper's approach is an erasure of — or reaction against — the personal and emotional characteristics of mid-century art and a turning to the "cold" impersonal banality of the mass-produced urban environment of the 1960s and 1970s. Leeper reduces the complexity of her designs to a minimum, concentrating on nonsensual, impersonal geometric configurations presented as natural objects without interpretation or artistic rationale. They are impeccably, flawlessly, and immaculately engineered forms.

As the artist herself affirms: "Today works of art are presented straightforwardly as objects rather than as mysterious renderings shrouded in metaphysical symbolism. I think this is enormously significant." Object, as both Martin and Leeper use the term, is more than a convenient designation for a non-representational piece; it alludes as well to invention in process, media, and space. Ahlander explains: "A salient aspect of contemporary art has been the combination of painting and sculpture into a third art form, in which the work becomes primarily an object in space. This new approach may be a three-dimensional work hanging from a wall, or it may be a free-standing form." The imposing compartmental constructions of Louise Nevelson fit the definition of the new-approach object, of course, as do the wall-mounted box modules of Donald Judd, the neon and glass creations of Keith Sonnier, the screens of Harry Bertoia, or the mixed-media assemblages of Robert Rauschenberg or Jasper Johns. In fact, the "movement" of conventional painting forward from the picture plane into three-dimensional space can be seen in the early twentieth-century collage and painted constructions of Picasso, Braque, Archipenko, Gabo, Tatlin, Malevitch, Arp, and numerous others.

While the viewer may at first read the Hunter Museum's untitled Leeper wall object (color plate 37) as essentially two-dimensional, a great measure of its visual effectiveness is in the multi-faceted, three-dimensional quality of the surface. The ten by twenty-five foot piece comprises 160 fifteen-inch square components. Each square in turn is made from six juxtaposed triangles. The center two isosceles triangles in each square unit form a two-color diamond, and occupy the back plane of the construct. Each diamond then is adjacent to four scalene triangles that incline forward to the corners opposite the long axis of the diamond, creating a shadow-box for each square and a saw-toothed effect in the abutment of squares one to another. Leeper employed eight color enamels to paint the individual triangular sections (all 960 of them). The diamond is always yellow ochre and dark brown, giving the composition a unifying grid. The surrounding triangles—in red, orange, green, dark blue, light blue, and light brown—are disposed in such a way as to set out intricate and carefully ordered patterns. If, for example, one concentrates on a single color, the orange say, one notes systematic, geometric progression. In eight places within the total composition (three left-center, two center, three right-center), cleverly alternated colors surround a single point (for example, orange-green-orange-green-etc.) on ascending and descending triangular planes so as to suggest four-point stars. In sum, the piece reveals a variety of design "surprises," and imparts extraordinary vitality with a sense of cadence and staccato beat.

The Hunter's wall relief was commissioned by the museum and conceived in advance for placement in the spacious entry foyer of the new building. Leeper began the project in March 1973; it was finished and installed in August 1975.

Leeper was born in 1929, and reared in Charlotte, North Carolina. Upon completing her bachelor's degree at Duke—for which she also earned membership in Phi Beta Kappa honor society—she returned to Charlotte and worked ten years as a commercial artist. In 1961 she elected to devote full time to her personal creative interests, whereupon she moved to Florida and established her present home and studio at Eldora, near New Smyrna Beach.

(color plate 37)

MODULAR WALL RELIEF IN EIGHT COLORS

Doris Leeper

1972-1974

enamel on polyester and fiberglass

120 x 300 x 4 inches

Museum commission

Provenance

Hunter Museum commission

Publications

Diana W. Suarez, *Bluff and the Magic Mansion, A Children's Guide to the Hunter Museum of Art,* Chattanooga: Hunter Museum of Art, 1980.

Robert Cottingham (b. 1935)

DR. GIBSON
Robert Cottingham
1974
lithograph, 39/50
36 x 36 inches
signed and dated lower right
Museum purchase with funds supplied in part by the National Endowment for the Arts, a Federal agency

Provenance

Landfall Press, Inc., Chicago Illinois (publishers)

Exhibitions

Contemporary Prints from the Collection of the Hunter Museum of Art, Dulin Gallery of Art, Knoxville, TN, Jan. 5-31, 1981; St. Andrews, Sewanee, TN, Oct. 1-31, 1981.

When Robert Cottingham, Richard Estes, Ralph Goings, Philip Pearlstein, and others emerged in the late 1960s as champions of a "new realism," many artists, critics, and dealers saw the development as a conservative backlash, a denial of the hard-won gains for credibility achieved in the abstract and non-objective movements that had dominated contemporary art since the end of World War II. This new work, after all, seemed to emphasize — even to the extreme — tangible objects in scenes of acute veristic detail. It seemed a revival of *trompe l'oeil* illusionism, only with latter-day themes and images. Yet stylistically the new realism, or "photo-realism," as the direction has also come to be designated, is substantially different from the *trompe l'oeil* of the nineteenth century, or from Hudson River School realism, or from the realism of such twentieth-century American artists as Edward Hopper, Charles Sheeler, or Andrew Wyeth. That which distinguishes the new realism is not solely its sharp-focus detailing, but rather too its underlying *abstraction*. Critic Gregory Battcock believes that photo-realism may be more closely related to abstract expressionism than to its more obvious affinity with pop art. And John Arthur explains: "The influence of abstract expressionism on the photo-realists can be seen in their incorporation of the physicality of the paint, abstract and/or expressive use of color, a more conceptual depiction of space and composition, and the large scale canvas as opposed to easel painting."

Pop art's influence was more thematic and technical. It had earlier demonstrated that everyday mundane things, movies and television, commercial art and advertising symbolism, provided effective motifs for making pointed comments about the materialism of contemporary American life. Further, the pop artists' adaptation of certain long-employed commercial art short cuts — the use of photographs, for example, and opaque or slide projectors to transmit photographic imagery to paper or canvas—suggested a modus operandi. The new realists also observed that *snapshot* photography especially, with its perfunctory viewfinder grouping, chance cropping, and flattened space, imparts an air of detachment that speaks to the impersonal nature of much of one's modern experience. Moreover, it prompted the artists to look dispassionately at shape, form, color, and their arrangement — elements that might otherwise be subordinated to story or narration. Again, it is the aesthetic impulse toward abstraction. Robert Cottingham, in point, builds his compositions on strong diagonals to achieve what he feels is an inherently more dynamic result. "I would like my paintings to radiate tension," he has said.

Cottingham's recurrent topic is the urban American iconography of storefronts, theatre marquees, and neon signs. Typically his visual access begins at what would be about ten feet above the ground, and, depending upon his distance from the facade, may extend upward to the equivalent of twenty to thirty feet. Often the wording on the signs is cropped in such a way as to leave new words: "me," "ha," "den," "oh," or droll nonsense syllables. At the same time, there is a touch of nostalgia and melancholy in his vision. The most elaborate and interesting facades, Cottingham believes, are from the 1930s, '40s and '50s, and consequently are likely to be found in the older areas of a town. For new subject ideas, the artist takes frequent bus trips to various cities, noting that bus depots in older and larger communities are often in areas that are faded reminders of a brighter and more prosperous time.

A sign for the walk-up office of an inner-city dentist is the subject of Cottingham's *Dr. Gibson*. The scroll-shaped contour of the sign and the architectural ornament immediately behind it recalls a pre-World War II fashion. The dominant brown, black, grey, and muted blue tonalities — though rich and harmonious in their own right — give scant notion of a live presence, and suggest that the doctor's practice is gone with the heyday of the neighborhood.

The Hunter's three-foot-square, new-method lithograph of 1974 accurately re-creates an original six-foot-square oil painting from 1971 (private collection). Technically remarkable, each print in the edition of fifty was "pulled" from aluminum plates in *eighteen* separate color "runs." The proper "registration" or allignment of the various color shapes to make a crisp and coherent image was a particularly exacting process.

Cottingham was born in Brooklyn, New York, in 1935. He studied at the Pratt Institute from 1959 to '64, completing an associate's degree in advertising art. At Pratt, he also worked as a graphic designer for New York's prestigious advertising firm of Young and Rubicam. And from '64 to '68 he was art director for the agency's Los Angeles branch. In 1969 and '70 he taught at the Art Center College of Design in Los Angeles. He lived in London from 1971 to '77, and now makes his home at Newton, Connecticut.

Albert Paley (b. 1944)

When sculptor/designer-craftsman Albert Paley joined the Artist Blacksmith Association of North America in 1975, he in effect affirmed what a major portion of his work essentially is about. Producing those objects of architectural ornament for which he has come to be recognized — including the Hunter Museum sculpture-garden fence and the separate gate piece installed outdoors on the walkway approach to the main entrance — involved traditional blacksmithing techniques: tapering, twisting, bending, punching, and reshaping metal that has been forge-heated to a malleable state. One senses "process" in the sinewy rod and bar components of Paley's finished constructs; no effort is made to mask, hide, or polish away evidence of the smith's manipulation.

HUNTER MUSEUM FENCE
Albert Paley
1975
mild steel, forged and
fabricated, two sections
117 x 336 x 27 inches
128 x 576 x 58 inches
stamped with name, left
section
Museum commission

Provenance

Hunter Museum commission

Publications

Robert A. Sobieszek, *The Metalwork of Albert
Paley*, Sheboygan, WI: John Michael Kohler
Arts Center of the Sheboygan Arts Foundation,
Inc., 1980, cover illus., illus. p. 28-29, no. 98, 99,
119, 120, 121, 122, 123, 124.

Barbaralee Diamonstein, *Handmade in America,
Conversations with Fourteen Craftmasters*, New
York: Harry N. Abrams, Inc., 1983, detail, p. 195.

Though Paley will have a preconceived composition in mind for the finished sculpture, and often makes elaborate preliminary drawings, the actual fabrication procedure becomes, in his own word, an "intuitive" response to opportunities afforded in the very course of working the material. The exaction of fire and the artist's command of appropriate tools reciprocate; the metal tugs and pulls, resists and yields, often suggesting in progress an amended design or structural effect. "The shape comes about," Paley asserts, "because when the iron is hot, it has a great deal of natural movement. It just flows into curves, and when it's cooled, the motion is frozen." In long, serpentine component elements or in the abrupt change of direction as the metal is bent, one senses undulation, acceleration, swift breaking to reverse course—in short, a rich interplay of movements, the very "frozen motion" of which Paley speaks. Art historians and critics have observed that the attenuated, rippling, "whiplash," linear result is reminiscent of the late nineteenth-century art nouveau. That, too, is all right with Paley. "I find the Art Nouveau shapes very seductive," he admits.

On a broader consideration, Paley is one of many contemporary artists, architects, and environmental designers who in the 1970s began to turn away from the pervasive influence of what is called the "International Style" — a design aesthetic originating at the German Bauhaus in the 1920s, and characterized by clean, functional, rectangular, sheer, unembellished shapes and spaces. "Less is more" is Ludwig Meis van der Rohe's oft-cited maxim for the International Style. Architect Richard Venturi and writer Tom Wolfe (*From Bauhaus to Our House*), among the more vocal, contend that, in actual application, less all too often is still *less*; moreover, it is frequently *dull*. Paley has contributed to the widespread rediscovery that artfully integrated ornament not only can fulfill modern design, but also may add a sense of warmth, elegance, and humanization.

Former Hunter Museum director Budd H. Bishop first approached Paley on the possibility of designing an enclosing decoration for a rooftop sculpture court in 1973, when architectural planning for the new museum building was in an early stage. Paley visited the site and studied the architect's drawings in early '74. By October of the same year, he submitted designs for a fence in two sections; totaling eighty feet in length, varying in height but averaging ten feet. The board of trustees formally awarded the commission the following month. With a team of assistants, Paley forged and fabricated the fence over a ten-month

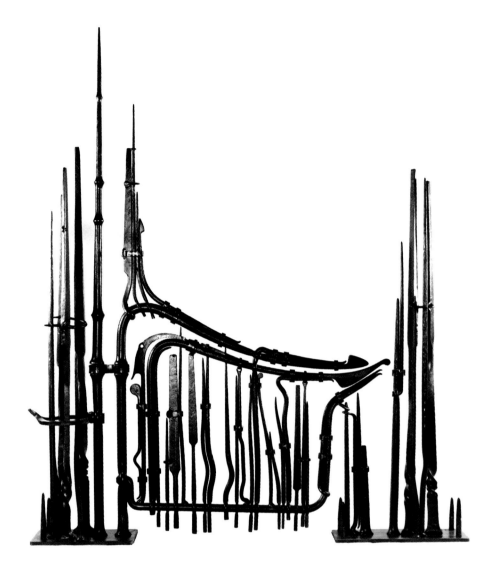

GARDEN GATE
Albert Paley
1976
mild steel, forged and
fabricated
115¾ x 102⅝ x 14½ inches
stamped with name and date
left gate-post, center
Gift of Ruth S. and A. William
Holmberg

Provenance

From the collection of the artist

Exhibitions

The Metalwork of Albert Paley, John Michael
Kohler Arts Center, Sheboygan, WI, April 13-
June 1, 1980; Hunter Museum of Art, Chat-
tanooga, TN, Oct. 19-Nov. 23, 1980.

Publications

Robert A. Sobieszek, *The Metalwork of Albert
Paley*, exhibition catalogue, Sheboygan, WI:
John Michael Kohler Arts Center of the
Sheboygan Arts Foundation, Inc., 1980, p. 8,
no. 78.

Barbarlee Diamonstein, *Handmade in America,
Conversations with Fourteen Craftmasters*, New
York: Harry N. Abrams, Inc., 1983, Illus. on title
page.

period. It was installed in August 1975 in time for the opening of the new facility. A twenty-five minute film documenting the design, fabrication, and installation of the fence was produced for National Educational Television by David Darby, then of KUED-TV in Salt Lake City.

The Hunter "gate"—though created as a totally separate conception in 1976—is sufficiently like the fence in style, proportion, and finish as to suggest that it was part of the original commission. Both pieces have the appearance of conventional wrought iron, but are actually of a related material called "mild" or "soft" steel. It is lower in carbon content than the iron and comparatively free from impurities.

Paley was born in Philadelphia in 1944. He earned a B.F.A. in sculpture in 1966, and an M.F.A. in goldsmithing in 1969, both degrees from Tyler School of Art at Philadelphia's Temple University. Even before completing his graduate work, he joined the faculty of the Tyler School's Evening Division to teach metalcrafting. After graduation in '69 he became an assistant professor in the School of American Craftsmen at Rochester Institute of Technology. Since 1972 he has taught at the State University of New York College at Brockport, a community about fifteen miles west of Rochester. He maintains his home and workshop in the larger city. 1972 was also the year that Paley entered the national competition to design a large portal double-gate for the Smithsonian's Renwick Gallery in

Washington, D.C. Winning the commission in '73 was pivotal to his career. Before that he had been mainly a designer of jewelry, flatware, and holloware. The success of the Renwick project gained him other notable architectural-scale commissions, including, of course, the Hunter fence, the Senate Chamber gates for the New York State Capitol at Albany in 1978, and thirty benches and nearly a thousand tree grates placed in 1982 along Washington's famed Pennsylvania Avenue.

James Rosenquist (b. 1933)

MARILYN
James Rosenquist
1974
lithograph, 69/75
image: 35½ x 27 inches
signed and dated lower right
Museum purchase with funds supplied in part by the National Endowment for the Arts, a Federal agency

Provenance

Petersburg Press, Inc., New York, New York (publishers)
Allan Frumkin Gallery, Chicago, Illinois

Exhibitions

Contemporary Prints from the Collection of the Hunter Museum of Art, St. Andrews, Sewanee, TN., Oct.1-31, 1981.

James Rosenquist's work of the 1960s and '70s was part of the phenomenon, at its height during those years, called "pop" (short for popular) art. The movement began as abstract expressionism was cresting, and in part may have been a reaction to that ethereal, non-objective, pure-design method. The fully earnest, though often facetious or sardonic pop artists' approach was to extract themes and motifs from what they believed were the basest, but at the same time most pervasive of contemporary visual stimuli: advertising art and product packaging, mass-produced industrial objects, automobiles, airplanes, fast foods, comic strips, glamour girls, pretentious movie and television personalities. The pop artists reasoned that these were the images that constituted "art" for the average John or Jane Q. Citizen. Why not then intensify such impressions, reorganize them, re-scale them, serve them up as "fine" art — and in the process make a commentary about the commercialism and resultant vulgarity of the age? In so bringing art down from its exalted pedestal, composer and aesthetic polemist John Cage first, and Robert Rauschenberg subsequently, expounded, the gap between art and everyday life could be bridged.

Each of the major artists identified with pop — Andy Warhol, Roy Lichtenstein, Richard Lidner, Robert Indiana, Tom Wesselman, Claes Oldenburg — remarkably came to the style separately and independently; initially each was unaware of what the others were doing. And each developed his own distinct form of expression. As a young man Rosenquist worked as a billboard painter, before and after stints at art school, for the General Outdoor Advertising Company in the Midwest between 1952 and '54, and for Artkraft Strauss in New York City from '58 to '60. In fact, on several occasions he worked on perhaps the most famous of all advertising boards, the enormous signs at Times Square. H. H. Arnason feels this was important to his later development as a painter and graphic artist:

> His experience painting huge signs, involving extreme close-ups of gigantic
> details of the human face and figure and of industrial objects, supplied the basis of
> his particular vision of pop art. From sign painting, he also drew his brilliant, often
> garish color pattern.

Inspired from billboard art though they may be, Rosenquist's pop creations are obviously more than clever takeoffs. One senses the influence both of cubist collage composition and the surrealist penchant for juxtaposing seemingly unrelated objects for their shock value, or for new, ingeniously observed associations, or simply for abstract design similarity. John Taylor describes Rosenquist's work as "a complex mosaic of visual patterns, recollections, perturbing configurations, and lyrical meanings." Then, regarding more specifically the artist's selection of motifs, Taylor goes on: "The images are left in the public domain, and yet are combined in such a way as to be transformed into a course for unique and personal rumination."

The public personna of Marilyn Monroe as packaged Hollywood sex-symbol was a pop preoccupation, nationwide if not worldwide, in the late '50s and early '60s, and it did not go unnoticed by several important artists of the time. Indiana and Warhol, as well as Willem de Kooning, each did his own interpretation of the actress. Rosenquist, too, completed his large painting, *Marilyn Monroe* (Museum of Modern Art), in 1962, the same year as the subject's untimely death. The nine-color lithograph, *Marilyn*, in the Hunter Museum collection is a smaller scale derivation after the painting that was custom printed in an edition of seventy-five in 1974. Cropped and rearranged facial features, the disturbing upside-down toothy smile, framed by stridently painted lips, the five letters *ARILY*, central to the name, gliding across the viewer's sight line and consciousness like a worded message flowing by on a street sign or television screen — all combine as a dynamic ensemble with potent visual impact.

Rosenquist was born at Grand Forks, North Dakota, in 1933. In 1948, when he was only fifteen years old, he was awarded a scholarship to attend the Minneapolis School of Art. He also attended the University of Minnesota in 1952 and the Art Students League in 1955. In 1957, though deriving his chief livelihood from billboard art, he established a studio for painting in New York. He continues to live and work in that city. In recent years he has experimented with conceptual art and large outdoor earthworks.

Sidney Goodman (b. 1936)

Philadelphian Sidney Goodman was first recognized as an important contemporary artist when the Museum of Modern Art included his work in its 1961 exhibition, *Return to the Figure*. As the title of that show implies, members of an emerging avant-garde were finding the still-dominant abstract expressionism either passé or simply unsuited to their creative ends. Goodman explained in an interview three years later: "What I want to do concerns more than just shapes, forms, and colors with no relation to a subject. There wasn't enough life in abstract art for me."

GIRL WITH A SHEET
Sidney Goodman
1974-1975
oil on canvas
71¾ x 53 inches
signed and dated lower left
Museum purchase with funds
provided by the Benwood
Foundation and the 1982
Collectors' Group

Provenance

Collection of the artist
Terry Dintenfass, Inc., New York, New York

Exhibitions

Sidney Goodman: Paintings, Drawings and Graphics, 1959-1979, Pennsylvania State University Museum of Art, University Park, PA, circulating exhibition: Pennsylvania State University Museum of Art, University Park, PA; The Queens Museum, Flushing, NY; Columbus Museum of Art, Columbus, OH; Delaware Art Museum, Wilmington, DE; July 5, 1980-June 14, 1981.

Publications

Richard Porter, *Sidney Goodman: Paintings, Drawings and Graphics, 1959-1979*, exhibition catalogue, University Park, PA: Pennsylvania State University, 1980, p. 52, no. 65.

William T. Henning, Jr., *Recent Acquisitions*, Chattanooga: Hunter Museum of Art, 1982.

Carolyn Mitchell, "The Hunter Museum, A Showcase for Modern American Art in Chattanooga." *Southern Accents*, May-June, 1984, illus. p. 122.

Goodman is a realist painter. But his is not the acute-focus realism of Richard Estes, Ralph Goings, Robert Cottingham, and others who use the photograph as a direct source of pictorial design; he does not employ a projector to transfer a photographic image to canvas for ready tracing. In the tradition of the distinguished Philadelphia patriarch-realists, Thomas Eakins and Thomas Anshutz, Goodman is interested in people as principal subject. Nearly all his paintings are subtle examinations of the human condition, and typically, they impart an air of mystery or enigma. Frederick R. Brandt contends: " . . . the meanings of his images are purposely left unclear to the viewer." Or, as George Bunker elaborates:

> The apparent simplicity of his subjects is deceptive . . . All the pictures share two
> things in common: the commonplace and a kind of mute foreboding; they are
> both casual and final, the everyday and its obverse self . . . In the end, Good-
> man's paintings invite our attention because we recognize their paradox, and our
> own.

Goodman's subjects are characteristically distant or remote. Faces are usually expressionless, averted, or turned completely away. When the artist allows the viewer to catch the glance of certain people, one feels like an intruder. Impersonality, isolation, withdrawal, disenfranchisement, unwillingness to get involved physically or emotionally—these predicaments of modern human relationship are the underlying themes of Goodman's art. And they may apply even to the potentially erotic situation. The Hunter Museum's 1974-75 oil, *Girl with a Sheet*, an apt example, is one of a series of nude or semi-nude female subjects the artist painted in the 1970s. The initial sight is highly provocative. From behind, the viewer observes a young woman, seductively holding a white sheet against her body, revealing the soft contours of her shoulders and arms. But on continued study, she seems profoundly inaccessible and clinically detached. The setting is plain and austere. A low, horizontal light source from the right models the torso effectively; the head, however, is left in shadow. One can just begin to glimpse the profile of the face as the head is turned slightly to the left. The pose, too, is ambiguous. Why is the woman standing as she is? Does she hold the sheet apart purely for compositional reasons? Is there an implication of impending action? Will she shortly wrap herself within the sheet. Taking the head position as a clue, is she about to turn toward the viewer?

For its metaphysical quality, some critics note a similarity in Goodman's painting to the surrealist visions of Giorgio DeChirico. And for geometric order as well as the play of light, his style has been compared to Edward Hopper. Goodman finds these resemblances superficial. Speaking especially of Hopper he declares:

> We're both interested in light, but the major difference is that there's a little more paranoia in my work, a little more anxiety, a darker, more ominous presence in the work. There is the light in it, but the concern is a little more subjective. There are really more differences than there are similarities.

Goodman does admit admiration for Diego Valasquez, Francisco Goya, Massacio, Piero della Francesca, and Jan Vermeer—artists whose work he first looked at seriously on a European tour in 1960. For graphic mood, he also acknowledges a debt to Italian filmmakers Frederico Fellini and Michelangelo Antonioni.

Goodman was born in Philadelphia in 1936. His parents, who had emigrated from Russia only a decade earlier, unenthusiastically approved his decision to become an artist. To placate their concern for his one day being able to earn a livelihood, he studied commercial illustration under Jacob Landau at the Philadelphia Museum College of Art. Though he never intended to become an illustrator, he stayed on in the program and graduated in 1958. A fascination with parody and the bizarre dominates his earliest painting. His work evolved through styles reminiscent of Goya, the German expressionists Max Beckman and George Grosz, English painter Francis Bacon, and American Ben Shahn. He arrived at his current style about 1965. He currently teaches at the venerable Pennsylvania Academy of the Fine Arts.

George Sugarman (b. 1912)

George Sugarman is one of America's foremost contemporary sculptors. His work to date falls mainly into two stylistic categories, both of which arise out of a long tradition of classically conceived formal abstraction. His best-known works, owing to several important large-scale architectural installations (Federal Court Building, Baltimore, Maryland; First National Bank, St. Paul, Minnesota; Xerox Data Systems Building, El Segundo, California), are multi-component ensembles of brightly colored, "jigsaw" free-form shapes. They suggest, as Sam Hunter observes, those "commercial artifacts and educational toys which test the rudimentary abilities of the child to connect parts to wholes." The works are indeed playful in their intent and visual result, though hardly childish in the intricacies of design and production.

To the second category belong works with a certain kinship to constructivism and minimalism. They are tight, essentially geometric configurations. Such a piece is *Red and Black Spiral*, of 1975. Around a *horizontal* axis four fan-fold or stair-step sections (indeed very much like a spiral stairway on its side) create a formation that is both helical and hyperbolic.

RED AND BLACK SPIRAL
George Sugarman
1975
painted, welded aluminum
69 x 128 x 44 inches
Museum commission with funds supplied in part by the National Endowment for the Arts, a Federal agency

Provenance
Hunter Museum commission.

The rotation of the two spiral sections on one side of the *vertical* axis moves counter to the two sections on the opposite side. From a narrow center footing, the counterbalanced members appear to spring in an undulating wave pattern. Interestingly, contours are reflected in the hard enameled surfaces so as to add another linear compositional element, and the play of shadows adds yet another. The profile of the work alters dramatically as the spectator changes vantage point. In one instance the stair units will be arched and convex; a moment later, as one moves a quarter way around, they become dished and concave. At broadside the sculpture seems more two-dimensional and self-contained, while from an oblique view it is dynamic and expansive. Order, mathematical progression, and serial unit structure — hallmarks of modern building art — mark the sum of impressions the sculpture provides.

Bold color has long been an aspect of Sugarman's work. His earliest sculptures were in wood. In mild frustration he elected to paint them to call attention to the form, thereby rebutting the many whose only comment to him previously had been about the beautiful grains of the natural material. What began as an arbitrary solution and a secondary design factor soon evolved to a state in which color is an integral and primary consideration. "In my sculpture the color is as important as form and space," Sugarman writes. ". . . The color is not used decoratively. It's not used to be pretty or attractive. It is used to articulate the sculpture in space." The artist has employed color to imply weight or density — or lack of it — and to regulate the sense of motion: analogous tones to speed up movement, contrasting or complementaries to slow it down.

Sugarman was born in New York City in 1912 and, except for periods of military service, art study abroad, extended travel and teaching, has lived his entire life there. He was graduated from City College (now University) of New York with a B.A. in 1938. In 1951-52 he studied with the Russian-French sculptor Ossip Zadkine and also attended the Académie de la Grand Chaumiere. He has taught at Hunter College of the City University. In 1967-'68 he was visiting professor at Yale.

Frank Stella (b. 1936)

NOWE MAISTRO (IV)
Frank Stella
1974
paper relief, dyed and collaged hand-colored paper, 3/25
24 x 21¼ x 1⅛ inches
Museum purchase with funds supplied in part by the National Endowment for the Arts, a Federal agency

Provenance

Tyler Graphics, Bedford Village, New York, New York (publishers)
Richard Gray Gallery, Chicago, Illinois

Exhibitions

Sears Bank Show, Sears Tower Building, Chicago, IL, March 1-April 30, 1976.

Probably no artist in the twentieth century, save perhaps Pablo Picasso, has come forth with so many different and original styles of expression as has Frank Stella. And whereas Picasso over the seventy years of his productive life worked alternately in figurative and semi-abstract modes, Stella's whole output in the twenty-five years of his career to this writing has been in totally non-objective, non-figurative invention. Art historian Philip Leider affirms: "He is of the first generation of American artists to have lived his entire creative life in abstraction." Stella himself finds that hardly extraordinary. "I see my work as being determined by the fact that I was born in 1936," he concludes simply.

What *is* astonishing, therefore, is that every few years—two to three on an average—Stella introduces a remarkably new visual thesis, discernably built on what has gone before, yet with novel divergence. Noting the cyclical pattern, critic and longtime Stella monitor Robert Rosenblum reflected in a 1983 article: "Every new show provided the same kind of jaw-dropping response . . . Once more it looked as if a totally fresh, youthful artist had appeared, almost from nowhere, to confront us with numbingly unfamiliar experiences that we could not blink away." Stella's work, thus, is organized into thematically related groups or "series" that generally have progressed from the minimal to the polyglot. Rosenblum continued:

He started as a young Savanarola who banished from the vocabulary of painting everything suggestive of pleasure, freedom, and impulse, leaving us only with a bare skeleton, immobilized in rectilinear patterns of noncolors (black, aluminum, copper). But now he pushed to the opposite extreme, assaulting us with an overwhelming glut of every color in the plastic rainbow, with hard-edged arabesques of decorative curves and serpentine circuits, with every imaginable ragged doodle and scribble in an alphabet of reckless graffiti.

The series titles, which derive from free association rather than specific description, intimate Stella's bent on increasing visual intricacy: from the simple, geometric *Irregular Polygon* series of 1965-66, through the *Pinstripe* of 1967-68; *Protractor* (probably his best-known work) of the late '60's; *Diamond Mine*, early '70s; *Polish Village*, 1973-74; *Brazilian*, 1974-75; *Exotic Bird*, 1976; *Indian Bird*, 1977-78; *Circuit*, 1980-81; *South African Mines*, 1982-83; and *Shards*, 1983-84. However superficially tumultuous an individual piece or a series may first appear, an underlying sense of order and method pervades all of Stella's work. Again, through graphic analogy, Rosenblum effectively summarizes: "Like escalating from an introductory lesson in plane geometry, where the ninety-degree angle and the circle reign supreme, to a course, taught by the same great mathematician, in advanced calculus, where beneath eye- and mind-boggling complexities, his consistent logic still obtains."

The Hunter Museum's Stella, *Nowe Miastro (IV)*, from 1974, is both a multiple and *not* a multiple. The handmade, cotton-pulp paper was pressed into its bas-relief design using molds specially constructed from hand-sewn brass screen and mahogany wood pieces. The process was repeated twenty-six times so that the same essential relief configuration resulted for each item in the "edition." But during the wet formation process, colored paper collage and dyes were applied differently from one paper to the next. After the papers had dried, each was further individually and distinctly hand colored by the artist with casiens or watercolors. Consequently, no two works in the edition are identical. What is more, *Nowe Miastro* is one of five relief designs—each produced in editions of twenty-six—that together constitute a larger project called *Paper Reliefs*. All totaled, the venture comprises 130 different works of art.

Paper Reliefs coincides with Stella's *Polish Village* series and is stylistically related to it. Improvising on certain distinctive architectural motifs from eighteenth- and nineteenth-century frame synagogues, straight lines and geometric shapes seem fitted or locked together in a construct that floats on the page. It is the characteristic relief pattern for *Nowe Miastro* as well as the four other edition designs. One's initial awareness—of structure, compactness, density—is mollified by the fibrous texture of the paper, the feathered and slightly irregular edges of the relief shapes, and the translucent stains of color. The result is a dichotomy of visual effects. Imparting an obvious incongruity, however, was the very basis of Stella's purpose, as he explains: "The *Polish Village* series was about the synagogues that were destroyed and about the obliteration of an entire culture. The culture was constructed in a perishable way . . ."

Stella was born in Malden, Massachusetts, and grew up in the Boston area. He attended the Phillips Academy at Andover, and Princeton University, from which he graduated in 1958. Later the same year he moved to New York City, where he rented a studio, but supported himself for a time working as a house painter. Recognition came quickly, and in 1960 Leo Castelli gave him his first one-man show. Stella has been visiting instructor or artist-in-residence at Dartmouth College in 1963, Cornell and Yale Universities in 1965, and Brandeis University in 1968. In the 1983-84 academic year, he delivered the prestigious Charles Eliot Norton lecture series at Harvard, a particular distinction in that he was the first artist invited to speak since Ben Shahn in 1956, and the first abstract artist ever.

Robert Rauschenberg (b. 1925)

By widespread critical consensus Robert Rauschenberg is one of the most important and most innovative artists in the world. Twenty-five years ago, however, when he was first achieving recognition, many even with modern art preferences thought him the *enfant terrible*, the bad boy of art whose works seemed coarse, incongruous, and, to many, thoroughly repulsive. "Pretty" or "appealing" results would have been the least, if not the antithesis, of Rauschenberg's concerns. And it substantially remains so to the present. He wants people seriously to examine their preconceptions of what art is and ought to be, to re-evaluate and re-order their perceptions so they might discern a new and vastly different dimension of meaning, significance, and even beauty in forms considered disparate or ugly in traditional contexts. Thus, using all manner of trash and discarded materials in a collage technique, along with photosilkscreen, photomontage, and conventional artists' paint, canvas, and panels — he fashions the "combine," a kind of visual tone poem or kaleidoscope of impressions. Through raw appearance and startling juxtaposition, the components of his designs generate, by their very contrast, forceful and provocative ideograms. Then, as Robert Hughes has observed, "absurdity, threat, delicacy, and extreme tension are packed into the image in a way that is Rauschenberg's and Rauschenberg's alone."

Rauschenberg's creative impulse has its roots partly in the dada movement's avowed purpose to destroy traditional standards of taste, partly in the ironic "ready-mades" of Marcel Duchamp, partly in Kurt Schwitter's bold collages, and partly in the aesthetic theories of his long-time friend, controversial artist and composer John Cage. Like certain of Duchamp's dictums or the recent conceptual art practice, Cage has insisted that art is more *process* of creating than the resulting object. By extension, the theory also explains art experiences for which time duration and direct viewer participation are integral factors, such as "happenings" and "environments." A subtle, further variation on this principle is the notion of "pregnant voids." Cage's own music often features long yet carefully measured spans of silence. But in actuality it is never a state of complete quiet. Noises from the audience, musicians, concert hall, or out-of-doors continue to invest and irregularly punctuate the interval.

An application for visual art is aptly demonstrated by Rauschenberg's *Opal Reunion* of 1976 (color plate 38). Voids dominate the central composition; figurative elements are chiefly relegated to the periphery. There is no obvious focal point unless it is the conspicuousness of the empty space itself. As Donald Kuspit interprets, the work is "a configuration of signs that converge into a vital entity that seems to have unity over time." Perceptively, albeit rather flowerily, Kuspit goes on:

> Unless the void existed, no constellation of signs could emerge. A void is the romantic's infinity of possible meanings – not actual meanings. The void is an essential part of the transcendental decorative . . . just as the blackness between the stars in the night sky becomes an essential part of the constellation that the stars are discovered to constitute.

The pictorial and real elements of the composition/constellation — a weatherbeaten oar, a set of bird wings extended as in flight, silkscreened bottles that repeat the spread formation of the wings — all set in a warm, sandy colored field, evoke the more specific awareness of sea and shore. It is perhaps an indirect reference to the areas surrounding the artist's home on Captiva Island, Florida. An unorthodox perpendicular end panel projects three feet toward the viewer, terminating the piece on the right, as it were, and giving a slight sense of enclosure. The inside plane, on the other hand, is faced with Mylar that reflects the entire piece and its immediate environment as a softly diffused mirror image. When looking into that surface the already large composition is effectively extended — in fact, doubled!

Rauschenberg was born in Port Arthur, Texas, in 1925. He studied at the Kansas City Art Institute, the Académie Julian in Paris, and at Black Mountain College in North Carolina, where his principal teacher was the noted former Bauhaus color expert, Josef Albers. It was at Black Mountain, too, that he met Cage and the avant-garde dance choreographer Merce Cunningham, with whom he later collaborated in several theatrical productions. Rauschenberg also studied at the Art Students League in New York. In 1964 he earned considerable

(color plate 38)

OPAL REUNION

Robert Rauschenberg

1976

mixed media combine, six panels

84 x 158 x 36 inches

signed lower left on second panel

Gift of the Benwood Foundation, Mr. and Mrs. Joseph H. Davenport, Jr., Ruth S. and A. William Holmberg, and Mr. and Mrs. Olan Mills, II

Provenance

From the collection of the artist through Heath Gallery, Inc., Atlanta, Georgia

Exhibitions

Out of the South, Heath Gallery, Inc., Atlanta, GA, Oct. 5-9, 1982.

Publications

Donald B. Kuspit, *Out of the South*, exhibition catalogue, Atlanta: Heath Gallery, Inc., 1982, pp. 20-21, no. 8.

Donald B. Kuspit, "Out of the South: Eight Southern-born Artists." *Art Papers*, Nov/Dec 1982, pp. 2-5.

John Howett, "Out of the South" exhibition review, *Art Papers*, Nov/Dec 1982, p. 20.

notoriety when he became only the third American ever to win the grand prize at the prestigious Venice Biennale exhibition.* His work has been acquired by major public and private collections throughout the world.

The other two were James A. M. Whistler and Mark Tobey.

Claes Oldenburg (b. 1929)

TONGUE CLOUD OVER LONDON WITH THAMES BALL
Claes Oldenburg
1976
soft-ground color etching, aquatint, inked a la puopee, 49/60
image: 31½ x 21¼ inches
signed and dated lower right
Museum purchase with funds supplied in part by the National Endowment for the Arts, a Federal agency

Provenance

Petersburg Press, Inc., London, England (publishers)
Allan Frumkin Gallery, Chicago, Illinois

Exhibitions

Contemporary Prints from the Collection of the Hunter Museum of Art, Dulin Gallery of Art, Knoxville, TN, Jan. 5-31, 1981; St. Andrews, Sewanee, TN, Oct. 1-31, 1981.

Claes Oldenburg is probably best known for his ludicrously outsized sculptures of ersatz foods and common household objects. Consequently he has been identified as a pop artist. Pop's major premise was debunking "high art" by raising ostensibly to the status of high art the mundane, mass-produced materials of popular culture (comic strips, advertising art, package design, movies, TV, etc.). Undeniably, Oldenburg fits the pop motivation. In fact, Dore Ashton feels that "of all the artists associated with pop, certainly Claes Oldenburg satisfied the largest number of criteria, whether social, technical, or artistic." Critic Lucy Lippard counts Oldenburg as one of the "New York five" pop artists (the others being Andy Warhol, Roy Lichtenstein, Tom Wesselman, and James Rosenquist). And Oldenburg's own, characteristically frank statement of purpose from 1961 verifies his finding creative validity and worthy social commentary in glorifying or farcifully exaggerating everyday, workaday things:

> I am for an art that is political-erotical-mystical, that does something other than sit on its ass in a museum. I am for an art that grows up not knowing it is art at all . . . I am for an art that involves itself with the everyday crap and still comes out on top. I am for an art that imitates the human, that is comic if necessary, or violent, for whatever is necessary. I am for an art that takes its form from the lines of life . . . and is sweet and stupid as life itself.

Still, unlike the other four New Yorkers' more literal conversion of daily life into pop imagery, Oldenburg represents a comparatively bizarre, surreal, dada-esque side of the movement. He sardonically re-interprets and re-forms depicted articles. Robert Doty observes: "The essence of his creative activity is in the perception, evocation, and association through which he alters conceptions and attitudes about common objects and the human body." Oldenburg looks specifically for the irony possible through contradiction and dislocation; thus he converts hard things to soft, large to small, small to large, the ordinary to the monumental. Such transformations, as John Russell notes, "always bring with them changes in implication." Sometimes the resultant artwork is an easy visual pun or amusing parody, other times a grotesque metamorphosis.

In the mid-1960s Oldenburg began illustrations for a series of improbable urban monuments and public works. (Though most exist only as plans and drawings, and were never meant to be taken seriously, several ideas *were* eventually realized, including the Yale University *Lipstick* of 1969, the Philadelphia *Clothespin* of 1976, and Chicago's *Batcolumn* of 1977.) Sam Hunter explains how they came about:

> These visionary inventions are grafts of the fantasies of childhood on an urban environment whose dehumanization, overcrowding and apparently hopeless problems of litter, traffic congestion, crime and pollution resist rational solution. The irrationality of the man-made environment, with its threat to human survival, makes Oldenburg's visual gibes seem humane and plausible by comparison.

One such make-believe project calls for a blimp-sized toilet flush-tank float ball to be placed in England's Thames River. The cursory suggestion of that bogus monument appears at the lower right in Oldenburg's color soft-ground etching and aquatint, *Tongue Cloud over London with Thames Ball*, from 1976. The composition, however, is dominated by a dark cloud overhead, out of which drops a long tongue, in a basic shape noticeably like that of a tornado or cyclone funnel. *Arts* magazine critic Noel Frackman finds the image "unmistakenly sexual," though he offers no additional explanation. The tongue, bright orange and slick, a vulgar elephantine leer, does seem both inherently lewd and disturbingly menacing. It is for just such works that Ashton applied the terse designation: "Rabelasian iconoclasm."

Oldenburg was born in Stockholm, Sweden, in 1929. His father, a career diplomat, took the family with him while on assignments of Oslo, Norway, New York City, and Chicago, where, after 1936, young Oldenburg grew up and attended school. Oldenburg first studied art at Yale, from which he graduated in 1950. He became a U.S. citizen in 1952. The same year he enrolled at the School of the Art Institute of Chicago, where he studied painting, anatomy, and figure drawing until 1954. He moved permanently to New York in 1956. Soon after his arrival he met other artists—particularly Jim Dine, Red Grooms, George Segal, and Allan Kaprow—who, like him, were questioning the primacy of the main avant-garde movement of the time, abstract expressionism, and the conventional boundaries between art and real life. By 1957 Oldenburg had abandoned the expressionist figurative style that typified his earlier work. He joined with the others in exploring the creative possibilities of environments and happenings—vehicles in which the encounter in process is as important, if not more important, than the finished object. (In fact, there might not be a tangible, finished piece.) He moved on to his more familiar pop experiments in the early '60s.

Philip Pearlstein (b. 1924)

TWO NUDES WITH OAK
STOOL AND CANVAS

Philip Pearlstein

1976

lithograph, 55/100

29 x 36¾ inches

signed lower left

Museum purchase with funds
supplied in part by the
National Endowment for the
Arts, a Federal agency

Provenance

Landfall Press, Inc., Chicago, Illinois (publishers).

How should one perceive Philip Pearlstein's depictions of nude men and women? Certainly they are not academic studies of the wondrous human anatomy, nor of the idealized physical perfection that ancient peoples ascribed to gods and heroes, nor of the Renaissance fascination with man as the measure of all things — and the well-formed physique of man as the measure of measures. But neither are Pearlstein's nudes blatantly sensual or pornographic (though to some, *any* picturing of the unclothed body is obscene). In fact, the subjects are remarkably indifferent to the state of their nudity. Presented without glamorization — without being necessarily good-looking, good-figured, enticing, or arousing — Pearlstein's people sit or recline passively, disinterestedly, dejectedly. "One knows that his models are tired," writes Robert Hughes. "Their faces sag in boredom, their muscles are barely awake." In scenes with more than one figure, each individual seems lost in him- or herself. While the people share the same time and restricted space, they do not interact. Hughes sees the effect as "a peculiar blend of remoteness and intimacy."

French poet and critic Charles Baudelaire in the mid-nineteenth century admonished artists to represent the nude in contemporary situations. Pearlstein has seemingly taken that charge to heart now, a century later. His models speak in a way of the detachment, loneliness, alienation, and apathy that characterize daily life for many, especially in larger cities. They are divested not just of clothing, but of vitality and personality as well. The harsh cropping of heads in many Pearlstein works is a kind of psychological decapitation that prompts the viewer to regard the models not so much as people whom one might wish to identify, but rather as stage properties the artist has arranged chiefly for compositional ends. The snapshot-like, viewfinder framing of the scene suggests an air of candor and immediacy, but the poses, visual angles, lighting, pattern contrasts, undulation of lines, positive and negative shapes — all are consciously coordinated. The scenes impart a convincing three-dimensional illusion into the shallow depth of the artist's studio, yet the strong patterns in the two dimensions of the picture plane are equally pronounced, probably a result of Pearlstein's long interest in oriental

TWO MODELS ON RED
OFFICE SWIVEL CHAIR
Philip Pearlstein
1985
oil on canvas
96 x 72 inches
signed and dated lower right
Museum purchase with funds
provided by the Benwood
Foundation and the 1985
Collectors' Group

Provenance
From the collection of the artist through
Hirschl & Adler Modern, New York, New York
Exhibitions
Philip Pearlstein, Hirschl & Adler Modern, New
York, NY, Feb. 9-March 9, 1985.

graphic arts. Richard S. Field notes the connection: "He has always loved Japanese prints and he has always sought to emulate the space . . . a space that loves the diagonal, the unexpected point of view, and the flatness of any particular form." The recurrent awkward pose and inordinate foreshortening or distortion of the model is in part an accommodation of that spatial concept, and in part a consequence of actually rendering from direct observation at close range. Unlike many other artists associated with the new realism, Pearlstein does not work from photographs. "It never occurred to me," he says, "that people would use photos, because I never had any difficulty drawing or painting."

To achieve a wider circulation and market for his work, the artist began etching and lithography in 1968. He has produced print editions regularly ever since, although painting is still his greater activity. The Hunter Museum's *Two Nudes with Oak Stool and Canvas*, an aluminum-plate lithograph from 1976, is characteristic Pearlstein. A laconic young woman sits on the floor to the right, while a head-cropped man sits uneasily on the strongly delineated stool at left. Each appears weary, preoccupied, scarcely aware of, much less attracted to, the other. Still, a design correspondence exists between the figures, as Field explains at length:

> Whereas the female figure implies deep recession, the male model juts uncomfortably close to the observer. Tensions between background and foreground are heightened by the unusually canted canvas. It provides a foil for the foreground figure whose modeling is a tour de force of dense crayon hatching . . . Thus the left half of the image pushes agressively towards the viewer in contrast to the relative quiessence of the right half. The female model occupies a space that is nearly parallel to the picture plane. Her body is brightly lit, washing out much of the detail and thereby reducing graphic activity. Her fullness extends to all her features, imparting needed conviction to the foreshortening of her extended right leg which incorporates and closes the total space of the left half of the image. This work embraces extremes of description and abstraction, and depth and surface.

Larger-than-life-sized female nudes appear apathetically to the viewer in Pearlstein's imposing oil, *Two Models on Red Office Swivel Chair*, from 1985. Organized along bold diagonals, the composition imparts a structural dynamic that subjectively counters the outward lethargy. The positioning of the models' legs left and right of the center axis is subtly reiterated in the metal legs of the chair, and below in inverted form by the zigzag decorative band of the floor covering. For design coherence, the artist has also sensitively repeated certain shapes and contours. The curvature of the model's calf at the right edge of the picture, for example, is almost exactly restated in the left outline of that portion of the dressing gown falling from the chair seat. All through the composition the two figures — the positive shapes, that is — by their poses circumscribe background areas so as to disclose visually appealing, abstract negative shapes. A stark, analytical light renders the flesh tones hard and decidedly unsensuous, though effectively contrasting the rich fabric patterns of robe and rug.

Pearlstein was born in Pittsburgh, Pennsylvania, in 1924. In 1949 he completed a B.F.A. degree at Carnegie Institute of Technology (now Carnegie-Mellon University), where Andy Warhol was both a classmate and roommate. He earned an M.A. in art history from the Institute of Fine Arts, New York University, in 1955. In the later '50s he evolved through a variety of styles — social realism, pre-pop, abstract-expressionist landscape. Then in 1958 he was awarded a Fulbright fellowship to study a year in Rome. It was a pivotal time in which he moved away from abstraction in order to record the ancient Italian monuments and ruins that he found fascinating. Returning to the United States, he was perturbed at seeing "the same de Kooning-derived work" that for a decade had been showing at contemporary galleries everywhere. "I felt the abstract/realist split then," Pearlstein recounts. Shortly he painted his earliest nudes. By 1970 critic Hilton Kramer confidently called Pearlstein "the foremost realist painter in America."

From 1959 to '63 Pearlstein was an instructor at the Pratt Institute in Brooklyn, New York. Simultaneously in '62 and '63 he was also visiting critic at Yale University. Since 1963 he has been distinguished professor of art at Brooklyn College.

Paul Jenkins (b. 1923)

Like an aurora in bright daylight, plumes of vivid color stream forth to the left and right from a source below the "horizon" at lower center in Paul Jenkins' striking abstract: *Phenomena Royal Violet Visitation* (color plate 39). The hues move out effortlessly, fluidly, with neither benefit nor necessity of brushstroke. The configuration seems expansive. The effect, however, is just the opposite of the way Jenkins achieved the image; he controlled the rendering from the sides inward. His technique was to pour paints that had been carefully prepared to suitable viscosity onto an unstretched, pre-moistened canvas. By tilting and manipulating the canvas he directed the paint to flow inward, then down and off the material (as it happens, into a collecting tray). Often in his painting Jenkins will use an ivory knife, sometimes attached to a long holder, to conduct the paints' course more deliberately, and to regulate the emerging result. In considerable measure, the outcome is directly attributed to the flexibility and extensibility of contemporary acrylic paints. As critic Alfred Frankenstein points out (with a dubious, or, more likely, indiscriminate allusion to destiny):

> There is one thing you can comprehend at once, with no more guidance than your naked eye: Paul Jenkins is one of those who were selected by fate to come into their own with the introduction of the acrylic medium. His mature work is inconceivable except in terms of acrylic, with its fluidity, its acquiescence in unconventional technique, and its range of luminosity in color.

Jenkins' painting style descends from abstract expressionism through color field abstraction to the so-called canvas stainers, or more specifically from the revolutionary pour-and-drip paint application of Jackson Pollock and Sam Francis, to Mark Rothko's spatial envelopes and mysterious luminosity, to Barnett Newman's vast panels of purely subjective and evocative color, to the translucent color veils of Morris Louis and the delicate tonal shapes of Helen Frankenthaler. Interestingly, Jenkins became a good friend of Pollock, Rothko, and Newman in the early 1950s shortly after he first went to New York, and in the ensuing years he has acknowledged a particular affinity with Louis and Frankenthaler. But whereas Louis and Frankenthaler tended to be more economical and subdued in their staining method, and usually applied their pigments to unprimed fabric, Jenkins typically employs a bold spectrum and prefers canvas primed and white for a brighter and truer color reflectivity.

It was also in the early 50's that Jenkins encountered various philosophical concepts that bore greatly on his creative temperament and growth. Albert Elsen has noted and commented upon these at length in his 1972 biography of the artist, but they are here recapitulated briefly: Through a series of public lectures Jenkins was introduced to the teachings of Russian esoteric philosopher Georges Gurdjieff, who contended that a human being has no permanent self; one is never the person one was a moment ago. Moreover, according to Gurdjieff, certain special individuals develop the capacity to transcend the physical body and assume a second, "astral" identity, a spiritual second self. "It was Gurdjieff who encouraged me to want to elevate the subjective in art," Jenkins relates, "to make that my purpose and to accept the notion of change in a new but not negative way." From reading the Confucian *I Ching (Book of Changes)*, Jenkins adopted the similar premise that continuous flux and transformation underlie all existence. On reading Carl Jung's *Psychology and Alchemy*, he took seriously the need to "repudiate the arrogant claim of the conscious mind to be the whole of the psyche, and to admit that the psyche is a reality which we cannot grasp with our present means of understanding." In the early '50s many people in New York intellectual and artistic circles had become interested in Zen, a school of Buddhist thinking that stresses that "enlightenment" can be attained through disciplined meditation and self-contemplation. Jenkins read Eugen Herrigel's *Zen in the Art of Archery*, an elaborate investigation on the importance in Japan of archery training on the mind. He learned of the "kendo stroke," a method of spiritual preparedness for an action—in archery, projecting one's astral self, psyche, or inner being to the arrow and target, thereby telekinetically controlling the flight and hitting the mark.

To Jenkins the application for painting seemed obvious. He soon spoke of creating a "metaphysical" rather than optical illusion, and he interpreted his creative role as that of automatist responding to extrasensory suggestion. "I paint the face of God," Jenkins says, "not as I would have him but as he chooses to come to me." Jenkins sees both process and product result of that process as "phenomena." In fact he refers to himself as a "visual phenominist" or "abstract phenominist," and since the late 1950s he has prefaced the titles for all his paintings with the word "phenomena" (the Hunter's piece to wit). He explains further:

> The word phenomenon came to me after finishing a painting which happened with no preconceived idea. The sensation of the experience happened within me, not outside me, as though it were done by a "medium." Within the act came the discovery, not arbitrarily before. I have to approach it indirectly through the meshes and foliage of darker memory and it comes in the working, in the discovery with paint; vortexes, shafts, pillars of light, images moving unceasingly, caught with purpose. Laws are made as one moves and method joins with meaning.

(color plate 39)

PHENOMENA ROYAL VIOLET VISITATION

Paul Jenkins

1977

acrylic on canvas

55 x 169 inches

signed and dated lower center

Gift of Ruth S. and A. William Holmberg

Provenance

From the collection of the artist through Gimpel & Weitzenhoffer, Ltd., New York, New York

Publications

Diana W. Suarez, *Bluff and the Magic Mansion, A Children's Guide to the Hunter Museum of Art,* Chattanooga: Hunter Museum of Art, 1980.

Carolyn Mitchell, "The Hunter Museum, A Showcase for Modern American Art in Chattanooga." *Southern Accents,* May-June, 1984, illus. p. 124.

Jenkins was born in Kansas City, Missouri, in 1923. After graduating from high school he studied briefly at the Kansas City Art Institute. However his stronger interest at the time was in drama. Before he was twenty, he worked at the Youngstown Playhouse in Ohio, and attended the prestigious Cleveland Playhouse on a scholarship. Two years' service with the Naval Air Corps interrupted his studies between 1943 and '45, but he went on for two additional years at the Drama School of Carnegie Institute (now Carnegie-Mellon University) in Pittsburgh. Jenkins admits that the early experience in theatre and dance, including a particular admiration for famed modern dancer and choreographer Martha Graham, has also had a bearing upon his painting. Truly one can sense the quality of dance movement in the undulating contours, blurred edges, and energetic twists and swirls that characterize his work. While at Carnegie, Jenkins also took art classes. In 1948 he elected to pursue painting full time and moved to New York to attend the Art Students League. He studied there nearly four years, chiefly with Yasuo Kuniyoshi.

In 1976 a number of Jenkins' paintings were used in the filming of the motion picture *An Unmarried Woman*, directed by Paul Mazursky. British actor Alan Bates, playing the part of a contemporary New York artist, learned in a month of instruction directly from Jenkins how to emulate the pour-and-flow method for scenes in the movie. "You lose yourself in the technique," Bates later reflected. "The kind of thing Jenkins produces looks so simple, but it comes from a very good mind and a very emotional soul. The man's a genius, of course."

Alex Katz (b. 1927)

Alex Katz' clever two-sided portrait of his wife, *Ada at Table*, from 1977, technically is sculpture in that it operates visually in three-dimensions. The piece is, however, truer in concept and format to painting—more specifically to two paintings, two flat two-dimensional images juxtaposed back to back in such a way as to represent, on opposite sides, the respective left and right profiles of the subject. Either profile might as readily have been painted over the background on a canvas. It is in fact from cutout figures in paper or board, shapes the artist would position temporarily on canvas in "trial" composition, that the idea for a separate sculptural application suggested itself. Katz first experimented with cutouts, both as aids to pictorial design and as independent three-dimensional objects, in the early 1950s; cutouts continue to the present as his only attempted sculptural idiom. Noting that it is obviously an extension of painting, Frank H. Goodyear, Jr. remarks: "The illusion of a Katz cutout figure in space—thin, compressed, flat, even if it is painted on both sides—is just that—a painted illusion."

It is, then, mainly as a painter that Katz has established his reputation as an important twentieth-century progressive, though his progressiveness was not so recognized in the 1950s, when abstract expressionism dominated modern art. Non-figurative artists had long spurned representational art, contending it was too conventional, too hackneyed, too easy. Katz countered with the stinging and well-founded charge that abstract expressionism had itself degenerated into a style overworked, mannered, and frought with cliché imitations of Willem de Kooning, Franz Kline, and other of the few major proponents of gestural painting. Perceiving a crucial point in modernism, Katz offered an alternative way in a novel form of realism. His solution was not a return to narrative illustration, nor a reversion to traditional landscape, portrait, still-life, or genre modes of the past. Instead, his realism was strongly to accord the actual two-dimensionality of the picture plane; he stressed flatness and design "on" rather than "into" the surface. Characteristically, plane volumes abut plane spaces. He has sought a simplified visual vocabulary, not in geometric reduction as did Cézanne, but in seemingly asking 'how much detail does a realistic picture require to impart convincing illusion?'—then painting *just* that amount. Avoiding commemoration, moralization, story-telling, even reference to particular time and place, Katz illuminates his images with a bold, smooth, directionless and timeless light—except, as he has stated, that he strives for "an absolute present-tense light." Again, avoiding sentimentality or emotional projection, Katz' subjects are, as John Perreault astutely summarizes: "peculiar, cool, neutral, detached, impersonal." Nonetheless, the people project psychological depth. Ada in the Hunter's piece, for example, is devoid of overt feeling, yet conveys a probing mental state.

Katz also typically works large, producing paintings that are six, eight, ten or more feet on a side. For impact on the viewer, such outsized scale is effectively akin to those forms of everyday popular American communication: billboards and movie screens. And with much the same sense of monumentality, immediacy, and arresting personal association, Katz frequently fills his picture area with one or two faces—in the compelling manner of the TV, movie, or advertising closeup.

A lifelong resident of New York, Katz was born in Brooklyn, in 1927, and reared in neighboring Queens. As a youth he had wanted to become a commercial artist. But he turned increasingly to fine art and to painting while attending New York's Cooper Union between 1946 and '49. There he studied with Robert Gwathmey, Morris Kantor, Peter Busa, and Carol Harrison. The 1949-50 academic year he attended the Skowhegan Art School in Maine, studying chiefly with Henry Varnum Poor. Subsequently he also taught at Skowhegan during the summer sessions of 1963 and '65. He taught regular terms at the Pratt Institute from 1962 to '65. From 1960 to '63, he was visiting critic at Yale University, and he served in a similar capacity in 1971 and '72 at the University of Pennsylvania. Katz' early paintings, from the 1950s, remind one of the abstract figurative styles of Milton Avery, Richard Diebenkorn, or Elmer Bishoff. When he turned in the late '50s to the spare, economical realism for which he has come to be recognized, he was a forerunner of both the "pop" realism of the '60s, and the super- or photo-realism of the later '60s, '70s, and '80s.

ADA AT TABLE
Alex Katz
1977
oil on cut-out aluminum
19 x 22 inches
Museum purchase with funds provided by the Benwood Foundation and the 1983 Collectors' Group

Provenance

From the collection of the artist through Robert Miller Gallery, Inc., New York, New York

Exhibitions

Susanne Hilberry Gallery, Birmingham, MI, 1979.
Mira Godard Gallery, Toronto, Canada, 1981.
John C. Stoller Gallery, Minneapolis, MN, 1982.

Publications

William T. Henning, Jr., *Recent Acquisitions*, Chattanooga: Hunter Museum of Art, 1983.

Kenneth Noland (b. 1924)

Witnessing the mannerist phase and steady decline of abstract expressionism in the late 1950s and early '60s, Kenneth Noland became a leading figure among a younger generation of abstract artists who sought viable new directions in purposefully anti-expressionist forms. What emerged was an art that is restrained, ordered, characteristically offering little sugges-tion of the artist's emotional transport in producing finished works. Thus, heavy calligraphic paint handling, or, in sculpture, tactile evidence of materials manipulation (that could graphically demonstrate an artist's temperament by idiosyncratic ways materials are

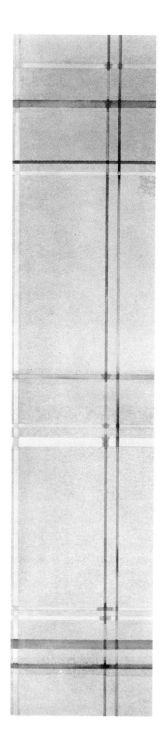

GOLD DOMAIN
Kenneth Noland
1972
oil on canvas
71⅝ x 16 inches
Gift of the artist

Provenance
From the collection of the artist.

wielded) was judged excessive, undisciplined, affected or melodramatic—and passé. Critic Clement Greenberg coined the term "post-painterly abstraction," in 1961, to signal the factor common to several reactionary, sometimes stylistically overlapping, trends: "minimalism," "hard edge" (both of which terms can be applied to two-dimensional art as well as sculpture), "op," and "color-field" (which apply to painting and printmaking). All of the movements tend to manifest a smooth, mechanized surface, evoking less the hand of the artist, more the emanation of some technological procedure; much less the feelings or moods of the artist, more an impersonal, yet timeless (in that the image is reduced to simple shapes and patterns) design.

Noland's paintings of the later '50s and '60s typically present—for inherent universality, avoidance of traditional associations, and an ambiguous illusionistic space—deceptively complex studies of geometric shapes—targets and chevrons—with bold, clean color. Toward the end of the period he devised wide panels of continuous horizontal stripes, a juxtapositioning of bright color bands that bring to mind how a musical chord might be displayed on a fanciful electronic scope. The majority of works aptly fit the criteria for minimalist and hard-edge painting. But in the early 1970s Noland steered his post-painterly style toward spatial illusion, informed by the sensory effects of color, in geometric bands that course both horizontally and vertically, appearing to superimpose in a plaid-like pattern. In fact, the several-years' production of paintings in this particular mode has been called the "plaid series." The principal format for plaid pieces is vertical, height two, three, even four times greater than width. Compared to the earlier horizontal-stripe paintings that the eye must scan in long side-to-side movements, the vertical plaid paintings work the eye both up-and-down and in short horizontal swipes. Hence the artwork is more immediate, more frontal; the eye is more active, the viewer's attention more focused. As critic Walter D. Bannard observes of the plaid canvases: "The thin vertical is a cautious shape, aiding coherence by 'stacking,' and by our innate perception of verticals as tight units."

As have some critics, the viewer may at first see Noland's plaids as derived from certain late paintings of Piet Mondrian, those the Dutch neo-plasticist produced in America, wherein he departed from his near-dogmatic use of black vertical and horizontal stripes against a white field, in favor of primary-color stripes (for example: *New York City I* and *New York City II*, both from 1942, private collections). But Mondrian, essentially a draftsman, employed the flattened grid to emphasize compositional structure, whereas Noland stresses color and space, or better perhaps, color *as* space. Critic Kenworth Moffett says of the plaid paintings:

> These pictures are exceptional in Noland's work in their coloristically varied field areas. The bands are kept close in color to the field or are set in complementary relationships to it so as to prevent it from falling away in an uncontrolled spatial way. Or sometimes the field is bled over the bands partly enveloping them atmospherically.

To augment a sense of color-space, that is, to render his color as insubstantial or vaporous as possible, Noland "stains" his paints directly into the unprimed canvas. The pigments thereby represent nothing corporeal, nothing in traditional illusionistic space; the paint appears not even to be sitting on the fabric. Color is free to "breathe" or expand, to advance and recede purely by its own optical propensity. Noland's stained canvases assert the fundamental premise of color-field painting, yet they also retain much of the geometric order of hard-edge or minimalism. Moffett adds: "The paintings come across like windows with panes of softly colored glass framed by bright mullions."

The Hunter Museum's *Gold Domain*, from 1972, is characteristic plaid-series painting. Four-and-a-half times taller than wide, it directly corresponds to, and confronts, the viewer's own axis. The "field" bands are mainly tones of pale yellow and yellow-orange, so that any quality of color movement or "breathing" is subtle. A system of taut vertical and horizontal stripes in pastel pinks and blues deploys in such a way as to divide the field into a remarkably varied pattern of rectangles, no two exactly the same. In one instance the lines appear to float above the field, in another the rectangles advance like tiles from the surrounding grout. The two long vertical stripes just right of center "bleed" at the intersection of certain horizontal lines, an effect that suggests a kind of vibration, like just-plucked strings of a harp. The visual "zing" additionally activates what at initial or casual observation seems a static image.

Noland was born at Asheville, North Carolina, in 1924. He studied art with Ilya Bolotowsky at Black Mountain College (near Asheville) from 1946 to '48, and with cubist sculptor Ossip Zadkine in Paris in 1948 and '49. On his return to the United States he settled in Washington, D.C., where he taught at the Institute of Contemporary Art from 1950 to '52 and Catholic University of America from 1953 to '59. Early in his Washington years, Noland became close friends with painter Morris Louis. In 1953, Clement Greenberg took the two men to visit Helen Frankenthaler's studio in New York City. Frankenthaler had just begun working in her highly personal method of soaking and staining paints directly into raw canvas, eliminating any brushwork. Duly impressed with the resultant visual effect, Noland and Louis adapted the technique to their own distinctly individual styles, and, at the same time, gave impetus to the group of artists who would later be known as the Washington Color School.*

Noland moved to New York in 1961, and currently lives in Shaftsbury, Vermont. In 1964 his work was represented in the prestigious Venice Biennale exhibition. While best known for painting, the artist has also produced sculpture, and, since the plaid series, his work has evolved to a simultaneously more painterly and more sculptural result, often involving irregularly shaped canvases, comparatively tactile surfaces, and compositions that echo or play off against the perimeter definition of such canvases.

*Including also Sam Gilliam, Gene Davis, Thomas Downing, Howard Mehring, and Paul Reed.

Jack Tworkov (1900-1982)

UNTITLED
Jack Tworkov
c. 1950
pencil and pastel on paper
23½ x 18 inches
Museum purchase with funds provided by the Benwood Foundation and the 1982 Collectors' Group

Provenance

Collection of the artist
Nancy Hoffman Gallery, New York, New York

Exhibitions

Jack Tworkov: Works on Paper, 1933-1982, Nancy Hoffman Gallery, New York, NY, March 26-April 28, 1982; The Mint Museum, Charlotte, NC, June 20-Aug. 15, 1982.

Publications

Jack Tworkov: Works on Paper, 1933-1982, exhibition catalogue, New York: Nancy Hoffman Gallery, 1982.

William T. Henning, Jr., *Recent Acquisitions,* Chattanooga: Hunter Museum of Art, 1982.

Jack Tworkov's mature work, that is, his production from the late 1940s until his death in 1982, is marked by two distinct and seemingly disparate styles, one following the other in time. The two Hunter Museum pieces illustrated in the catalogue are representative of each. The untitled pencil and pastel drawing from 1953 is characteristic of the artist's abstract expressionistic period. Tworkov was part of the "action painting" wing of abstract expressionism, represented by such figures as Franz Kline, Robert Motherwell, and Willem de Kooning. H. H. Arneson has written: "Of the brush-gesture painters after de Kooning, Jack Tworkov is the most individual." It is a fitting comparison, especially in that Tworkov and de Kooning began a friendship about 1940, and the two shared a studio in the late '50s.

Tworkov's was a "subdued" gestural manner. "Abstract expressionism never meant to me an esthetic of disorder," he asserted. His work in the style is typified by even and regular strokes of the brush (or, as in the case of the museum's drawing, pencil, pastel, or crayon), predominantly vertical or inclining slightly to the right, like a handwriting slant. A single brushstroke has been called "flame-like;" many strokes juxtaposed seem to coalesce into squarish panels that in turn are organized on a tight, near-geometric, vertical-horizontal substructure. The surface is restless, yet the composition is controlled and restrained.

In the late 1960s, Tworkov began to move from what Andrew Forge calls "'hot' gestural painting" to "'cool' measured painting," the second of his major styles. The former vigorous brush technique is reduced to an overall pattern of small modulated dashes, set within geometric configurations formed as straight lines extend back and forth across the plane, dividing it into component rectangles, trapezoids, and triangles. While most of the surface remains a continuous monochromatic color field, certain few of the geometric shapes are set out in contrasting hues, which provide a sense of design emphasis or direction, and in some cases — as with Q3-78-#3 (color plate 40) — a subtle dynamism as colors optically "pull" one against another. Though the brushwork is a whisper of its earlier abstract-expressionist effect, one can still feel a delicate surface animation, accented by periodic flickers of light, as along the vertical line in the lower center.

Comparing and critically evaluating the two phases of Tworkov's production, Forge summarizes:

> . . . it seems to me that we are drawn into two universal modes of perception, the storming unities of infancy, its rages and enveloping comforts – and the anxious responsibility of later experience with its mature recognition of a freestanding reality with its acceptance of potential loss.

Tworkov was born at Biala, Poland, in 1900. He came with his family to the United States at age thirteen, settling in New York City. From 1920 to '23 he attended Columbia University, where he majored in English. But he also had opportunity there to take art courses. He transferred in '23 to the National Academy of Design, where he worked mainly with Charles Hawthorne. He transferred a second time in 1925 to the more progressive Art Students League, studying two years with Boardman Robinson and Guy Pene du Bois. He became an American citizen in 1928. Though he made his permanent home at New York City and Provincetown, Massachusetts, he was often away for extended periods because he was a popular, sought-after teacher. He served as artist-in-residence at numerous colleges, including: Pratt Institute, Queens College, New York University, American University, Black Mountain College, Indiana University, University of Minnesota, University of Mississippi, and Yale University. In 1981, a year before his death, he was elected to membership in the American Academy and Institute of Arts and Letters.

Jack Youngerman (b. 1926)

Painter and sculptor Jack Youngerman, who was born in Louisville, Kentucky, in 1926, came of age and artistic maturity in the years immediately following World War II, when progressive American art was dominated by abstract expressionism. But his development—including studies at the University of North Carolina from 1944 to '46 and the University of Missouri, from which he earned a B.A. degree in 1947—evidences only peripheral involvement with the abstract-expressionist movement. He encountered

(color plate 40)

Q3-78- #3

Jack Tworkov

1978

oil on canvas

54 x 54 inches

signed on reverse

Museum purchase with funds provided by the Benwood Foundation and the 1983 Collectors' Group

Provenance

The collection of the artist
Nancy Hoffman Gallery, New York, New York

Exhibitions

Jack Tworkov: Fifteen Years of Painting, The Solomon R. Guggenheim Museum, New York, NY, April 5-June 20, 1982.

Publications

Jack Tworkov: Fifteen Years of Painting, exhibition catalogue, New York: The Solomon R. Guggenheim Museum, 1982, cover illus. and on p. 43.

William T. Henning, Jr., *Recent Acquisitions,* Chattanooga: Hunter Museum of Art, 1983.

Carolyn Mitchell, "The Hunter Museum, A Showcase for Modern American Art in Chattanooga." *Southern Accents,* May-June, 1984, illus. p. 128.

MECOX BAY
Jack Youngerman
1978
acrylic on wood, two-sided
72 x 96 x 1⅜ inches
initialed lower right
Gift of Mr. and Mrs. R.B.
Davenport, III

Provenance

From the collection of the artist through Heath Gallery, Inc., Atlanta, Georgia

Exhibitions

Out of the South, Heath Gallery, Inc., Atlanta, GA, Oct. 5 - 9, 1982.

Publications

Donald B. Kuspit, *Out of the South,* exhibition catalogue, Atlanta: Heath Gallery, Inc., 1982, pp. 28-29, no. 18.

Donald B. Kuspit, "Out of the South: Eight Southern-born Artists." *Art Papers,* Nov/Dec. 1982, pp. 2-5.

John Howett, "Out of the South," exhibition review, *Art Papers* Nov/Dec 1982, p. 20.

it, then virtually by-passed it en route to the familiar hard-edge, simple-configuration design that typifies his style and has made him a prominent figure among the "post-painterly abstractionists."

Upon graduation Youngerman lived abroad, and, significantly, *away* from the contemporary American art scene for the duration of his twenties, from 1947 to '56. With his base at Paris, he traveled extensively in Europe and the Near East. He studied briefly at the École des Beaux Arts, where he was introduced to constructivism, as well as the related structural refinement of Piet Mondrian, the bold-silhouette, dada-esque forms of Hans Arp, and the decorative patterning in the late work of Henri Matisse, an artist he especially admired. Between 1952 and '56 Youngerman also worked periodically with architect Michael Ecochard on building projects in Lebanon and Iraq, where he gained an awareness of the geometricized or foliate arabesque ornament of traditional Islamic art.

Youngerman was aptly fitted, therefore, upon his return to the United States in '56, to identify with the still-germinal anti-expressionist movement. In New York City, where he settled and has continued to reside, he associated with a group of hard-edge painters that included Al Held, Ellsworth Kelly, Leon Polk Smith, and Frank Stella. His work is noticeably different from that of his fellow "hard-edge-its," however, by virtue of his favoring organic or irregular shapes. His production of the late '50s and '60s featured two or three ragged, interlocking shapes in strongly contrasting colors on large canvasses. Often black registers as foreground, while a high-keyed hue suggests depth—just the opposite of the usual color spatial-illusion property. Despite the post-painterly determination to avoid the emotionally evocative, Youngerman's works of the period "feel" powerful, aggressive, even menacing.

Youngerman is different, too, from other hard-edge artists in his thorough preoccupation with the visual tension between the "positive" figure and the "negative" ground or field against which the positive image is placed. He strives for a kind of reciprocal relationship that is alternately active and passive. The artist explains: "The active shape transfers its dynamism to the previously passive space that it seizes. The surrounding space is animated and it seizes the shape in its turn." Critic Carter Ratcliff informs from the viewer's perspective: "The distinction between figure and ground is so elegantly clear that a limit of clarity is reached, then crossed, and then the elements shift roles—figures become fragments of ground, ground breaks up into figure . . . Every form can finally be read with ease as either positive or negative."

In the 1970s Youngerman moved away from the jagged-shaped imagery toward either more fluid designs with gently rolling, streamlined contours or curvilinear, centripetal forms. The former effect is reminiscent of Art Nouveau stylisms. As Ratcliff observes: "These whiplash curls are quite close to those of Hector Guimard and his many followers." The latter disklike motifs derive from the artist's long interest in Eastern meditative design figures—more specifically, the Yantra, a sign-device upon which the viewer concentrates systematically, sometimes in a linear progression, more often from the outside in on a circular form, eventually to achieve an acute spiritual focus for contemplating the divinity.

Both design elements are presented in the Hunter Museum's *Mecox Bay*, an acrylic painted, bi-fold wood screen, from 1978. The screen is in itself an intimation of something Oriental. But to it have been added, front and back, motifs of a decided Far Eastern character. Large spiral disks, an abstracted variation on the mandala format, mirror one another in bright red-orange, a Chinese vermilion against the natural varnished wood background, on the two outside panels (not illustrated). The continuous image of a broad undulating wave-like form in vivid cerulean blue sweeps across the two inside or front panels. At the onset of viewing the blue seems convincingly positive. After one's attention has been fixed (for a length of time that varies with the individual), however, the warm tones of the wood ground become assertive, and, as with a click, the artist's desired reciprocal tension and equilibrium is established. The lone wave as a motif of "heroic" proportions recalls yet another, and not so subtle Oriental connotation: Japanese master printmaker Katsushika Hokusai's famous *Wave at Kanagawa*, of 1823-29.

Rutgers University professor Donald B. Kuspit submits a thoughtful critical analysis of *Mecox Bay*:

> *Ostensibly a folding screen and so, from a conventional viewpoint, clearly having a decorative purpose, it in fact clearly articulates a sense of temporal movement. There is a slow unfolding of movement on the screen's back. The* Japonisme *of both sides is self-evident, with the design expanding beyond the frame without bursting it, a potential implicit in the flat, brightly colored surfaces of Japanese prints. The use of a single color in a broad flat plane takes us right back to Gauguin's idea of decorative abstraction from nature and his idea of using such a plane of color to sum up 'everything . . . in one instant.' There is the same interest in what Gauguin called the 'inner force of color.'*

In the 1980s Youngerman has proceeded to create large relief objects—wall-mounted, yet a combination of painting and sculpture—of shaped polystyrene construction. The brightly colored artworks in some examples appear like great abstracted butterflies. More often the pieces are round swirl or pinwheel designs that seem again to address the Yantra premise.

Jack Beal (b. 1931)

Jack Beal's highly realistic oil from 1981, *The Painting Lesson*, can be passably studied and appreciated as reproduced in this catalogue (color plate 41). But for optimum effectiveness, the spectator really must confront the seven-by-eight-foot painting firsthand. Then one realizes fully that the people depicted are life-sized, and that the studio interior (despite the exaggerated, tipped-up perspective) appears as a continuation from the observer's real space. Because scale both within and without the painting is approximately the same, one can emphatically project into the scene far more readily than were the piece smaller. An awareness comes quickly that what the teacher and his students are looking at so intently — presumably the subject or set-up they are trying to capture on their canvases — is none other than the viewer. Involving the observer as an active participant is a characteristic of much Beal work. He acknowledges: "Communications with the audience has become for me as necessary a factor as the aesthics of the picture."

In *The Painting Lesson*, Beal and the viewer communicate in a subtle yet direct and personal way. The stocky, blond, bespectacled instructor, who leans forward to point out something in the woman student's work, is the artist's own likeness. During a 1983 informal conversation with Richard N. Gregg, director of the Allentown Art Museum, Beal further explained the idiosyncratic imagery of the painting: The two students are also real individuals. The woman, whose name is Ellen Hutchenson, actually is not a painter, but rather Beal's bookkeeper. The bearded man is artist-friend Dean Hartung. Amidst the seeming clutter of the room, one may find fragmentary visual references to works by eighteen artists whom Beal admires, including: David, Velásquez, Rembrandt, Rubens, Titian, Caravaggio, Millet, Corot, and Manet. The plastic "Visible Man" at lower left center is, according to Beal, an important personal symbolic device, to suggest that beauty originates from within the self. The curious dark painting on the easel in the background, upper right corner, is another self-portrait. That he here appears to be "stabbed in the back" by the blade-like edge of an artwork alludes to an unpleasant experience he had while teaching at the Skowhegan Art School in Maine. Beal and his wife are frequent flea-market patrons, and some of the items they have acquired are part of the disarray. All of these "props" are components in a carefully staged arrangement of shapes, textures, angles, and directions. Moreover, the heavily tactile, richly colored, and dramatically lighted tableau is mildly reminiscent of the Dutch still-life tradition, for which Beal developed considerable enthusiasm after seeing many such works on a 1980 European trip. "I am making twentieth-century pictures," he said in an interview, "but I've learned a lot from my sixteenth- and seventeenth-century colleagues." He went on to reveal:

> My whole painting career I've searched for an equitable balance between human needs and aesthetic needs. It's a very exciting conflict. Clearly I'm a modern painter, but my interests are extremely varied and I try to draw stimulation from all kinds of sources . . . I'm trying to paint people and things the way I think most people see people and things. And I am trying to paint them as they are.

Beal divides his residency between New York City and his farm near Oneonta in upstate New York. He was born in Richmond, Virginia, in 1931. He attended the College of William and Mary and later the Art Institute of Chicago, where he received his bachelor's degree. At the time of his graduation, the abstract-expressionist movement was nearing its height, and Beal was working accordingly in an abstract style. Eventually he rejected non-objective art in favor of the realistic manner that has typified his painting since the late 1960s. Though he prefers to call himself a "life artist" rather than a realist, he is undeniably one of the principal figures responsible for the revival of realist and narrative art as valid and critically recognized contemporary expression.

(color plate 41)

THE PAINTING LESSON

Jack Beal

1980-1981

oil on canvas

84 x 96 inches

signed and dated lower right inscribed: For W.M.

Gift of Mr. and Mrs. John T. Lupton

Provenance

From the collection of the artist through Allan Frumkin Gallery, New York, New York

Exhibitions

The Artist's Studio in American Painting, 1840-1983, Allentown Art Museum, Allentown, PA, Sept. 25, 1983-Jan. 8, 1984.

Publications

Nicolai Cikovsky, *The Artist's Studio in American Painting, 1840-1983,* exhibition catalogue, Allentown, PA: Allentown Art Museum, 1983, no. 63.

Sean Bronzell, "Bios—Jack Beal." *American Artist,* Nov. 1983, illus. p. S30.

Louise Nevelson (1899-1988)

Prominent modern sculptor Louise Nevelson is probably best known for large modular wood "walls" (and, in some cases, complete environments) of architectonically arranged compartments, into each of which have been fixed all manner of found materials — bits of old furniture, newel posts, balusters, chair slats, barrel staves, and the like — what Wayne Anderson calls a "disparate array of societal debris." Dealer Arnold G. Glimcher adds: "Nevelson gleans the forms from the detritus of society that satisfy the selectivity of her eye and from which, in a system of interdependency, she creates new images." While the tendency is to see the finished ensemble as an appeal to nostalgia based on one's personal response to the various items of attrition, Nevelson asserts strongly that original function or history of objects has no bearing upon their use in the construct. What *is* of paramount importance is the abstract shape, the design, the pattern. Despite the artist's avowed non-representational purpose, it is doubtful that a viewer can ever fully disassociate prior utility. But the outcome is far from inappropriate, as Sam Hunter explains:

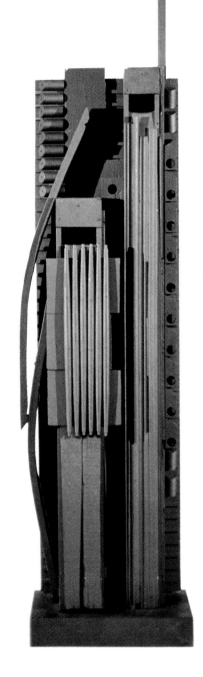

CASCADES-PERPENDICULARS
XXVII
Louise Nevelson
1980-1982
painted wood
90 x 22 x 13 inches
Museum purchase with funds
provided by the Benwood
Foundation and the 1984
Collectors' Group

Provenance

From the collection of the artist through The
Pace Gallery, New York, New York

Exhibitions

*Louise Nevelson: Cascades Perpendiculars Si-
lence Music*, The Pace Gallery, New York, NY,
Jan. 14-Feb. 19, 1983.

Publications

*Louise Nevelson: Cascades Perpendiculars Si-
lence Music*, exhibition catalogue, New York:
The Pace Gallery, 1983, detail illus. on cover.

*Effects of weathering and aging and marks of human use persist to a degree, and
surround the fragments with an aura of privileged status. The fact that discarded
objects, taken out of the stream of life and use, have been assembled with such
lucid precision creates a subtle interplay between personal identification and the
overriding consideration of design. The repeating, only slightly varied structures
within the larger whole suggest continuing mental effort . . . as if a problem had
yet to be restated and did not admit of final solution. Nevelson's ensembles*

245

function finally with the "metaphysical" ambiguity of a de Chirico still life, where geometric style acts as a source of poetic mystery rather than of clarity and precision.

Rosalind K. Krauss sees the meter and cadence Hunter describes as a "sequential piling up of moments . . . to create the sensation of real time," an effect similar to that achieved in certain cubist works, notably Marcel Duchamp's *Nude Descending a Staircase* (1912, Philadelphia Museum of Art). Of interest, cubisim is the only earlier stylistic influence that Nevelson acknowledges.

Rather than employing wide textural variety, bold colors, or strong contrast, Nevelson achieves rhythmic result by repetition of shape and tonal nuance. Indeed, she calls herself an "architect of shadows." Building each sculpture in a single hue for coherence and unity, she paints her stock of components *before* assembling, so that she is predisposed to regard them in terms of an abstract vocabulary, ready for inventive manipulation. She has produced series of sculptures in white and in gold, and for a brief time in clear plexiglas, but the predominant number have been black, her favorite color. Writing in her autobiography, *Dawns and Dusks* (published by Scribner's in 1976), Nevelson relates: "There was something in me drawing me to the black. I actually think that my trademark and what I like best is the dark, the dusk." And when asked in an interview if her use of black was connected with death, she replied:

> *Yes, if you want to get philosophical, death means peace, completeness, black – it's only an assumption of the western world that it means death; for me it may mean finish, completeness, maybe eternity.*

Thus Nevelson's sculptures, notwithstanding their essential abstraction, are capable of generating in the viewer levels of subjective awareness. *Death* is one of three prevailing themes in the artist's oeuvre that Laurie Wilson has identified in her 1978 doctoral dissertation at Columbia University. It is, Wilson feels, both a speculative preoccupation and a kind of sustained expression of mourning — long denied on the conscious plane — over three losses in the mid 1940s that troubled Nevelson deeply: her mother in 1943, father in '46, and her first dealer and spiritual patriarch, Karl Nierendorf, in 1947. With particular consideration of the titles Nevelson has given her pieces, Wilson perceives the other two principal topics as *royalty* and *marriage*, and, in many examples, the three themes are combined. Black, for instance, the artist finds inherently aristocratic (in the same way a black limousine or tuxedo is intrinsically elegant), hence, regal. The designations "king" or "queen" in the titles of many Nevelson columnar, free-standing sculptures project an anthropomorphic intent not sought in the wall ensembles. Wilson notes that in psychoanalysis royal figures are standard symbols for parents (again perhaps, the lost mother and father) and indirectly of the married state. The frequent pairing of columnar pieces and the words "bride" and "wedding" incorporated in several titles infer to Wilson the artist's continual longing toward an idyllic concept of matrimony, tempered by the admission that her own marriage had been unfulfilling, and that her mother, too, had never been happy in a union of convenience. Finally, Wilson ascertains considerable formal similarity between the columnar pieces and monumental totemic stelae Nevelson admired on visits to the Mayan ruins at Quirigua, Guatemala, in the 1930s. The stelae, moreover, present a thematic association in that they feature memorial depiction of royal figures, carved in relief, as though occupying open sarcophagi.

Cascades – Perpendiculars XXVII, fashioned in black between 1980 and '82, is an ingenious assemblage of characteristic Nevelson wood parts, plus a novel integration of small organ pipes from a razed church. Though standing in the round, the piece is essentially frontal, in which respect it is akin to the wall sculptures. The back presents a simpler, secondary design dominated by four large, flat disks placed one above the other. The narrower sides, squarish in silhouette and otherwise lacking definition, are conspicuously flanks to move past in order to square one's view on the main configurations.

The artist was born Louise Berliawsky in Kiev, Russia, in 1899. When she was six, her family emigrated to the United States and settled at Rockland, Maine. At age twenty she married Charles Nevelson of New York City, a wealthy shipping merchant. Their only child, a son, Michael, was born in 1922. They divorced in 1931. From 1928 to '30 she studied at the Art Students League, chiefly with Kenneth Hayes Miller. She went on to study with Hans

Hofmann at his school in Munich in 1931, and with him again at the League in 1932. Later that same year, she was chosen by Diego Rivera to assist in painting the murals for the New Workers School in New York. It was at Rivera's urging that she subsequently traveled extensively in Mexico and Central America. Her sculpture of the late '30s and '40s reflects primitive and pre-Columbian sources. Over a twenty-year span Nevelson also studied theatre, voice, and dance — all of which have contributed to what Wilson calls the artist's "public self-dramatization" and "majestic public personna" through her forceful manner, proud bearing, and well-known exotic attire.

Harold Tovish (b. 1921)

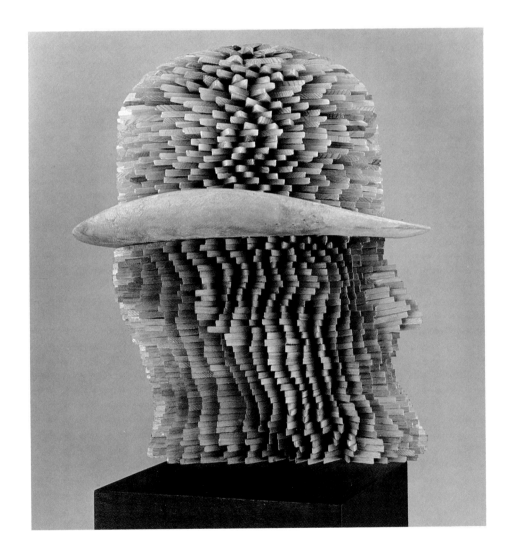

HOMAGE TO MAGRITTE
Harold Tovish
1981
pine
11¾ x 9⅞ x 10½ inches
initialed and dated top of base, right rear corner
Museum purchase with funds provided by the Benwood Foundation and the 1982 Collectors' Group

Provenance
From the collection of the artist through Terry Dintenfass, Inc., New York, New York

Publications
William T. Henning, Jr., *Recent Acquisitions*, Chattanooga: Hunter Museum of Art, 1982.

Sculptor Harold Tovish has long had an interest in the aesthetic and inventive possibilities of the life-sized human head. "He has studied the illusive structure of the head, its minute intervals which seem to shift even as the sitter holds his pose," writes artist and *Arts* magazine critic Michael Mazur. Though Tovish's heads may indeed suggest actual likenesses, manifestly they are more the effect of ingenious technique, along with symbolic portrayals of various human conditions. However abstracted, a Tovish head is subjectively provocative; it generates in the viewer awarenesses of disposition and character—pathos perhaps, or resoluteness, or fatigue, or resignation.

Between 1977 and '80, Tovish produced a set of fourteen head inventions that he called the "Transformation Series." Each piece serves a consistent concept, specifically, the artist's own image. Yet each is different—a different material (bronze, plaster, wood), a different stylistic variation (from realistic, to cubistic, to greatly simplified formal abstraction). The Hunter Museum's *Homage to Magritte*, from 1981, while not part of the Transformation group, is derived from it. The sculpture is near-identical in technique to one of the variations. Except for the hat brim, the later work is composed of hundreds of small, flat, triangular wood pieces that have been systematically cemented—butt ends in, points out—to an internal solid wood core. The fabrication is a mild "inside" joke or pun; fellow artists will recognize at once that the small wood components are the pegs or "keys" that painters employ in the tongue-and-groove corner joinings of canvas stretchers, in order to tap out, by expanding the corner, the slack or loosening that invariably befalls canvas with seasonal changes or with age. Remarkably, the loci of projecting points disclose volume, contours, convexity and concavity—in sum, the features of head, hat, and face.

The "Magritte" alluded to in the title of the sculpture is Belgian surrealist painter Rene Magritte (1898-1967), whose work Tovish admires for some of the same qualities he himself often attempts to impart: irony, visual incongruities, fantasy, riddles. The bowler-topped male figure is the protagonist in many of Magritte's dream-like pictures. Moreover, the image in those pictures is Magritte's own likeness, and the character is a projection of his own personna. But whereas Magritte's actor is clean-shaven, Tovish's man is clearly bearded, as Tovish is bearded. The slightly hooked shape of the nose and hollow of the cheeks are Tovish's features too. Hence Tovish puts on the guise of Magritte's man; the "homage" is stated alter ego to alter ego.

Tovish was born in New York City in 1921. He studied at Columbia University from 1940 to '43, the Zadkine School of Sculpture and Drawing in Paris in 1949 and '50, and the Académie de la Grande Chaumiere, Paris, in 1950 and '51. He has taught at the New York State College at Alfred, University of Minnesota, Boston Museum School, and University of Hawaii. In 1966 he was sculptor-in-residence at the American Academy in Rome. He received a Guggenheim Foundation fellowship the following year, and in 1967-68 he was a Fellow at the Center for Advanced Visual Studies, Massachusetts Institute of Technology. Since 1971 he has been a member of the art department faculty of Boston University.

In his most recent work, Tovish has experimented with mixed-media enclosures—"cells" he calls them—into which he fixes objects that are replicated and endlessly extended by systems of one-way mirrors. True to his fascination with visual perplexities, the created illusions belie the real physical properties and dimensions of the respective arrangements.

Robert Bechtle (b. 1932)

Californian Robert Bechtle is one of the leading members of a distinct West Coast group of new realist or, as the movement is also called, photo-realist painters that includes Don Eddy, Ralph Goings, Richard McLean, and Paul Wonner, to name several of the better known. With his 1964 oil, *'56 Chrysler*, Bechtle was in fact the first artist of that region to produce a "true" photo-realist painting. "True" is obviously not to say that he was the only artist at the time working realistically, but rather that he had already grasped the aesthetic premise of a new contemporary style. With its roots partly in pop art, it is characterized by a dispassionate look at current popular society, a cognizance of the cluttered urban environment, and a preoccupation with gaudy material possessions and commercial objects: motor vehicles, storefronts, billboards, marquees and shop signs, toys, geegaws, and the like. The various artists' penchant for incisive, sharp-focus realism is likewise an outgrowth of modern business and technology. As Bechtle unashamedly admits: "Pop Art led to an awareness of commercial art techniques which is where the license for use of photographs and projectors came from for me." To the surprise of few, the new realists indeed usually employ opaque or slide projectors to throw a photographic image onto a canvas or paper while they meticulously trace the forms, highlights, and shadows. Is it cheating? No; these artists would contend that advertising designers use such tricks all the time and that the camera therefore is as acceptable a tool to do art as a calculator is to do mathematics. Using

SUNSET PAINTER
Robert Bechtle
1981
watercolor on paper
9⅞ x 14¾ inches
initialed and dated lower right
Museum purchase with funds
provided by the Benwood
Foundation and the 1982
Collectors' Group

Provenance
From the collection of the artist through O. K.
Harris Gallery, New York, New York

Publications
William T. Henning, Jr., *Recent Acquisitions*,
Chattanooga: Hunter Museum of Art, 1982.

an airbrush to reproduce the smooth gradations of tone is also a typical new realist effect. Little wonder then that most of their paintings are astonishingly like snapsnot enlargements; it is latter-day *trompe l'oeil*!

Nonetheless, each new realist artist has his or her values, points-of-view, and rendering mannerisms that set apart the work of one from the other. Bechtle is different chiefly in two ways: Unlike those who so minimize their brushwork as to simulate the slick or matte finish of photo printing, Bechtle's surfaces do not hide the method of paint application, remaining ever-so-slightly tactile. Second, he edits his visual information; he does not insist that every element or object in a composition be given equal importance or focus. "I see my paintings," he has said, "as being essentially still lifes that deal with such classical concerns as balance, shape, color, tension, et cetera." And though Bechtle relates to the scenes he paints and cannot help but have made editorial pre-judgments in the selection and organization of topic imagery, he avoids dramatics or romanticizing, praise or ridicule. He endeavors to remain characteristically new realist neutral.

Bechtle has been predominately concerned with two topics. The automobile is a central motif in many of his paintings. Accordingly he has noted: "The automobile is a very important part of our life, probably *the* most important single object—especially here in California." One sees a car parked in the driveway at the right of the Hunter's *Sunset Painter* of 1981. Essentially, however, the smoothly brushed watercolor is representative of Bechtle's other favored study — the sun-bathed suburban communities of the San Francisco Bay area, (including the residential district called Sunset, hence the designation in the title), with their homogeneous middle-class stucco and frame dwellings. Usually the scene is set at mid-depth, with frontal, even lighting and bland, soft colors. As a camera often foreshortens the illusion of three-dimensionality, so the houses here overlap, producing a pattern of geometric shapes unavoidably reminiscent of Hopper, an admiration for whose work Bechtle acknowledges. Hopper-like, too, is the painting's subjective quietude.

In 1984 Bechtle again took inspiration from the Sunset neighborhood for his large (56 x 120 inch) oil on canvas—or more accurately, three laterally abutted canvases—*Sunset Intersection*. The scene is dominated by a wide, almost empty residential street that recedes in one-point perspective. Strong diagonals leading to the vanishing point at off-center-left reinforce an illusion of deep space. At the same time, the artist "contrapuntally" develops the surface plane through his characteristic foreshortening, use of flat, unmodeled shapes, and by the curious long, horizontal, overhead telephone wires that effectively lace all three panels together. But why the seemingly contrived triptych device? Perhaps it was just

whim—though Bechtle has made each section a remarkably adequate, independent composition, with pictorial business all its own. The novelty, then, may be in demonstrating that the whole truly *is* greater than the sum of its parts.

ArtNews magazine critic Eric Jay reads *Sunset Intersection* in sober philosophical terms that Bechtle may or may not have consciously considered: "In a mysterious chasm at the end of the boulevard is a solid sheet of blue sea. This is where Bechtle leaves us: secure and comfortable in our surroundings, facing an unsure drop. The intersection is that of life and death, the eternal present and the finite future."

Bechtle was born in San Francisco in 1932. He attended the California College of Arts and Crafts in Oakland, where he received a B.A. in 1954 and an M.F.A. in 1958. He has taught at the University of California campuses at Berkeley and Davis. He is on the faculty of San Francisco State University and lives in Berkeley.

SUNSET INTERSECTION
Robert Bechtle
1984
oil on canvas (triptych)
56 x 40 inches each panel
Museum purchase with funds provided by the Benwood Foundation and the 1984 Collectors' Group

Provenance

From the collection of the artist through O. K. Harris Gallery, New York, New York

Exhibitions

Robert Bechtle, O. K. Harris Gallery, New York, NY, May 5-26, 1984.

John R. Henry (b. 1943)

"Like Zeus playing pick-up sticks" is Chicago art critic Henry Hanson's picturesque analogy for artist John Henry's production. Henry is one of the principal figures involved in the large outdoor sculpture movement that has grown steadily in the United States since the early '60s, and includes such other notables as David Smith, Tony Smith, George Sugarman, Claes Oldenberg, Mark di Suvero, Richard Serra, and Alexander Calder. Working in what can be fairly termed "architectural scale," Henry has created pieces as great as two hundred twenty-five feet in horizontal span, and nearly sixty feet in height. The "sticks" are fabricated steel or aluminum, hollow square beams in various lengths, that are bolted together at

LARGO
John R. Henry
1981
painted aluminum
171 x 74 x 183 inches
stamped with name and date
on one joint bolt
Museum purchase

Provenance
From the collection of the artist.

overlapping end-plates and cantilivered at subtle angles from the ground and from other beams within the structure. The result is a study of force and equilibrium, as dealer Jim Fuhr explains:

> *The formal power of John Henry's sculpture is generated in the torsion and lift among elements that, although straight, wind about one another with the sweep and movement of arcs and curves. The elements grip one another at connectors that hold the entire piece together. The strength required to raise each element into its space-generating relationships with other elements is spread throughout the structure. The forces that drive through each element are active from the ground up. Those elements that make contact with the ground generally rest on corners, rather than along edges. This helps visually to spring the piece up from the earth, and accelerates the circulation of forms within the work.*

Henry completes each piece in a single bold-color enamel that not only enlivens the composition, but also emphasizes the work's man- and machine-made character in advancing the latter twentieth-century industrial and commercial aesthetic of slick bright packaging, as in finishes for motor vehicles, appliances, and other manufactured objects.

For most artwork in three dimensions, and modern sculpture in particular, the viewer must progress around the piece for the optimum experiencing of it. With a Henry sculpture, the viewer is invited to enter into its volumes and articulated spaces, its stresses and thrusts, its surges and sweeps—all of which unfold in ever modulating designs as the vantage changes. Truly, the viewer activates or energizes the work.

Titles hold little more significance for Henry than as matters of convenient identification and differentiation. "I don't like titles," he says flatly. "People run around a piece of sculpture to find a bronze plate, because as soon as they have found it, all the questions are answered. What a sculpture does and where it is placed is more important that the actual designation of a piece." One should not be surprised to learn, therefore, that *Largo*—the Hunter Museum's fourteen-foot-tall, bright yellow Henry work from 1981—is not necessarily meant to generate in the observer associations of slow or solemn music. Nothing symbolic was intended. Henry's simple exposition: "I came back from sailing down Key Largo, and named the piece." He allows as all right, too, a friend's tagging the work "over-sized french fries."

"My parents swore up and down that when they named me they never gave a thought to the song *John Henry*," relates the artist, who was born in Lexington, Kentucky, in 1943. Working as a young man in his father's construction business would have considerable bearing upon his later development as a sculptor. Initially, however, he began his career in art as a painter. He attended the University of Kentucky and the University of Washington before studying at the School of the Art Institute of Chicago, from which he graduated in 1969. He has since also studied at the University of Chicago and the Illinois Institute of Technology. Henry has been visiting instructor at the University of Chicago, University of Iowa, University of Wisconsin—Green Bay, and Aquinas College in Grand Rapids, Michigan. At this writing, he maintains studios in Chicago and Miami, and divides his time seasonally between the two cities.

Sol LeWitt (b. 1928)

Sol LeWitt is variously identified with the constructivist, minimal, and conceptual art movements. The latter direction particularly is based on the supposition that the essence of an artwork is its underlying "concept" and organizational scheme, rather than the methods and processes of formation or the finished work. The thesis is in part an extension of Marcel Duchamp's dictum that art is experience, not object—a notion foreign to most viewers who are conditioned to require a tangible piece as the final and necessary fulfillment of the idea. As art historian and critic Sam Hunter points out, it is also a reaction by many creative figures to the materialism with which society is so preoccupied and to the commercialism that dominates and dictates the serious art world. In the mid-1960s, for example, when early conceptual art theories were just being advanced, op and pop art became high fashion in near-overnight flurry, while a painting by any one of the better-known abstract expressionists could fetch hundreds of thousands of dollars. In an atmosphere of what was seen as synthetic validities and inflated prices, this new avante-garde asserted that art need not and indeed should not be treated as a commodity. One obvious way to de-emphasize a commodity, of course, is to de-emphasize the permanent physical object. Thus art could become a self-justifying act of aesthetic inquiry, unperturbed by dealer whims and the commercial market. Related contemporary developments—earthworks, happenings, performance art, body art, process art—whatever the formal label, share a common avoidance of the immutably finished piece. LeWitt effectively summarizes:

> Conceptual art is made to engage the mind of the viewer rather than his eye or emotions. The conceptionalist artist would want to ameliorate this emphasis on materiality as much as possible or to use it in a paradoxical way (to convert it into an idea). This kind of art then should be stated with the greatest economy of means.

For LeWitt's purposes, that most parsimonious of means is abstractly embodied in the square and cube. "The most interesting chacteristic of the cube," LeWitt explains, "is that it is relatively uninteresting." Writing about LeWitt's work, Lucy Lippard further expounds:

13/4
Sol LeWitt
1981
painted balsa wood
31⅜ x 31⅜ x 31⅜ inches
Museum purchase with funds
provided by the Benwood
Foundation and the 1983
Collectors' Group

Provenance

From the collection of the artist through John
Weber Gallery, New York, New York

Publications

William T. Henning, Jr., *Recent Acquisitions,*
Chattanooga: Hunter Museum of Art, 1983.

Carolyn Mitchell, "The Hunter Museum, A
Showcase for Modern American Art in Chattanooga." *Southern Accents,* May-June, 1984,
illus. p. 122.

Compared to any other three-dimensional form, the cube lacks any aggressive force, implies no motion, and is least emotive. Therefore it is the best form to use as a basic unit for any more elaborate function, the grammatical device from which the work may proceed. Because it is standard and universally recognized, no intention is required of the viewer. It is immediately understood that the cube represents the cube, a geometric figure uncontestably itself. The use of the cube obviates the necessity of inventing another form and reserves it for invention.

True to his conceptual logic, LeWitt's large, white, skeletal, open cube "structures" (he dislikes their being called sculptures), which he has been producing since 1964, are manifestations of predetermined modular arrangements. "Experiencing" a work like the Hunter's painted balsa *13/4*, of 1981, is partly contemplating the system of permutations and progressions and partly discovering the constantly changing geometric patterns that appear and disappear within the piece as one varies the vantage point or moves around the construct. This latter phenomenon is perhaps an unanticipated visual wonder. For all the intended simplicity and professed denial of conventional tangibility, LeWitt's art, as critic Robert Rosenblum almost apologetically allows, "has turned out to be stunningly beautiful." In fairness, by the way, one cannot fully discern or appreciate the operative effects of the work in looking at a still photograph.

LeWitt was born in Hartford, Connecticut, in 1928. After his father's death in 1934, the family moved to New Britain, where he attended elementary and high schools. He was graduated from Syracuse University with a B.F.A. in 1949. He has taught at the Museum of Modern Art School, The Cooper Union, the School of Visual Art, and New York University. Though now working independently, he still resides in New York City. An articulate and prolific writer, LeWitt has also published more than fifty books and articles about his own work and about conceptual art in general.

William King (b. 1925)

ADOLESCENCE
William King
1982
aluminum
107 x 39 x 87 inches
Gift of Sara Jo and Arthur J.
Kobacker in honor of Abe
and Bertha Borisky

Provenance

From the collection of the artist through Terry
Dintenfass Gallery, New York, New York

Sara Jo and Arthur J. Kobacker, Columbus,
Ohio

Exhibitions

Outdoors, Terry Dintenfass, Inc., New York,
NY, April 27-May 20, 1982.

Chicago Art Fair, Chicago, IL, May 5-25, 1982.

State University of New York, Potsdam, NY,
Aug. 26-Oct. 5, 1982.

Critic Hilton Kramer has called William King "the most autobiographical of all living sculptors." A man of droll, self-effacing humor, King's creative approach is akin to a skilled cartoonist who identifies, simplifies, and exaggerates certain physical forms, postures, and gestures to produce effective caricature. Not every King sculpture suggests the artist's own lanky build and idiosyncratic facial features as descriptively as the Hunter Museum's *Adolescence* from 1982 (a number, in fact, depict women), but all present an aspect of his personal feeling and experience, of his alter ego. The characteristic King figure,

Kramer continues, "may be awkward and ridiculous, caught unaware in the unlikely contraption of his own physique and decked out with accoutrements that only succeed in amplifying an innate absurdity." Kramer further observes: "There is a quality that is almost Chaplinesque in King's work—a mockery that remains sweet to the taste, a satirical vision that does not exempt the artist himself from the reach of its criticism."

With an affinity to shop-sign cutouts, weathervanes, whirligigs, tinwork, and the like, King's style and technique echo American primitive and folk art. One sees the same frankness, naiveté, and indifference to pedantic discourse, the same untutored freshness in design and fabrication. "He developed a style involving witty figurative interpretations of American folk genre," Wayne Anderson notes, though finding further that King's work is also "tempered formally by the modernist sensibility of Elie Nadelman." Kramer, too, marks King's debt to that important Polish-American sculptor, mainly of the late teens, '20s, and '30s, "whose painted wood carvings and papier-mâché figures—at once so light-hearted, so elegant, so original, and so fully articulated—have provided King with a vision and an ideal of craftsmanship against which to measure his own accomplishment and aspiration."

Kramer points out additionally that artists who deal in humor, satire, and parody—Nadelman and King, certain of the works of Picasso, Calder, the pop artists generally (not to mention comedic performing artists, playwrights, and authors)—share in the dilemma of not being regarded seriously for the aesthetic merits of their discipline. "Thus any sculptor aspiring to the comic mode has had to prove himself on purely formal grounds as well as on the basis of his particular vein of comic invention."

King is a master of streamlined expressive silhouette and of articulate negative space. Yet his work is tightly organized and economical in the number and use of component shapes that make up his individual figures. Aluminum plates that appear to have been cut by a jigsaw and slotted for easy assembly purposely remind the viewer of those simple cutout toys or models that children delight in putting together. The effect is engagingly childlike—which is not to say child-ish. For *Adolescence* King has also used cast aluminum for the figure's more definitive face and hands, giving the slightest suggestion of ears, cheekbones, eye sockets, knuckles, and skin creases. Though the visage is King in adulthood, the curious stiff-seated pose, with arms uncomfortably outstretched, hands tapping restlessly on the knees, bespeak a youth, fidgety and ill-at-ease.

King was born in Jacksonville, Florida, in 1925. He attended the University of Florida from 1942 to '44. He then studied architecture at the Cooper Union in New York from 1945 to '48. The following year he was awarded a Fulbright scholarship to attend the Academia dei Belli Arte in Rome, where he remained through 1950. In 1952 he attended the Central School of Arts and Crafts in London. From 1953 through '59, he was instructor of sculpture at the Brooklyn Museum of Art School. He has also taught or been artist-in-residence at the University of California at Berkeley (1965-66), Art Students League, New York (1968-69), and University of Pennsylvania (1972-73). In the early stages of his career, King worked predominantly in carved and painted wood, clay, terra cotta, and bronze—even then creating in a pseudo-primitive style satiric characters drawn from everyday observance. He began moving toward his more familiar plate-metal pieces in the early '60s.

Lin Emery

No still photograph like the one accompanying this article can adequately record the design totality of Lin Emery's sculpture. In proper operation her work *moves*, propelled by air currents or human touch; the component arrangement is in flux; multiple flashes of light and color reflecting from the polished metal surfaces enliven the display; spaces in which the motion takes place are continually rearticulated. In short, visible motion is an integral part of ever-changing composition. Emery fulfills in her work the basic premise for *kinetic* sculpture that Russian-American artist Naum Gabo propounded as early as 1920: "Constructive sculpture is not only three-dimensional, it is four-dimensional insofar as we are striving to bring the element of time into it."

FLAME
Lin Emery
1982
fabricated aluminum
53 x 41 x 14 inches
(61 inch orbit)
signed on base
Museum purchase with funds provided by the Benwood Foundation and the 1984 Collectors' Group

Provenance

From the collection of the artist through Max Hutchinson Gallery, New York, New York

Exhibitions

Lin Emery, Max Hutchinson Gallery, New York, NY, Oct. 9-30, 1982.

Publications

Lin Emery, exhibition catalogue, Max Hutchinson Gallery, New York, NY, 1982, illus.

Gabo was in part specifically defending a motorized mechanical piece he had devised. Others who experimented early with sculpture purposely designed to move in some way include dada master Marcel Duchamp in his *Bicycle Wheel* "ready-made" of 1913, Italian futurists Giacomo Balla and Fortunato Depero at nearly the same time, and Bauhaus teacher Laszlo Moholy-Nagy, whose *Lichtrequisit*, or "light machines," motorized revolving plates integrated with electric light bulbs from the 1920s and '30s. But more recent and direct antecedents for Emery's innovations may be seen in Australian-American Len Lye's motor-activated splay of elastic steel wire, Alexander Calder's air-propelled mobiles of petal-like shapes suspended from wire rods, and George Rickey's pivoting blades, driven by natural air currents so as to cut geometric arcs in space. Yet Emery's work, despite superficial similarities (as, say, to Calder's biomorphic shapes or to Rickey's base-lifted kinetic mechanism), is substantially her own aesthetic and motive system.

The streamlined elements that make up an Emery piece, though non-representational, may remind the viewer of birds, fish, or leaves—among the most aerodynamic and graceful of organic shapes. They suggest figures in organized flight or systematically gliding through water. Their performance, like birds or fish, may be sometimes swift and effortless, other times slow or erratic. E. John Bullard, director of the New Orleans Museum of Art and author of an expository essay on Emery's work, declares: "She has attempted to express in her kinetic sculpture the underlying unity and harmony that she perceives in nature." The artist herself affirms: "My forms are derived from symmetries found in nature and I borrow natural forces (wind, water, gravity) to set them in motion." Bullard, reflecting on the unpredictability of the "activating force," that is, of air current or human touch, addresses fortuity as a positive factor. "Chance," he says "gives to Emery's sculptures the spontaneous impulse which creates an infinitely variable movement—*exactly the condition found in nature*." (Italics added.) Emery also acknowledges that a longtime interest in theatre bears upon her art, and that she tends to equate the component units of her sculpture to individual dancers. Again, Bullard relates: "Emery consciously designs her sculptures in a way similar to a choreographer composing a ballet." And the artist admits: "Often I am surprised as the finished work invents an added dance of its own."

Though Emery has cast elements in bronze, her preferred material has been sheet marine aluminum, cut and welded together, then ground and polished. Predetermining weights, counterbalances, clearances, and probable kinetic action, she joins one graceful unit to another at a critical balancing point by a connecting cylindrical stem containing a ball-bearing assembly. Each principal element can thereby rotate a full 360 degrees, and in that the components are interconnected, the movement of parts is progressive. When one section moves, so in the shifting of weights does it transfer momentum through the ball-bearing couplers to the components joined to it.

Emery was born in New York City. In 1950 she was in Paris, where she studied with the Russian-expatriate, cubist-derived sculptor, Ossip Zadkine. Like Gabo, Zadkine stressed that sculpture must be conceived and perceived in terms of space and time, and he insisted that every sculpture has a thousand profiles. Emery produced her first kinetic work in 1956, a water-propelled bronze fountain piece, the first in a series of what she calls "aquamobiles." It was not until 1978 that she began to concentrate on air-propelled works. The Hunter Museum's *Flame*, with its flowing S-curved elements, was created in 1982. Larger works in the same idiom are aptly suited to outdoor and architectural placement, and she has received several such commissions: City Hall Plaza in Lawrence, Kansas; the Fidelity Bank of Oklahoma City; South Central Bell offices in Birmingham, Alabama; and the New Orleans Museum of Art. The artist has lived in New Orleans since 1962.

Janet Fish (b. 1938)

Janet Fish can be numbered among the contemporary American New Realist group, though she prefers to call herself a "perceptual" realist rather than be strictly identified with the so-called Photo- or Super-Realists. Indeed, her approach and resultant work differ from the New Realists in two significant ways. First, she does not work directly from photographs or projections of photographic images to the canvas from which the painted forms are, for all practical purposes, traced. For her well-known still lifes, Fish actually sets up the subject arrangement and paints from direct observation — usually without elaborate preliminary drawing. Most often her source of illumination is the natural daylight streaming through studio windows. Sometimes she will wait upon a particular time of day when the intensity, tone, and angle of the light suit her intent. Second, Fish does not strive for a photoprint smooth surface that would tend to eliminate or minimize one's awareness of the picture plane. Rather, she allows the oil medium to remain comparatively tactile; her brushwork is dexterous and painterly.

Early in her career, in the early 1960s, Fish worked briefly in an abstract expressionist style. But she was uncomfortable with it. "Abstract painting didn't have any meaning for me," she recalls. "I was just arranging paint according to predetermined rules." A period of landscape painting followed, but gradually she became interested in "objects" and the organization of the objects as still life. What gives her work the distinctive Janet Fish stamp is her selection of subject materials — not for allegorical or sentimental association — but for shape dynamics, design relatedness, and most especially for potential activity in light. Many of her favorite motifs have been glass or plastic vessels that reflect, refract, and distort light and adjacent forms in visually stimulating patterns. Again Fish explains:

(color plate 42)
ORANGE LAMP AND ORANGES
Janet Fish
1982
oil on canvas
65⅞ x 50 inches
signed and dated lower right
Museum purchase with funds provided by the Benwood Foundation and the 1982 Collectors' Group

Provenance

From the collection of the artist through Robert Miller Gallery, Inc., New York, New York

Publications

William T. Henning, Jr., *Recent Acquisitions*, Chattanooga: Hunter Museum of Art, 1982, cover illustration.

The vitality and constant motion of light have always fascinated me. Glass seemed to trap and contain these qualities. I like the play of movement between the solid and transparent forms – the shapes of the reflections conveyed an energy and provided an opportunity for the play of color.

Vivid, high-keyed colors and strong contrasts reinforce the artist's concept of energetic design. Further, she likes to work on a large scale so that the commonplace things she pictures take on drama and monumentality. Each painting manifests an effective combination of larger and smaller gestures, of big sweeps and shapes and within those "petite set pieces of the light's doing and the painter's attentiveness," as Fish's friend Barry Yourgrau so keenly describes it.

In the Hunter Museum's *Orange Lamp and Oranges* of 1980 (color plate 42), one feels a rhythmic composition based on a system of circles and ovals. There is an intended tension in the grouping as the shapes, both objects and reflections, seem to pull through and across the rounded body of the glass decanter near the center. A diagonal axis is suggested from lower left to upper right (through the oranges, bottle, and lampshade) and another counter to it from upper left to lower right (grapes, bottle, and lamp reflection in the glass table top). One notes too a structural similarity between the orange sections, lamp reflection, and the interior base of the decanter. The partially crumpled plastic wrap at right center, a quite unusual device, provides a small riot of abstract linear design and in its busyness helps balance the scallop-edged fruit dish and grapes to the left.

Fish was born in Boston in 1938. She attended Smith College in Northampton, Massachusetts, receiving a B.A. degree in 1960. At Smith she studied with Leonard Baskin, who recommended that she continue her academic work at Yale University. In the course of completing an M.F.A. there in 1963, she studied under Philip Pearlstein and Alex Katz, the latter of whom she particularly acknowledges as having had a profound influence upon her developing style. Now, except for summers at a home in Vermont, Fish lives in New York City where she maintains a SoHo studio.

Paul Wonner (b. 1920)

As the title *Dutch Still Life with Art Books and Field Guide to Western Birds* (color plate 43) suggests, Paul Wonner's depiction of a room dominated by a table top that is meticulously spread with curious and oddly related articles adapts various pictorial attributes from the grand style of seventeenth and early eighteenth century Netherlandish interior and still life painting: precise detail, smooth finish, soft yet radiant lighting. Jan Vermeer, Claes Heda, Jan de Heem, Jan van Huysum, and the numerous others who refined the mode can be seen as proper forebearers. But Wonner, of course, belongs to the realist revival that has been an important trend in American art since the late 1960s. Unlike many of the new realists, however, whose imagery and composition proceed directly from photographic sources — and whose subject matter usually favors the mundane, emotionally detached, even sardonic — Wonner's contemporary variation on the earlier Dutch fashion is consciously allied to the long historic tradition of representational art. His ordered vistas are carefully disposed, one might say "staged," with a keen eye to the abstract values of shape, color, substructure, spatial interval, rhythmic repetition, and balance. The objects rendered have a *design* significance at least equal in merit to their role as recognizable entities. Seeking an appropriate term by which to categorize Wonner's style, critics Suzaan Boettger, Sandy Ballatore, and George W. Neubert, in separate writings, have fittingly called him an *abstract realist*.

An insight into Wonner's method for devising the Hunter Museum's painting can be gained from an explanation of his approach, which he wrote in 1981:

(color plate 43)

DUTCH STILL LIFE WITH ART BOOKS AND FIELD GUIDE TO WESTERN BIRDS

Paul Wonner

1982

acrylic on canvas

72 x 50 inches

signed lower right

Museum purchase with funds provided by the Benwood Foundation and the 1983 Collectors' Group

Provenance

From the collection of the artist through Hirschl & Adler, Modern Gallery, New York, New York

(Continued on page 259)

I first set a background and a "floor" plane, then paint the objects separately, one by one, not arranged ahead of time. I seldom know what will come next, and the final result is always somewhat of a surprise to me. I try to bring everything together by subjective linear designs, each object or shadow leading to another throughout the painting. Drawing and perspective are altered to support the linear composition. Objects usually do not overlap; each is to be seen as much alone as in context with others. They are painted approximately life-sized and are selected at random from things around the house that I'm familiar with and like or commercial products that I use frequently whose packaging or design interest me.

Wonner was born in 1920 at Tucson, Arizona, where he lived until age seventeen. From 1937 to '41, he attended the California College of Arts and Crafts in Oakland, completing a B.A. degree. Following service in the U.S. Army during World War II, he moved to New York City in 1946, where he worked as a package designer for the House of Haley and where he studied part-time at the Art Students League under Robert Motherwell. He returned to California in 1950 to attend the University of California, Berkeley. He received a second B.A. degree from the University in 1952, and stayed on to complete an M.A. the following year. He also earned a Master of Library Science degree at Berkeley in 1955, and in the late '50s worked as chief catalogue clerk at the main library of the University of California, Davis. His paintings of the same time, and into the mid 1960s, were dexterously brushed, highly structured figurative (this is, human figure) compositions, strongly similar to contemporary works by the so-called California figurative painters: David Park, Elmer Bischoff, and Richard Diebenkorn. About 1966 he began working in the realist style that typifies his current work, but initially he limited to two or three the number of objects in his pictures. Multi-item compositions were introduced about 1977. Wonner has taught or been artist-in-residence at the University of California at Davis, U.C.L.A., California State University in Long Beach, the Otis Art Institute, the Art Center in Los Angeles, and the University of Hawaii. Since 1976 he has lived in San Francisco.

Miriam Schapiro (b. 1923)

Stylistically, Miriam Schapiro's work since about 1970 belongs to a movement in contemporary art called "pattern painting," characterized by intricate, systematic, often symmetrical or near symmetrical, highly decorative, surface-oriented design. Thematically, her work expresses through personal symbol and allegory her dedicated feminism. One might suppose that a woman so staunch in her preoccupation would take an iconoclastic stance and would disavow images suggestive of old-fashioned spousal and maternal domesticity. But Schapiro finds archetypal female emblems not in the oft "neuterizing" drive for parity of the sexes, but rather in those conventional roles women have performed almost exclusively and superlatively to men. Traditional feminine handicrafts (sewing, piecing, quilting), traditional apparel (frills, lace, brocade, embroidery, etc.), traditional domains (home, nursery), and matters of the heart and emotions are variously celebrated in Schapiro's art. Some critics have pooh-poohed the underlying sentimentality in her work. She in turn asserts that she does not seek to impart sentiment for its sake alone, but that women *are*, after all, essentially more romantic, more feeling, more given to nostalgia than men.

Unapologetically then, Schapiro richly embellishes what she believes are the most elegant and traditionally feminine materials. In a combination of fabric collage and painting — a technique she had dubbed "femmage" to imply its suitability to her basic purpose — she fashions designs in which house silhouette, flower, fan, and heart motifs have been among her favorite formats. The works are usually large because, as Melinda Wortz explains, "Schapiro sees scale as important in elevating imagery often associated with kitsch to the more hallowed halls of high art." In their imposing size, strict formal arrangement, and consistent reference, the artworks may be seen as contemporary feminist icons.

(Continued from page 258)

Publications

William T. Henning, Jr., *Recent Acquisitions,* Chattanooga: Hunter Museum of Art, 1983.

Carolyn Mitchell, "The Hunter Museum, A Showcase for Modern American Art in Chattanooga." *Southern Accents*, May-June, 1984, illus. p. 126.

(color plate 44)

IN HER OWN IMAGE
Miriam Schapiro
1983
acrylic and fabric on canvas
60 x 100 inches
signed bottom, right of center
Museum purchase with funds provided by the Benwood Foundation and the 1983 Collectors' Group

Provenance

From the collection of the artist through Barbara Gladstone Gallery, New York, New York

Exhibitions

Birmingham Museum of Art, Birmingham, AL, Jan. 5-Feb. 6, 1984.

Publications

William T. Henning, Jr., *Recent Acquisitions,* Chattanooga: Hunter Museum of Art, 1983.

(Continued on page 260)

About 1979 Schapiro began what she labels the "vestiture" series, inspired in part by Matisse's designs for chasubles. "The new woman needs a new set of royal robes," Schapiro declares. The striking *In Her Own Image* (color plate 44) of 1983 seems indeed a kind of abstracted ceremonial garment (for a latter-day priestess of the Earth Mother, perhaps). It is more than a metaphor on clothing, however. The bowed lines and swelling contours of the main configuration are inherently buxom, fecund, and by psychological association womanly. In this and other works of the series, the "robe" parts so as to reveal a bold upward-pointing triangle. Again, the artist has commented on feminine symbolism associated with the form: communication from the earth, seen as female, upward to the heavens, or the more mundane connotation of the *mons veneris*. Interestingly, Schapiro incorporates in the vestiture works needlework, embroidery, and other hand-finished materials that have been given to her by women throughout the world.

Schapiro was born in Toronto, Canada, in 1923, but she is an American citizen. Her father, Theodore, was an artist and industrial designer, and (with curious implication for the femmage works) her paternal grandfather was a tailor in New York City. She grew up in Brooklyn and lives today in Manhattan's SoHo. She earned B.A., M.A., and M.F.A. degrees from the University of Iowa, where she studied with James Lechay, Stuart Edie, Lester Longman, and Mauricio Lasansky. In 1970 she met and soon collaborated with the unreserved feminist artist, Judy Chicago, to produce the "Woman House," an "environment" for the Feminist Art Program at the California Institute of the Arts in Valencia. In '71 she joined the faculty at the Institute, remaining through '75, when she and her husband returned to New York. The College of Wooster, in Ohio, organized a major retrospective of her work that showed there and at eight other art museums between September 1980 and May 1982. In May 1983 she participated in the important exhibition, "At Home," at the Long Beach Museum of Art, which examined a decade of significant feminist art in southern California.

Edward Moulthrop (b. 1916)

"The purchase verifies that my work has improved a lot," Edward Moulthrop quipped in 1982, on the occasion of the Museum of Modern Art's buying one of his large turned wooden bowls for its permanent collection. But then, reflecting on the broader implications of the purchase, he continued in a more serious vein: "It means that my bowls are more than just collectibles for the lay public—that they are acceptable to the highest-level design museum in the U.S." Moulthrop's stressing "design" in his categorization of the Modern museum is a key to perceiving that which sets his work apart from the interminable woodworkers who produce hackneyed salad, nut, or fruit bowls that can be bought at craft fairs anywhere in the nation. In an effort to bridge the commonly applied, though admittedly ill-defined, distinctions between handicraft and "fine" art, critics more and more use the term "designer-craftsman" (or craftsperson) to identify artists of Moulthrop's originality and technical skill. In point, *Atlanta Journal* critic W. C. Burnett writes: "It's his sensitive artist's eye for figures in the wood grain, relationships of width to height, the degree of curvature of the shape, the quality of the surface and the color of the finished wood that makes a bowl by Moulthrop a work of art."

Moulthrop bowls tend to simple streamlined designs: shallow wide-mouthed hemispherical forms, thick-walled doughnuts, bulbous cylinders, or the shape for which he is best known, the small-mouthed hollow globe. And though he has made smaller utilitarian bowls, his notoriety is mainly based on outsized works, for which the fashioning process is a tour-de-force. He has produced bowls up to forty inches in diameter. The Museum of Modern Art's piece has a thirty-three inch diameter. The Hunter's striking tulipwood bowl from 1983, no small example, is twenty-four inches across at its greatest swell.

(Continued from page 259)

Carolyn Mitchell, "The Hunter Museum, A Showcase for Modern American Art in Chattanooga." *Southern Accents*, May-June, 1984, illus. p. 124.

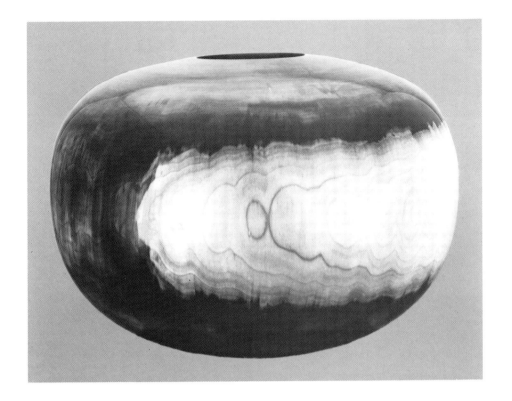

BOWL
Edward Moulthrop
1983
figured tulipwood
15½ inches high, 24 inches diameter
signed and dated on bottom
Museum purchase with funds provided by Mr. and Mrs. E. Y. Chapin, III, Ruth S. and A. William Holmberg and Mr. and Mrs. Phil B. Whitaker

Provenance
From the collection of the artist.

Like Michelangelo, who was said to discern a potential sculpted figure in a block of quarrystone, Moulthrop declares: "Each bowl already exists in the tree trunk, and my job is simply to uncover it and take it out." The larger bowls begin as massive trunk sections that may weigh up to 1,500 pounds. "I love the heft and the solidness of those huge blocks," the artist explains. "I love to feel their weight as they resist the leverage of a big cant-hook, or to sense the tug of gravity as the hoist slowly separates a block from the ground." Moulthrop uses only woods native to the Southeast—tulip poplar, white pine, wild cherry, magnolia, persimmon, black walnut—finding the respective colorings and grain patterns amply distinctive.

After squaring the ends of a trunk section with an electric chainsaw, Moulthrop bolts a large faceplate to the center of what will eventually become the base of the bowl. Then, using a hoist to lift the block to a heavy-duty lathe that the artist has himself designed, the faceplate is attached to the headstock. While the variable-speed lathe turns the block between fifty and a hundred revolutions per minute, Moulthrop carves the wood with sharp cutting tools he has also specially designed or modified, what is called a "lance" for the exterior, and a "loop" for hollowing out the interior. Bracing the implements on a rest bar and against his thigh, he reduces the block to a "roughed out" state. Next he removes the block from the lathe and transfers it to a large vat where it will steep in a polyethylene-glycol solution from eight to sixteen weeks, depending upon the size of the block and the season of the year (longer in cold months). The chemical bath arrests shrinkage and prevents splitting or cracking. After letting the block dry for about two weeks, it is remounted to the lathe and the final carving is completed. Upon removing the faceplate and filling the bolt holes in the base underside, carefully matching color and grain, each bowl is finished with polyurethane varnish, hand rubbed with fine steel wool between coats, followed by an application of tripoli compound and rouge, and additional buffing.

Moulthrop was born in Cleveland, Ohio, in 1916. The carpentry and wood turning he learned as a youth of fourteen sustained a lifelong avocation. After studying architecture at Princeton University, he came to Atlanta in 1941 to teach at the Georgia Institute of Technology. He remained on the faculty until 1949, after which he practiced architecture privately in Atlanta until 1974. He then elected to devote full time to his bowl-crafting art.

The Catalogue

A Complete Catalogue of the American Collection

Abeles, Sigmund (b. 1934)
Nude in Bed
1978
lithograph, 22/25
image: 8 x 11¾ inches
Gift of Dr. and Mrs. Frederick P. Nause

Paul
1978
lithograph, 22/25
image: 23 x 18 inches
Gift of Dr. and Mrs. Frederick P. Nause

Princeton Nude
1977
lithograph, 10/25
21 x 17 inches
Gift of Dr. and Mrs. Frederick P. Nause

Print Dealer and His Lamp
1979
lithograph, 23/25
22½ x 15 inches
Gift of Dr. and Mrs. Frederick P. Nause

Self-Portrait with Cap
1977
lithograph, 9/125
image: 8 x 6 inches
Gift of Dr. and Mrs. Frederick P. Nause

Space Issue #3
1977
lithograph, 16/125
image: 30 x 22 inches
Gift of Dr. and Mrs. Frederick P. Nause

Space Issue #3, Northwood
1978
etching, 4/25
image: 7 x 5¾ inches
Gift of Dr. and Mrs. Frederick P. Nause

Tiger Lilly
1978
lithograph, 22/25
image: 14 x 21 inches
Gift of Dr. and Mrs. Frederick P. Nause

Weekend Guests
1977
lithograph, 24/125
image: 22 x 15 inches
Gift of Dr. and Mrs. Frederick P. Nause

Adams, Ansel (1902-1984)
Moonrise, Hernandez, New Mexico, 1941
1941
gelatin silver print photograph
15 x 19½ inches
Gift of Dr. and Mrs. Bruce E. Dahrling, II and
Museum purchase

*Mount Williamson, Sierra Nevada, from
Manzanar, California, 1944*
1944
gelatin silver print photograph
15⅜ x 18¼ inches
Gift of Dr. and Mrs. Bruce E. Dahrling, II and
Museum purchase

*Oak Tree, Snowstorm, Yosemite National Park,
California, 1948*
1948
gelatin silver print photograph
9¾ x 15½ inches
Gift of Dr. and Mrs. Bruce E. Dahrling, II and
Museum purchase

Allen, Walter H.
Diathesis I
1972
acrylic paint, plastic and bolts on shaped
canvas
37 x 55 x 1¾ inches
Museum purchase

Antreasian, Garo (b. 1922)
Project I
1977
lithograph, 20/25
20¼ x 26 inches
Gift of Dr. and Mrs. Frederick P. Nause

Project II
1978
lithograph, 10/25
21 x 26½ inches
Gift of Dr. and Mrs. Frederick P. Nause

Untitled (79-12-2)
1980
lithograph, 4/25
image: 6 x 6 inches
Gift of Dr. and Mrs. Frederick P. Nause

Untitled (79-12-3)
1980
lithograph, 4/25
image: 6 x 6 inches
Gift of Dr. and Mrs. Frederick P. Nause

Untitled (79-12-4)
1980
lithograph 4/25
image: 6½ x 6 inches
Gift of Dr. and Mrs. Frederick P. Nause

Untitled (79-12-5)
1980
lithograph, 4/25
image: 7½ x 8 inches
Gift of Dr. and Mrs. Frederick P. Nause

Untitled (79-12-6)
1980
lithograph, 4/25
image: 7½ x 6 inches
Gift of Dr. and Mrs. Frederick P. Nause

Anuszkiewicz, Richard (b. 1930)
Inflexional II
1966
acrylic on masonite
36 x 36 inches
Gift of the artist

Spectrum 9
1976
silkscreen on plastic modules
54 x 54 inches
Gift of the Commerce Union Bank,
Chattanooga

Volumes
1970
silkscreen on plastic, 47/150
nine interchangeable panels: 3 squares, 19⅝ x
19⅝ inches each; 6 diamonds, 36 x 15 inches
each
Gift of Ruth S. and A. William Holmberg

Arneson, Robert (b. 1930)
Cherry Pie
1975
lithograph, 8/38
22½ x 30 inches
Museum purchase with funds supplied in part
by the National Endowment for the Arts, a
Federal agency

Arnholm, Ronald (b. 1939)
Vivaldi
1968
polymer on board
18 x 24 inches
Museum Purchase

Audubon, John James (1785-1851)
Putorius Vison, Linn (Mink)
1844
lithograph, no. 7, pl. 23
image: 20 x 25 inches
Gift of Dr. L. H. Lassiter

Audubon, John Woodhouse (1812-1862)
Ursus Americanus, Pallas (Cinnamon Bear)
1847
lithograph, no. 26, plate CXXVII
image: 19 x 25¼ inches
Gift of Dr. L. H. Lassiter

Avery, Milton (1885-1965)
March by the Sea
1945
oil on canvas
28 x 36⅛ inches
Gift of the Benwood Foundation

Young Girl in Blue
1939
oil on canvas
33 x 26 inches
Gift of Mr. and Mrs. Roy R. Neuberger

Baisden, Frank (b. 1904)
Florida Fishermen
1946
watercolor on paper
18½ x 22¾ inches
Museum purchase

Barber, Judy (b. 1943)
Life/Depth/Red
1969
polymer on canvas
67¾ x 67¾ inches
Museum purchase award — Tenth Hunter
Annual Exhibition, 1969

Bardin, Jesse (b. 1923)
Flight Into Autumn
1963
oil on canvas
50 x 40 inches
Museum purchase award — Fourth Hunter
Annual Exhibition, 1963

Barnet, Will (b. 1911)
Waiting (from the *Kent Bicentennial Portfolio*)
1975
lithograph, 101/125
37 x 39½ inches
Gift of the Lorillard Company

Bartlett, Paul Wayland (1865-1925)
Untitled (grouping of seven oil sketches)
1920-1921
oil on canvas
sizes vary from 3 x 5½ inches to 7½ x 5⅝ inches
Gift of the artist's daughter, Mrs. Armistead
Peter, III, through the Corcoran Gallery

Baskin, Leonard (b. 1922)
Man of Peace
1952
woodcut on paper
image: 59½ x 30¾ inches
Museum purchase with funds supplied in part
by the National Endowment for the Arts, a
Federal agency

Baumgart, Isolde (b. 1935)
Ember Days
1980
etching, 4/25
image: 10 x 7¾ inches
Gift of Dr. and Mrs. Frederick P. Nause

Beal, Jack (b. 1931)
The Painting Lesson
1980-1981
oil on canvas
84 x 96 inches
Gift of Mr. and Mrs. John T. Lupton

The Trout
1976
lithograph, 44/102
image: 20 x 25½ inches
Museum purchase with funds supplied in part
by the National Endowment for the Arts, a
Federal agency

Beattie, George (b. 1919)
Departure of Apollo
c. 1960
mixed media
24 x 36 inches
Gift of the American Academy of Arts and
Letters, Childe Hassam Fund

Bechtle, Robert (b. 1932)
Sunset Intersection (triptych)
1984
oil on canvas
each panel: 56 x 40 inches
Museum purchase with funds provided by the
Benwood Foundation and the 1984 Collectors'
Group

Sunset Painter
1981
watercolor on paper
9⅞ x 14¾ inches
Museum purchase with funds provided by the
Benwood Foundation and the 1982 Collectors'
Group

Bellows, George (1882-1925)
Elsie, Emma and Marjorie
1921
lithograph
image: 9⅜ x 12⅛ inches
Gift of the Art Study Club in memory of
Anna C. Turner

The Model, Early Study
1917
lithograph, 8
11½ x 7⅝ inches
Museum purchase in memory of Evelyn Oakes

Benes, Barton Lidice (b. 1942)
Burnt-Out
1982
found objects, paper and ink on paper
30¼ x 22¾ inches
Museum purchase with funds provided by the
Benwood Foundation and the 1982 Collectors'
Group

Benson, Frank Weston (1862-1951)
Lilies and Laurel in a Blue Vase
1929
oil on canvas
30 x 25 inches
Gift of Mr. and Mrs. John T. Lupton

Benton, Thomas Hart (1889-1975)
The Wreck of the Ole '97
1943
egg tempera on gessoed masonite
28½ x 44½ inches (sight)
Gift of the Benwood Foundation

Berry, Bill (b. 1941)
Beverly
1978
watercolor on paper
40 x 30 inches
Museum purchase award from the 1978 Tennessee Watercolor Society Exhibition, made
possible by a contribution from Scott L.
Probasco, Jr.

Berry, John (b. 1943)
Ali
1976
acrylic on canvas
51 x 36 inches
Museum purchase award — Sixteenth Hunter
Annual Exhibition, 1977

Beyer, Al (b. 1947)
Harrington Hotel
c. 1976
oil on canvas
68 x 32 inches
Museum purchase award — Fifteenth Hunter
Annual Exhibition, 1976

Untitled
c. 1972-1974
oil on canvas
36 x 68 inches
Museum purchase award — Fourteenth
Hunter Annual Exhibition, 1974

Bierstadt, Albert (1830-1902)
Across the Prairie
1864
oil on canvas
12⅞ x 19¼ inches
Museum purchase with funds donated
anonymously

Bingham, George Caleb (1811-1879)
Elizabeth Carpenter Griffin
c. 1860
oil on canvas
40 x 32¼ inches
Gift of Mr. and Mrs. Walter T. Wood

John R. Griffin
c. 1860
oil on canvas
40 x 32¼ inches
Gift of Mr. and Mrs. Walter T. Wood

Bireline, George (b. 1923)
Island
1966
polymer on canvas
60¼ x 48 inches
Museum purchase award — Seventh Hunter
Annual Exhibition, 1966

Black, Richard (b. 1932)
August Song One
1980
lithograph, 4/25
image: 18 x 12 inches
Gift of Dr. and Mrs. Frederick P. Nause

August Song Two
1980
lithograph, 4/25
image: 18 x 12 inches
Gift of Dr. and Mrs. Frederick P. Nause

August Song Three
1980
lithograph, 4/25
image: 18 x 12 inches
Gift of Dr. and Mrs. Frederick P. Nause

Blossoms in Mid-Air: A
1978
etching, 22/25
image: 9¾ x 7¾ inches
Gift of Dr. and Mrs. Frederick P. Nause

Blossoms in Mid-Air: C
1978
etching, 22/25
image: 9¾ x 7¾ inches
Gift of Dr. and Mrs. Frederick P. Nause

Blossoms in Mid-Air: L
1978
etching, 22/25
image: 9¾ x 7¾ inches
Gift of Dr. and Mrs. Frederick P. Nause

Blossoms in Mid-Air: O
1978
etching, 22/25
image: 9¾ x 7¾ inches
Gift of Dr. and Mrs. Frederick P. Nause

Blossoms in Mid-Air: R
1978
etching, 22/25
image: 9¾ x 7¾ inches
Gift of Dr. and Mrs. Frederick P. Nause

Ezekiel's Wheel
1978
etching, 22/25
image: 8¾ x 11¾ inches
Gift of Dr. and Mrs. Frederick P. Nause

October Song
1980
etching, 4/25
image: 12 x 14¾ inches
Gift of Dr. and Mrs. Frederick P. Nause

September Song
1980
etching, 4/25
image: 14¾ x 12 inches
Gift of Dr. and Mrs. Frederick P. Nause

Weaver's Blue Dream
1980
lithograph, 4/25
image: 18 x 12 inches
Gift of Dr. and Mrs. Frederick P. Nause

Blakelock, Ralph Albert (1847-1919)
Landscape With Moon
c. 1885-1890
oil on canvas
20 x 30 inches
Gift of the Benwood Foundation
(by exchange)

Blauvelt, Charles F. (1824-1900)
The Immigrants
c. 1850
oil on canvas
21¼ x 17 inches
Museum purchase

Bluemner, Oscar (1867-1938)
*Form and Light, Motif in West
New Jersey (Beattiestown)*
1914
oil on canvas
30 x 40⅛ inches
Gift of the Benwood Foundation

Untitled landscape studies, New Jersey
(group of 3)
1920-1921
pencil on paper
4⅞ x 7½, 4⅛ x 6½, 4⅞ x 7¼, inches (sight)
Museum purchase in memory of
James M. Bishop

Boggs, Frank M. (1855-1926)
The Seine, Outside Paris
1885
oil on canvas
15⅛ x 22⅛ inches
Museum purchase with funds provided by
Mr. and Mrs. Llewellyn Boyd and
Mr. and Mrs. Scott L. Probasco, Jr.

Bopp, Emery (b. 1924)
Table D'Hote
1964
oil on canvas
35 x 40 inches
Museum purchase award — Sixth Hunter
Annual Exhibition, 1965

Botkin, John (b. 1940)
Washington Park
c. 1965-67
acrylic on canvas
31 x 25 inches
Museum purchase award — Eighth Hunter
Annual Exhibition, 1967

Bowen, Dale A.
Raspberry-Lime
1970
acrylic on canvas
48 x 60 inches
Museum purchase award — Eleventh Hunter
Annual Exhibition, 1970

Bowen, Helen Eakins
Retreat
1965
oil on canvas
30 x 24 inches
Gift of the artist in memory of her
grandmother, Lucy Jane Eakins Pruett

Boxer, Stanley (b. 1926)
Argumentofnoavail
1976
etching with aquatint, 2/28
image: 12 x 10⅞ inches
Museum purchase with funds supplied in part
by the National Endowment for the Arts, a
Federal agency

Bradford, William (1823-1892)
Arctic Scene
undated
oil on canvas
27 x 20 inches
Gift of Philip Claflin

Breverman, Harvey (b. 1934)
Mike
1980
lithograph, 4/25
image: 18 x 13 inches
Gift of Dr. and Mrs. Frederick P. Nause

Paul
1980
lithograph, 4/25
image: 23 x 18 inches
Gift of Dr. and Mrs. Frederick P. Nause

S.P. (self-portrait)
1980
lithograph, 4/25
15 x 22½ inches
Gift of Dr. and Mrs. Frederick P. Nause

Sinclair
1980
lithograph, 4/25
22¼ x 15 inches
Gift of Dr. and Mrs. Frederick P. Nause

Briselli, Susanna (b. 1945)
Untitled #94
1982
handcolored photograph
15⅞ x 19¾ inches
Museum purchase with funds provided by the
Benwood Foundation and the 1982 Collectors'
Group

Brown, John George (1831-1913)
Business Neglected
c. 1884
etching on Japan paper, 52/250
image: 13¼ x 9½ inches
From *Twenty Original American Etchings* pub-
lished under the auspices of the New York
Etching Club, 1884
Gift of Elizabeth Glascock in memory of Miles
White, Jr.

Solid Comfort
c. 1881
oil on canvas
30 x 25 inches
Gift of Mr. and Mrs. John T. Lupton

Browning, Colleen (b. 1929)
Union Mixer (from the *Kent Bicentennial
Portfolio*)
c. 1976
lithograph, 65/125
23 x 35 inches
Gift of the Lorillard Company

Bruce, Thomas
Untitled
c. 1976
acrylic on paper
40½ x 30¼ inches
Museum purchase award — Fifteenth Hunter
Annual Exhibition, 1976

Bry, Edith (b. 1898)
Equations
1970
paper collage
42 x 36 inches
Gift of the artist (by exchange)

Exodus
undated
lithograph
image: 11¾ x 9⅛ inches
Gift of the artist (by exchange)

Pompeii
1938
pastel on paper
16½ x 23½ inches
Gift of the artist (by exchange)

Woman of the Night I
1945
ink on paper
11 x 8½ inches
Gift of the artist (by exchange)

Woman of the Night II
1945
ink on paper
11 x 8½ inches
Gift of the artist (by exchange)

Bryant, Jack (b. 1929)
Daddy's Little Boys
1975
bronze, 4/20
13 x 12 x 7½ inches
Gift of Dr. Bruce E. Dahrling, II

Hitching Post
1975
bronze, 4/20
12½ x 20 x 6¼ inches
Gift of Dr. Bruce E. Dahrling, II

Monarch of the Plains
1975
bronze, 5/20
20 x 13 x 8 inches
Gift of Dr. Bruce E. Dahrling, II

Burchfield, Charles E. (1893-1967)
Coal Mine – End of the Day
1920
watercolor on paper
17¼ x 30⅞ inches (sight)
Gift of the Benwood Foundation

Dead Zinnias (study)
1946
charcoal on paper
11 x 17 inches
Gift of the Kennedy Galleries, New York

December Sun
1940
watercolor on paper
36 x 53 inches
Gift of the Benwood Foundation

Gateway to September
1946-1956
watercolor on paper
42½ x 56 inches
Gift of the Benwood Foundation

Pioneer Evening
1961-1966
watercolor on paper
49 x 55 inches
Gift of the Benwood Foundation

Two Ravines
1934-1943
watercolor on paper
36½ x 61⅛ inches (sight)
Gift of the Benwood Foundation

Burelbach, M. J.
Apples
c. 1939-1941
gelatin silver print photograph
10¼ x 13¼ inches (sight)
Gift of Miss Dorothy Kuster

Archer
c. 1939-1941
gelatin silver print photograph
13¼ x 10¼ inches
Gift of Miss Dorothy Kuster

Beach Grass
c. 1939-1941
gelatin silver print photograph
10¼ x 13¼ inches (sight)
Gift of Miss Dorothy Kuster

Concords
c. 1939-1941
gelatin silver print photograph
10 x 13 inches (sight)
Gift of Miss Dorothy Kuster

Flight
c. 1939-1941
gelatin silver print photograph
10¼ x 13¼ inches (sight)
Gift of Miss Dorothy Kuster

Oxen
1939
gelatin silver print photograph
9½ x 11½ inches (sight)
Gift of Miss Dorothy Kuster

Sea Gull
c. 1939-1941
gelatin silver print photograph
13 x 10¼ inches (sight)
Gift of Miss Dorothy Kuster

Showing Off
c. 1939-1941
gelatin silver print photograph
10¼ x 13¼ inches (sight)
Gift of Miss Dorothy Kuster

Skyward
c. 1939-1941
gelatin silver print photograph
13¼ x 10¼ inches (sight)
Gift of Miss Dorothy Kuster

Solo
c. 1939-1941
gelatin silver print photograph
13 x 10¼ inches (sight)
Gift of Miss Dorothy Kuster

Sunburst
c. 1939-1941
gelatin silver print photograph
10¼ x 13¼ inches (sight)
Gift of Miss Dorothy Kuster

Thunderhead
c. 1939-1941
gelatin silver print photograph
9¾ x 11½ inches (sight)
Gift of Miss Dorothy Kuster

Untitled (lighthouse)
c. 1939-1941
gelatin silver print photograph
9¼ x 11½ inches (sight)
Gift of Miss Dorothy Kuster

Untitled (oxen pulling cart)
1939
gelatin silver print photograph
10¾ x 9 inches (sight)
Gift of Miss Dorothy Kuster

Untitled (statue)
c. 1939-1941
gelatin silver print photograph
13½ x 9¼ inches (sight)
Gift of Miss Dorothy Kuster

Untitled (three gulls)
c. 1939-1941
gelatin silver print photograph
10⅛ x 11⅛ inches (sight)
Gift of Miss Dorothy Kuster

Work Horses
1941
gelatin silver print photograph
9 x 11¼ inches
Gift of Miss Dorothy Kuster

Burk, George (b. 1938)
Blind/Phase
1977
lithograph, 19/25
image: 10 x 7⅝ inches
Gift of Dr. and Mrs. Frederick P. Nause

Enchantment/Lakeside
1977
lithograph, 10/25
image: 10½ x 7¾ inches
Gift of Dr. and Mrs. Frederick P. Nause

Night/Lilies
1977
lithograph, 17/25
image: 10 x 7⅛ inches
Gift of Dr. and Mrs. Frederick P. Nause

Satelites/Tiny
1977
lithograph, 16/25
image: 9⅝ x 6⅝ inches
Gift of Dr. and Mrs. Frederick P. Nause

Screened/Match
1977
lithograph, 16/25
image: 9½ x 7 inches
Gift of Dr. and Mrs. Frederick P. Nause

Union
1977
lithograph, 17/25
image: 10½ x 7½ inches
Gift of Dr. and Mrs. Frederick P. Nause

Untitled
1981
bronze, 10/15
9¾ x 18 x 8 inches
Gift of Dr. and Mrs. Frederick P. Nause

Burks, Myrna R. (b. 1943)
Landscape
c. 1969
acrylic and gouache on paper
13⅞ x 18⅛ inches
Museum purchase award — Eleventh Hunter
Annual Exhibition, 1970

Burnley, Gary (b. 1950)
Untitled (hemisphere)
1981
della robbia glaze on hydrostone with wood
dowels
15⅜ x 15⅜ x 12 inches
Museum purchase with funds provided by the
Benwood Foundation and the 1982 Collectors'
Group

Burns, J. Bradley (b. 1951)
*Demolished Garage, Chattanooga, Tennessee,
1975* (from *Portfolio I*)
1975
gelatin silver print photograph, 4/20
7¾ x 9¾ inches
Gift of Mr. and Mrs. Scott L. Probasco, Jr.

Detail, Railroad Bridge, Chattanooga, 1975
(from *Portfolio I*)
1975
gelatin silver print photograph, 4/20
7¾ x 9¾ inches
Gift of Mr. and Mrs. Scott L. Probasco, Jr.

Evening, Volcano, California, 1974
(from *Portfolio I*)
1974
gelatin silver print photograph, 4/20
7¾ x 9¾ inches
Gift of Mr. and Mrs. Scott L. Probasco, Jr.

Female Nude, 1980 (from *Portfolio I*)
1980
gelatin silver print photograph, 4/20
7¾ x 9¾ inches
Gift of Mr. and Mrs. Scott L. Probasco, Jr.

Mill Dam, Winterport, Maine, 1978
(from *Portfolio I*)
1978
gelatin silver print photograph, 4/20
7¾ x 9¾ inches
Gift of Mr. and Mrs. Scott L. Probasco, Jr.

Plant Stems, Neah Bay, Washington, 1976
(from *Portfolio I*)
1976
gelatin silver print photograph, 4/20
7¾ x 9¾ inches
Gift of Mr. and Mrs. Scott L. Probasco, Jr.

Pond, Sierra Nevada Mountains, California, 1976
(from *Portfolio I*)
1976
gelatin silver print photograph, 4/20
9¾ x 7¾ inches
Gift of Mr. and Mrs. Scott L. Probasco, Jr.

Vines, Chattanooga, Tennessee, 1980
(from *Portfolio I*)
1980
gelatin silver print photograph, 4/20
7¾ x 9¾ inches
Gift of Mr. and Mrs. Scott L. Probasco, Jr.

Walkway, Northeast Harbor, Maine, 1978
(from *Portfolio I*)
1978
gelatin silver print photograph, 4/20
9¾ x 7¾ inches
Gift of Mr. and Mrs. Scott L. Probasco, Jr.

Wall Detail, Viola, Tennessee, 1981
(from *Portfolio I*)
1981
gelatin silver print photograph, 4/20
7¾ x 9¾ inches
Gift of Mr. and Mrs. Scott L. Probasco, Jr.

Burt, Charles (1823-1892)
Bargaining for a Horse
(after William Sidney Mount)
1851
engraving
image: 10 x 10 inches
Printed by the American Art Union
Museum purchase

Byrd, Byron Keith (b. 1956)
Campbells Soup
1983
serigraph, 5/90
42¾ x 30¼ inches
Gift of the artist in honor of Mrs. Barbara Byrd
Lawhorn

Calder, Alexander (1898-1976)
Pregnant Whale
1963
painted steel plate
126½ x 105 x 88 inches
Gift of the Benwood Foundation
(by exchange)

Cameron, Brooke (b. 1941)
Miss Willie
1977
etching, 10
19½ x 16 inches
Gift of Dr. and Mrs. Frederick P. Nause

Cameron, James (1817-1882)
*Colonel and Mrs. James A. Whiteside, Son
Charles and Servants*
c. 1858-1859
oil on canvas
53 x 75 inches
Gift of Mr. and Mrs. Thomas B. Whiteside

View of Moccasin Bend, Chattanooga
1857
oil on canvas
40 x 60 inches
Gift of the Chattanooga Public Library

Cannon, Howard (b. 1943)
High Latitudes, No. 77
1983
oil on canvas
29¼ x 29 inches
Gift of the artist

Caponigro, Paul (b. 1932)
*Running White Deer, Wicklow County,
Ireland, 1967*
1967
gelatin silver print photograph
5¼ x 13½ inches
Museum purchase

Carlsen, Emil (1853-1932)
Connecticut Hillside
c. 1915 (printed from original plates in 1978)
sepia ink etching on handmade paper, 97/200
image: 3¾ x 4⅜ inches
Gift of Dr. Kotcho Solacoff

Connecticut Landscape
c. 1915 (printed from original plates in 1978)
sepia ink etching on handmade paper, 97/200
image: 3⁵/₁₆ x 4⅜ inches
Gift of Dr. Kotcho Solacoff

Still Life with Copper and Onions
c. 1915 (printed from original plates in 1978)
sepia ink etching on handmade paper, 97/200
image: 4⁵⁄₁₆ x 3⁷⁄₁₆ inches
Gift of Dr. Kotcho Solacoff

Still Life with Vase and Bottle
c. 1915 (printed from original plates in 1978)
sepia ink etching on handmade paper, 97/200
image: 3¹⁵⁄₁₆ x 2¹⁵⁄₁₆ inches
Gift of Dr. Kotcho Solacoff

Three Studies
c. 1915 (printed from original plates in 1978)
sepia ink etching on handmade paper, 97/200
image: 2⅞ x 3¹³⁄₁₆ inches
Gift of Dr. Kotcho Solacoff

Tree Study
c. 1915 (printed from original plates in 1978)
sepia ink etching on handmade paper, 97/200
image: 4¾ x 5⅞ inches
Gift of Dr. Kotcho Solacoff

Carr, Samuel S. (1837-1908)
Untitled (pastoral scene)
undated
oil on canvas
14 x 20⅛ inches
Gift of Mr. and Mrs. James C. Stites

Carrithers, Mary Baker (b. 1943)
The Poet's Typewriter
1975
acrylic on wood
10½ x 11½ inches
Museum purchase award — 22nd Annual
Chattanooga Area Painting Exhibition, 1975

Carsman, Jon (b. 1944)
Whirling Shapes
1974
watercolor on paper
20 x 14 inches
Anonymous gift

Cash, Harold (1895-1977)
D'a-lal
1929
bronze
65 x 15 x 12½ inches
Museum purchase with funds supplied in part
by the National Endowment for the Arts, a
Federal agency

Doctor Lyle Battey West
undated
bronze
13 x 7½ x 9 inches
Gift of Mr. L.W. Oehmig

Emile Compard
1929-1930
bronze
19¼ x 4¾ x 4 inches
Museum purchase

Head of Monte Caldwell
c. 1950
bronze
14¼ x 8 x 7½ inches
Gift of Miss Mary Gardner Bright

Cassatt, Mary (1845-1926)
Baby Bill in His Cap and Shift, Held by His Nurse
c. 1890
pastel on paper
16⅞ x 15⅛ inches
Gift of the Benwood Foundation (by
exchange)

Casselli, Henry (b. 1946)
The End
1980
pastel on paper
20½ x 28½ inches
Gift of Mr. and Mrs. Frank E. Fowler

Sad Mime
1980
watercolor and gouache on board
5⅜ x 3⅝ inches (sight)
Gift of Gay Fowler in memory of her mother,
Sally R. Zimmermann

Castellon, Federico (1914-1971)
Stop him and strip him I say
undated
lithograph, 51/60
13½ x 9⅝ inches
Museum purchase

Central State Numismatic Society
*Three commemorative medals (one-hundredth
anniversary of the death of Abraham Lincoln)*
1965
1 silver, 1 bronze, and 1 aluminum
2 x 2 inches each
Gift of Philip J. More

Christensen, Ron and Darryl Hudak (designers)
Garden benches (four)
1985
Honduras mahogany
17¼ x 71½ x 16¾ inches
17 x 71¾ x 16¼ inches
17 x 72 x 16½ inches
17 x 71 x 16¼ inches
Constructed by students from the Appalachian Center for Crafts, Smithville, Tennessee.
Museum commission with funds provided by
Ruth S. and A. William Holmberg

Christo (Javacheff) (b. 1935)
Museum of Contemporary Art – Chicago
1972
lithograph, 59/60
42 x 32 inches
Museum purchase with funds supplied in part
by the National Endowment for the Arts, a
Federal agency

Church, Frederick Stuart (1842-1923)
A Symphony, Nineteenth Century
1884
etching on Japan paper, 52/250
image: 8¹³⁄₁₆ x 12⅜ inches
From *Twenty Original American Etchings*, pub-
lished under the auspices of the New York
Etching Club, 1884
Gift of Elizabeth Glascock in memory of Miles
White, Jr.

Clark, Joan
Neon Night
c. 1975
watercolor on paper
8¾ x 10¾ inches
Museum purchase award — 22nd Annual
Chattanooga Area Painting Exhibition, 1975

Clemens, Jonathan (b. 1947)
Prayer I
1977
woodcut, 10/25
image: 11⅛ x 9 inches
Gift of Dr. and Mrs. Frederick P. Nause

Prayer II
1977
woodcut, 10/25
image: 11 x 9 inches
Gift of Dr. and Mrs. Frederick P. Nause

Prayer III
1977
woodcut, 10/25
image: 11⅛ x 9 inches
Gift of Dr. and Mrs. Frederick P. Nause

Silver I
1977
woodcut, 7/25
image: 18 x 13¾ inches
Gift of Dr. and Mrs. Frederick P. Nause

Silver II
1977
woodcut, 7/25
image: 18 x 13¾ inches
Gift of Dr. and Mrs. Frederick P. Nause

Silver III
1977
woodcut, 10/25
image: 10¾ x 7 inches
Gift of Dr. and Mrs. Frederick P. Nause

Coffelt, James F. (b. 1953)
Lidded bowl
1984
turned holly wood
5½ x 8 inches diameter
Gift of the artist

Collins, Debbe (b. 1951)
Midnight Lace
1982
bronze
5 x 7 x 9½ inches
Gift of Mr. and Mrs. Scott L. Probasco, Jr.

Collins, Jim (b. 1934)
Cedar Breeze
1969-1972
cedar, copper, cast brass, paint
45 x 16½ x 16 inches
Museum purchase

Paper Watcher
1980
handmade rag paper
19¼ x 15¼ x ⅞ inches
Museum purchase

Weather Watcher
1978
painted carbon steel and cast iron
51 x 19¾ x 40½ inches
Gift of Mrs. Arthur Hays Sulzberger

Colman, Samuel (1832-1920)
The Olive Trees of the Riviera
c. 1884
etching on Japan paper, 52/250
image: 11⅝ x 14⅝ inches
From *Twenty Original American Etchings*, pub-
lished under the auspices of the New York
Etching Club, 1884
Gift of Elizabeth Glascock in memory of Miles
White, Jr.

Cone-Skelton, Annette (b. 1942)
Untitled
1974
acrylic and pencil on canvas
48 x 65¾ inches
Museum purchase award — Fifteenth Hunter
Annual Exhibition, 1976

Cooke, S. Tucker (b. 1941)
Infant Trilogy
1969
oil on canvas
49 x 49 inches
Museum purchase award — Tenth Hunter
Annual Exhibition, 1969

Cottingham, Robert (b. 1935)
Dr. Gibson
1974
lithograph, 39/50
36 x 36 inches
Museum purchase with funds supplied in part
by the National Endowment for the Arts, a
Federal agency

Coughlin, Jack (b. 1932)
Waiting for the Moon
c. 1966
etching, 9/100
image: 9⅞ x 14 inches
Museum purchase

Cox, Ralph
Six Views of Multiple Forms
1972
enamel on paper
35½ x 46 inches
Museum purchase award — Twelfth Hunter Annual Exhibition, 1972

Craft, David (b. 1945)
Post Meridian – Edge
1975
pencil on illustration board
3 x 4 inches
Museum purchase award — 22nd Annual Chattanooga Area Graphics and Photography Exhibition, 1976

Crane, Robert Bruce (1857-1937)
November
undated
oil on canvas
25 x 30 inches
Gift of Dr. Arch Y. Smith

Crawford, Spencer (b. 1944)
Executive Rattle
1982
laminated woods with rattle mechanism
15½ inches high x 3½ inches diameter
Museum purchase

Cress, George A. (b. 1921)
Broken Light
1953
oil on canvas
36 x 18¼ inches
Museum purchase

Outdoor Bouquet
1965
oil on canvas
25¼ x 33 inches
Gift of Louise Howell

Palisades
1982
pencil on paper
10 x 11¾ inches (sight)
Gift of the artist

Serpentine Marshes
1977
pencil on paper
18½ x 23 inches
Gift of Mr. and Mrs. Scott L. Probasco, Jr.

Croft, L. Scott (b. 1911)
Untitled
undated
oil on masonite
12 x 16 inches
Gift of the artist and Roger J. Welter

Cropsey, Jasper Francis (1823-1900)
Untitled (rural landscape)
1867
watercolor on paper
20½ x 28 inches (sight)
Gift of Carl D. Hagaman and museum purchase funds

Cucaro, Pascal (b. 1915)
Venice
1967-1968
acrylic on canvas
48 x 24 inches
Gift of the artist

Currier, Nathaniel (publisher)
John Adams
undated
handcolored lithograph
image: 13⅛ x 9¼ inches
Gift of Gordon M. Scott

John Quincy Adams
undated
handcolored lithograph
image: 13⅜ x 9¼ inches
Gift of Gordon M. Scott

American Country Life
F. F. Palmer (illustrator)
1855
handcolored lithograph
image: 18⅝ x 24 inches
Gift of Mr. and Mrs. Eugene Thomasson

James Buchanan
undated
handcolored lithograph
image: 12⅜ x 8½ inches
Gift of Gordon M. Scott

Daniel in the Lion's Den
undated
handcolored lithograph
image: 13⅛ x 9¼ inches
Gift of Dr. and Mrs. A. M. Patterson

Death of Andrew Jackson
1845
handcolored lithograph
image: 13¾ x 8⁹/₁₆ inches
Gift of Dr. and Mrs. A. M. Patterson

Millard Fillmore
1848
handcolored lithograph
image: 12¾ x 8⅝ inches
Gift of Gordon M. Scott

Fruits and Flowers
1848
handcolored lithograph
image: 12¾ x 8½ inches
Gift of the Estate of Marian Daniel West

General Taylor at the Battle of Resca de la Palma
1846
handcolored lithograph
image: 9 x 12⅝ inches
Gift of Dr. and Mrs. A. M. Patterson

William Henry Harrison
undated
handcolored lithograph
image: 13 x 9⅛ inches
Gift of Gordon M. Scott

Indian Hunter
1846
handcolored lithograph
image: 12½ x 8⅝ inches
Gift of Mrs. A. M. Patterson and Elizabeth Patterson

Thomas Jefferson
undated
handcolored lithograph
image: 13³/₅ x 9¼ inches
Gift of Gordon M. Scott

Julia
1845
handcolored lithograph
image: 12⅝ x 8⅜ inches
Gift of Mr. and Mrs. Eugene Thomasson

James Madison
undated
handcolored lithograph
image: 13⅜ x 9⅜ inches
Gift of Gordon M. Scott

Margaret
1848
handcolored lithograph
image: 12½ x 8⅜ inches
Gift of Mr. and Mrs. Eugene Thomasson

James Monroe
undated
handcolored lithograph
image: 13 x 9 inches
Gift of Gordon M. Scott

Franklin Pierce
1852
handcolored lithograph
image: 12⅜ x 8⅞ inches
Gift of Gordon M. Scott

The Road – Winter
1853
handcolored lithograph
image: 19¼ x 26⅜ inches
Gift of Mr. and Mrs. Eugene Thomasson

Zachary Taylor
1848
handcolored lithograph
image: 13⅜ x 8¹⁵/₁₆ inches
Gift of Gordon M. Scott

John Tyler
undated
handcolored lithograph
image: 12⅞ x 9 inches
Gift of Gordon M. Scott

Martin Van Buren
undated
handcolored lithograph
image: 13⅝ x 9¾ inches
Gift of Gordon M. Scott

George Washington
undated
handcolored lithograph
image: 12¾ x 9⅛ inches
Gift of Gordon M. Scott

Currier and Ives (publishers)
Battle of Chattanooga
undated
handcolored lithograph
image: 9¼ x 12⅜ inches
Gift of Mrs. A. M. Patterson and Elizabeth Patterson

Caught on the Fly
1879
handcolored lithograph
image: 9½ x 14¼ inches
Gift of Mr. and Mrs. Eugene Thomasson

The Celebrated Clipper Ship, "Dreadnought"
undated
handcolored lithograph
image: 9½ x 13½ inches
Gift of Mr. and Mrs. Eugene Thomasson

Cottage by the Cliffs
undated
handcolored lithograph
image: 9¼ x 12½ inches
Gift of Mr. and Mrs. Eugene Thomasson

Emma
undated
handcolored lithograph
image: 13½ x 7¼ inches
Gift of Mr. and Mrs. Eugene Thomasson

Fly Fishing
1878
handcolored lithograph
image: 9¾ x 13¾ inches
Gift of Mr. and Mrs. Eugene Thomasson

Fruits of a Golden Land
1871
handcolored lithograph
image: 9½ x 13 inches
Gift of Miss Mary Gardner Bright

Fruits of the Tropics
1871
handcolored lithograph
image: 9¼ x 12½ inches
Gift of the Estate of Marian Daniel West

Good Times on the Old Plantation
undated
handcolored lithograph
image: 9¼ x 12½ inches
Gift of Dr. and Mrs. A. M. Patterson

A Home in the Wilderness
1870
handcolored lithograph
image: 8⅝ x 12½ inches
Gift of Miss Mary Gardner Bright

The Home of Washington, Mt. Vernon
undated
handcolored lithograph
image: 9 1/16 x 12½ inches
Gift of Mr. and Mrs. Eugene Thomasson

Home Sweet Home
undated
handcolored lithograph
image: 9¼ x 12½ inches
Gift of Mr. and Mrs. Eugene Thomasson

Andrew Jackson – Seventh President
undated
handcolored lithograph
image: 11½ x 9 inches
Gift of Mrs. A. M. Patterson

Landing a Trout
1879
handcolored lithograph
image: 9½ x 13½ inches
Gift of Mr. and Mrs. Eugene Thomasson

Landscape, Fruit and Flowers
F. F. Palmer (illustrator)
1862
handcolored lithograph
image: 21⅛ x 27½ inches
Gift of Mr. and Mrs. Eugene Thomasson

Abraham Lincoln
1860
handcolored lithograph
image: 13⅛ x 8 11/16 inches
Gift of Gordon M. Scott

The Little Brothers
1875
handcolored lithograph
image: 12⅜ x 8½ inches
Gift of Mr. and Mrs. Eugene Thomasson

The Little Sisters
undated
handcolored lithograph
image: 12½ x 8½ inches
Gift of Mr. and Mrs. Eugene Thomasson

Lookout Mountain Tennessee and the Chattanooga Railroad
F. F. Palmer (illustrator)
1866
handcolored lithograph
image: 16¼ x 20½ inches
Gift of Mrs. Arthur Hays Sulzberger in memory of William McKenzie

Lookout Mountain Tennessee and the Chattanooga Railroad
F. F. Palmer (illustrator)
1866
handcolored lithograph
image: 16¼ x 20½ inches
Gift of the Estate of Marian Daniel West

Moonlight on Long Island Sound
undated
handcolored lithograph
image: 9½ x 12½ inches
Gift of Miss Mary Gardner Bright

Niagara Falls from Canada
undated
handcolored lithograph
image: 9⅛ x 12½ inches
Gift of Mrs. A. M. Patterson

Noah's Ark
undated
handcolored lithograph
image: 8 9/16 x 12½ inches
Gift of the estate of Marian Daniel West

The Old Mill in Summer
undated
handcolored lithograph
image: 9¼ x 12½ inches
Gift of Mr. and Mrs. Eugene Thomasson

Peaches and Grapes
1870
handcolored lithograph
image: 13¾ x 9 inches
Gift of the estate of Marian Daniel West

Skating Scene – Moonlight
1868
handcolored lithograph
image: 8⅝ x 12½ inches
Gift of Mr. and Mrs. Eugene Thomasson

The Village Blacksmith
undated
handcolored lithograph
image: 10¼ x 15⅜ inches
Gift of Mr. and Mrs. Eugene Thomasson

Winter Morning
F. F. Palmer (illustrator)
1861
handcolored lithograph
image: 12½ x 15⅜ inches
Gift of Mr. and Mrs. Eugene Thomasson

Yacht "Sappho" of New York, 310 tons
undated
handcolored lithograph
image: 9⅝ x 12⅝ inches
Gift of Mr. and Mrs. Eugene Thomasson

Dagnan, Gary (b. 1946)
October Evening
1975
watercolor on paper
31½ x 41 inches
Museum purchase award — Fifteenth Hunter Annual Exhibition, 1976

Daingerfield, Elliott (1859-1932)
Untitled (landscape)
undated
watercolor on paper
12¼ x 16¼ inches
Museum purchase

D'Andrea, Bernard (b. 1923)
Pequest #2
1982
oil on masonite
20⅛ x 27 inches
Gift of the artist

Davies, Arthur B. (1862-1928)
Juno and the Three Graces
1902
oil on canvas
16 x 20⅛ inches
Museum purchase

Dee, Leo (b. 1931)
Truro
1974
silverpoint
14 x 18½ inches
Gift of Charles Z. Offin Art Fund, Inc.

de Kooning, Elaine (b. 1920)
Athens, Greece
1974
charcoal on paper
16½ x 22¾ inches (sight)
Gift of the artist

de Kooning, Willem (b. 1904)
Untitled 1969
1969
oil on paper, mounted on board
41⅜ x 30⅛ inches
Museum purchase with funds provided by the Benwood Foundation, Mr. and Mrs. Joseph H. Davenport, Jr., Mr. and Mrs. Scott L. Probasco, Jr., and Mr. and Mrs. Phil B. Whitaker

Dement, Mike
Pat and His Friends – Don and Carol
c. 1968
acrylic on shaped canvas
72 x 65¾ inches
Museum purchase award — Ninth Hunter Annual Exhibition, 1968

Denton, Jack (b. 1949)
Morning On M. L. King
1984
oil on canvas
36 x 60 inches
Gift of the artist

Dine, Jim (b. 1935)
Paint Brush
1971
etching, 29/75
image: 54 x 50 inches
Museum purchase with funds supplied in part by the National Endowment for the Arts, a Federal agency

di Suvero, Mark (b. 1933)
For Rilke
1976
lithograph, 11/26
48 x 32 inches
Museum purchase with funds supplied in part by the National Endowment for the Arts, a Federal agency

Dodd, Lamar (b. 1909)
July Surf: Lobster Point
1955
watercolor on paper
15½ x 22½ inches
Gift of the Chattanooga Area Alumni of the University of Georgia, and friends of the artist

Shanties – LaGrange, Georgia
1932
watercolor on paper
15 x 18¾ inches (sight)
Gift of Mr. and Mrs. Scott L. Probasco, Jr.

Doughty, Thomas (1793-1856)
Near Little Point, Catskill Mountains
c. 1840
oil on canvas
36 x 50 inches
Gift of the Benwood Foundation

Driggs, Elsie (b. 1898)
Nudes
c. 1920-1925
watercolor and pencil on paper
11 x 9 inches
Gift of Coe Kerr Gallery, New York

du Bois, Guy Pene (1884-1958)
Central Park
c. 1940
pastel and oil on paper
15 x 21 inches (sight)
Gift of the Benwood Foundation

Shopper in a Red Hat
1939
oil on canvas
30⅛ x 25 inches
Gift of the Benwood Foundation

Ecker, Robert (b. 1936)
Connections
1978
mezzotint, 22/25
image: 4 x 4 inches
Gift of Dr. and Mrs. Frederick P. Nause

Dark Glasses 2
1978
mezzotint, 24/25
image: 2 x 2 inches
Gift of Dr. and Mrs. Frederick P. Nause

Dark Glasses 3
1978
mezzotint, 22/25
image: 2 x 2 inches
Gift of Dr. and Mrs. Frederick P. Nause

Dark Glasses 5
1978
mezzotint, 22/25
image: 2 x 2 inches
Gift of Dr. and Mrs. Frederick P. Nause

Drawer
1978
mezzotint, 23/25
image: 4 x 4 inches
Gift of Dr. and Mrs. Frederick P. Nause

The Historical View
1978
mezzotint, 22/25
image: 4 x 4 inches
Gift of Dr. and Mrs. Frederick P. Nause

Melancholia II
1978
mezzotint, 22/25
image: 4 x 4 inches
Gift of Dr. and Mrs. Frederick P. Nause

Monument
1978
mezzotint, 22/25
image: 2 x 2 inches
Gift of Dr. and Mrs. Frederick P. Nause

Reflections
1978
mezzotint, 22/25
image: 4 x 4 inches
Gift of Dr. and Mrs. Frederick P. Nause

Relic
1978
mezzotint, 23/25
image: 2 x 2 inches
Gift of Dr. and Mrs. Frederick P. Nause

Strange But True
1978
mezzotint, 22/25
image: 4 x 4 inches
Gift of Dr. and Mrs. Frederick P. Nause

The Tragic View
1978
mezzotint, 22/25
image: 4 x 4 inches
Gift of Dr. and Mrs. Frederick P. Nause

Edwards, John W. (b. 1958)
New Street, Johnson City
1982
gelatin silver print photograph
10 x 8 inches
Gift of the artist

Untitled (Hunter Mansion facade)
1983
gelatin silver print photograph
image: 13½ x 10½ inches
Gift of the artist

Elliott, Charles Loring (1812-1868)
Joseph Howe
1847
oil on canvas
29¾ x 24¾ inches
Museum purchase

Maria Howe (Mrs. Joseph Howe)
1847
oil on canvas
29⅞ x 24¾ inches
Museum purchase

Ellis, Frank (Bud) (b. 1936)
Not All Toys Are Made for Kids
1972-1973
brass and aluminum
25 x 24¼ x 12 inches
Museum purchase

Emery, Lin
Flame
1982
fabricated aluminum
at rest: 53 x 41 x 14 inches (61 inch orbit)
Museum purchase with funds provided by
the Benwood Foundation and the 1984 Collectors' Group

Evergood, Philip (1901-1973)
Girl with Sunflowers
1965
etching, 111/150
image: 8⅛ x 5⅞ inches
Gift of Mr. and Mrs. Joseph H. Davenport, Jr.

Love on the Beach
1937
oil on canvas
30¼ x 37¼ inches
Gift of the Benwood Foundation

Farrer, Henry (1843-1903)
Evening, New York Harbor
1884
etching on Japan paper, 52/250
image: 9⅝ x 13½ inches
From *Twenty Original American Etchings*, pub-
lished under the auspices of the New York
Etching Club, 1884
Gift of Elizabeth Glascock in memory of Miles
White, Jr.

Feinstein, Lillian Brown (1908-1983)
Benediction
1968
bronze
13¾ x 6½ x 3 inches
Museum purchase

Filmus, Michael (b. 1943)
Early Spring
1983
oil on canvas
44 x 60 inches
Gift of Mr. and Mrs. John T. Lupton

Fish, Janet (b. 1938)
Orange Lamp and Oranges
1982
oil on canvas
65⅞ x 50 inches
Museum purchase with funds provided by the
Benwood Foundation and the 1982 Collectors'
Group

Flack, Audrey (b. 1931)
Fourth of July Stillife (From the *Kent Bicentennial Portfolio*)
1975
serigraph with die cut foil laminates, 61/125
40 x 40 inches
Gift of the Lorillard Company

Fleming, Frank (b. 1940)
Frog's Dining Room
c. 1979-1980
unglazed porcelain, nine pieces
8½ x 29½ x 26 inches, assembled
Anonymous gift in honor of Jim Odom

Florsheim, Richard (1916-1979)
Bridge
1977
lithograph, 10/25
image: 8 x 16 inches
Gift of Dr. and Mrs. Frederick P. Nause

City Moon
1977
lithograph, 10/25
image: 16¼ x 8¼ inches
Gift of Dr. and Mrs. Frederick P. Nause

Departure
1977
lithograph, 10/25
image: 10 x 14 inches
Gift of Dr. and Mrs. Frederick P. Nause

Flags
1978
lithograph, 4/25
image: 21¼ x 15¾ inches
Gift of Dr. and Mrs. Frederick P. Nause

Morning Birds
1977
lithograph, 11/25
image: 10 x 14 inches
Gift of Dr. and Mrs. Frederick P. Nause

Parade
1977
lithograph, 16/25
image: 8 x 16 inches
Gift of Dr. and Mrs. Frederick P. Nause

Sand Flats
1978
lithograph, 4/25
image: 21¼ x 15¾ inches
Gift of Dr. and Mrs. Frederick P. Nause

Spray
1977
lithograph, 9/25
image: 10⅛ x 14 inches
Gift of Dr. and Mrs. Frederick P. Nause

Fräbel, Hans Godo (b. 1941)
Crowded
1970
blown borosilicate crystal
19½ x 6 x 5½ inches
Gift of the artist

Francis, Sam (b. 1923)
White Bone
1971
lithograph, 55/69
27⅝ x 39⅝ inches
Museum purchase with funds supplied in part by the National Endowment for the Arts, a Federal agency

Frankenhauser, Neil (b. 1939)
Big Dream Dialog No. 3
1968
acrylic on canvas
24 x 24 inches (sight)
Museum purchase award — Tenth Hunter Annual Exhibition, 1969

Frankenthaler, Helen (b. 1928)
Dream Walk
1977
lithograph, 30/47
26 x 35 inches
Museum purchase with funds supplied in part by the National Endowment for the Arts, a Federal agency

The Franklin Mint
Official Big Game Medals (set of 40)
1973
20 silver, 20 bronze
2 inches diameter each
Gift of Philip J. More

Fraser, James Earle (1876-1953)
End of the Trail
1915 (cast 1965)
bronze, 5/24
34 x 30³⁄₈ x 10 inches
Cast from original plaster models by Modern Art Foundry of Long Island, New York, under the supervision of Syracuse University
Museum purchase

Frishmuth, Harriet Whitney (1880-1980)
Crest of the Wave
1926
bronze
66 x 16 x 15 inches
Gift of Mr. and Mrs. Cartter Lupton

Fuller, Kevin (b. 1943)
Wisp River, 1981
print, 1983
gelatin silver print photograph
2¹⁵⁄₁₆ x 8 inches
Gift of the artist

Furr, Jim (b. 1939)
Black Drawing #40: Untitled
1976
charcoal on paper with collage
41¼ x 29⅜ inches
First Tennessee Bank Award — Seventeenth Hunter Annual Exhibition, 1978

Gaugengigl, I. M. (1855-1932)
Bellissima
c. 1884
etching on Japan paper, 52/250
image: 8³⁄₁₆ x 7⁷⁄₁₆ inches
From *Twenty Original American Etchings*, published under the auspices of the New York Etching Club, 1884
Gift of Elizabeth Glascock in memory of Miles White, Jr.

Getchell, Edith Loring Pierce (1855-1940)
Solitude
c. 1884
etching on Japan paper, 52/250
image: 5¾ x 8⅝ inches
From *Twenty Original American Etchings*, published under the auspices of the New York Etching Club, 1884
Gift of Elizabeth Glascock in memory of Miles White, Jr.

Gibson and Company (publishers)
Capture of Fort Donelson
undated
handcolored lithograph
15¾ x 19 inches
Gift of Dr. and Mrs. A. M. Patterson

Gifford, Sanford Robinson (1823-1880)
South Bay, On the Hudson, Near Hudson, New York (also known as *Autumn Sailing*)
1864
oil on canvas
12¼ x 25¼ inches
Museum purchase

Gilchrist, Doug
Radii
c. 1969
acrylic on canvas
62 x 74½ inches
Museum purchase

Gilliam, Sam (b. 1933)
The Great American Quilt Series
1975
cloth, buttons and pigment incorporated into handmade paper, 25
13½ x 19 inches
Museum purchase with funds supplied in part by the National Endowment for the Arts, a Federal agency

Glackens, William (1870-1938)
Miss Olga D.
1910
oil on canvas
32 x 26 inches
Gift of the Benwood Foundation

Glick, John Parker (b. 1938)
Tea Set
1969
glazed stoneware
9 inches high (teapot)
Gift of The Johnson Wax Company

Golub, Leon A. (b. 1922)
Head XXV
1959
lacquer on canvas
48 x 38 inches
Museum purchase with funds provided by the Benwood Foundation and the 1983 Collectors' Group

Goodman, Ken (b. 1950)
Pet
1984
oil on canvas
72 x 72 inches
Museum purchase with funds provided by the Benwood Foundation and the 1985 Collectors' Group

Goodman, Sidney (b. 1936)
Girl with a Sheet
1974-1975
oil on canvas
71¾ x 53 inches
Museum purchase with funds provided by the Benwood Foundation and the 1982 Collectors' Group

Sitting by the Sea (also known as *Two Figures*)
1980
watercolor on paper
15 x 22½ inches
Museum purchase with funds provided by the Benwood Foundation and the 1982 Collectors' Group

Goodwin, Richard LaBarre (1840-1910)
The Huntsman's Door
c. 1890
oil on canvas
50½ x 30¼ inches
Gift of Mrs. Otto K. LeBron in memory of her husband, Otto K. LeBron

Gorky, Arshile (1904-1948)
In the Garden
1938-1941
oil on canvas
16 x 20 inches
Museum purchase with funds provided by the Benwood Foundation and the 1984 Collectors' Group

Greenbaum, Dorthea (b. 1893)
Straw Hat
undated
painted plaster composition
10 x 5¾ x 6½ inches
Gift of Adam Hochschild

Sunbonnet
1970
bronze, edition of six
13 x 8 x 9 inches
Gift of Mrs. Arthur Hays Sulzberger in memory of Mr. Arthur Hays Sulzberger

Griffin, Walter (1861-1935)
Old Mill at South Waterford, Maine
1918
oil on board
13 x 15⅞ inches
Gift of Harold and Regina Simon

Grooms, Red (b. 1937)
Bicentennial Bandwagon (From the *Kent Bicentennial Portfolio*)
1976
serigraph, 107/125
29 x 41 inches
Gift of the Lorillard Company

Grosz, George (1893-1959)
Landscape
c. 1940
lithograph
11½ x 15½ inches
Gift of Frederick Woodworth Pattison III

Guberman, Sidney (b. 1936)
The Heart of the Park
1983
serigraph, 49/58
image: 18⅜ x 26¼ inches
Gift of Louise Guberman in memory of Morris Guberman

Guerriero, Henry (b. 1929)
iii Self: c – Collision: Kill Daddy! (From *Age of Confrontation Portfolio*)
1971
lithograph, 13/20
20 x 15 inches
Gift of Georganne Aldrich Heller

Gundaker, Ellen Grey (b. 1950)
Strata
1973
oil pastel and acrylic on canvas
36 x 36 inches
Museum purchase award — Fourteenth Hunter Annual Exhibition, 1974

Guy, Seymour Joseph (1824-1910)
The First Needlework
c. 1884
etching on Japan paper, 52/250
image: 8 15/16 x 11 5/8 inches
From *Twenty Original American Etchings*, published under the auspices of the New York Etching Club, 1884
Gift of Elizabeth Glascock in memory of Miles White, Jr.

Hanton, Charles K. R. (b. 1935)
Lemon Tree
1969
painted welded steel
65½ x 35 x 34½ inches
Gift of Jay and Rosalind Solomon

Primordialis
1967
welded steel
12 x 21 x 13½ inches
Gift of Jay and Rosalind Solomon

Hardy, DeWitt (b. 1940)
Two Trains Passing in the Rain
1978
drypoint, 22
image: 20 x 16 inches
Gift of Dr. and Mrs. Frederick P. Nause

Hardy, Pat (b. 1940)
Arrangement with Cassatt
1977
lithograph, 10/25
image: 12½ x 16 inches
Gift of Dr. and Mrs. Frederick P. Nause

Gloves at Lake Michigan
1977
lithograph, 4/25
image: 16 x 12 inches
Gift of Dr. and Mrs. Frederick P. Nause

Model in Studio
1977
lithograph, 9/25
image: 6⅛ x 4⅛ inches
Gift of Dr. and Mrs. Frederick P. Nause

Nautilus I
1977
etching, 16/25
image: 8 x 9¾ inches
Gift of Dr. and Mrs. Frederick P. Nause

Nautilus II
1977
etching, 16/25
image: 9¾ x 8 inches
Gift of Dr. and Mrs. Frederick P. Nause

Nautilus III
1977
etching, 17/25
7¾ x 9¾ inches
Gift of Dr. and Mrs. Frederick P. Nause

Harman, Maryann (b. 1935)
Southwest Mountains
c. 1972-1974
oil and acrylic on canvas
46 x 71 inches

Harrington, Bryan (b. 1953)
Floating Fear
1982
mixed media and collage on paper
17⅜ x 14⅝ inches
Museum purchase with funds provided by the Benwood Foundation and the 1982 Collectors' Group

Harris, A.
Landscape with Animals
undated
oil on canvas
20 x 25 inches
Gift of Mrs. A. M. Patterson and Elizabeth Patterson

Hart, William M. (1823-1894)
Autumn Landscape
1870
oil on canvas mounted on panel
14½ x 24¼ inches
Gift of Dr. Arch Y. Smith

Hartley, Marsden (1877-1943)
Chanties to the North
1938-1939
oil on board
28¼ x 22⅜ inches
Gift of the Benwood Foundation

Harvey, André (b. 1941)
The Portrait Sitter
1977
bronze, 34/60
7 x 14 x 5 inches
Gift of Dr. and Mrs. Bruce E. Dahrling, II

The Relic
1979
bronze, 18/60
7½ x 26 x 7 inches
Gift of Dr. and Mrs. Bruce E. Dahrling, II

The Wing Chair
1979
bronze, 3/30
15 x 16 x 11¾ inches
Gift of Dr. and Mrs. Bruce E. Dahrling, II

Haskell & Allen (publishers)
The Old Mill Dam at Sleepy Hollow
undated
handcolored lithograph
image: 8⅛ x 13¼ inches
Gift of Mrs. A. M. Patterson

Hassam, Childe (1859-1935)
French Tea Garden (also known as *The Terre-cuite Tea Set*)
1910
oil on canvas
35 x 40¼ inches
Gift of the Benwood Foundation

Side panels (From *The Flower Girl* triptych)
1888
oil and gold leaf on board
16½ x 7½ inches each
Gift of Hirschl and Adler Galleries, New York

Spring, the Dogwood Tree
1921
oil on canvas
43 x 46 inches
Gift of the Benwood Foundation

Hatcher, Flo (b. 1937)
A Box with a Sky Window
1977
lithograph, 4
7 x 5 inches
Gift of Dr. and Mrs. Frederick P. Nause

British War Relief Society
1977
lithograph, 10
image: 7⅜ x 5⅜ inches
Gift of Dr. and Mrs. Frederick P. Nause

Hatcher, Keith (b. 1934)
Bay Colony Secrets
1977
lithograph, 9
15¼ x 13¾ inches
Gift of Dr. and Mrs. Frederick P. Nause

Boston Bay Blower
1977
lithograph, 10
14⅞ x 21¾ inches
Gift of Dr. and Mrs. Frederick P. Nause

Hawthorne, Charles (1872-1930)
Lake at Sunset
c. 1928
watercolor on paper
10¼ x 14¼ inches
Gift of Ruth S. Holmberg

Hayes, David (b. 1931)
Study for Landscape Sculpture – Beachforms
1982
ink and gouache on paper
22¼ x 30 inches
Gift of the artist

Healy, George P. A. (1813-1894)
Portrait of a Man
c. 1850-1860
oil on canvas
30 x 25⅛ inches
Gift of Dr. and Mrs. Cecil E. Newell

Heliker, John (b. 1909)
Landscape, Maine
1979
watercolor on paper
7⅞ x 11⅝ inches (sight)
Gift of the Thornton Memorial Fund in memory of Russell Thornton

Hendricks, Edward Lee (b. 1952)
1981-XX
1981
aluminum, stainless steel, magnesium
23 x 234 x 12 inches
Gift of George Barber, Jr.

Henri, Robert (1865-1929)
Pet (also known as *Wee Annie Lavelle*)
1927
oil on canvas
24 x 20 inches
Gift of the Benwood Foundation

Woman in Pink on Beach
1893
oil on canvas
18 x 24 inches
Gift of the Benwood Foundation

Henry, John R. (b. 1943)
Largo
1981
painted aluminum
171 x 74 x 183 inches
Museum purchase

Untitled (BRS 80-28)
1980
aluminum
10⅝ x 13 x 9 inches
Gift of Cleve K. Scarbrough

Hill, Thomas (1829-1908)
Untitled
1898
watercolor on paper
9 x 20 inches
Gift of John L. Petty

Hirsch, Joseph (1910-1981)
The Boston Tea Party (from the *Kent Bicentennial Portfolio*)
c. 1975-1976
lithograph
28 x 19⅛ inches
Gift of the Lorillard Company

Hoffman, Malvina (1887-1966)
Fidelia Lamson Hoffman
1918
marble
16½ x 9½ x 7¾ inches
Gift of Mrs. Arthur Hays Sulzberger

Hofmann, Hans (1880-1966)
Scintillating Blue 38-30
1956
oil on canvas
38 x 30 inches
Museum purchase with funds provided by Ruth S. and A. William Holmberg, Mr. and Mrs. Olan Mills, II, Mr. and Mrs. Scott L. Probasco, Jr., and Mr. and Mrs. Phil B. Whitaker

Hogan, Ed (b. 1937)
Blue Quartet
1980
lithograph, 15/25
15 x 16½ inches
Gift of Dr. and Mrs. Frederick P. Nause

Chitlin Supper
1980
lithograph, 4/25
image: 20½ x 14 inches
Gift of Dr. and Mrs. Frederick P. Nause

Reclining Nude
1980
lithograph, 4/25
image: 11 x 15 inches
Gift of Dr. and Mrs. Frederick P. Nause

Sitting Nude
1980
lithograph, 4/25
image: 10¾ x 8¼ inches
Gift of Dr. and Mrs. Frederick P. Nause

Hollander, Irwin (b. 1927)
B Bear
1978
lithograph, 22/25
image: 10 x 7 inches
Gift of Dr. and Mrs. Frederick P. Nause

Mann
1978
lithograph, 22/25
image: 16½ x 10½ inches
Gift of Dr. and Mrs. Frederick P. Nause

Holty, Carl (1900-1973)
Untitled
undated
watercolor on paper
11½ x 9⅛ inches (sight)
Gift of the Thornton Memorial Fund in memory of Russell Thornton

Homer, Winslow (1836-1910)
Eight Bells
1887
etching
image: 18⅞ x 24⅜
Gift of Mr. and Mrs. Scott L. Probasco, Jr.

Shepherdess and Sheep
1879
pencil and gouache on paper
9½ x 14⅞ inches
Bequest of Margaret Caldwell Morrison (1895-1984)

The Sun Dial
c. 1885
ink on paper
3¼ x 4⅝ inches
Gift of Michael F. McGauley

Time and Tide
c. 1885
ink on paper
3⅛ x 4¼ inches
Gift of Michael F. McGauley

Young Lady in Woods
1880
watercolor on paper
8½ x 11⅛ inches
Museum purchase

Hope, James (1818-1892)
Chattanooga from Lookout Mountain
1878
oil on canvas
25¼ x 20⅛ inches
Museum purchase

Hopper, Edward (1882-1967)
House and Boats (also known as *Seaside House*)
c. 1923
watercolor on paper
13⅞ x 20 inches
Gift of the Benwood Foundation

Horton, William S. (1865-1936)
Punch on the Beach at Broadstairs, England (also known as *The Beach at Broadstairs – Punch Amid the Trippers,* and *Broadstairs, England*)
1920
oil on canvas
25⅜ x 30¾ inches
Gift of M. R. Schweitzer in memory of Robert L. Maclellan (by exchange)

Howe, Harold B. (b. 1934)
DVO #27
c. 1976
acrylic on paper
38¼ x 50¼ inches
Museum purchase award — Fifteenth Hunter Annual Exhibition, 1976

On the Death of My Father
1967
acrylic on canvas
44¼ x 58¼ inches
Museum purchase award — Tenth Hunter Annual Exhibition, 1969

Hudak, Darryl
(See listing under Ron Christensen)

Huggins, Victor (b. 1936)
Soft Center
1969
acrylic and acrylic stain on unprimed, shaped canvas
21½ x 62¼ inches
Museum purchase award — Eleventh Hunter Annual Exhibition, 1970

Hunt, Richard (b. 1935)
Paper Piece I
1978
five color lamination, 4/25
16 x 21 inches
Gift of Dr. and Mrs. Frederick P. Nause

Paper Piece II
1978
three color lamination, 22/25
16¼ x 21¼ inches
Gift of Dr. and Mrs. Frederick P. Nause

Paper Piece III
1978
four color lamination, 21/25
16 x 20½ inches
Gift of Dr. and Mrs. Frederick P. Nause

Paper Piece IV
1978
six color lamination, 22/25
17 x 21 inches
Gift of Dr. and Mrs. Frederick P. Nause

Paper Piece V
1978
two color lamination, 1/25
18½ x 23 inches
Gift of Dr. and Mrs. Frederick P. Nause

Untitled
1978
lithograph, 22/25
11½ x 15½ inches
Gift of Dr. and Mrs. Frederick P. Nause

Untitled
1978
lithograph, 22/25
11¼ x 15 inches
Gift of Dr. and Mrs. Frederick P. Nause

Untitled
1978
lithograph, 23/25
13 x 17½ inches
Gift of Dr. and Mrs. Frederick P. Nause

Untitled
1978
lithograph, 22/25
15¾ x 11¼ inches
Gift of Dr. and Mrs. Frederick P. Nause

Untitled
1978
lithograph, 22/25
15 x 22½ inches
Gift of Dr. and Mrs. Frederick P. Nause

Untitled (RH 879A)
1979
lithograph, 8/25
22½ x 15 inches
Gift of Dr. and Mrs. Frederick P. Nause

Untitled (RH 879B)
1979
lithograph, 8/25
17 x 22½ inches
Gift of Dr. and Mrs. Frederick P. Nause

Hunter, John (b. 1934)
Carnival
1978
lithograph, 22/25
22½ x 15 inches
Gift of Dr. and Mrs. Frederick P. Nause

Childhood
1979
lithograph, 9/25
22½ x 15 inches
Gift of Dr. and Mrs. Frederick P. Nause

Death and Transfiguration
1978
lithograph, 22/25
22½ x 15 inches
Gift of Dr. and Mrs. Frederick P. Nause

The Litho Daemon
1978
lithograph, 21/25
11¼ x 15 inches
Gift of Dr. and Mrs. Frederick P. Nause

Love
1978
lithograph, 4/25
22½ x 15 inches
Gift of Dr. and Mrs. Frederick P. Nause

The Printsellers
1978
lithograph, 4/25
22½ x 15 inches
Gift of Dr. and Mrs. Frederick P. Nause

Self-Portrait at 45
1979
lithograph, 8/25
15 x 22 inches
Gift of Dr. and Mrs. Frederick P. Nause

Vaudeville 1978
1978
lithograph, 20/25
11¼ x 15 inches
Gift of Dr. and Mrs. Frederick P. Nause

Ikegawa, Shiro (b. 1933)
Issa
1966
intaglio
24 x 18 inches
Gift of the Container Corporation of America

Indiana, Robert (b. 1928)
Jimmy Carter (from the *Presidential Portfolio*)
1980
serigraph, 41/150
image: 21 x 18⅛ inches
Anonymous gift

Liberty (from the *Kent Bicentennial Portfolio*)
1975
serigraph, 75/125
36 x 40 inches
Gift of the Lorillard Company

Inness, George (1825-1894)
Near Milton
1880
oil on panel
16¼ x 23¾ inches
Gift of Mr. and Mrs. Scott L. Probasco, Jr.

Rosy Morning
1894
oil on canvas
30 x 45 inches
Gift of the Joseph H. Davenport, Jr. family in memory of Laura Voigt and Joseph Howard Davenport

Ippolito, Angelo (b. 1922)
Midwest
1967
oil on canvas
65½ x 65½ inches
Gift of Dr. John Q. Durfey in memory of John C. Durfey, John M. Callaway, and T. Grady Parham

Jackson, H. Dan (b. 1919)
Fish Monger
1982
welded steel
19 x 8 x 13¼ inches
Gift of the artist

Jans, Candace (b. 1952)
Via Giuseppe Verdi
1981
oil and magna on masonite
12⅞ x 10⅜ inches
Museum purchase with funds provided by the Benwood Foundation and the 1983 Collectors' Group

Jenkins, Paul (b. 1923)
Phenomena Royal Violet Visitation
1977
acrylic on canvas
55 x 169 inches
Gift of Ruth S. and A. William Holmberg

Jennerjahn, Elizabeth (b. 1923)
Golden Lace
1965
fabric appliqued collage, cotton organdy, lace and silk on natural linen
69 x 54 inches
Gift of The Johnson Wax Company

Johns, Jasper (b. 1930)
Untitled (triptych)
1969
ink on synthetic vellum
20¾ x 56¼ inches (sight)
Gift of the Benwood Foundation

Johnston, W. Medford (b. 1941)
Grouping #V-2
1969
acrylic on canvas
36 x 60 inches
Museum purchase award — Tenth Hunter Annual Exhibition, 1969

Jones, Frances Williams (1874-1964)
View of Chattanooga, 1910
1910
oil on canvas
12 x 29½ inches
Gift of the family of Frances W. Jones in her memory

Jones, Lynne A. (b. 1951)
Untitled
1973
acrylic on canvas
9¾ x 13¾ inches
Museum purchase award — Fourteenth Hunter Annual Exhibition, 1974

Katz, Alex (b. 1927)
Ada at Table
1977
oil on cut-out aluminum
19 x 22 inches
Museum purchase with funds provided by the Benwood Foundation and the 1983 Collectors' Group

Tiger Lilies
1972
lithograph, 39/90
19 x 19½ inches
Gift of Jacqueline M. Holmes

Untitled
1978
lithograph, 57/100
27½ x 36⅛ inches
Gift of the Friends of the New Jersey State Museum

Young Washington (from the *Kent Bicentennial Portfolio*)
c. 1976
lithograph, 76/125
20 x 40 inches
Gift of the Lorillard Company

Kellogg, Edward (b. 1944)
Late Summer, Self Portrait
1976
oil on canvas
48 x 66 inches
Museum purchase award — Seventeenth Hunter Annual Exhibition, 1978

Undercurrent
1981
linocut, reduction printing on mulberry paper, 1/75
15 x 18 inches
Museum commission in commemoration of the 30th anniversary of the Hunter Museum of Art

Kellogg and Comstock (publishers)
Double Fishing
undated
lithograph
14 x 10 inches
Gift of Mrs. A. M. Patterson

Kelly, Ellsworth (b. 1923)
Colored Paper Image: XXI
1978
colored pulp lamination to handmade paper, 9/10
32¼ x 31¼ inches
Museum purchase with funds supplied in part by the National Endowment for the Arts, a Federal agency

Kensett, John Frederick (1816-1872)
View at Conway
c. 1850
oil on panel
12 x 10 inches
Museum purchase

Kerciu, G. Ray (b. 1933)
Polka Dots and Moon Beams
1980
lithograph, 4/25
image: 17 x 12½ inches
Gift of Dr. and Mrs. Frederick P. Nause

King, Clinton (1901-1978)
French Farm
1977
lithograph, 10/25
17⅛ x 22 inches
Gift of Dr. and Mrs. Frederick P. Nause

King, William (b. 1925)
Adolescence
1982
aluminum
107 x 39 x 87 inches
Gift of Sara Jo and Arthur J. Kobacker in honor of Abe and Bertha Borisky

Klein, Jody W.
Royal Family
1966-1967
four wall hangings, dyed cotton fabric, wool and cotton thread, yarn and beads, batiked, quilted and appliqued overall
29 x 34½ inches
Gift of The Johnson Wax Company

Kohlmeyer, Ida (b. 1912)
Microcosms
1978
serigraph, 4/75
22 x 30 inches
Museum purchase with funds supplied in part by the National Endowment for the Arts, a Federal agency

Kolbrener, Bob (b. 1942)
Stop, Benton, California
undated
gelatin silver print photograph
10½ x 13⁷⁄₁₆ inches
Gift of the artist

Koos, Vivian (b. 1927)
Red and Black
1958
vitreous enamel on iron
17¾ inches diameter
Gift of The Johnson Wax Company

Kuhn, Walt (1877-1949)
In the Women's Tent
1929
ink and wash on paper
6 x 9 inches
Gift of Kennedy Galleries, New York

Model Reclining on Back
1930
ink on paper
8½ x 10¼ inches
Gift of Kennedy Galleries, New York

The Rider
1924
oil on canvas
50⅛ x 33⅜ inches
Gift of the Benwood Foundation

Kuniyoshi, Yasuo (1893-1953)
The Acrobat
1938
lithograph, proof 15
16 x 13 inches
Gift of Grey Phillips

LaFarge, John (1835-1910)
Books and Owl
c. 1859
oil on wood panel
13¼ x 7 inches
Gift of Mr. and Mrs. Noel Wadsworth

Spring and *Autumn*
c. 1896
stained glass windows (pair)
43⅝ x 36 inches
44⅛ x 36 inches
Gift of Mrs. Arthur Hays Sulzberger

Lane, Fitz Hugh (1804-1865)
The "Constitution" in Boston Harbor
c. 1848-1849
oil on canvas, mounted on panel
15¾ x 23¼ inches
Museum purchase

Lasansky, Mauricio (b. 1914)
Amana Girl in Black Winter Coat
1967
intaglio, 15/70
47⅛ x 21⅝ inches
Museum purchase with funds supplied in part by the National Endowment for the Arts, a Federal agency

Lawrence, Jacob (b. 1917)
The Apartment
1943
gouache on paper
21¼ x 29¼ inches
Museum purchase with funds provided by the Benwood Foundation and the 1982 Collectors' Group

The 1920's . . . The Migrants Cast Their Ballots (from the *Kent Bicentennial Portfolio*)
1974
silkscreen, 49/125
32 x 25 inches
Gift of the Lorillard Company

The Swearing In (from *The Inaugural Portfolio*)
1977
serigraph, AP 15/20
17⅞ x 28 inches
Gift of Frank E. Fowler and funds provided in part by the National Endowment for the Arts, a Federal agency

Lawson, Ernest (1873-1939)
The Old Tulip Tree, Long Island
undated
oil on canvas
25¾ x 30⅝ inches
Gift of the Benwood Foundation

LeDoux, David G. (b. 1926)
Gravity's Rainbow II
c. 1976
mixed media on canvas
50½ x 41½ inches
Museum purchase award — Fifteenth Hunter Annual Exhibition, 1976

Leeper, Doris (b. 1929)
Diamond Parallelogram: 7
1970
enamel on masonite
42 x 58 inches
Museum purchase

Modular Wall Relief in Eight Colors
1972-1974
enamel on polyester and fiberglass
120 x 300 x 4 inches
Museum commission

Untitled
1976
silkscreen on canvas, two sections
36 x 144 inches and 36 x 73 inches
Gift of Commerce Union Bank, Chattanooga

Lee-Smith, Hughie (b. 1915)
Confrontation
c. 1970
oil on canvas
33 x 36 inches
Gift of the National Academy of Design, H. W. Ranger Fund

Leland, Whitney E. (b. 1945)
None I
1973
watercolor on paper
30 x 22¼ inches
Museum purchase award — Thirteenth Hunter Annual Exhibition, 1973

Leslie, Alfred (b. 1927)
Richard Bellamy
1974
lithograph, 31/50
40 x 30 inches
Museum purchase with funds supplied in part by the National Endowment for the Arts, a Federal agency

Frank Fata
1974
lithograph, 31/50
40 x 30 inches
Museum purchase with funds supplied in part by the National Endowment for the Arts, a Federal agency

Alfred Leslie
1974
lithograph, 31/50
40 x 30 inches
Museum purchase with funds supplied in part by the National Endowment for the Arts, a Federal agency

Levine, Jack (b. 1915)
Prisoner
1965
lithograph, 62/100
16 x 20 inches (sight)
Museum purchase

LeWitt, Sol (b. 1928)
13/4
1981
painted balsa wood
31⅜ x 31⅜ x 31⅛ inches
Museum purchase with funds provided by the Benwood Foundation and the 1983 Collectors' Group

Lichtenstein, Roy (b. 1923)
Untitled (From *The Inaugural Portfolio*)
1977
serigraph, AP 15/20
image: 16 x 26 inches
Gift of Frank E. Fowler and funds provided in part by the National Endowment for the Arts, a Federal agency

Lovejoy, Rupert Scott (1885-1975)
Gaspe, Canada
undated
oil on canvas
11¼ x 13½ inches
Gift of Sessions Hootsell, Jr.

Luks, George Benjamin (1867-1933)
Allen Street
c. 1905
oil on canvas
32 x 45 inches
Gift of Miss Inez Hyder

Dr. Wynkoop
1909
oil on canvas
78 x 38 inches
Gift of Dr. and Mrs. Yutaka Kato

Malone, Robert (b. 1933)
Afternoon
1978
lithograph, 22/25
image: 19¾ x 12¼ inches
Gift of Dr. and Mrs. Frederick P. Nause

Closed
1979
lithograph, 8/25
13½ x 22½ inches
Gift of Dr. and Mrs. Frederick P. Nause

Evening
1978
lithograph, 22/25
image: 12½ x 20 inches
Gift of Dr. and Mrs. Frederick P. Nause

Morning
1978
lithograph, 22/25
image: 12½ x 19¾ inches
Gift of Dr. and Mrs. Frederick P. Nause

Night
1978
lithograph, 23/25
image: 12½ x 19¾ inches
Gift of Dr. and Mrs. Frederick P. Nause

Through the Window
1978
lithograph, 22/25
image: 12½ x 20 inches
Gift of Dr. and Mrs. Frederick P. Nause

Marin, John (1870-1953)
City Movement, Downtown Manhattan #2
1936
watercolor and ink on paper
25⅜ x 20⅝ inches (sight)
Gift of the Benwood Foundation

Four Sail Boats
undated
pencil on paper
10¼ x 7¼ inches
Gift of Kennedy Galleries, New York

Marisol (Escobar) (b. 1930)
Women's Equality (From the *Kent Bicentennial Portfolio*)
1975
lithograph, 20/125
41½ x 29½ inches
Gift of the Lorillard Company

Marsh, Reginald (1898-1954)
(Gaiety) Burlesque (also known as *Irving Place Burlesque*)
c. 1930-1933
egg tempera on canvas, mounted on masonite
36 x 48 inches
Gift of the Benwood Foundation

Subway – 14th Street
1930
egg tempera on canvas, mounted on masonite
36 x 48 inches
Gift of the Benwood Foundation

Switch Engine LVRR
1931
etching on laid paper, first state of two
image: 5 x 7 inches
Museum purchase

Maruyama, Wendy (b. 1952)
Garden benches (pair)
1983
African mahogany
17 x 72 x 14½ inches
16 x 72 x 18 inches
Constructed by students from the Appalachian Center for Crafts, Smithville, Tennessee
Museum commission with funds provided by the Hunter Museum Volunteer Associates

Massey, Charles, Jr. (b. 1942)
Chance Hanging, Skyhook Finding
1973
mixed media on paper
29¼ x 21¾ inches
Museum purchase award — Thirteenth Hunter Annual Exhibition, 1973

Maurer, Alfred H. (1868-1932)
Still Life with Muffins
c. 1929-1930
oil on board
18¼ x 21¾ inches
Gift of Ione and Hudson D. Walker

McAdoo, Donald (b. 1929)
Tied Down
undated
graphite on paper
8¾ x 12 inches (sight)
Gift of Arthur Gene Finch

McCord, Jane (b. 1915)
Shapes in Space #2
1971
acrylic on canvas
60½ x 48 inches
Museum purchase award — Twelfth Hunter Annual Exhibition, 1972

McCormick, Jim (b. 1936)
Collaboration: Assistant
1979
lithograph, 23/25
image: 8 x 13 inches
Gift of Dr. and Mrs. Frederick P. Nause

Collaboration: Press
1979
lithograph, 8/25
image: 13 x 8 inches
Gift of Dr. and Mrs. Frederick P. Nause

Collaboration: Printer
1979
lithograph, 8/25
image: 8 x 13 inches
Gift of Dr. and Mrs. Frederick P. Nause

Collaboration: Slab
1979
lithograph, 9/25
image: 13 x 8 inches
Gift of Dr. and Mrs. Frederick P. Nause

Collaboration: Visitor
1979
lithograph, 8/25
image: 8 x 13 inches
Gift of Dr. and Mrs. Frederick P. Nause

WC: EL
1980
lithograph, 4/25
image: 10½ x 14½ inches
Gift of Dr. and Mrs. Frederick P. Nause

WC: Inside Out
1980
lithograph, 4/25
image: 10½ x 14½ inches
Gift of Dr. and Mrs. Frederick P. Nause

WC: Way Out
1980
lithograph, 4/25
image: 14½ x 10½ inches
Gift of Dr. and Mrs. Frederick P. Nause

McIver, John (b. 1931)
The Bridge
1968
watercolor on paper
22 x 30 inches
Gift of the artist

McMahon, Ken
Untitled
c. 1976
watercolor on paper
28½ x 18½ inches
Museum purchase award — Fifteenth Hunter Annual Exhibition, 1976

Miller, Elis F.
A Summer Afternoon
1882
etching on Japan paper, 52/250
image: 6¾ x 10 inches
From *Twenty Original American Etchings*, published under the auspices of the New York Etching Club, 1884
Gift of Elizabeth Glascock in memory of Miles White, Jr.

Minick, Roger (b. 1944)
A & W Palms (from the *Southland* series)
1975
gelatin silver print photograph
11 x 14 inches
Museum purchase

Two Chairs (from the *Hills of Home: the Rural Ozarks of Arkansas* series)
1972
gelatin silver print photograph
10⅝ x 13¾ inches
Gift of the artist

W. C. Corey (from the *Hills of Home: the Rural Ozarks of Arkansas* series)
1968
gelatin silver print photograph
11 x 14 inches
Museum purchase

Mitchell, Sue (b. 1923)
Green
1961
oil on canvas
48½ x 71 inches
Chattanooga Times Purchase Award — Second Hunter Annual Exhibition, 1961

Monson, Jim (b. 1943)
Totem
1980
etching, 4/25
image: 10 x 9½ inches
Gift of Dr. and Mrs. Frederick P. Nause

Moran, Edward (1829-1901)
Burning of the "Philadelphia"
c. 1897
oil on canvas
20 x 16 inches
Gift of Mrs. Robert Toombs Wright

English Coastal Scene
undated
oil on canvas
12 x 22 inches
Gift of Philip J. More and Mr. and Mrs. Eugene Thomasson (by exchange)

Moran, (John) Leon (1864-1941)
A Japanese Fantasy
c. 1884
etching on Japan paper, 52/250
image: 11½ x 8 inches
From *Twenty Original American Etchings*, published under the auspices of the New York Etching Club, 1884
Gift of Elizabeth Glascock in memory of Miles White, Jr.

Moran, Mary Nimmo (1842-1899)
Gardiner's Bay, Long Island, Seen From Fresh Pond
1881
etching on Japan paper, 52/250
image: 7⅞ x 11½ inches
From *Twenty Original American Etchings*, published under the auspices of the New York Etching Club, 1884
Gift of Elizabeth Glascock in memory of Miles White, Jr.

Moran, (Edward) Percy (1862-1935)
An Interesting Chapter
c. 1884
etching on Japan paper, 52/250
image: 11⅜ x 7¾ inches
From *Twenty Original American Etchings*, published under the auspices of the New York Etching Club, 1884
Gift of Elizabeth Glascock in memory of Miles White, Jr.

Moran, Peter (1841-1914)
The Pool
c. 1884
etching on Japan paper, 52/250
image: 8 x 11⅞ inches
From *Twenty Original American Etchings*, published under the auspices of the New York Etching Club, 1884
Gift of Elizabeth Glascock in memory of Miles White, Jr.

Moran, Thomas (1837-1926)
The Castle of San Juan De Ulua Vera Cruz
1884
etching on Japan paper, 52/250
image: 11⅜ x 9⅝ inches
From *Twenty Original American Etchings*, published under the auspices of the New York Etching Club, 1884
Gift of Elizabeth Glascock in memory of Miles White, Jr.

Morris, George L. K. (1905-1975)
Arizona Altar
1949
oil and pencil on unprimed cotton
53 x 40½ inches
Gift of Ruth S. Holmberg

Motherwell, Robert (b. 1915)
Gesture 1
1976
color, sugarlift, aquatint, 46/75
19½ x 15¾ inches
Museum purchase with funds supplied in part by the National Endowment for the Arts, a Federal agency

Moulthrop, Edward (b. 1916)
Bowl
1983
figured tulipwood
15½ inches high, 24 inches diameter
Museum purchase with funds provided by Mr.
and Mrs. E. Y. Chapin, III, Ruth S. and A.
William Holmberg and Mr. and Mrs. Phil B.
Whitaker

Mullen, Philip (b. 1942)
Moving Sentinel in Studio
undated
acrylic, graphite and wood on masonite
60 x 48 inches
Gift of Nancy and Max Underwood

S #5 (Center Vest)
1969
graphite on illustration board
39 x 29¼ inches
Museum purchase

Woman Under Glass
1973
mixed media on masonite
60 x 48 inches
Museum purchase award — Thirteenth
Hunter Annual Exhibition, 1973

Murphy, J. Francis (1853-1921)
The Glory of Evening
1888
oil on board
3½ x 5¼ inches
Museum purchase

Summer Time
1908
oil on canvas
24¼ x 36 inches
Gift of William J. Flather, Jr.

Musick, Rosemary (b. 1952)
Tassel & Copper
1975
copper and sisal
67 x 13 inches
Museum purchase award — 22nd
Chattanooga Area Crafts and Sculpture
Exhibition, 1976

Musser, Margaret Akers (1819-1917),
Musser, Samantha (1849-1877),
Musser, Charlotte (1853-1909)
Basket quilt
c. 1865
quilted cotton fabric, cotton batting
79 x 68 inches
Quilted by Mrs. Joseph Schwartz and her
daughters
Gift of Mrs. Merrill Brinson

Nakashima, Tom (b. 1941)
Untitled
1977
lithograph, 5/25
image: 12 x 10 inches
Gift of Dr. and Mrs. Frederick P. Nause

Nalls, Gayil (b. 1953)
American Altar/Unmistakable
1981
gold leaf and oil on masonite
6⅛ x 8⅛ inches
Museum purchase with funds provided by the
Benwood Foundation and the 1983 Collectors'
Group

The Embarrassment in Nature/Failures of Art
1982
gold leaf and oil on masonite
6¹/₁₆ x 8¹/₁₆ inches
Museum purchase with funds provided by the
Benwood Foundation and the 1983 Collectors'
Group

Formulas for Harmony and Volkswagons
1982
gold leaf and oil on masonite
6¹/₁₆ x 8¹/₁₆ inches
Museum purchase with funds provided by the
Benwood Foundation and the 1983 Collectors'
Group

The Pleasant Sense of Contradiction
1982
gold leaf and oil on masonite
6⅛ x 8¹/₁₆ inches
Museum purchase with funds provided by the
Benwood Foundation and the 1983 Collectors'
Group

Natkin, Robert (b. 1930)
Intimate Lighting
1973
acrylic on paper
36 x 58 inches
Museum purchase

Nevelson, Louise (1899-1988)
Cascades – Perpendiculars XXVII
1980-1982
painted wood
90 x 22 x 13 inches
Museum purchase with funds provided
by the Benwood Foundation and the
1984 Collectors' Group

Nice, Don (b. 1932)
Double Sneaker
1975
lithograph, 18/50
34 x 47¾ inches
Museum purchase with funds supplied in part
by the National Endowment for the Arts, a
Federal agency

Nicholson, Peter (b. 1928)
Interpenetrating Cubes
1973
chromed brass, 9/10
33 x 6⅜ x 7⅜ inches
Museum purchase with funds supplied in part
by the National Endowment for the Arts, a
Federal agency

Nicoll, James Craig (1846/47-1918)
Harbor Scene
1884
etching on Japan paper, 52/250
image: 9 x 12⅛ inches
From *Twenty Original American Etchings*, pub-
lished under the auspices of the New York
Etching Club, 1884.
Gift of Elizabeth Glascock in memory of Miles
White, Jr.

Noland, Kenneth (b. 1924)
Gold Domain
1972
oil on canvas
71⅝ x 16 inches
Gift of the artist

Nutting, Wallace
The Mills at the Turn
undated
hand-colored photograph
10⅜ x 13¼ inches
Gift of Mrs. A. M. Pennybacker

Offin, Charles Z. (b. 1889)
Milk Lady, Mallorca
1931
etching, 27/35
image: 4⅞ x 6⅞ inches
Gift of the artist

The Morning Catch, Mallorca
1931
etching, 13/40
image: 7¾ x 11 inches
Gift of the artist

Planters, Mallorca
1931
etching, 4/25
image: 7¾ x 6⅛ inches
Gift of the artist

Pottery Maker, Mallorca
1931
etching, 4/25
image: 6⅞ x 4⅞ inches
Gift of the artist

Twisted Branches, Mallorca
1931
etching, 19/20
image: 10 x 8¾ inches
Gift of the artist

Oldenburg, Claes (b. 1929)
*Tongue Cloud Over London
with Thames Ball*
1976
soft-ground color etching, aquatint, inked à la
puopee, 49/60
image: 31½ x 21¼ inches
Museum purchase with funds supplied in part
by the National Endowment for the Arts, a
Federal agency

Oliveira, Nathan (b. 1928)
Ryan 66
1981
monoprint with handcoloring
image: 19¾ x 17¾ inches
Museum purchase with funds provided by the
Benwood Foundation and the 1982 Collectors'
Group

Ozaki, Emi (b. 1939)
Microscope as Telescope
1968
acrylic on canvas
18 x 18 inches
Gift of the artist

Paley, Albert (b. 1944)
Garden Gate
1976
mild steel, forged and fabricated
115¾ x 102⅝ x 14½ inches
Gift of Ruth S. and A. William Holmberg

Hunter Museum Fence
1975
mild steel, forged and fabricated,
two sections
117 x 336 x 27 inches
128 x 576 x 58 inches
Museum commission

*Working sketch for Hunter Museum Fence,
Section I*
1974
pencil, ink, ink wash on paper
23 x 35 inches
Museum commission

*Working sketch for Hunter Museum Fence,
Section II*
1974
pencil, ink, ink wash on paper
23 x 35 inches
Museum commission

*Working sketch for Hunter Museum Fence,
Section III*
1974
pencil, ink, ink wash on paper
23 x 35 inches
Museum commission

Working sketch for *Hunter Museum Fence*,
Corner Section
1974
pencil, ink, ink wash on paper
19¼ x 13 inches
Museum commission

Paone, Peter (b. 1936)
Crying Man (from *My Father Suite*)
undated
lithograph, 2/100
21½ x 15½ inches
Gift of Mr. and Mrs. Lawrence A. Fleischman

Park, David (1911-1960)
Boy-Girl
1959
oil on canvas
50 x 58 inches
Museum purchase with funds provided by the
Benwood Foundation and the 1983 Collectors'
Group

Parrish, Stephen (1846-1938)
Mills at Mispek
c. 1884
etching on Japan paper, 52/250
image: 8⅝ x 11⅝ inches
From *Twenty Original American Etchings*, pub-
lished under the auspices of the New York
Etching Club, 1884
Gift of Elizabeth Glascock in memory of Miles
White, Jr.

Pascin, Jules (1885-1930)
Portrait d'une jeune fille assise
undated
oil on canvas
32 x 25¾ inches
Gift of the Benwood Foundation

Paxton, William McGregor (1869-1941)
Harry P. Meikleham
1937
oil on canvas
40¼ x 35¼ inches
On loan from Monticello, Thomas Jefferson
Memorial Foundation, Inc., Charlottesville, VA

Peale, James (1749-1831)
Zachariah Poulson (?)
c. 1808
oil on canvas
36 x 28½ inches
Museum purchase with funds donated
anonymously

Pearlstein, Philip (b. 1924)
Two Models on Red Office Swivel Chair
1985
oil on canvas
96 x 72 inches
Museum purchase with funds provided by the
Benwood Foundation and the 1985 Collectors'
Group

Two Nudes with Oak Stool and Canvas
1976
lithograph, 55/100
29 x 36¾ inches
Museum purchase with funds supplied in part
by the National Endowment for the Arts, a
Federal agency

Pembrooke, Theodore K. (1865-1917)
Untitled (landscape)
undated
oil on canvas
25¼ x 30¼ inches
Gift of Ruth S. Holmberg

Pennell, Joseph (1860-1926)
Below Chestnut Street
1884
etching on Japan paper, 52/250
image: 11¾ x 9¾ inches
From *Twenty Original American Etchings*, pub-
lished under auspices of the New York Etching
Club, 1884
Gift of Elizabeth Glascock in memory of Miles
White, Jr.

Perry, Lilla Cabot (1848-1933)
A Stream Beneath Poplars
c. 1890-1900
oil on canvas
25¾ x 32 inches
Gift of Mr. and Mrs. Stuart P. Feld

Peterson, Jane (1876-1965)
Luna Park
undated
gouache on paper
17⅜ x 23⅜ inches
Gift of Mr. and Mrs. Stuart Feld

Pfitzer, Charles (b. 1954)
The Doorway
1975
oil on canvas
48 x 70¼ inches
Museum purchase award — 22nd
Chattanooga Area Painting Exhibition, 1975

Pierschalla, Michael (b. 1955)
Garden benches (pair)
1983
African mahogany
17⅛ x 70½ x 16½ inches
17½ x 70½ x 19½ inches
Constructed by students from the Appalachian Center for Crafts, Smithville, Tennessee
Museum commission with funds provided by
the Hunter Museum Volunteer Associates

Platt, Charles A. (1861-1933)
Rye, Sussex, England
1884
etching on Japan paper, 52/250
image: 6¼ x 9⅜ inches
From *Twenty Original American Etchings* pub-
lished under the auspices of the New York
Etching Club, 1884
Gift of Elizabeth Glascock in memory of Miles
White, Jr.

Polansky, Lois (b. 1939)
Parterre To Wear
1984
handmade paper, mixed media
44 x 63 x 2¼ inches
Museum purchase with funds provided by the
Benwood Foundation and the 1984 Collectors'
Group

Ponce de Leon, Michael (b. 1922)
Once Upon a Journey
1979
lithograph, 8/25
image: 15¼ x 22¼ inches
Gift of Dr. and Mrs. Frederick P. Nause

Poons, Lawrence (b. 1937)
Sunnyside Switch
1963
acrylic on canvas
80 x 80 inches
Gift of the Museum Purchase Fund Collection,
established by Gloria Vanderbilt, under the
auspices of the American Federation of Arts

Porter, Liliana (b. 1941)
Untitled
1982
gouache, photosilkscreen, pencil and collage
on paper
40⅜ x 60 inches
Museum purchase with funds provided by the
Benwood Foundation and the 1982 Collectors'
Group

Potthast, Edward Henry (1857-1927)
In the Far Northwest — Montana
c. 1913
oil on canvas
50 x 40 inches
signed lower right
Gift of Mr. and Mrs. Scott L. Probasco, Jr. and
Mrs. Elizabeth L. Davenport

Powers, Don (b. 1950)
Two Timucua Spear-Fishermen
1977
egg-tempera on paper
23½ x 28 inches
Gift of Mr. and Mrs. Thomas B. Hooker

Prendergast, Maurice (1859-1924)
Gloucester Harbor
1918
oil on canvas
19⅝ x 26½ inches
Gift of the Benwood Foundation

Prior, William Matthew (1806-1873)
George Washington
c. 1850
reverse glass painting
24 x 18 inches
Gift of Mrs. A. M. Patterson and Elizabeth
Patterson

Quest, Charles F. (b. 1904)
Studio Interior #1
1978
oil on canvas
48⅛ x 68 inches
Gift of the artist

Raffael, Joseph (b. 1933)
Eternity
1985
watercolor on paper
42½ x 89½ inches
Museum purchase with funds provided by the
Benwood Foundation and the 1985 Collectors'
Group

Ramsey, Milne (1847-1915)
Sunset on a Pond
1906
watercolor on paper
20½ x 12 inches
Gift of Dr. Bruce E. Dahrling, II

Ransom, Henry C. (b. 1942)
Chairs
undated
graphite on paper
41½ x 34¾ inches
Gift of the artist

Rauschenberg, Robert (b. 1925)
Opal Reunion
1976
mixed media combine, six panels
84 x 158 x 36 inches
Gift of the Benwood Foundation, Mr. and Mrs.
Joseph H. Davenport, Jr., Ruth S. and A.
William Holmberg, and Mr. and Mrs. Olan
Mills, II

Untitled (from *The Inaugural Portfolio*)
c. 1976
lithograph, 15/20
30½ x 21¾ inches
Gift of Frank E. Fowler and funds provided in part by the National Endowment for the Arts, a Federal agency

Raymo, Ann (b. 1939)
Two
1977
fabric applique
64 x 60 inches
Gift of Mrs. Ann Robinson

Richards, William Trost (1833-1905)
The Lion Rock
1885
oil on canvas
34 x 60 inches
Gift of Mr. and Mrs. Scott L. Probasco, Jr.

Rivers, Larry (b. 1923)
Signing of the Declaration of Independence (from the *Kent Bicentennial Portfolio*)
1975
lithograph/serigraph, 106/125
31½ x 41½ inches
Gift of the Lorillard Company

Rivituso, Arthur (b. 1928)
River Bend
c. 1970-1972
watercolor on paper
21 x 24 inches
Museum purchase award — Twelfth Hunter Annual Exhibition, 1972

Roberts, Priscilla (b. 1916)
Family Bible
c. 1940
oil on board
13⅝ x 16 inches
Gift of Edna and Clarence Shaw

Robinson, Alan James
Richard Wagner
undated
etching, AP, first state I
image: 24 x 17¾ inches
Gift of Colon W. York

Tchaikovsky
undated
etching, AP, VIII
image: 24 x 17¾ inches
Gift of Colon W. York

Robinson, Boardman (1876-1952)
Portrait of a Negro
undated
pencil and ink wash on paper
15 x 11 inches (sight)
Gift of the Thornton Memorial Fund in memory of Russell Thornton

Rosenquist, James (b. 1933)
Marilyn
1974
lithograph, 69/75
image: 35½ x 27 inches
Museum purchase with funds supplied in part by the National Endowment for the Arts, a Federal agency

Ross, Alan (b. 1948)
Solar Telescope, Kitt Peak, 1976
print, 1978
gelatin silver print photograph
15¼ x 19⅜ inches
Gift of the artist

Ruscha, Edward (b. 1937)
America, Her Best Product (from the *Kent Bicentennial Portfolio*)
1974
lithograph, 97/125
31⅜ x 23½ inches
Gift of the Lorillard Company

Ryan, Mark
Unit III
1976
acrylic on canvas
46 x 46 inches
Museum purchase award — Fifteenth Hunter Annual Exhibition, 1976

Ryder, Albert Pinkham (1847-1917)
Plodding Homeward
c. 1878
oil on canvas
11 x 16½ inches
Gift of Mr. and Mrs. Llewellyn Boyd

Sacklarian, Stephen (b. 1899)
Reality of Unreality XIII
1973
oil on canvas
40 x 49 inches
Gift of Dr. Arthur F. Furman

Sakoguchi, Ben (b. 1938)
What Man's Mind Can Create, Man's Character Can Control
undated
etching, 8/10
image: 35½ x 24 inches
Gift of the Container Corporation of America

Santore, Joseph (b. 1945)
The Red House
1983-1984
oil on canvas
42 x 42 inches
Gift of Frances M. Hostetler and children in memory of Louis James Hostetler

Sargent, John Singer (1856-1925)
Figure study for *Chiron and Achilles*
c. 1922-1924
charcoal and pencil on Berville paper
19 x 24 inches
Gift of Mr. and Mrs. Colin M. Curtis

Figure study for *The Winds*
1921
charcoal on paper
14½ x 17½ inches
Gift of Mr. and Mrs. Colin M. Curtis

Sarkisian, Paul (b. 1928)
Untitled
1977
acrylic and graphite on paper
22½ x 30 inches
Gift of Joel and Anne Ehrenkranz

Schapiro, Miriam (b. 1923)
In Her Own Image
1983
acrylic and fabric on canvas
60 x 100 inches
Museum purchase with funds provided by the Benwood Foundation and the 1983 Collectors' Group

Schlump, John (b. 1933)
Expose
1979
silkscreen, 8
image: 5 x 15 inches
Gift of Dr. and Mrs. Frederick P. Nause

Surf Forms
1979
silkscreen, 8
image: 4¼ x 15 inches
Gift of Dr. and Mrs. Frederick P. Nause

Scholder, Fritz (b. 1937)
Bicentennial Indian (from the *Kent Bicentennial Portfolio*)
c. 1976
lithograph, 37/125
22 x 30 inches
Gift of the Lorillard Company

Stillwater a 7
1977 etching, 10/25
image: 9¾ x 7⅞ inches
Gift of Dr. and Mrs. Frederick P. Nause

Schwartz, Carl (b. 1935)
RG a XII
1977
soft ground etching and aquatint, 17/25
image: 7⅞ x 10¾ inches
Gift of Dr. and Mrs. Frederick P. Nause

Rushing Water a 6
1977
etching, 16/25
image: 5⅞ x 8¾ inches
Gift of Dr. and Mrs. Frederick P. Nause

Shoreline
1977
etching, 19/25
image: 7⅞ x 10¾ inches
Gift of Dr. and Mrs. Frederick P. Nause

Shrimp Fleet I
1980
lithograph, 4/25
image: 12¾ x 20 inches
Gift of Dr. and Mrs. Frederick P. Nause

Shrimp Fleet II
1980
lithograph, 4/25
image: 12¾ x 20 inches
Gift of Dr. and Mrs. Frederick P. Nause

Shrimp Fleet III
1980
lithograph, 4/25
image: 12¾ x 20 inches
Gift of Dr. and Mrs. Frederick P. Nause

Shrimp Fleet IV
1980
lithograph, 4/25
image: 12¾ x 20 inches
Gift of Dr. and Mrs. Frederick P. Nause

Shrimp Fleet V
1980
lithograph, 4/25
image: 12¾ x 20 inches
Gift of Dr. and Mrs. Frederick P. Nause

Shrimp Fleet VI
1980
lithograph, 4/25
image: 12¾ x 20 inches
Gift of Dr. and Mrs. Frederick P. Nause

Stillwater a 5
1977
etching, 17/25
image: 7⅞ x 9¾ inches
Gift of Dr. and Mrs. Frederick P. Nause

Stillwater a 7
1977
etching, 10/25
image: 9¾ x 7⅞ inches
Gift of Dr. and Mrs. Frederick P. Nause

Seawright, James (b. 1936)
Mirror V
1985
fiberglass, reinforced cement and mirrors
66½ x 66½ x 4 inches (assembled)
Museum purchase with funds provided by the Benwood Foundation and the 1985 Collectors' Group

Sellers, Anna (1824-1905)
Girl in Blue with Tablet
undated
watercolor on paper
8¾ x 5¾ inches
Gift of Mr. and Mrs. Scott L. Probasco, Jr.

Sleeping Papal Swiss Guard
c. 1870
watercolor on paper
9½ x 6¼ inches
Gift of Mr. and Mrs. Scott L. Probasco, Jr.

Sexauer, Donald (b. 1932)
Cervantes' Gift (folio of 9 prints)
1969
intaglio, 29/50
each print measures 22⅜ x 14⅞ inches
Gift of Cleve K. Scarbrough

Shahn, Ben (1898-1969)
The Handshake
1942
serigraph
19 x 24½ inches
Gift of Mr. and Mrs. Mark Pluiguian

Shinn, Everett (1876-1953)
Actress in Red Before Mirror
c. 1910
pastel on paper
25½ x 14⅝ inches (sight)
Gift of the Benwood Foundation

Shook, Georg (b. 1934)
Lattice Work
1979
watercolor on paper
36⅝ x 28¼ inches (sight)
Gift of Mr. and Mrs. Scott L. Probasco, Jr.

Shumacker, Elizabeth (1912-1993)
Orchard
1977
acrylic collage
21 x 21 inches
Gift of the artist

Siegel, Alan (b. 1938)
Big Julie
1981
enameled and stained birch and walnut (two pieces)
49¾ x 26½ x 44 inches
Museum purchase with funds provided by the Benwood Foundation and the 1982 Collectors' Group

Sloan, John (1871-1951)
Fifth Avenue Critics
1905
etching
image: 4½ x 6¾ inches
Gift of Douglas James

Night Windows
1910
etching
8 x 9½ inches
Gift of the Art Study Club in memory of Anna C. Turner

Smith, Linda Thern (b. 1946)
Para Los Dioses: Por Favor y Gracias
1979
slate, wood, clay, copper wire, found objects
23 x 10½ x 8⅜ inches
Gift of Ralph D. Smith

Snelson, Kenneth (b. 1927)
V-X II
1973-1974
stainless steel, 1/3
97 inches high x 161 inches diameter
Museum commission with funds supplied in part by the National Endowment for the Arts, a Federal agency

Snyder, Lewis
Untitled
1973
paint on ceramic
28 x 16¼ x 12 inches
Gift of Mr. and Mrs. Scott L. Probasco, Jr.

Solomon, Rosalind (b. 1930)
Jimmy Carter, Chattanooga, Tennessee
1975
gelatin silver print photograph
15 x 15¼ inches
Gift of the artist

Chinese Food Basket
undated
type C color print photograph
10⅜ x 3⅜ inches
Gift of the artist

Junction Box
undated
gelatin silver print photograph
13¾ x 9¼ inches
Gift of the artist

Mannequins
undated
gelatin silver print photograph, mounted on masonite
14¼ x 21¾ inches
Gift of the artist

Mannequins
undated
type C color print photograph
11 x 16½ inches
Gift of the artist

Rabbi Abraham and Lillian Feinstein
1975
gelatin silver print photograph
15 x 14⅞ inches
Gift of the artist

Untitled (tree bark)
undated
gelatin silver print, mounted on masonite
13¼ x 20 inches
Gift of the artist

Sonntag, William Louis (1822-1900)
Chenago Valley, New York
c. 1865-1870
oil on canvas
30 x 50 inches
Museum purchase with funds donated anonymously

Soyer, Moses (1899-1974)
Two Men
undated
oil on canvas
25 x 20 inches
Gift of Mr. and Mrs. David Soyer

Soyer, Raphael (b. 1899)
Untitled (seated nude)
undated
ink and pastel on paper
9⅞ x 7½ inches
Gift of Brabson House Galleries and William Smith Interior Design

Untitled (standing female figure)
undated
ink and pastel on paper
9⅞ x 7½ inches
Gift of Brabson House Galleries and William Smith Interior Design

Stack, Frank (b. 1937)
Disturbed Sleep
1979
lithograph, 8/25
image: 16½ x 11¼ inches
Gift of Dr. and Mrs. Frederick P. Nause

Dresser Mirror
1978
lithograph, 22/25
image: 11¾ x 8 inches
Gift of Dr. and Mrs. Frederick P. Nause

Jean
1978
lithograph, 22/25
image: 14½ x 9½ inches
Gift of Dr. and Mrs. Frederick P. Nause

Kim
1979
lithograph, 8/25
image: 9¾ x 6 inches
Gift of Dr. and Mrs. Frederick P. Nause

Mirror Nude
1978
lithograph, 2/25
image: 11¾ x 8 inches
Gift of Dr. and Mrs. Frederick P. Nause

Sleepwatcher
1979
lithograph, 8/25
image: 15¾ x 11¼ inches
Gift of Dr. and Mrs. Frederick P. Nause

Sleepwatchers
1979
lithograph, 7/25
image: 17¾ x 10 inches
Gift of Dr. and Mrs. Frederick P. Nause

Tina
1978
lithograph, 22/25
image: 15 x 11 inches
Gift of Dr. and Mrs. Frederick P. Nause

Tree
1978
lithograph, 22/25
image: 9¾ x 7¾ inches
Gift of Dr. and Mrs. Frederick P. Nause

Two Women
1978
lithograph, 22/25
image: 11¾ x 17¾ inches
Gift of Dr. and Mrs. Frederick P. Nause

Stackhouse, Robert (b. 1942)
Listings and Sailings
1982
watercolor and charcoal on paper
84½ x 120¼ inches
Museum purchase with funds provided by the Benwood Foundation and the 1983 Collectors' Group

Stauffer, Edna Pennypacker (1882-1956)
After the Shower, the Inn at Steele Hill
undated
lithograph
8¾ x 11¾ inches
Gift of Mrs. John S. Dixon

Avignon
undated
etching
6¾ x 5¾ inches
Gift of Mrs. John S. Dixon

Bird of the Hurricane
undated
lithograph
9⅜ x 12¼ inches
Gift of Mrs. John S. Dixon

Bruges Houses
undated
etching
5 x 3½ inches
Gift of Mrs. John S. Dixon

Captive Dryki
undated
lithograph
9⅛ x 10½ inches
Gift of Mrs. John S. Dixon

Jackie Coogan and the Cop
undated
etching
10 x 8 inches
Gift of Mrs. John S. Dixon

Florentine Housetops and Guitto's Tower
undated
crayon and charcoal on paper
10½ x 7⅞ inches
Gift of Mrs. John S. Dixon

Gloucester Harbor
undated
etching
8 x 6 inches (sight)
Gift of Mrs. John S. Dixon

Jungle Bound, Nassau in the Bahamas
undated
lithograph
12⅞ x 9⅞ inches
Gift of Mrs. John S. Dixon

Macchu Picchu
undated
lithograph
9¾ x 12¾ inches
Gift of Mrs. John S. Dixon

March in Bermuda
undated
lithograph
8⅝ x 13⅞ inches
Gift of Mrs. John S. Dixon

Off Cape Hatteras
undated
lithograph
11¼ x 16½ inches
Gift of Mrs. John S. Dixon

Orchestra Pit
undated
charcoal on paper
12 x 15⅝ inches (sight)
Gift of Mrs. John S. Dixon

Passing Storm, Venice
undated
lithograph
7¾ x 9½ inches
Gift of Mrs. John S. Dixon

Portofino, Late Afternoon
undated
lithograph
7¾ x 9¾ inches
Gift of Mrs. John S. Dixon

The Postman
undated
etching
7 x 5 inches
Gift of Mrs. John S. Dixon

Poupee Paderewski
undated
etching
8 x 6 inches
Gift of Mrs. John S. Dixon

Segovia, Spain
undated
watercolor and pencil on paper
12⅞ x 9⅝ inches (sight)
Gift of Mrs. John S. Dixon

Street In Marblehead – Gloucester
undated
etching
9 x 7 inches
Gift of Mrs. John S. Dixon

Sun Rise, Amalfi, Italy
undated
lithograph
11½ x 14 inches
Gift of Mrs. John S. Dixon

Tree Under Which Hippocrates Taught, Kos, Mediterranean Sea
1932
lithograph
6¼ x 7¼ inches
Gift of Mrs. John S. Dixon

Untitled
undated
charcoal on paper
12 x 15⅜ inches
Gift of Mrs. John S. Dixon

Untitled
undated
watercolor on paper
13¾ x 19¼ inches
Gift of Mrs. John S. Dixon

Untitled (reclining nude)
undated
pencil on paper
8¼ x 13¾ inches (sight)
Gift of Mrs. John S. Dixon

War De Hant
1953
pastel and charcoal on paper
15¼ x 10½ inches (sight)
Gift of Mrs. John S. Dixon

Warm Springs, Virginia
undated
lithograph
9¼ x 12½ inches
Gift of Mrs. John S. Dixon

West Virginia
undated
pencil and crayon on paper
10⅛ x 13½ inches
Gift of Mrs. John S. Dixon

Stella, Frank (b. 1936)
Nowe Miastro (IV)
1974
paper relief, dyed and collaged hand-colored paper, 3/25
24 x 21¼ x 1⅛ inches
Museum purchase with funds supplied in part by the National Endowment for the Arts, a Federal agency

Stevens, W. Lester (1888-1969)
The Bridge
undated
oil on masonite
30 x 24 inches
Gift of Mr. and Mrs. Heiman G. Gross

Stockdale, John (b. 1936)
Stores, New York City
undated
type C color prints, 14-image photographic composite
26½ x 6⅞ inches (sight)
Museum purchase

Sublett, Carl C. (b. 1919)
Bluff
1972
watercolor on paper
35¾ x 27¼ inches
Museum purchase award — Twelfth Hunter Annual Exhibition, 1972

Sugarman, George (b. 1912)
Red and Black Spiral
1975
painted, welded aluminum
69 x 128 x 44 inches
Museum purchase with funds supplied in part by the National Endowment for the Arts, a Federal agency

Sully, Thomas (1783-1872)
Juvenile Ambition (also known as *Grandfather's Hobby*)
1825
oil on canvas
36¼ x 28¾ inches
Gift of Mrs. Roana B. Hayes in memory of her husband, Henry H. Hayes

Martha Wade Young (also known as *Mrs. Benjamin Young*)
1835
oil on canvas
25 x 30 inches
Gift of Mr. Jo Conn Guild, Jr. in memory of May Young Guild

Suttman, Paul (b. 1933)
Still Life
1968
bronze bas-relief
10 x 7¼ inches
Gift of the American Federation of Arts through a grant from the Edward John Noble Foundation

Taylor, Ronald (b. 1938)
Witness
1964
oil on canvas
60½ x 48½ inches
First Flight Company Purchase Award — Fifth Hunter Annual Exhibition, 1964

Thiebaud, Wayne (b. 1920)
Glassed Candy (from the *Presidential Portfolio*)
1980
lithograph, 41/150
image: 20½ x 17¼ inches
Anonymous gift

Thomas, Howard (1899-1971)
July 4th
1961
gouache on paper
21⅞ x 32 inches
Gift of Mrs. Howard Thomas

Wolf Fork Valley
c. 1950
gouache on paper
15¼ x 22 inches
Museum purchase

Thrift, Walter (b. 1922)
Pavilion
c. 1960-1962
oil and collage on canvas
36 x 40 inches
Museum purchase

Tiffany, Louis C. (1848-1933)
Bowl
c. 1900-1910
favrile glass
3 inches high x 7 inches diameter
Gift of Mrs. R. B. Orme

Tovish, Harold (b. 1921)
Homage to Magritte
1981
pine
11¾ x 9⅞ x 10½ inches
Museum purchase with funds provided by the Benwood Foundation and the 1982 Collectors' Group

Townsend, Stan (b. 1947)
Bluff View
1981
serigraph, 1/75
12 x 15¾ inches
Museum commission in commemoration of the 30th anniversary of the Hunter Museum of Art

Trapp, Wayne
Maquette for *River's Wedge*
1985
black marble
11 x 16¾ x 9¼ inches
Museum purchase

Traylor, Bill (1854-1947)
Three Figures—Man Stealing Liquor
c. 1940
pencil and poster paint on cardboard
11½ x 8 inches
Museum purchase with funds provided by the Benwood Foundation and the 1985 Collectors' Group

Trebilcock, Paul A. (1902-1982)
George Thomas Hunter
1954
oil on canvas
36 x 28¼ inches
Museum commission

Trova, Ernest (b. 1927)
F. M. Manscapes, 1969
1969
silkscreen, 175/175
28 x 28 inches
Anonymous gift

Falling Man Suspended
1969
brass on plexiglass, 83/175
11⅞ x 11 inches
Gift of Dr. Edward E. Reisman, Jr.

Trumbull, John (1756-1843)
Bartholomew Dandridge
c. 1800
oil on canvas
29⅜ x 23⅜ inches
Anonymous gift

Twachtman, John Henry (1853-1902)
Boats and River (also known as *River and Bridge*)
c. 1890
oil on canvas
20¼ x 16¼ inches
Gift of the Benwood Foundation

House with Trees
c. 1898
pencil on paper
7¾ x 9¾ inches
Gift of Mr. and Mrs. Lawrence Fleischman

Untitled
c. 1890
watercolor
13½ x 8 inches
Gift of Mr. and Mrs. Frank Fowler in memory of his father, Calvin Fowler

Tworkov, Jack (1900-1982)
L.P. #2-Q2-75
1975
lithograph
30 x 33¾ inches
Museum purchase with funds supplied in part by the National Endowment for the Arts, a Federal agency

Q3-78-#3
1978
oil on canvas
54 x 54 inches
Museum purchase with funds provided by the Benwood Foundation and the 1983 Collectors' Group

Untitled
c. 1950
pencil and pastel on paper
23½ x 18 inches
Museum purchase with funds provided by the Benwood Foundation and the 1982 Collectors' Group

Underhill, William (b. 1933)
Untitled vessel
1963
bronze
24 x 20½ x 16 inches
Gift of The Johnson Wax Company

Underwood, Mary Earl (1838-1919)
Quilt top (*Rose of Sharon with Feathers* pattern)
c. 1865
cotton fabric and linen, appliqued
101 x 99½ inches
Gift of Mary Lou Kell Camp

The United States Mint
United States Presidential Series (set of 39 medals)
1820 to the present
bronze
3 inches diameter each
Gift of Philip J. More

Unknown artist
Cameron Hill and Union Military Bridge
c. 1865
handcolored photograph
18½ x 23½ inches (sight)
Gift of Dr. L. H. Lassiter

Unknown artist
Girl with a Bird and Cage
c. 1735-1740
oil on canvas
36½ x 24½ inches
Gift of Mr. and Mrs. Harold Cash

Unknown artist
Market Street, Chattanooga
c. 1862
handcolored photograph
17 x 24½ inches (sight)
Gift of Dr. L. H. Lassiter

Unknown artist
Mrs. Harriet Peters Phelps Gibson
undated
oil on canvas
35 x 28 inches
Gift of Miss May Archibald

Unknown artist
Portrait of a Gentleman
c. 1845-1850
oil on canvas
30 x 25 inches
Gift of Mrs. A. M. Patterson and Elizabeth Patterson

Unknown artist
Portrait of a Lady
c. 1845-1850
oil on canvas
30 x 25 inches
Gift of Mrs. A. M. Patterson and Elizabeth Patterson

Unknown artist
The View of Knoxville, 1871
1871
oil on canvas
14¼ x 41¼ inches
Gift of Norman Hirschl

Unknown artist
Rose Applique Quilt
c. 1830-1840
cotton, pieced and quilted
107 x 109 inches
Gift of Mrs. Lesley Wallace Colburn

Unknown artist
Untitled (figure under a tree)
c. 1855
oil on canvas
17¾ x 14½ inches
Museum purchase

Unknown shop
American empire secretary
c. 1870
mahogany and mahogany veneer
95 x 53 x 25½ inches
Gift of the Estate of Mrs. Charles Roberts Thomas

Unknown shop (attributed to Boston)
American empire sofa
c. 1820-1830
mahogany and mahogany veneer on pine, velvet upholstery
39 x 72 x 26½ inches
Gift of Dr. and Mrs. Edwin Lindsay

Unknown shop
American empire sofa
c. 1835-1838
mahogany and mahogany veneer on pine, brocade upholstery
34½ x 90 x 22 inches
Gift of Miss Margaret Thomasson and Mr. Eugene Thomasson

Unknown shop
American empire sofa
late nineteenth century
mahogany veneer, brocade upholstery
38 x 80¼ x 32⅝ inches
Gift of Mrs. Harry Maxwell Shoemaker

Unknown shop (attributed to Philadelphia)
American empire banquet table
1815-1825
mahogany
56 x 105½ x 27½ inches
Gift of Dr. and Mrs. Edward Newell in memory of Georgia Wilson Newell

Unknown shop
American Renaissance-Revival secretary
c. 1870-1880
southern black walnut
110 x 50 x 21 inches
Gift of the estate of Mrs. Charles Roberts Thomas

Unknown shop
Petticoat tables (pair)
c. 1910
various hardwoods, beige and rose veined marble
34 x 43 x 18¾ inches each
Anonymous gift

Unknown shop
Pier mirror
c. 1900
gilded gesso over wood, marble, glass mirror
102 x 37½ inches, base: 15½ x 40½ x 16 inches
Gift of the Estate of John L. Hutcheson

Unknown shop (attributed to Philadelphia)
Pier mirrors (pair)
c. 1865
gilded gesso, white marble, glass
144 x 38 inches each
Gift of Mrs. George S. Elder

Unknown shop (attributed to New England)
Three-part mirror
c. 1890-1900
wood, gold leaf
60 x 60 inches
Gift of the Estate of Katherine Patton Johnson in memory of Mr. and Mrs. T. L. Montague

Unknown artist
Quaker shawl
undated
silk
57 x 55 inches
Gift of Miss Zillah K. Hickox

Uzilevsky, Marcus (b. 1937)
Aquarelle
c. 1982
watercolor
22½ x 30¾ inches
Gift of the artist

First Movement of the Ambient Sonata in A Minor
1982
watercolor on handmade Inclusion des Florales paper
18¾ x 30 inches
Gift of the artist

Madrigal for Maryann
1982
serigraph, 147/175
image: 16 x 34¼ inches
Gift of the artist

Springtime Sonata
1982
serigraph, 43/190
image: 35⅜ x 20⅛ inches
Gift of the artist

Vanderhoof, Charles A. (-1898)
The Thames at Limehouse
c. 1884
etching on Japan paper, 52/250
image: 5⅞ x 11⅜ inches
From *Twenty Original American Etchings*, published under the auspices of the New York Etching Club, 1884
Gift of Elizabeth Glascock in memory of Miles White, Jr.

Van Elten, H. D. Krusman (1829-1904)
The Cottage by the Sea
c. 1884
etching on Japan paper, 52/250
image: 9¾ x 13⅝ inches
From *Twenty Original American Etchings*, published under the auspices of the New York Etching Club, 1884
Gift of Elizabeth Glascock in memory of Miles White, Jr.

Van Suchtelen, Adrian (b. 1941)
Cherries
1978
etching, 23/25
image: 5¾ x 8¾ inches
Gift of Dr. and Mrs. Frederick P. Nause

Cherries
1978
lithograph, 22/25
image: 4½ x 10 inches
Gift of Dr. and Mrs. Frederick P. Nause

Daybreak
1980
etching, 4/25
image: 7¼ x 11¾ inches
Gift of Dr. and Mrs. Frederick P. Nause

Four Graces
1978
etching, 24/25
image: 7½ x 10¾ inches
Gift of Dr. and Mrs. Frederick P. Nause

Indian Summer
1980
lithograph, 4/25
image: 9¾ x 7 inches
Gift of Dr. and Mrs. Frederick P. Nause

K
1980
lithograph, 4/25
image: 11 x 9 inches
Gift of Dr. and Mrs. Frederick P. Nause

Perfume Delight
1980
mezzotint, 4/25
image: 4¾ x 6 inches
Gift of Dr. and Mrs. Frederick P. Nause

Pomegranates
1978
etching, 23/25
image: 6¾ x 11¾ inches
Gift of Dr. and Mrs. Frederick P. Nause

Seven
1978
shaped paper lamination, handmade, 23/25
12½ x 20 inches
Gift of Dr. and Mrs. Frederick P. Nause

Stillife
1980
lithograph, 4/25
image: 9¾ x 15¾ inches
Gift of Dr. and Mrs. Frederick P. Nause

Target
1978
etching, 22/25
image: 8¾ x 11¾ inches
Gift of Dr. and Mrs. Frederick P. Nause

Three Lilies
1978
etching, 23/25
image: 5¾ x 8¾ inches
Gift of Dr. and Mrs. Frederick P. Nause

Three Trees
1978
etching, 23/25
image: 5¾ x 8¾ inches
Gift of Dr. and Mrs. Frederick P. Nause

Time Out
1978
etching, 22/25
imge: 23½ x 17½ inches
Gift of Dr. and Mrs. Frederick P. Nause

Unleashed
1980
lithograph, 4/25
image: 11 x 16 inches
Gift of Dr. and Mrs. Frederick P. Nause

Wade, David (b. 1947)
Window Watching
1977
watercolor on paper
26 x 36 inches
Gift of Mr. and Mrs. Scott L. Probasco, Jr.

Wagner, J. E.
Landscape with Rocky Summitt
undated
oil on canvas
29 x 36 inches
Gift of John Graham

Warhol, Andy (1928-1987)
Jackie (one in an edition titled *11 Pop Artists of 1965)*
c. 1965
serigraph on foil paper
40 x 30 inches
Museum purchase

Lillian Carter
1977
serigraph, 23/50
39¼ x 29¾ inches
Gift of Frank E. Fowler

Jimmy Carter III (from *The Inaugural Portfolio)*
1977
lithograph, AP 15/20
28¼ x 20½ inches
Gift of Frank E. Fowler and funds provided in part by the National Endowment for the Arts, a Federal agency

Warner, Doug (b. 1930)
August Pyramid
1977
lithograph, 10/25
18¼ x 24 inches
Gift of Dr. and Mrs. Frederick P. Nause

Double V
1978
two part shaped paper piece, lamination, 10/25
13 x 23 inches
Gift of Dr. and Mrs. Frederick P. Nause

Double X
1978
lithograph, 21/25
11 x 15 inches
Gift of Dr. and Mrs. Frederick P. Nause

Homage/L.V.B.
1979
lithograph, 8/25
18 x 15 inches
Gift of Dr. and Mrs. Frederick P. Nause

Screenscape
1978
lithograph, 22/25
20¼ x 15 inches
Gift of Dr. and Mrs. Frederick P. Nause

Two Plus
1978
shaped paper piece, lamination on
handmade paper, 22/25
11½ x 22¼ inches
Gift of Dr. and Mrs. Frederick P. Nause

Two Pyramids
1978
shaped paper piece, lamination on
handmade paper, 23/25
12 x 21½ inches
Gift of Dr. and Mrs. Frederick P. Nause

Untitled
1978
lithograph, 22/25
image: 6½ x 4¾ inches
Gift of Dr. and Mrs. Frederick P. Nause

Untitled
1978
lithograph, 22/25
image: 6½ x 4¾ inches
Gift of Dr. and Mrs. Frederick P. Nause

Untitled
1978
lithograph, 4/25
11 x 15 inches
Gift of Dr. and Mrs. Frederick P. Nause

Untitled
1978
lithograph, 22/25
15 x 15 inches
Gift of Dr. and Mrs. Frederick P. Nause

X Shift
1978
shaped paper piece, lamination on
handmade paper, 22/25
15 x 21¾ inches
Gift of Dr. and Mrs. Frederick P. Nause

Weaver, Robert (b. 1935)
MTK 313
1977
lithograph, 16/25
image: 22¾ x 16¼ inches
Gift of Dr. and Mrs. Frederick P. Nause

Nudes
1980
lithograph, 4/25
image: 15 x 21½ inches
Gift of Dr. and Mrs. Frederick P. Nause

Nude on a Couch
1980
lithograph, 4/25
image: 13 x 20¾ inches
Gift of Dr. and Mrs. Frederick P. Nause

Nude on a Pool Table
1980
lithograph, 4/25
image: 15 x 21½ inches
Gift of Dr. and Mrs. Frederick P. Nause

Standing Nude
1980
lithograph, 4/25
image: 19½ x 13¾ inches
Gift of Dr. and Mrs. Frederick P. Nause

Weege, William III (b. 1935)
Cowomonoco
1978
paper image collage, cotton fiber,
hand-painted lamination, 2
21 x 21 inches
Gift of Dr. and Mrs. Frederick P. Nause

Grubtsoo
1979
paper image collage, cotton fiber,
hand-painted lamination, 8
18 x 19 inches
Gift of Dr. and Mrs. Frederick P. Nause

Hsokhso
1979
paper image collage, cotton fiber,
hand-painted lamination, 8
18 x 19 inches
Gift of Dr. and Mrs. Frederick P. Nause

Oconomowoc
1979
paper image collage, cotton fiber,
hand-painted lamination, 8
18 x 23 inches
Gift of Dr. and Mrs. Frederick P. Nause

Oostburg
1979
paper image collage, cotton fiber,
hand-painted lamination, 8
14½ x 21 inches
Gift of Dr. and Mrs. Frederick P. Nause

Oshkosh
1979
paper image collage, cotton fiber,
hand-painted lamination, 8
22 inches diameter
Gift of Dr. and Mrs. Frederick P. Nause

Weir, J. Alden (1852-1919)
Helen Weir Sturgis
c. 1878
oil on canvas
49 x 36 inches
Gift of M. R. Schweitzer in honor of his friends
and clients in Chattanooga

Wells, Kimball (1939-1979)
Burger Queen
1977
lithograph, 16/25
23 x 17 inches
Gift of Dr. and Mrs. Frederick P. Nause

Wengenroth, Stow (1906-1978)
Lanesville Harbor
1976
lithograph, Ed/50
12 x 16 inches
Museum purchase

Twilight Clearing
1971
lithograph, Ed/70
10½ x 15 inches
Museum purchase

Weston, Brett (b. 1911)
Canal, Netherlands, 1971
print, 1972
gelatin silver print photograph
18 x 14¼ inches (sight)
Museum purchase

A Temple Facade, Japan, 1970
print, 1972
gelatin silver print photograph
10½ x 10½ inches
Museum purchase

Weston, Edward (1886-1958)
Dunes, Oceano, 1936
print, c. 1977, by Cole Weston
gelatin silver print photograph
7½ x 9½ inches
Museum purchase

Kelp, China Cove, Point Lobos, 1940
print, c. 1977, by Cole Weston
gelatin silver print photograph
9½ x 7½ inches
Museum purchase

Nude, 1936
print, c. 1977, by Cole Weston
gelatin silver print photograph
9½ x 7½ inches
Museum purchase

Oak, Monterey County, 1929
print, c. 1977, by Cole Weston
gelatin silver print photograph
7½ x 9½ inches
Museum purchase

Shell, 1927
print, c. 1977, by Cole Weston
gelatin silver print photograph
9¼ x 7⁵⁄₁₆ inches
Museum purchase

Whistler, James Abbott McNeill (1834-1903)
Gray and Gold – The Golden Bay
1900
oil on panel
5½ x 9¼ inches
Gift of Mr. and Mrs. Scott L. Probasco, Jr.

White, E. Alan (b. 1946)
Figure in a Megalithic Landscape
1976
intaglio, AP
image: 17½ x 19⅞ inches
Museum purchase award — 22nd Annual
Chattanooga Area Graphics and Photography
Exhibition, 1976

Whittredge, Thomas Worthington (1820-1910)
Trout Fishing in the Adirondacks
c. 1862
oil on canvas
22¼ x 18¼ inches
Museum purchase and partial gift of Leon
and Marjorie H. Marlowe, Miss Margaret
Thomasson and the Estate of Billie
Fitts Durham (by exchange)

Wiley, William T. (b. 1937)
Mr. Unatural
1975
lithograph, 13/65
36 x 25 inches
Museum purchase with funds supplied in part
by the National Endowment for the Arts, a
Federal agency

Wilkinson, Lucille Jordon (1908-1968)
Playa d'Oro
1967
collage on paper
16 x 22 inches (sight)
Gift of the artist's friends

Wollaston, John (c. 1710-c. 1770)
Portrait of an Unknown Gentleman
c. 1755
oil on canvas
22⅛ x 18⅛ inches
Gift of Hirschl & Adler Galleries, New York

Wonner, Paul (b. 1920)
*Dutch Still Life with Art Books and Field Guide to
Western Birds*
1982
acrylic on canvas
72 x 50 inches
Museum purchase with funds provided by the
Benwood Foundation and the 1983 Collectors'
Group

Wood, Thomas Waterman (1823-1903)
Thinking It Over
1884
etching on Japan paper, 52/250
image: 13¹⁵/₁₆ x 9¾ inches
From *Twenty Original American Etchings*, published under the auspices of the New York Etching Club, 1884
Gift of Elizabeth Glascock in memory of Miles White, Jr.

Wotherspoon, William Wallace (1821-1888)
Scene Outside a Southern Schoolhouse
c. 1855
oil on canvas
12½ x 18½ inches
Museum purchase with funds donated anonymously

Wyeth, Andrew (b. 1917)
The Lobster-Man
1937
watercolor
21½ x 29 inches (sight)
Gift of the Benwood Foundation

Wyeth, Jamie (b. 1946)
Bee Shadows (from *The Farm* portfolio)
1980
etching and drypoint, 22/150
image: 9 x 11¾ inches
Gift of Joseph F. and Rachel S. Decosimo

Chicken Basket (from *The Farm* portfolio)
1980
etching and drypoint, 22/150
image: 16⅞ x 13⅞ inches
Gift of Joseph F. and Rachel S. Decosimo

91, 75, 86, 93, 83 (from *The Farm* portfolio)
1980
etching and drypoint, 22/150
image: 9¾ x 9¾ inches
Gift of Joseph F. and Rachel S. Decosimo

Runaway Pig (from *The Farm* portfolio)
1980
etching and drypoint, 22/150
image: 9⅞ x 13½ inches
Gift of Joseph F. and Rachel S. Decosimo

The Scythe
1961
watercolor on paper
19⅜ x 24½ inches
Gift of the Benwood Foundation

Untitled (from *The Inaugural Portfolio*)
c. 1976
lithograph, AP 15/20
image: 20 x 23 inches
Gift of Frank E. Fowler and funds provided in part by the National Endowment for the Arts, a Federal agency

Wyeth, N. C. (1882-1945)
"Just as the baby's feet cleared the ground Padfoot leaped into the air and buried his teeth into the feathers of his old enemy." (Illustration from *Grace of the Dim Strain*)
c. 1923
oil on canvas
45 x 24 inches
Gift of Miss Carolyn Wyeth

Public Health and Morale (study for Squibb display poster)
1944
pencil on paper
36 x 32½ inches
Gift of Miss Carolyn Wyeth

The Seth Parker
undated
pencil and watercolor on paper
42 x 47½ inches
Gift of Mr. Frank E. Fowler

Untitled (gentleman before map of Delaware)
undated
pencil on paper
25¼ x 18½ inches
Gift of Miss Carolyn Wyeth

Untitled (porch scene)
undated
pencil on paper
42¼ x 46¾ inches
Gift of Miss Carolyn Wyeth

Untitled (seascape)
undated
oil on canvas
37¾ x 53¼ inches
Gift of Miss Carolyn Wyeth

Untitled (seascape)
undated
oil on canvas
37¾ x 53¼ inches
Gift of Miss Carolyn Wyeth

Yon, Erin (b. 1954)
Untitled
1978
stained glass
19¼ x 14½ inches
Gift of Joe H. Wheeler

Youkeles, Anne
Gemini
undated
serigraph, cut and folded, 13/100
19½ x 20 inches
Gift of Dr. Bruce E. Dahrling, II

Youngerman, Jack (b. 1926)
Mecox Bay
1978
acrylic on wood, two-sided
72 x 96 x 1⅜ inches
Gift of Mr. and Mrs. R. B. Davenport, III

Zapkus, Kes (b. 1938)
Study in Warm White
1974
watercolor, acrylic, pencil and vinyl screen on paper
22½ x 41¼ inches
Museum purchase

Index of Featured Artists

(Page numbers in italics refer to illustrations.)

All photographs by J. Bradley Burns except the following: Robert W. Scott, courtesy of *Southern Living Classics*, page 12; Photography, Inc., pages 48, 95, 97, 98, 99, 103, 109, 147, 148, 150, 151, 153, 158, 175, 177, 200, 204, Cover; Robert B. Wright, pages 76, 172, 245, 250, 256; Hirschl & Adler Modern, page 233; Terry Dintenfass, Inc., page 254.